Structure and Process in Southeastern Archaeology

JOFFRE LANNING COE

Structure and Process in Southeastern Archaeology

EDITED BY

Roy S. Dickens, Jr. and H. Trawick Ward

A DAN JOSSELYN MEMORIAL PUBLICATION

WITH AN EPILOGUE BY

James B. Griffin

THE UNIVERSITY OF ALABAMA PRESS

Library of Congress Cataloging in Publication Data

Main entry under title:

Structure and process in southeastern archaeology.

Includes index.
1. Indians of North America—Southern States—Antiquities—Addresses, essays, lectures. 2. Excavations (Archaeology)—Southern States—Addresses, essays, lectures. 3. Southern States—Antiquities—Addresses, essays, lectures. I. Dickens, Roy S., 1938– II. Ward, H. Trawick, 1944–
E78.S65S77 1985 975′.01 84-23
ISBN 0-8173-0216-6

0-8173-1188-2 (pbk: alk. paper)

To

Joffre Lanning Coe

Contents

Figures

Tables

Preface

The unifying theme of this volume is Southeastern archaeology and the influence of Joffre Coe in shaping its course. All of the contributors studied with Joffre at some point in their formative years, and we asked them to develop, in the context of their current research, chapters that would manifest this important aspect of their training.

The chapters in Section I reflect a strong concern for proper evaluation of the matrices in which archaeological materials occur. Thus, context and site formation processes (both cultural and physical) are explicitly addressed. Many of these intrasite chapters also draw on data obtained from long-term, carefully managed excavations at single sites. Coe is noted for these projects, which have resulted in large, systematic collections that will be used and reused by generations of thankful researchers.

The chapters in Section II broach problems on an intersite level. There are some useful and up-to-date summaries of regional and subregional cultural sequences, the kinds of syntheses of which Coe's *Formative Cultures* stands as a classic example. Not merely culture histories, these syntheses suggest reasons for the regularities and variability found in the subject assemblages. Chronology and typology, and interrelationships between the two, also are given mindful attention.

In an epilogue to the book, James B. Griffin gives an overview of Coe's career, which spans the WPA era as well as the developmental years of the "new archaeology." Dr. Griffin's keen and sensitive discussion makes us aware of the magnitude of the accomplishments of the founding fathers of modern Southeastern archaeology.

ROY S. DICKENS, JR.
H. TRAWICK WARD

Chapel Hill, North Carolina

Acknowledgments

We would like to thank Leland Ferguson, Jeff Reid, and Mike Trinkley for their advice and assistance during the planning of this volume, and we express special appreciation to Sally Coe and James B. Griffin for their many efforts throughout its development. We are also grateful to Barton Wright for his excellent pen-and-ink drawings. And, of course, we thank the authors for timely responses to our many requests and for continued encouragement. Sincere thanks are also due Estella Stansbury, Carol Dickens, and Steve Davis for their help in editing and typing the manuscript.

Portions of the funding for this publication were provided by grants from the University Research Council and the College of Arts and Sciences' Endowment for Scholarly Publications, Artistic Exhibitions, and Performances of the University of North Carolina, Chapel Hill.

Structure and Process in Southeastern Archaeology

Introduction · ROY S. DICKENS, JR. AND H. TRAWICK WARD

Within the general structure-and-process theme of this compendium, the authors have focused on either *intrasite problems* (those dealing with the formation and structure of a site, type of site, or type of feature) or *intersite problems* (those dealing with behavioral organization and process as developed from comparative site data). This approach is clearly in keeping with Joffre Coe's interests over the years. He has devoted much attention to intensive, long-term investigations of sites or site groups, those that he has felt were keys to understanding an area or cultural period. Examples of these long-term site-specific investigations include Town Creek, Hardaway, and Upper Saratown in the North Carolina Piedmont; and Garden Creek, Coweeta Creek, and Warren Wilson in the Appalachian Summit. Never content only to interpret individual sites, however, Joffre has proceeded to develop areal syntheses and cultural-chronological reconstructions based on multisite data. These larger constructs are well exemplified in his Archaic-Woodland chronology for the Piedmont, and his reconstructions of Cherokee culture history in the Appalachian Summit.

The papers in this volume also reflect research conducted in what several of the authors have termed the "Coe style." On the surface, it might seem easy to define that style, since to almost any Southeastern archaeologist the name Joffre Coe brings to mind an image of quality field and laboratory work and of sound interpretations. But there is much more to that style; it involves a set of approaches and philosophies for which Joffre has stood strongly during his career. He has practiced and taught that interpretations of the archaeological record are only as good as the observations on which they are based, and the observations only as good as the technical skills and perceptive abilities of the archaeologist in the field. This approach requires patience, and an important part of Joffre's philosophy has been to instill in young archaeologists the need for patience, care, and thoughtful attention to detail in their excavations, recovery procedures, record keeping, and laboratory work.

The other basic elements of the "Coe style" are consistency and comparability. Joffre's methods and techniques in the field have assured consistency and comparability both within and between projects. These qualities have carried over into the laboratory, and Coe the curator has been as dominant as Coe the excavator. There has always been order in Joffre's lab. Many a visitor to the Research Laboratories of Anthropology has marveled at how neat and clean he managed to keep the dirty business of archaeology. Crisp brown paper always covered the tables, and bags of specimens were lined in parade formation as if ready to be trooped by their commander.

Even during two massive moves between 1973 and 1975, there was order. Handtrucks rolled continuously across campus from Person Hall to Alumni Building, while pickup trucks ferried boxes from warehouses in Chapel Hill to warehouses in Durham. Boxes and specimens were counted, ordered, and reinventoried at each stage of the moves. For two years, materials and equipment, accumulated over a span of four decades, were marched across town and campus by lab staff and students with drill-team precision. As a consequence of Joffre's concern for order and consistency, all of the records and collections housed at the Research Laboratories are in a form that can be retrieved, understood, and *used* by future archaeologists.

Joffre's requirements of rigor, technical excellence, and consistency should not imply that he has been inflexible or has lacked the dimension of innovation. His innovations have been numerous, especially in the area of field techniques, but he has gone about them in a characteristically quiet and unassuming way. He has not been anxious to introduce a catch phrase or flashy bit of jargon into the literature. He has been much more concerned with what we do and how we go about doing it, than with what we call it. His innovative side is reflected time and again in the papers in this volume.

Thus, the "Coe style" must be viewed as a composite, a blend of quality, consistency, and innovation. Each of us contributing to this volume hopes that a little of that style has rubbed off.

Beyond these comments on basic themes, the chapters deserve some individual discussion, and in several instances it is useful to compare two or more of them when they present complementary approaches to the same problem or differing interpretations of the same or similar data.

The first chapter in the intrasite section, by Jefferson Reid, discusses the fundamental nature of the interpretation of site formation in archaeological research. He stresses the necessity of considering formation processes during all stages of research. His points are succinctly illustrated in a reexamination of ceramics from Coe's 1937–1938 excavations of the substructure mound at the Town Creek site in south-central North Carolina. Assemblage relationships between different proveniences are explored to test hypotheses about the sequence and behavioral consequences manifest in the formation processes responsible for the mound.

Roy Dickens examines the contexts of garbage deposition at late prehistoric and historic Southeastern aboriginal sites. He proposes that although fill in a pit may not be directly related to the pit's function, there is an indirect relationship represented through circumstances of abandonment. By examining the archaeobotanical remains from 22 features, representing eight functional pit categories, Dickens demonstrates that function affects the time of abandonment. Garbage subsequently used to fill the pits usually produced seasonally specific archaeobotanical profiles, a fact which supports his hypotheses about function and abandonment. Although he views the large pits at Upper Saratown as representing subterranean food-storage facilities, in contrast to Trawick Ward who sees them more as places to cache possessions during periods of village abandonment, both interpretations can be supported by their respective data.

Jack Wilson's paper is a detailed discussion of activity structure reflected in different zones of fill from functionally distinct features. Using archaeobotanical remains from some of the same features discussed by Dickens, Wilson takes the position that fill from pits often has little to do with the primary function of these features. He further proposes that since the cultural and natural formation processes responsible for the final filling episodes were complex, the resulting strata require meticulous excavation and recovery procedures, as well as detailed analyses. The paper ends on a somewhat pessimistic note by suggesting that we may never succeed in ferreting meaning about specific cultural activities from some depositional contexts because of the range of behaviors and natural forces that could have contributed to their formation. Wilson's discussion complements that of Dickens, although the two authors apply different approaches to distinct, yet related, problems and arrive at somewhat different conclusions.

Trawick Ward, as with Dickens and Wilson, uses feature data to interpret behavioral patterns. Southeastern archaeologists once considered pits merely as receptacles for artifacts, rather than as functional components of site structure and, therefore, as key variables for interpreting settlement and subsistence patterns. Ward proposes that differences in the frequencies of storage pits and in certain artifact categories between late prehistoric Cherokee sites and early historic Siouan sites in North Carolina reveal differences in social organization, settlement patterns, and subsistence practices of the respective groups. This kind of comparative study, which uses data spanning nearly 20 years of research, would not have been possible without the rigorously systematic procedures of Joffre Coe.

Michael Trinkley's chapter is a succinct examination of the formation processes involved in shaping Early Woodland shell rings on the Carolina and Georgia coasts. Following Coe, he stresses the need for block excavations to interpret site structure and correctly asserts that although scattered sampling may provide an overall picture of site content, it usually does not yield the kind of information necessary to determine functionally distinct activity loci. Trinkley's block excavations resulted in the identification of architectural features and depositional patterns, from which he reconstructs the events and activities that contributed to the development of the shell rings.

Using data from historic sites, Alexander Morrison reinforces Trinkley's comments on the need for extensive block excavations to interpret architectural relationships and intrasite variability. By carefully excavating and analyzing postmolds and postholes from seventeenth-century timber structures, in the context of total structures, he succeeds in identifying four distinct construction types that reflect varying social, economic, and demographic factors in early Colonial American culture.

Jefferson Chapman's chapter, which begins the intersite section, proposes that our notions about the distributions and frequencies of Archaic sites in certain larger river valleys of the Southeast have been grossly distorted by circumstances of discovery related to depositional patterns in the late Pleistocene and early Holocene. He notes that in the Little Tennessee Valley, and possibly other parts of the Ridge-and-Valley physiographic province, archaeologists should expect Paleoindian occupational surfaces to have been destroyed, and Early to Middle Archaic surfaces to have become deeply buried. The deeply buried sites, with their intact stratified sequences, offer considerable potential for the study of activity patterning and adaptive processes during the Archaic period. Chapman's interpretations of site location and preservation relative to geomorphologic and hydraulic phenomena closely follow Coe's early work on site formation in the Yadkin River Valley of North Carolina.

Stephen Davis, also working in the Little Tennessee Valley, assesses intersite assemblage variability using a model of contemporary hunter-gatherers developed primarily by Lewis Binford. Functional and temporal dimensions of artifacts are explored in an effort to reconstruct adaptive shifts and resulting settlement pattern changes. The settlement analysis relies on a nonsite probabilistic sampling scheme facilitated by plowing sample units to insure comparability. Davis' position regarding the reliability of surface samples for predicting site structure and activity must be evaluated in light of Reid's and Ward's suggestions that surface and plowzone artifact configurations often can only be properly evaluated after a site's subsurface structure has been defined.

The chapter by Veletta Canouts and Albert Goodyear provides an important complement to the studies by Chapman and Davis. Whereas the latter provided new data on and interpretations of site location and settlement pattern within a large river valley, Canouts and Goodyear examine the same phenomena in an upland setting. They argue that the upland sites have retained more structural integrity than previously thought, and that only through consideration of these sites can archaeologists expect to comprehend the entire cultural-environmental systems of prehistoric Southeastern societies. Since some of their assumptions pertaining to contextural integrity of small, shallow sites can be disputed, their approaches should be tested through further work in upland situations.

Billy Oliver, following Coe's landmark studies of typology and technological evolution, suggests that within a generalized Piedmont Tradition of tool manufacture, one can recognize significant spatial and temporal variation. As with Egloff's ceramic analysis, Oliver proposes that technological variation reflects differential information exchange and retention within regional adaptive patterns. Oliver hypothesizes that a western (Blue Ridge) technological pattern allowed for the persistence of small stemmed points longer than in the Piedmont, where there was a more rapid adoption of triangular points. This difference, according to Oliver, may be interpreted as a reflection of an earlier use of the bow-and-arrow by Piedmont people, who were located closer to sources of information about this Early Woodland innovation.

Kit Wesler's discussion of the Archaic sequence in Maryland, as with Chapman's for Tennessee, relies heavily on recent reassessments of both the archaeological and paleoenvironmental records. Wesler focuses on the need for cultural reconstructions to be based on well-defined artifact typologies and chronologies. Like Oliver, he feels that the use of superficial typological analogies tends to limit interpretation of regionally distinct technological trends. Wesler also stresses the need to recognize the human and nonhuman factors that affect the formation and archaeological "visibility" of sites. His settlement-subsistence model is one in which Paleoindian and Archaic cultures continually shifted their strategies to maximize efficiency as environmental factors changed, rather than simply becoming increasingly efficient through time. Finally, he recognizes that his interpretations are tentative and that they must be tested through excavations of sites with intact deposits, rather than being formulated solely on surface data.

The chapter by Keith Egloff traces the development of ceramic ware groups in the Coastal Plain of Virginia during the Woodland period. He proposes that, throughout this development, there existed "spheres" of cultural interaction, which can be observed in the ceramic record through distributions of attributes and attribute clusters. The formation of ceramic boundaries early in the Woodland period may, according to Egloff, represent the coalition of cultural-natural areas that were maintained into the historic period. He does not propose one-to-one correlations between prehistoric ceramic wares and historically defined tribes. Rather, he suggests that ceramics can be used to measure cultural interaction and as an indirect reflection of adaptive patterns. His interpretations, as with those of the other authors, are based on securely documented and clearly defined artifact taxonomies.

John Walthall presents a fresh and intriguing interpretation of ritual behaviors associated with Hopewell centers. Using ceramic and settlement data, he clearly establishes a link between the Middle Woodland vacant ceremonial centers of Ohio and contemporary habitation sites with Hopewell artifacts in the South Appalachian Highlands. Though smaller and less elaborate, the South Appalachian sites show evidence of being functionally equivalent to the Ohio centers. Walthall's synthesis and interpretation should be of interest not only to Hopewell scholars but to all archaeologists who study cultural interaction and information exchange.

Stanley South and Michael Hartley make a strong case for an interrelationship between the physiographic features of deep water and high ground in the choice of settlement sites by seventeenth-century coastal Carolinians. As the authors note, this proposal resembles Coe's "narrows hypothesis" for predicting settlement locations of prehistoric Piedmont Carolinians. South and Hartley were highly successful in their search for seventeenth-century sites by combining information from historic maps, modern topographic maps, and surface artifact collections. The patterns they point out illustrate the continuity between prehistoric and historic cultures in selecting settlement locations.

In conclusion, we believe that the chapters in this volume succeed in reflecting the Joffre Coe style of archaeology. The authors develop their propositions and interpretations on foundations of solid data, and although there is a strong inductive flavor, there is also attention to theoretical issues and to the development of behavioral interpretations. Those who may disagree with the methods chosen for exposition of some of the data or with some of the conclusions reached can nevertheless rest assured that the procedures under which the data were acquired, and the treatment of these data in the laboratory, were of Coe quality.

Section I

Intrasite Structure and Formation Processes

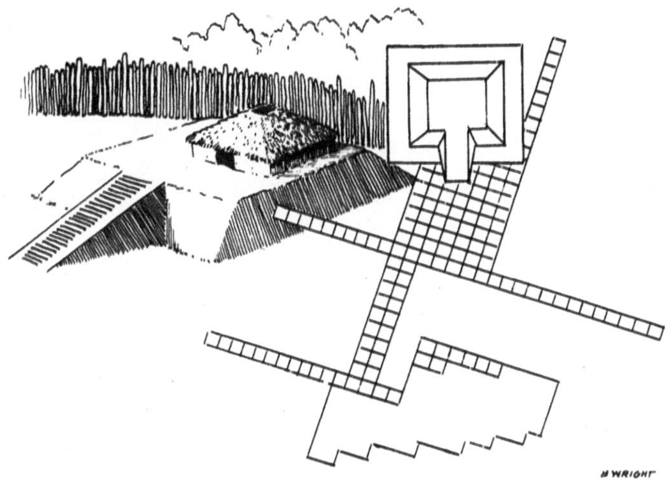

1 • J. JEFFERSON REID

Formation Processes for the Practical Prehistorian: An Example from the Southeast

Introduction

Concern with the processes that conspire to form the archaeological record has been noticeable in archaeology for many years. Indeed, archaeology as a discipline is predicated on a recognition of the need to reconstruct the behaviors that formed that record. In earlier periods of the discipline's growth, when discussion of methodological matters was less likely to reach the literature, knowledge of these processes was considered by the better archaeologists to be a necessary ingredient of sound data collection, the stuff of which good fieldwork was made. And this knowledge, like much of the craft at that time, was passed from the experienced fieldworker to the student. Now, due largely to the work of Schiffer (1972, 1976), in some measure Clarke (1973), and more recently Binford (1977, 1978a, 1981), one may consult a substantial archaeological literature on formation processes. Some of this literature codifies and much of it expands upon methodological considerations once handed down in the apprenticeship process made obsolete by rapid growth in the number of archaeologists, in the amount of archaeological information, and in the specificity of our questions about the past.

One prominent feature of this recent literature is the elemental role accorded formation process identification in the reconstruction and explanation of past behavior. "Knowledge of the past is accessible only when formation processes are considered" (Schiffer 1976:27). The logical unassailability and simple reasonableness of this assertion may be partially gauged by the introductory archaeology texts that now treat the topic (e.g., Rathje and Schiffer 1982) and the treatment it receives in a recent history of the discipline (Willey and Sabloff 1980). Although these latter authors regard formation process study as low-level theory, it is so only in the analogous sense that the wheel is a simple device.

The fundamental nature of formation processes is fully appreciated by those archaeologists who have experienced the full spectrum of research activities and who, having grappled with reconstructing past behavior from its traces, have found that archaeology cannot be done without an understanding of these processes.

Increased exposure to ethnographic literature and cultural anthropology under the standard of "archaeology as anthropology" expanded appreciation of behavioral possibilities while whetting appetites for asking more interesting and more complicated questions about the past. Forays into the literature of related disciplines revealed ideas and models that could be applied to new sets of observations and to realignments of data. The resulting need for a better understanding of the processes that form the prehistoric record spawned a multitude of studies of ethnographic, historic, and modern cultural contexts in order to provide some of this information.

However, despite a respectable methodological antiquity, the logical explicitness of the recent literature, and its experiential obviousness, the identification of formation processes is not well established in prehistoric investigations, certainly less well than in ethnoarchaeology, historic sites archaeology, and modern material culture studies. Why does this seeming paradox exist? Perhaps prehistorians await archaeologists of the present to develop the methods for studying the past. I sketch an argument that encourages prehistorians to study the formation of the archaeological record.

It is obvious that the correlation of behavior with materials and their associations is best achieved where both may be observed in context. Thus, ethnoarchaeology can inform on processes and possibilities not directly observable in the prehistoric record. However, the prehistorian would be ill advised to postpone study of formation processes until ethnoarchaeologically derived solutions are available. After all, the ethnoarchaeologist, while increasing our appreciation of possibilities, can only inform on general behavioral principles. Although essential to many areas of reconstruction and theory building, such principles are insufficient alone for dealing with the past. That this is so becomes clearer when one looks at the general categories of behavior operating to form the record of the past. These behaviors may be seen to divide into those that are idiosyncratic, those that are historical (or culturally specific), and those that are universal. The latter two are more germane to present concerns.

Universal behaviors are those that conform to general principles, behavioral regularities, or laws. They function importantly to permit explanation when initial conditions are met. They may not, however, account for a significant proportion of the relevant processes that formed a specific past record, and they cannot be assumed to be universal unless they are demonstrated to be nonhistorical. Anthropologists as a group become much involved with the people they study, and archaeologists, in maintaining this affection, often err in extrapolating from their own limited site or region to interpret behavior on a universal scale. However, one's people, site, or region may not represent the universal behaviors one supposes.

Historical behaviors are those specific to a single community, a group of communities, an ethnic group, or a culture, and though one might wish to subdivide and label these further, it is sufficient to recognize a category of recurrent behaviors that is neither idiosyncratic nor universal. It is unknown how much of the past record is a result of historical behaviors, though it probably is substantial. For the moment the important point is that these historical behaviors contribute to the formation of the prehistoric record, and their identification must be made in the context of that record (cf. Whittlesey 1978).

Prehistorians are encouraged by the research of colleagues pursuing other strategies within an interrelated behavioral archaeology (Reid, Schiffer, and Rathje 1975). They should not, however, ignore the study of formation processes under the false hope that these colleagues will solve their problems. Furthermore, a reticence to explore formation processes more fully in the prehistoric record may stem from insufficient attention to the practical issues of articulating an abstract notion of these processes with the different stages of archaeological research. In response to reticence and false hope, this paper seeks a resolution to the paradox by addressing the practical issues of studying formation processes as they apply to the archaeology of the prehistoric record.

The remainder of this paper is divided into two parts. The first part emphasizes that prehistoric archaeologists must seek to identify formation processes in all stages of research. Select applications pertinent to the design, collection, classification, analysis, and exposition stages of research are presented and illustrated. The second part comprises a limited reexamination of ceramics from the mound at the Town Creek site in Montgomery County, North Carolina. This analysis attempts to underscore that differential formation of proveniences precludes treating the associated ceramics as equivalent analytic units. The inclusion of examples from both the American Southwest and Southeast serves less as a reflection of personal experiences than as an indicator of the general applicability of formation process considerations.

Discussion of these issues is appropriate to the theme of this volume in that Joffre Coe has always maintained a practical grasp of formation processes and their application to the study of the past. His long-term program of investigation at Town Creek illustrates the importance of understanding site formation in the structure and conduct of fieldwork. His research on the formative cultures of the Carolina Piedmont (Coe 1964) demonstrates the analytic power of research grounded in control of the relevant processes affecting that particular prehistoric record.

Formation Processes and the Goals of Behavioral Archaeology

Much attention has been directed over the past decade to the proper conduct of archaeology, and, though fad and fashion have at times been distracting, the discipline has made significant progress in expanding domains of investigation, refining analytic tools and procedures, as well as providing a clearer vision of what archaeologists strive to achieve. Without detailing the achievements or excesses of the more tumultuous years, a summary is provided in a rearticulation of the goals of archaeological research (see Reid 1982 for further discussion).

Borrowing structure and content from the threefold division of Binford (1968), the goals of archaeology could be articulated as (1) accounting for the formation of the archaeological record, (2) reconstructing human behavior, and (3) explaining human behavior. Although these goals are logically sequential—behavior must be reconstructed before it can be explained—valid research contributions are made without straining always for explanatory relevance. The identification of formation processes functions as an independent goal of research as well as the essential basis for sound behavioral reconstructions. By signaling formation process studies as a legitimate goal of research, we begin to come to grips with the special features of the data that set archaeology apart from other behavioral sciences. Archaeology as archaeology establishes an appropriate frame of reference for theory building of a uniquely important kind (Reid 1973; Gumerman and Phillips 1978).

Although the theoretical structure for the investigation of formation processes has been well framed by Schiffer (1972, 1976), a brief review of essential features serves to orient subsequent discussion. A moderate degree of interpretive license is intended to augment appreciation of these processes and their applications.

It is well understood that the archaeological record is not simplistically equivalent to the past behavioral system that in large part produced it (Schiffer 1976). It is not as well understood precisely how archaeologists go about interpreting the past from its traces. Development of the requisite procedures is unlikely to be achieved without a knowledge of the formation processes that gave rise to these traces or the methods by which archaeologists observe them.

The pristine archaeological record is formed, and only formed, by cultural and natural processes. Specific terminology is not the issue; it is of little import whether one begins consideration of these processes as "n-transforms" and "c-transforms" (Schiffer 1976), or in terms of "predepositional," "depositional," and "postdepositional" theory (Clarke 1973). The purpose of such considerations is to model the formation of the record in order to reduce distortions that otherwise impair reconstructions of past behaviors that are the target of research. If archaeologists' collection and analytic procedures were sufficiently sensitive and their models of formation principles sufficiently precise, their image of past behavior would be sharp and undistorted. But their procedures are not so precise and, so, their image of the past *is* distorted. In this sense one may speak of distortions in perceptions caused by ignorance of relevant formation processes and their effects. Therefore, the identification of formation processes functions to reduce distortions, to enhance the image of past behavior. This point deserves repeating. *The archaeological record is only formed. Distortions in the record appear as a result of inadequate observation of the effects of relevant formation processes. As these processes are identified and their effects controlled, distortions diminish and our view of the past becomes clearer.* For such a seemingly simple reason, these processes are highly critical to archaeological research.

In a practical sense, the degree of perceptual distortion is inversely related to experience, to one's knowledge, implicit or explicit, of the record's formation. To the neophyte, much, if not all, of the record is a blur; differentiating plain pottery sherds from sandstone chips is perceptually agonizing. In time, the experienced archaeologist develops at least an intuitive grasp of formation processes. However, if left at this subconscious level, such expertise poses the danger of a relaxed vigilance toward devastatingly distorting effects of processes too subtle for intuitive recognition. The explicit identification of formation processes and their effects must occupy the investigator throughout all stages of research, from design through data collection, classification, analysis, and exposition. Discussion now turns to a consideration of the practical issues in studying formation process at these critical stages of research.

Research Applications

A large number of processes, both natural and cultural, obvious and subtle, potentially contribute to the formation of a site. How does the experienced archaeologist approach this welter of possibilities in the organization and implementation of research? To approximate an answer to this question requires that research be separated into its constituent stages with specific applications and examples pertinent to each. Rather than being an exhaustive catalog, these applications underscore the general point that consideration of formation processes must accompany research throughout all of its stages.

Design Stage

Knowledge of formation processes permits more appropriate articulation of research problems with the archaeological context to be investigated.

This application has been discussed as site-problem matching, where, regardless of which comes first, there must be a reasonable fit between the two (Lipe 1974; Reid 1975). To achieve this fit requires specification of requisite data and an evaluation of a site's potential for producing those data. An accurate evaluation is contingent upon knowledge of relevant formation processes that operated in the past to produce the site. This knowledge provides the basis for estimating the probability that certain material remains or configurations will or will not be found.

A fine example of this application is Coe's research on defining the Carolina Piedmont Archaic. In "the development of a hypothesis that will increase the probability of finding stratified sites in the river flood plains," Coe (1964:13), generates a model incorporating both natural and cultural processes responsible for the formation of stratified sites. Briefly, the natural processes include the physiographic and depositional factors peculiar to the narrows of Piedmont rivers, while cultural processes include the movement of people along river courses and the redundancy of campsite locations.

Not all formation processes relevant to the execution of a piece of research can be known prior to the initiation of data collection.

It is safe to say that all sites were not formed in similar ways. And even though categories of sites may share certain natural and behavioral processes in their formation, there is some truth to the claim that each prehistoric site is unique. Though certainly not students of the unique, archaeologists at the design stage of research must confront the fact that all relevant processes and their sequential or combinatorial effects cannot be identified prior to investigation. Archaeologists face the necessity, therefore, of being alert throughout research to the identification of relevant processes and their effects upon the items and associations of the record. In like manner archaeologists must be sensitive to the effects *they* may have upon the record both in terms of distorting their own data and in terms of distorting that same record to be investigated by others in the future. The only way by which one might account for the unknown is to design a sufficiently flexible research program to permit identification during subsequent research stages.

For example, younger archaeologists are no longer embarrassed to admit that chronology, essential to estimates of rate, sequence, and movement, is a primary research concern. Few archaeologists, even in the American Southwest, can determine beforehand what kinds of materials will be present at a site and whether they will provide a date. In anticipating this uncertainty in the Grasshopper Region of Arizona, where the coveted tree-ring sample is not as common as nonsouthwesterners might imagine, one must be prepared to recover or record all tree-ring samples, all archaeomagnetic samples, ceramics for cross-dating and seriation, ceramics for room abandonment computations, standard vertical stratigraphy, and the horizontal stratigraphy of pueblo wall relationships.

Since one cannot presume to know all relevant formation processes prior to the initiation of data collection, research must be designed with enough flexibility to test what is suspected as well as to identify and incorporate new information.

Data Collection Stage

Knowledge of formation processes and possibilities is essential to accurate field identification, and, therefore, to data collection.

In the data collection phase of research, one interacts with artifacts, features, and their associated matrix to resolve ambiguities toward the establishment of identifications and interpretations. One proceeds with a knowledge of general and local processes which are weighted according to their probability of occurrence.

My clearest recollection of first applying this knowledge was at Town Creek, where Bennie Keel and Ed Gaines, having exposed undisturbed soil in a 10 by 10-foot square, were testing dark, circular discolorations to distinguish postholes from root holes, rodent burrows, and plow scars. Ed instructed me in the necessary and sufficient conditions for making discriminations between culturally and naturally formed features. He could have expressed this lesson in terms of testing alternative formation hypotheses, replete with test implications, had he been familiar with such modes of discourse, but it would not have altered our task of identifying the processes responsible for the dark configurations in the soil.

Identifying postholes required the excavation of all smaller discolorations, while identifying burials within the category of large pits did not. Both procedures were predicated on a knowledge of how these features were formed and what was required for identification. In the case of burial pits, as Coe explained to his students, the top of the freshly troweled fill differs visibly from nonburial pits in being a mottled, less homogeneous composition of contrasting soils. This property of burial pits results when a deep hole, excavated through contrasting soils such as humus and subsoil, is filled with the mixed soil. Similar identifications are possible in all instances where the initial conditions are met. In the excavation of a large southwestern pueblo, for example, knowledge of this process has permitted burial identification at point of pit origin in complicated deposits, an identification essential to burial analysis (Whittlesey 1978). In addition it has led to the discovery of burial chamber forms not recognized when these features are discovered at the point where shovel contacts bone.

Knowledge of formation processes assists in targeting more precisely the data to be collected, and in refining collection strategies to assure recovering items from relevant data populations.

The application of this knowledge permits a closer articulation between collection units and the research questions being investigated. Clearly, one cannot always be certain even with experience that a particular provenience will produce all data relevant to one's research, yet an experienced appraisal of context formation will permit one to increase the probability that this is so. In simplest terms, application of formation process information permits more precise, more efficient, data collection. As collection procedures become increasingly complicated and costly, such considerations are not without advantage.

At Grasshopper Pueblo, as detailed elsewhere (Reid 1973; Reid, Schiffer, and Neff 1975), temporal differences in patterns of refuse disposal were isolated sufficiently early in the research to direct the selection of excavation units toward the resolution of specific problems. It can be shown that early constructed rooms were more often abandoned, their floor artifacts removed, and then filled with refuse. In contrast, late constructed room floors were abandoned with complete artifact arrays and little refuse in the fill. Because of the processes producing this situation, all floor-associated artifact assemblages are not comparable. Late household ceramic assemblages, for example, are complete and found as whole vessels on late abandoned room floors. On the other hand, early ceramic assemblages, since early floors are relatively bare, can only be approximated from sherd material collected from proveniences of the appropriate early period of occupation. Such knowledge permits one to target more accurately those excavation units most likely to contain relevant ceramic data. The need to employ probability sampling strategies as a discovery technique is often replaced by expertise expressed as a knowledge of relevant formation processes and their effects (Reid, Schiffer, and Neff 1975).

One might imagine that the identification of formation processes is best achieved in the field during data collection. For those processes most visible in the field context this is true though quite often not the case. Clearly, the majority of *natural formation processes* should be isolated in the field. Even when circumstance precludes adequate field identification, being attuned to formation process regularities permits identifications to be made in the laboratory.

Classification Stage

The formats by which archaeologists record, code, and classify material can be structured to identify relevant formation processes.

Many formation processes are more effectively identified during classification. One reason for this is that crucial information is not usually available until after a certain level of data reduction or synthesis has been achieved. Distributional data by provenience or artifact class, for example, are generally unavailable during the field phase of data collection. Classification can and should be structured to facilitate the identification of relevant formation processes.

Archaeologists recognize that different processes operate to reduce whole vessels into sherds of different sizes and characteristics. In partial compensation for the effects of these processes ceramic classification includes separation of body sherds from rims, bowl sherds from jars, and recording both number and weight. Until these data are matched with additional information such as provenience, there is often not a clear basis for identifying distortion effects. Such data are used, for example, to compensate for the disproportionate contribution large jars make to a sherd collection.

Analysis Stage

Analysis, especially that aimed at behavioral reconstruction, must include the identification of processes that could distort the reconstructions.

Analysis as the research activity of describing pattern and variability in past behavior, is a further stage in the research process where distortion effects can be identified. It is also the stage of research where cultural formation processes as distortion-producing behaviors include or merge with behaviors that are themselves the subject of research. Important at this stage is the need to identify the interactive effects of these different behaviors so that they may be accounted for during interpretation.

For example, it is a widely held assumption that a probability sample of surface ceramics approximates critical qualitative and quantitative values of the ceramic assemblage at a site. Accordingly, frequency distributions of ceramic assemblages are assumed to represent a site's ceramic signature, often to be used in comparison with similar signatures from other sites. In cases where equivalent discard probabilities exist, this assumption is probably workable. This assumption is invalid, however, in large Southwestern neolithic communities where different ceramic types participated in different use-contexts and possessed nonequivalent disposal probabilities.

At Grasshopper Pueblo, ceramic types occur in frequencies specific to the context of use and discard. In effect, there is a mortuary assemblage, a domestic household assemblage, a community assemblage, and a *discard assemblage*. It is this latter assemblage that may influence most the composition of the surface collection. Thus, the surface-derived distribution does not reflect these different use-contexts and cannot be assumed to represent quantitative values of the past ceramic assemblages. The distortion effects on the surface assemblage of ceramics participating in different use-contexts appeared well into the analysis and are themselves significant behaviors contributing to the generation of higher order interpretations.

Exposition Stage

Formation processes can function to structure the presentation and, thus, to enhance understanding past behavior.

Regardless of the fact that archaeological analysis can go on indefinitely, there comes a time when a piece of work is to be presented. At this stage in research, formation processes can serve to structure the narrative, thereby contributing to clarification of interesting patterns. Even to express past behavior patterns in terms of processes assumed to have operated, but not demonstrated, increases one's understanding of behavioral interactions and encourages further research to demonstrate the extent of the proposed effects. In this sense, a retroactive application of principles, formation processes function to structure exposition.

An example is that of the room abandonment measure developed for Grasshopper Pueblo to order temporally the abandonment of rooms. The pattern was discovered during the mundane activity of computing excavation figures for an annual report. Regardless of the context of discovery, the model appears to work. Its exposition has been enhanced by employing cultural formation processes that remain undemonstrated.

According to the model, the following processes are assumed to have operated at Grasshopper (Reid 1973; Reid, Schiffer, and Neff 1975:217; cf. Ciolek-Torrello 1978):

1. When a habitation room is abandoned while the pueblo is still occupied, usable objects will be retained in moving to another nearby habitation room.
2. Even if all usable objects are not retained, habitation room floors abandoned while the pueblo is still occupied maintain a high probability of being scavenged for usable items.
3. Abandoned habitation rooms may be used for secondary refuse disposal.
4. The last habitation rooms abandoned will not be scavenged nor used as dumps.

The combined effects of these processes that permit the relative ordering of room abandonment events are expressed as follows:

1. Rooms abandoned while the pueblo was still occupied contain little or no de facto refuse on the last utilized habitation floor but may contain a high density of secondary refuse in the room fill above the floor.
2. Rooms abandoned at or near the time of pueblo abandonment have a high density of de facto refuse on the last utilized habitation floor and a low density of secondary refuse in the room fill above the floor.

The pattern of artifact distribution incorporated in this model is made more comprehensible when expressed in terms of cultural formation processes that provide a reasonable, yet undemonstrated, account of this variability in the archaeological record.

Afterthought

Given that the magnitude of potential cultural and natural processes operating to form the record is great and that a substantial number are beyond current techniques of identification, archaeologists must endure incomplete knowledge as they go about contributing to the cumulative understanding of these processes.

A large number of processes could potentially have operated to form the record as viewed here, many of which are too subtle or leave too weak a trace for confident, consistent identification. However, the dismal truth of this situation is provisional and instead of retarding research should serve to focus it. Certainly it cannot be used as a justification for summarily dismissing consideration of formation processes.

One must effect a workable adjustment to the condition of being unable to identify and monitor all formation processes relevant to specific research. One can view the possible multitude of unmeasurable processes as being not dissimilar to the multitude of human behaviors which, though currently beyond our ability to isolate, are subsumed in the general patterns of behavior offered as reconstructions. Archaeologists do isolate patterns of recurrent behavior, while knowing that clarity is diminished by behaviors for which they cannot control, many of which turn up as residuals in various analytic procedures. In like manner, it is possible, even requisite at this point in our understanding, to concentrate on those processes that produce major distortions in the record and assume that the effects of minor processes are themselves minor. The recognized danger here, but one we must partially endure, is that major processes may be defined as the most visible, the ones most readily identified rather than the ones with the greatest effect upon data configurations.

Before turning to a more lengthy example of applications, a comment should be made concerning a significant restraint on research into the nature and operation of formation processes in the prehistoric record.

It is disheartening that the reward structure of American archaeology, favoring as it does grand schemes and facile reconstructions, does not easily accommodate much needed basic research. In the rush to achieve immediate solutions to complex problems, to build theories of the intermediate and ethereal range, to apply hackneyed interpretive formulas, archaeologists have neglected the cumulative development of basic concepts and tools that characterizes mature sciences. Until this structure and this ambience shift emphasis, young practitioners, upon whom depends the future of the discipline, will be reticent to defer immediate compensation in order to pursue more distant solutions to the persistent, fundamental, and mundane questions that confront archaeology.

Formation Processes and the Mound at Town Creek

The processes that have formed substructure mounds in the American Southeast have been tacitly understood since the days of Cyrus Thomas. Nevertheless, it is quite clear that this understanding has not been consistently translated into the interpretations of past behavior and events derived from information in these mounds. Critical proveniences often are not identified during data collection or, if so, they are treated in the ceramic analysis as equivalent. These equivalence assumptions, disregarding as they do the processes forming mounds and provenience-associated ceramics, give rise to potentially erroneous interpretations of the past. The following sketch of mound formation, linked to possible ceramic use and discard behaviors, establishes a framework for examining assemblage nonequivalence.

The purpose of this discussion is not to present a reanalysis of Town Creek ceramics. Rather, it is to illustrate a point made 14 years ago under Coe's tutelage that mound proveniences differ in formation and thus in the character of associated ceramics, and that the nature of these differences must be considered in analysis. One may now frame this observation in terms of formation processes.

The Mound

The Town Creek mound-and-village site is located on the west bank of Little River above its junction with Town Creek in Montgomery

County, North Carolina. It represents the northernmost extension on the Piedmont of the pervasive late prehistoric Southern Appalachian Mississippian development (Griffin 1967; Ferguson 1971). The lifeway manifested at Town Creek is designated the Pee Dee culture (Coe 1952, 1964).

It is worth pointing out that the excavation of the Town Creek mound well illustrated the field identification of behaviorally meaningful proveniences, a task described today as being facilitated by knowledge of formation processes. Further note should be made of the fact that the data recovery strategy designed by Coe for the ceremonial precinct and village did not include the excavation of all features. Very briefly, the general strategy was one of excavating and screening the plowsoil in 10 by 10-foot squares down to undisturbed subsoil. Remnants of undisturbed midden deposits overlying subsoil were isolated separately. Features evident in the subsoil were mapped, photographed, the postholes excavated, the square covered with white sand to mark excavation limits, and then backfilled. This excavation strategy, combined with a special photographic technique developed by Coe, has made possible the construction of a composite, whole-site photograph of subsurface features. The site exists today as an ideal laboratory for exploring a variety of research questions.

The utility of applying formation principles in data collection is glimpsed in a brief presentation of mound formation at Town Creek summarized from Coe's field notes. In addition, this outline of the major construction and use episodes establishes the framework for examining the associated ceramics.

A humus zone (Premound Humus) extended under the mound. Upon this surface were constructed at least two mortuary houses. Post-dating the mortuary houses was a structure (Earth Lodge) banked laterally with dirt revealed in the excavation as a laminated earthen embankment. Nearby, and perhaps contemporary with the Earth Lodge, was a small structure (Trash Bin) constructed of posts surrounded on the exterior walls and capped with clay.

After razing the Earth Lodge, a retaining wall was constructed and filled (Mound Fill) providing the platform for the first temple structure (Temple 1). There is evidence of only one more structure (Temple 2) separated from the first by a shallow fill. Temple 2 was partially covered and preserved by spoil dirt from a post-aboriginal disturbance. The flanks of the mound contained remnants of an undisturbed refuse layer (Debris) discarded when the temples were in use. A humus layer (Top Soil) constituted the youngest soil, one formed by erosion and plowing. Each of the field-identified proveniences contained a variety of artifacts, the most conspicuous of which were sherds (Table 1-1). A large number of smaller proveniences are lumped as General.

The mound ceramics were examined in the spring of 1967 as a master's thesis project (Reid 1967). In retrospect, that examination reflects youthfulness in its definition of problem—a description of and changes through time in Pee Dee ceramics and in classification and analytic techniques. The archaeological climate of that time and place was also characterized by analysis framed in terms of probable processes responsible for forming mound provenience units and thus influencing the character of the ceramic assemblages. A portion of that thesis is quoted below to underscore the point that Coe, as the one directly influencing the structure and content of that climate, was aware and taught the importance of formation processes and their effects.

> Some caution must be used in making comparisons between these two units [Premound Humus and Debris], and other archaeological units also, for rarely are such units equally comparable in their cultural significance even though they are recognized in the same mound. Discounting the temporal factor, [one recognizes that] the material from the premound humus probably differs from that found in the later debris layer by containing the residue of aboriginal activities both before and after this plot of ground was regarded as special by being designated sacred or ceremonial. Once this space was defined, only a limited range of activities could take place. Thus the premound humus exhibits a potentially wider range of activities, both pre-ceremonial and ceremonial, while the later debris layer can be interpreted as producing refuse material of ceremonial activities that took place when the temples were in use. Such differences are more significant when dealing with cultural groups exhibiting a greater divergence between ceremonial and utilitarian goods. Pee Dee ceramics are thought not to be so specialized; yet these factors should be considered as possible indicators of difference rather than time alone (Reid 1967:56–57).

Ceramics Reexamined

A reexamination of ceramics from the mound, though limited by the information available in the original thesis, serves nevertheless to il-

Table 1-1. Distribution of Body Sherds by Mound Provenience and Surface Finish (from Reid 1967, Table 1).

	Premd. Humus	Earth Lodge	Trash Bin	Md. Fill	Temple 1	Temple 2	Debris	Top Soil	Gen	Total
Filfot, 2 bar	2							1		3
Filfot, 4 bar	1					1			12	14
Filfot, 5 bar	7			11		2	2	3	20	45
Filfot, 6 bar	1						1		1	3
Filfot, 7 bar	11			1			4	1	24	41
Filfot, 8 bar		1							1	2
Filfot scroll	2							1	1	4
Misc. filfot	214	7	1	59	5	19	60	74	223	662
TOTAL FILFOT	238	8	1	71	5	22	67	80	282	774
Concentric circle	393	14	5	93	2	8	35	124	238	912
Quartered circle	178	18	2	13			5	14	36	266
Arc-angle	106	1	2	26		1	13	21	48	218
Herring bone	95			45		3	14	18	100	275
Split diamond	53			3		1	1	3	9	70
Line block	2			3					9	14
Quartered cross	6						4	1	36	47
Arc-angle variant	12						1	2	1	16
Misc. rectilinear	929	37	9	216	6	27	113	409	529	2275
Misc. curvilinear	885	29	15	185	18	32	76	386	408	2034
Misc. unidentifed	1196	39	9	248	23	21	105	531	570	2742
TOTAL COMPLICATED STAMP	4093	146	43	903	54	115	434	1589	2266	9643
Textile wrapped	42	1		50	1	6	30	71	124	325
Check stamped	19			9		2	3	6	10	49
Cordmarked	21			6		1	4	5	11	48
Corncob	3	3					1		3	10
Plain, rough	4		1	5					3	13
Plain, smooth	105	2	3	32	3	1	14	52	92	304
Burnished	654	23	2	149	3	15	161	347	477	1831
Polished	18	3		1				1	8	31
TOTAL PLAIN	781	28	6	187	6	16	175	400	580	2179
Non PeeDee	280	10	9	70	32	5	28	168	151	753
Misc. indeterminate	215	9		71	6	9	15	113	158	596
TOTAL	5454	197	58	1296	99	154	690	2352	3303	13603

lustrate the role played by formation process considerations in archaeological research. At the most general level, the proveniences may be separated into architectural and nonarchitectural associations as follows:

Architectural	Nonarchitectural
Temple 2	Top Soil
Temple 1	Mound Fill
Trash Bin	Premound Humus
Earth Lodge	Debris

The ceramics associated with these two provenience classes may be taken to reflect different ranges of behavior, which may be conceptualized as differences in types of refuse—primary refuse associated with architecture, and secondary refuse associated with nonarchitectural proveniences (Schiffer 1976). The primary refuse may be taken *provisionally* to represent activities performed within those structures. The secondary refuse reflects behaviors of a potentially much wider range, and not necessarily associated with mound use. This latter range of behaviors, depending on the origin of the construction dirt, may result from domestic or other activities taking place in the areas later used for borrow. On this basis alone one can propose a set of relationships for analytic exploration.

If one assumes initially, for the sake of simplicity, that activities taking place in structures changed little during the mound's use and that the ceramics recovered represent consistent proportions of those activities, then the following series of provisional relationships can be generated for the ceramic assemblages defined by provenience.

1. Temple 1 ceramics are similar to Temple 2 ceramics.
2. Since the Debris layer was interpreted in the field to be associated with refuse from Temples 1 and 2, then one would expect that Temples 1 and 2 ceramics are similar to Debris ceramics.
3. Earth Lodge ceramics are similar to Temples 1 and 2 ceramics.
4. If the Trash Bin is associated with the Earth Lodge, then one would expect that the Earth Lodge ceramics are similar to Trash Bin ceramics.
5. Trash Bin ceramics are similar to Debris ceramics.

In like manner, if the nonarchitectural proveniences contain ceramics reflecting use and discard behaviors similar among themselves but dis-

Table 1-2. Aggregated Distribution of Body Sherds Used in Analysis.

	Premd. Humus	Earth Lodge	Trash Bin	Md. Fill	Temples 1 & 2	Debris	Top Soil
1. Total filfot	238	8	1	71	27	67	80
2. Concentric circle	393	14	5	93	10	35	124
3. Quartered circle	178	18	2	13		5	14
4. Arc-angle	106	1	2	26	1	13	21
5. Herring bone	95			45	3	14	18
6. Split diamond	53			3	1	1	3
7. Textile wrapped	42	1		50	7	30	71
8. Plain	109	2	4	37	4	14	52
9. Burnished-polished	672	26	2	150	18	161	348

similar to the structure-associated behaviors, then one would expect the following:

6. Premound Humus, Mound Fill, and Top Soil ceramics are similar.
7. Premound Humus, Mound Fill and Top Soil ceramics are not similar to ceramics from Temples 1, 2, Earth Lodge, Trash Bin, and Debris.

These relationships establish an initial framework for evaluating the results of a pair-wise comparison of all provenience-defined ceramic assemblages using the Pearson *r* correlation coefficient. The purpose is to explore interassemblage variablity toward verifying previously hypothesized relationships. This analysis tests whether different mound proveniences contain equivalent artifact assemblages.

The frequency distribution of all ceramics from the mound in Table 1-1 provides the data from which more appropriate distributional tables are constructed. In Table 1-2 the number of ceramic categories is reduced to nine. The nine provenience categories in Table 1-1 are reduced to seven in Table 1-2. The provenience labeled "General" constitutes a miscellaneous category of numerous small proveniences about which the notes are unilluminating, and, thus, it is eliminated. Temples 1 and

Table 1-3. Correlation Coefficients of Mound Proveniences Using All Ceramic Surface Finishes (Items 1 through 9 in Table 1-2).

	Premd. Humus	Earth Lodge	Trash Bin	Md. Fill	Temples 1 & 2	Debris	Top Soil
Premd. Humus	1.0						
Earth Lodge	.88	1.0					
Trash Bin	.41	.16	1.0				
Md. Fill	.91	.68	.30	1.0			
Temples 1 & 2	.58	.41	.04	.71	1.0		
Debris	.89	.71	.07	.92	.73	1.0	
Top Soil	.93	.76	.24	.94	.59	.96	1.0

Table 1-4. Correlation Coefficients of Mound Proveniences Using Complicated-stamped Surface Finishes (Items 1 through 6 in Table 1-2).

	Premd. Humus	Earth Lodge	Trash Bin	Md. Fill	Temples 1 & 2	Debris	Top Soil
Premd. Humus	1.0						
Earth Lodge	.70	1.0					
Trash Bin	.87	.35	1.0				
Md. Fill	.85	.30	.60	1.0			
Temples 1 & 2	.51	.17	.09	.69	1.0		
Debris	.61	.21	.23	.79	.98	1.0	
Top Soil	.95	.46	.76	.94	.66	.75	1.0

2 are combined to form a larger sample on the basis of architectural similarities and a Brainerd-Robinson coefficient of 171.42. (Recall that the Brainerd-Robinson coefficient ranges from 0 to 200 and more faithfully responds to the zeros so frequent in archaeological data arrays.)

In Tables 1-3 and 1-4, one sees the extent of dissimilarity among assemblages and further that the provisional relationships listed above are not all supported.

Relationship 1, that Temples 1 and 2 ceramics are similar, is assumed to be true on the basis of the Brainerd-Robinson test, and the ceramics are combined for a more reliable comparison with other assemblages.

Relationship 2, that Temples 1 and 2 ceramics are similar to the Debris ceramics, is not supported at a very convincing level in Table 1-3, but in Table 1-4 the correlation shows the highest coefficient in that table. This interesting result leads not only to partial validation of the field identification of the Debris, but also to the suggestion that complicated stamped vessels, and perhaps even specific designs, played a prominent ceremonial role in Pee Dee culture.

Relationship 3, that the Earth Lodge is similar to Temples 1 and 2, is not supported. Neither are relationships 4 and 5. In fact the ceramic assemblages associated with Temples 1 and 2, the Earth Lodge and the Trash Bin appear unrelated, which prompts consideration of possible functional changes in ceramic use during the ceremonial history of Town Creek.

Relationship 6, that Premound Humus, Mound Fill, and Top Soil are similar, is supported by the coefficients presented in both Tables 1-3 and 1-4, thus reinforcing the suggestion that these proveniences represent similar, perhaps nonspecific, secondary refuse deposits. It is noteworthy that the Debris assemblage is similar to this group in the Table 1-3 coefficients. This correlation, contrasting with that of Table 1-4, highlights further the possible ceremonial function of complicated stamped ceramics.

Relationship 7, that the nonarchitectural provenience ceramics are dissimilar to those associated with structures, receives mixed support in the analysis and indicates a more complex depositional pattern than can be accounted for using this set of relationships and available data.

This brief analysis provides information to which one could add additional data in order to generate a revised set of relationships and a more appropriate model of mound formation. In addition, it poses questions to be explored further in the data from the mound or with material from other behaviorally relevant proveniences. For example, the suggested functional specificity of complicated stamped ceramics could be further explored using burial urns associated with mortuary houses.

The purpose of this analytic exercise is to illustrate that, due to the operation of potentially different formation processes, the provenience-associated ceramic assemblages are nonequivalent. Thus, they cannot be used to generate interpretations requiring analytic unit equivalency. Neither specific formation processes nor all important assemblage characteristics are claimed to have been explored. Such specifications await a reanalysis of the ceramics using the full range of information.

Conclusions

The theme of the preceding discussion is that reliable reconstructions of the past can be achieved only when the archaeologist explicitly considers, throughout all stages of research, the identification of formation processes and their distortion effects. In order that archaeologists might attend the difficult tasks confronting our attempts to reconstruct and explain past behavior, the issues and nonissues surrounding discussions of formation processes are briefly summarized. If one's concern is with understanding the past, with developing those techniques and skills that make this goal feasible, then:

1. It is immaterial whether knowledge of formation processes is deeply rooted in the methodological history of the discipline. This is a concern for the historians and philosophers of science.
2. It is irrelevant whether the current literature is laden with a new vocabulary thought to be jargonistic or whether one uses the labels of the new vocabulary.
3. It matters little to the actual practice of archaeology whether one believes in laws of human behavior or in the law character of many formation processes.

On the other hand, it is requisite to proper archaeological research that one comprehend the role played by formation processes in producing the archaeological record and, in turn, the role an understanding of these processes plays in making possible knowledge of the past. What is called to our attention is not just that the archaeological record is formed by cultural and natural processes, but that the processes often are complicated in their distorting effects, often regular in these effects and, most important, discoverable through conscientious research. Furthermore, prehistorians must devote increased attention to resolving the practical problems of identifying for themselves the processes operating to form the record of past behavior.

These considerations, even if labelled low-level theory, are essential to the building of a behavioral science wherein the behaviors studied are believably reconstructed. Only after we have presented reliable reconstructions of past behavior may we presume to explain it. At this point archaeologists compete with all other social and behavioral scientists to explain pattern and variability in human history. To do otherwise, to treat lightly or to ignore formation processes, is to perpetuate antiquarianism partially disguised in the currently fashionable vocabulary.

Acknowledgments

For their insightful comments and helpful suggestions, I wish to thank Stephanie Whittlesey, Michael Schiffer, Roy Dickens, Trawick Ward, and the following participants in a graduate seminar in archaeology at the University of Arizona: John Andresen, Laverne Conway, Michael Jacobs, Julie Lowell, Michael McComas, and Charlotte Williams.

2 · ROY S. DICKENS, JR.

The Form, Function, and Formation of Garbage-filled Pits on Southeastern Aboriginal Sites: An Archaeobotanical Analysis

Introduction

During the past half century, American archaeologists have become increasingly aware of the importance of context when interpreting the human material record. It now seems almost incredulous that, as late as 1948, Walter Taylor needed to urge his colleagues to recognize and utilize contextual relationships.

> There is one source of archaeological data . . . rarely mentioned or fully utilized in archaeological literature. I refer to what may be called the *affinities* existing between the material remains: between individual cultural objects, between groups of objects, between objects and the natural environment. These affinities are as much facts and as much integral parts of the archaeological data as are the material objects themselves. . . . If the archaeologist does not specifically search for, and consciously make use of these affinities, he is overlooking a great proportion of his meager data. Often they lie hidden to the casual eye within the cultural and natural contents [contexts] of an archaeological site [Taylor 1948:111–112].

The lesson in Taylor's statement was surprisingly slow to be learned, however, and it has only been in the past 15 to 20 years that archaeologists have begun to treat context not just as a locational phenomenon, but as a complex set of variables in the interaction of human behavior and the formation of the material record of that behavior. Joffre Coe (1964) was one of the first archaeologists in the southeastern United States to rigorously apply field techniques that would allow accurate interpretation of context, and he was one of the first to discuss site formation processes.

More recently, Binford (1978 a and b), Schiffer (1977), and others have attempted to define explicitly the physical and cultural processes by which archaeological contexts are formed. They have noted (e.g., Schiffer 1977) that culturally produced materials are, in fact, *transformed* from their systemic contexts to their archaeological contexts through complex and varied activities that may or may not be related to the original functions of the materials or their original locations of use.

In this paper, the contexts of garbage deposition on several late prehistoric and historic aboriginal sites in the Southeast will be examined.[1] Garbage-filled features are classified, regardless of age or site, in categories based on form and function, to propose from the functions expected seasonal abandonment and filling processes, and finally to test these propositions with one component of the garbage—the botanical remains. In general, it is hypothesized that if a feature were designed to fulfill a specific function, it is probable that the feature would be abandoned and thus become a potential garbage repository within seasonal parameters. Such an interpretation further suggests that while the garbage in an archaeological feature may not be related *directly* to the original function of that feature, it nevertheless may be related to circumstances surrounding abandonment of the feature and therefore *indirectly* to its original function.

If seasonal patterning can be demonstrated for feature fills, the possibilities become numerous for investigating activity variability within specific sites, and for comparing activities between sites of the same culture and through time within a cultural continuum. It would also indicate that archaeologists should consider feature type in selecting samples for archaeobotanical and zooarchaeological analyses, and that they should avoid lumping data from different types of features in reporting and interpreting their findings.

Feature Form

The 22 archaeological features used in this study were excavated at seven archaeological sites (Figure 2-1). The Henderson, Nuyaka, Warren Wilson, and Plum Grove sites were excavated by the author between 1966 and 1979. The Little Egypt site was excavated by David Hally (1981), the Upper Saratown site by Jack Wilson (1977), and 38AN8 by W. Dean Wood (1981). The Warren Wilson and Upper Saratown

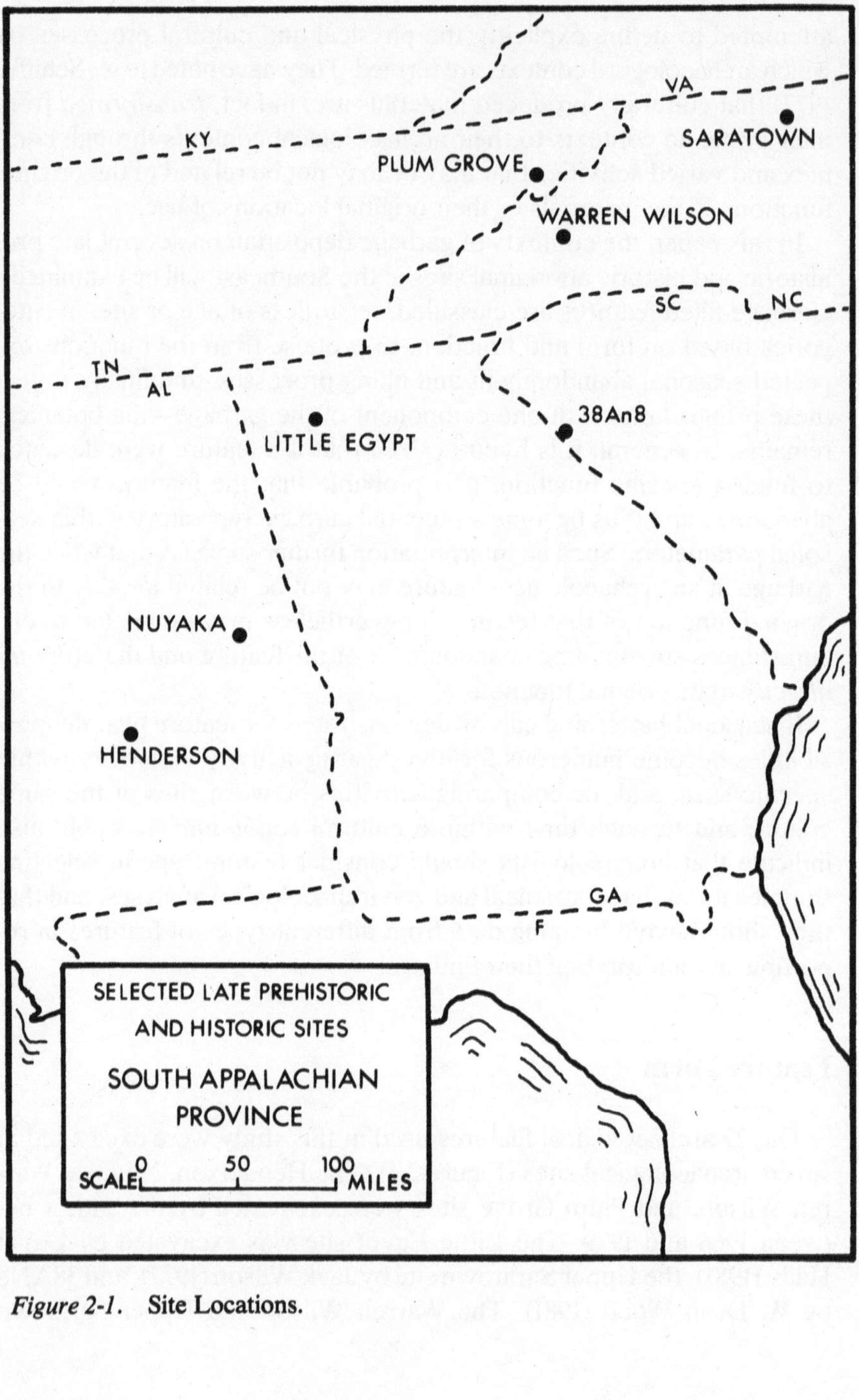

Figure 2-1. Site Locations.

Table 2-1. Site Information.

Site	Location	Cultural Affiliation	No. of Features	Source
Henderson (1LO32)	Alabama Upper Costal Plain	Late Woodland Henderson Phase (A.D. 500–700)	2	Dickens (1971)
Warren Wilson (31BN29)	North Carolina Appalachian Summit	Late Mississippian Pisgah Phase (A.D. 1200–1400)	6	Dickens (1976)
Plum Grove (40WG17)	Tennessee Ridge and Valley	Late Mississippian Pisgah Phase (A.D. 1300–1500)	2	Wilson (1980)
Little Egypt (9MU102)	Georgia Ridge and Valley	Late Mississippian Barnett (Lamar) Phase (A.D. 1500–1700)	3	Hally (1981)
38AN8	South Carolina Piedmont	Late Mississippian Lamar Phase (A.D. 1200–1400)	1	Wood (1981)
Upper Saratown (31SK1)	North Carolina Piedmont	Historic Siouan (ca. A.D. 1680)	5	Wilson (1977)
Nuyaka (1TP3)	Alabama Piedmont	Historic Creek (ca. A.D. 1795)	3	Vaught (1979)

projects were under the overall direction of Joffre Coe. The locations, cultural affiliations, and written sources (published or unpublished) for the sites are given in Table 2-1.

These features had two things in common: all were pits, and all contained garbage in their fill. The term garbage is used here specifically to stand for that type of refuse (discarded or abandoned materials) resulting from general household activities, especially food preparation and consumption. On late prehistoric Southeastern sites, garbage consists of a relatively dense mixture of pottery sherds, animal bones, wood charcoal, charred seeds and other plant parts, mollusk shells, heat-fractured rocks, debitage from tool making, abandoned or broken tools of clay, stone, and bone. Although these materials will be present in varying ratios and combinations, most of the categories usually will be represented. Many of the features included in this study seem to have served intentionally as garbage repositories, even though they may have had only small amounts (probably incidental inclusions) of some of the materials listed above. For example, only one burial pit was included, as these pits usually were backfilled with relatively sterile soil rather than with garbage.

Several formal categories could be discerned within the 22 features (Figure 2-2 and Table 2-2). Form refers to the shape (plan and profile), size,[2] and associations (covering, lining, postmold pattern, human skeletal remains, etc.) of a feature. The eight feature types in the study group are as follows:

Type 1. a pit with a relatively small (60–140 cm) circular orifice; is deep (60–130 cm); has straight-sided or bell-shaped profile; and occasionally may contain a rock slab that served as a covering.

Type 2. a pit with a relatively large (160–280 cm) circular or oval orifice; is shallow (20–60 cm); has a basin-shaped profile; and has no lining or other structural associations.

Type 3. a depression with a large (5–10 m) square to rectangular orifice; is shallow (10–40 cm); has basin- or dish-shaped profile; and may have hard-packed floor, hearth(s), postmolds, and other associated features.

Type 4. a pit or depression with a relatively small (40–100 cm) circular orifice; is shallow (5–15 cm); has a basin-shaped profile; may be lined with rocks or burnt clay; and may be associated with a Type 3 feature.

Type 5. a pit with a medium to wide (100–200 cm) orifice; relatively shallow (10–60 cm); has a straight-sided or basin-shaped profile; and may have burnt areas and/or concentrations of fire-cracked rock.

Type 6. a ditch or linear pit with wide (120–180 cm) orifice; usually has shallow (30–80 cm) sloping sides; and may have an adjacent postmold alignment.

Type 7. a pit with a small (5–30 cm) circular orifice; shallow to medium depth (10–120 cm); round to pointed bottom; straight sides; and may occur individually, in an aligned pattern or within a narrow trench.

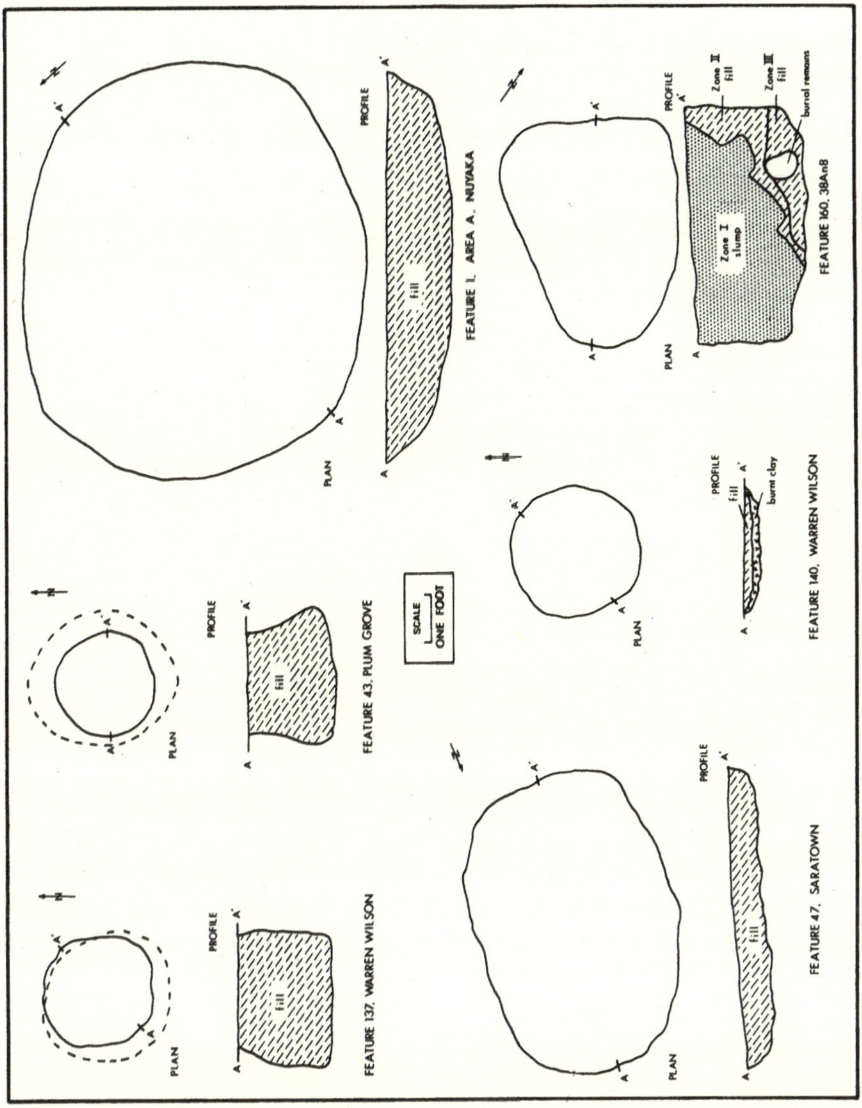

Figure 2-2. Selected Feature Plans and Profiles.

Table 2-2. Feature Types by Site.

	Henderson	Warren Wilson	Plum Grove	Little Egypt	38AN8	Saratown	Nuyaka	Total
Storage Pit (Type 1)	2	2	2			3		9
Borrow Pit (Type 2)						2	3	5
Structural Floor (Type 3)				3				3
Hearth (Type 4)		1						1
Cooking Pit (Type 5)		1						1
Ditch/Moat (Type 6)		1						1
Postmold/Wall Trench (Type 7)		1						1
Burial Pit (Type 8)					1			
Total	2	6	2	3	1	5	3	22

Type 8. a pit with a medium (80–160 cm) oval or rectangular orifice; deep (50–120 cm); straight sided or undercut, and contains human remains (smaller dimensions for subadult burials).

These types do not include all forms of pit features found on Southeastern aboriginal sites but only those types within the sample group of features available for this study.

Feature Function

Type 1 features, which are found on sites of the Archaic through the Historic periods in the Southeast, often have been called "storage pits" (e.g., Dickens 1971, 1976; Cobb and Faulkner 1978; Wilson 1977). This functional interpretation seems justified on the basis of historic descriptions of similar features being used for food storage by Southeastern Indians (e.g., Bartram 1940:57; Lawson 1967:34–35, 105; Swanton 1946:379), and by Plains and Southwestern Indians (e.g., Forde 1934:249, 256–257;

Lowie 1954:23–24). It is probable that in the Southeast these pits were used mostly for the storage of hard seeds and nuts, as the climates and moist soils would have encouraged above-ground (crib) storage of maize and other "soft" vegetables. Herein, therefore, Type 1 features will be classed functionally as *storage pits*, although this may not have been the sole function of these pits.

Type 2 features have a temporal distribution in the Southeast from the Late Woodland to the Historic periods. These pits usually are referred to as "circular basins," "shallow basin-shaped pits," "simple pits," or by some other formal, rather than functional, designation (e.g., Cobb and Faulkner 1978; Dunnell et al. 1971; Wilson 1977). Most such pits probably were dug to acquire clay for construction and repair of buildings. This interpretation is supported somewhat by the fact that this type of pit is rare on sites that predate a permanent-village settlement pattern in the Southeast. Elsewhere (Dickens 1976:51–66, 1979a:83–100), proposals have been made that these pits should be classed functionally as *borrow pits*. Five such features are grouped in this category for the present study.

Type 3 features, because of the association of postmold patterns, hearths, burial pits, etc., leave no doubt of their function as floors of houses or other structures. Some of these features seem to have been purposefully excavated by the aborigines to lower the floor below the existing ground surface, whereas in other cases the depression may have resulted from repeated cleaning of a floor. Three *structural floors*, all from the Little Egypt site in northwestern Georgia (Hally 1981), are included in the present study.

Type 4 and 5 features, because of their formal characteristics and associations, may be interpreted functionally as *hearths* and/or *cooking pits*. The smaller versions of these features, usually located on structural floors and having burnt-clay linings, leave little doubt that they functioned as hearths. Other versions, often larger and not located on floors, but having rock linings or interior burnt areas, may be classed as cooking pits (sometimes, borrow pits may have functioned as cooking pits following their excavation). Pits of the latter type usually are found adjacent to structures. One hearth and one cooking pit are included in the present study.

Type 6 features, classed as *ditches*, usually are found enclosing, or partly enclosing, villages of the Late Woodland and Mississippian periods in the Southeast (e.g., Dickens 1976; Dunnell et al. 1971; Hally et al. 1975). Often these ditches are quite shallow, and they may even be discontinuous. Usually, there is an associated postmold pattern for a palisade. Wide, deep, and more formalized versions of these features have been termed "moats" at some large Mississippian ceremonial centers, where they probably functioned for defense (Larson 1972). The less formal versions seem mostly to have been byproducts of palisade construction (to obtain clay for daubing or reinforcing the wall). A portion of one such ditch, at the Warren Wilson site in North Carolina, is included in this study (see Ward, this volume).

Type 7 features can be classed functionally as *postholes* and *wall trenches*. Such features are ubiquitous on most late prehistoric and historic sites in the Southeast. They resulted from the use of upright posts in the construction of buildings, palisades, and other facilities. Posts were either set in individual holes or in narrow trenches.

Type 8 features, because they contain human skeletal remains and associated mortuary artifacts, are classed functionally as *burial pits*. Usually the fill of these pits does not contain garbage or any other kind of refuse. Occasionally, however, there will be garbage in the upper portion of such a pit, in a pocket created when the fill slumped following decay of the corpse and its associated wrappings, coverings, etc. Rarely, the original burial fill will contain garbage. Both the slump zone and fill zones of a single burial pit used in this study, Feature 160 at site 38AN8 in South Carolina, contained garbage.

Feature Content and Formation Processes

As previously stated, all of the features included in this study contained some amount of garbage in their fill. The *storage pits* (Type 1 features) uniformly had rather dense and undifferentiated fill. Even where distinct layers were present, the fill seemed to represent a relatively short-term accumulation, as evidenced by the presence of sherds from the same pots in different layers.

It is probable that abandoned storage pits, with their small orifices, large below-ground capacities, and locations near dwellings, would have been highly desirable repositories for waste materials. Once filled, there would have been little chance of dispersal of the garbage by animals and human traffic. And, protected in such pits, the garbage would have attracted fewer vermin. The most likely time for storage pits to have been abandoned, and thus to have become available for garbage disposal, would have been at the time they were determined unsuitable for reuse, that is, when they were found to have become contaminated (e.g., water-filled, soured, or vermin infested).[3] With pits used for storing nuts, inspection for reuse probably would have occurred in the fall to early winter (September–November), when the year's nut crop was ready for collection. One could hypothesize, therefore, that storage pits would have been abandoned and filled with garbage in the fall and early winter more often than at other times of the year. Such an interpretation certainly would not exclude the possibility of these pits being filled occasionally at other seasons.

Since borrow pits (Type 2 features) would not have been dug to serve a purpose themselves, but only to be used as clay sources, they would have been available for use as garbage receptacles immediately after their excavation. Since these pits were shallow and open, the garbage placed in them would have been susceptible to scattering by animals and to some mixing with surrounding surface material by erosion and human traffic. In short, the fill in this type of feature will probably be less homogeneous and have more lensing and intrusions than the fill of storage pits.

The fill in borrow pits should exhibit seasonal patterning if the clay being borrowed was for use in building repairs and construction. It is probable that repairs and construction that required clay daub or chinking would have taken place in the summer and early fall, prior to the onset of cold weather. For Southeastern agriculturalists, an especially good time for such repairs and construction would have been in the months following spring planting and before late summer–fall harvests. One could hypothesize, therefore, that garbage remains in Type 2 pits will exhibit summer to early fall seasonality.

A structural floor (Type 3 feature), following abandonment of the associated structure, might have become a receptacle for garbage if the hole were not already filled with unwanted structural debris. Like borrow pits, however, the fill of such features would have been susceptible to post-depositional contamination, mixing, and erosion. In the cases of burned or collapsed structures, the fill would contain materials present on the floor at the time of destruction.

It is probable that structures, especially dwellings, would not have been purposefully abandoned during colder months. Accidental burning, however, may have occurred more frequently during the cold months, when fires burned hotter and longer within the structures. Seasonality for remains on structural floors, especially dwellings, should be expected to exhibit a spring-to-fall pattern for abandoned structures, and a late fall-to-winter pattern for burned structures. Certainly, however, one should expect exceptions to these patterns.

Hearths and cooking pits (Type 4 and 5 features), probably would have fallen into disuse at the time of abandonment of their associated structures, especially those located on the floors of structures. As with Type 2 and 3 features, these pits would have been open and unprotected, thus making their fill susceptible to post-depositional mixing through erosion, foot traffic, etc. Further, because of their relatively small size, these pits probably were not often used for purposeful garbage deposition, but became filled with more incidental accumulations of such material.

Season of filling would be somewhat variable for these features, unless they were located within a structure, in which case they would conform to the patterns proposed for structural floors. Those containing fill that accumulated incidentally, rather than through rapid deposition, might represent more than one season.

Ditches (Type 6 features) probably would have become available for both purposeful and incidental garbage accumulation immediately after they were opened, except for the more formalized versions, which may have been kept relatively free of refuse (Larson 1972). Ditch fill usually exhibits lensing and intrusive disturbances, which suggest that the materials accumulated erratically and slowly. The remains, therefore, can be expected to cross-cut seasons, although there may be pockets or lenses of seasonally specific remains.

A posthole or wall trench (Type 7 features) would have become a trap or repository for garbage at the time its associated structure was abandoned, or at the time of repairs to the structure. It also would have been possible for some garbage to become trapped around posts while the structure was still in use. For most postholes and wall trenches, the garbage contents should reflect warm-month deposition, unless the structure had burned.

Burial pits (Type 8 features), as noted earlier, seldom were purposefully used as garbage repositories. Garbage sometimes accumulated in the slumped portions of old burials, however, and occasionally garbage-laden soil was used as part of the fill. When garbage is present in the fill, it should reflect the season of burial, whereas the slump fill should represent a period several months subsequent to the interment.

Archaeobotanical Analysis

Seasonality for each of the 22 features was determined from an examination of the charred plant remains extracted from the fill. At the Henderson, Warren Wilson, Plum Grove, Upper Saratown, and Nuyaka sites, the recovery process consisted of fine-screening (lightly hosing the fill through window screen) in the field, and separation of the plant remains by flotation at the laboratory. The Little Egypt and 38AN8 remains were obtained through field flotation.

All or sample portions of the plant remains from each feature were then identified and quantified by an archaeobotanist. Materials from the Henderson and Warren Wilson sites were analyzed by Richard Yarnell, the Plum Grove and Upper Saratown sites by Jack Wilson (under the direction of Richard Yarnell), the Little Egypt site by Richard Yarnell and Gary Crawford, the 38AN8 site by Paul Gardner (under the direction of Richard Yarnell), and the Nuyaka site by Claire C. B. Vaught (with the assistance of Roy Dickens and Elizabeth Sheldon).

Procedures for sorting and classification were comparable between observers. Quantification differed only in that Vaught (Nuyaka site) reported seeds by weight, whereas Yarnell and his students (all other sites) listed them by number. This difference did not present a major problem for this study, however, since the final comparisons were of percentages not frequencies.

The remains from each feature were listed by species (or genus when species-level identification was not possible) under one of three seasons of availability: Late Spring–Early Summer (April–June), Late Summer–Early Fall (July–September), or Late Fall–Early Winter (October–December).[4] This list is given in Table 2-3. It should be noted that assignment to a particular season was made on the basis of availability of the seed, and not necessarily on when other useful parts of the plant are available. Pokeweed seeds, for example, were assigned to Late Fall–

Table 2-3. Plant Remains from Archaeological Features, by Season.[1]

	Henderson		Warren Wilson						Plum Grove		Little Egypt			38AN8	Upper Saratown					Nuyaka		
	Fea. 4	Fea. 5	Fea. 7	Fea. 54	Fea. 57	Fea. 136	Fea. 137	Fea. 140	Fea. 43	Fea. 45	Str. 1	Str. 2	Str. 3	Fea. 160	Fea. 11	Fea. 47	Fea. 23	Fea. 63	Fea. 92	Fea. 1	Fea. 4	Fea. 9
LATE SPRING–EARLY SUMMER																						
Weeds & Grasses																						
Maygrass (*Phalaris caroliniana)*	—	—	—	—	—	—	—	—	—	—	—	—	—	—	—	—	—	—	—	0.04	—	0.03
Fruits																						
Maypop (*Passiflora incarnata)*	—	—	2	1	1	—	—	13	—	—	2	2	6	12	2	4	1	3	2	0.77	0.60	0.07
Strawberry (*Fragaria virginiana)*	—	—	—	—	—	—	—	—	—	—	—	—	—	12	—	—	—	—	—	—	—	—
LATE SUMMER–EARLY FALL																						
Weeds & Grasses																						
Amaranth (*Amaranthus* sp.)	—	—	—	—	—	—	—	—	—	—	—	—	—	—	—	—	—	—	—	0.03	—	—
Bearsfoot (*Polymnia uvedalia)*	—	—	—	—	—	—	—	—	—	—	—	28	23	—	—	—	—	—	—	—	—	—
Bedstraw (*Galium* sp.)	—	—	—	—	—	1	1	—	1	—	—	—	—	—	—	—	—	—	2	0.04	0.07	0.02
Buttonweed (*Diodia teres)*	—	—	—	—	—	—	—	—	—	—	—	—	—	—	—	—	—	—	—	0.07	0.02	0.08
Copperleaf (*Acalypha virginica)*	—	—	—	—	—	—	—	—	—	—	—	—	—	—	—	1	—	—	—	0.01	—	—
Knotweed (*Polygonum* sp.)	—	—	—	—	—	—	1	1	—	—	—	—	3	—	—	1	—	—	—	—	0.02	—
Morning Glory (*Ipomoea* sp.)	—	—	—	—	—	—	—	—	—	—	—	—	—	—	—	—	—	—	—	0.21	0.04	0.09
Partridge Pea (*Cassia fascicalata)*	—	—	—	—	—	—	—	—	—	—	—	—	—	—	—	—	—	—	—	0.02	0.02	0.01
Ragweed (*Ambrosia artemesiifolia)*	—	—	4	1	2	—	—	—	—	—	—	—	—	—	—	—	—	1	—	—	—	—
Cultigens																						
Beans (*Phaseolus vulgaris)*	—	—	—	—	4	2	—	—	1	1	2	1	—	—	—	3	—	—	—	0.01	—	—
Corn (*Zea mays)*	—	—	2.20	0.62	4.52	3.14	0.34	0.69	4.30	1.03	64.90	4.76	34.43	14.78	26.75	35.01	1.86	2.46	1.20	0.36	1.41	0.02
Peach (*Prunus persica)*	—	—	—	—	—	—	—	—	—	—	—	—	—	—	apprx. 119	apprx. 17	apprx. 1	3	1	—	1.39	—
Squash (*Cucurbita pepo)*	—	—	1	—	1	1	—	—	—	—	—	—	—	—	—	1	—	—	—	—	—	—

Sumpweed *(Iva annua)*	—	—	—	—	2	1	—	—	—	—	—	—	—	—	—	—	—	—	—	—	—	—
Sunflower *(Helianthus annus)*	—	—	—	—	—	—	—	—	—	—	—	—	—	—	—	—	—	—	1	—	—	—
Fruits																						
Blackberry *(Rubus* sp.)	—	—	—	—	—	—	—	—	—	—	—	—	—	1	—	—	—	1	—	—	—	—
Honey Locust *(Gleditsia triacanthos)*	1	—	—	—	—	—	—	—	—	—	120	2	22	—	—	—	—	—	—	—	—	—
Plum *(Prunus* sp.)	—	—	—	—	—	—	—	—	—	—	4	—	2	—	—	1	—	—	1	—	—	—
Nuts																						
Hazelnut *(Corylus americana)*	0.10	—	—	—	—	—	—	—	0.08	1.86	—	—	—	—	—	0.12	—	0.02	—	—	—	—
LATE FALL–EARLY WINTER																						
Weeds & Grasses																						
Chenopod *(Chenopodium* sp.)	—	—	—	1	1	—	—	—	—	—	—	—	—	1	—	—	—	—	—	—	—	—
Hog Peanut *(Amphicarpa bracteata)*	—	—	—	—	—	—	—	—	1	—	—	—	—	—	—	—	—	—	—	—	—	—
Pokeweed *(Phytolacca americana)*	—	—	—	—	—	1	—	—	—	—	2	—	36	—	—	5	—	—	—	—	—	0.05
Fruits																						
Grape *(Vitis* sp.)	—	—	8	—	2	9	4	2	—	1	15	10	26	1	9	64	—	2	3	0.01	0.03	—
Hackberry *(Celtis occidentalis)*	2	—	—	—	—	—	—	—	—	—	—	—	—	—	—	—	—	—	—	—	—	—
Hawthorn *(Crataegus rotundifolia)*	5	3	—	—	—	—	—	—	—	—	—	—	—	—	—	2	—	—	—	—	—	—
Persimmon *(Diospyros virginiana)*	6	2	—	—	1	1	—	—	—	—	280	1	—	24	5	12	4	1	—	—	—	—
Nuts																						
Acorn *(Quercus* sp.)	2.20	2.82	0.30	0.50	1.12	0.19	—	—	1.67	1.89	2.90	0.50	0.53	0.25	0.02	0.47	0.09	0.41	0.41	—	0.44	—
Butternut *(Juglans* sp.)	—	—	0.24	0.07	—	0.03	—	—	—	—	3.41	0.05	—	—	—	—	—	—	—	—	—	—
Hickory *(Carya ovata)*	53.10	26.70	3.41	7.71	3.14	19.70	2.20	0.52	9.57	45.92	197.35	9.91	4.55	28.00	3.46	101.88	1.21	11.42	0.63	0.76	1.28	0.02
Walnut *(Juglans nigra)*	0.27	0.36	0.41	0.13	0.54	0.13	0.17	0.07	1.21	3.85	3.04	0.50	2.12	—	—	—	0.10	—	—	—	—	—
Nut (unidentified)	—	—	—	—	—	—	—	—	—	—	—	—	—	—	—	—	0.01	0.01	—	0.31	4.55	0.55

[1]All seeds are listed by number (except for Nuyaka features); all corn and nuts are listed by gram weight.

Early Winter, because that is the season when the berry ripens and the mature seed is available. Edible parts (shoots and leaves) of the poke plant, however, would have been available from late spring to midsummer, before the seed matures. Poke seeds probably got into the garbage either incidentally (because the plants were growing around the habitations), or as byproducts of use of the berries for a medicine, dye, or fish stunner.

From the tabulations, percentage profiles by season were constructed for each feature. On these profiles, the major storable food plants (corn and nuts) are presented separately from the other plant types. It was felt that without this separation, the profiles would have provided less sensitive indications of seasonality. This is not to say, however, that corn and nuts were the only plants preserved across seasons.

The archaeobotanical profiles for the 22 features are shown in Figures 2-3 to 2-8. On these graphs, the hatched columns represent the percentages of major storable foods (corn and nuts) by season, whereas the darkened columns represent all other seeds by season. This type of representation is useful in that it can provide a suggestion of season even when all of the remains do not fall within a single season. For example, a profile on which 25 percent of the seeds (nonmajor storable foods) are in the Late Spring–Early Summer group, 70 percent are in the Late Summer–Early Fall group, and 5 percent are in the Late Fall–Early Winter group, one would be safe in proposing a Late Summer deposition. In short, the tendency on this profile would be toward the first part of the Late Summer–Early Fall period.

Features classed in the *storage pit* (Type 1) category (Figure 2-3) consisted of two from the Late Woodland period (Henderson site), four from the Mississippian period (Warren Wilson and Plum Grove sites) and three from the Historic period (Upper Saratown). The two Henderson features (Figure 2-3, A and B), the two Warren Wilson features (Figure 2-3, C and D), and one of the Upper Saratown features (Figure 2-3, G) have strong Late Fall–Early Winter profiles. The two Plum Grove features, (Figure 2-3, E and F) and two of the Upper Saratown features (Figure 2-3, H and I) show a tendency toward Late Summer–Early Fall seasonality. The profiles for Plum Grove features may not be reliable because of the small number of seeds identified for each of them.[5]

The late summer to early winter tendencies for the storage pits is

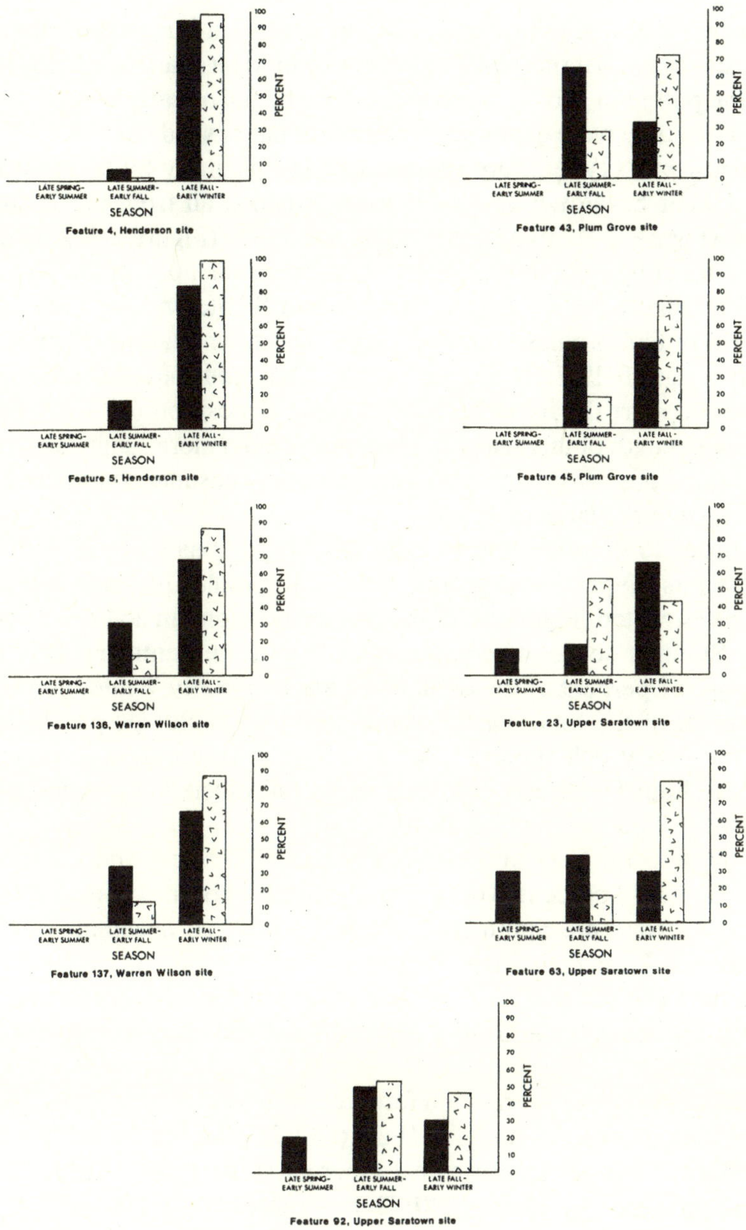

Figure 2-3. Seasonal Profiles for Archaeobotanical Remains from Storage Pits.

consistent with the hypothesis developed early in this paper. That hypothesis stated that these pits most often would be abandoned, and thus become potential garbage repositories, in the fall or early winter, at the time when they were examined for reuse in nut or seed storage.

Borrow pits (Type 2) are represented in this study by two features from Upper Saratown and three from Nuyaka, all from the Historic period (Figure 2-4). Two of the Nuyaka features (Figure 2-4, A and B) exhibit a strong Late Spring–Early Summer profile, one of the Nuyaka features (Figure 2-4, C) and one from Upper Saratown have Late Summer–Early Fall profiles, and one Upper Saratown feature (Figure 2-4, E) has a Late Fall–Early Winter profile. Thus, four out of five of these profiles support the hypothesis of summer deposition for this type of pit. The strength of this seasonal tendency is even more significant given the possibilities for mixing, and thus for cross-seasonal contamination, of the fill in these large open pits.

In order to compare the storage pits (Type 1) as a group with the borrow pits (Type 2) as a group, composite profiles for each category were constructed (Figure 2-5). The storage pits contain no Late Spring–Early Summer seeds, whereas species from Late Summer–Early Fall comprise 33 percent of the total, and Late Fall–Early Winter comprise 67 percent of the total. Of the major storables in storage pit fill, Late Summer–Early Fall species (corn and hazelnut) represent 12 percent, whereas Late Fall–Early Winter species (all other nuts) represent 88 percent. For borrow pits, seeds from Late Spring–Early Summer comprise 47 percent, Late Summer–Early Fall 36 percent, and Late Fall–Early Winter 17 percent. Major storable foods in borrow pits consist of 36 percent for Late Summer–Early Fall (corn and hazelnuts) and 64 percent for Late Fall–Early Winter (all other nuts). Seasonal differences between the two types of features are significant for frequencies of both the seeds (x^2 48.68 df 2 $p < .001$) and the major storable foods (x^2 33.23 df 1 $p < .001$).

Archaeobotanical information for three *structural floors* (Type 3) were available from a recent study by Hally (1981:723–742) of the Little Egypt site (Barnett phase) in northwest Georgia (Figure 2-6). These floors were interpreted by Hally (1981:724) as representing domestic structures. Two of the houses (Structures 1 and 3) had burned while in use, whereas the other (Structure 2) had been abandoned. The fill of the two burned structures cannot be classed as garbage, since most of the re-

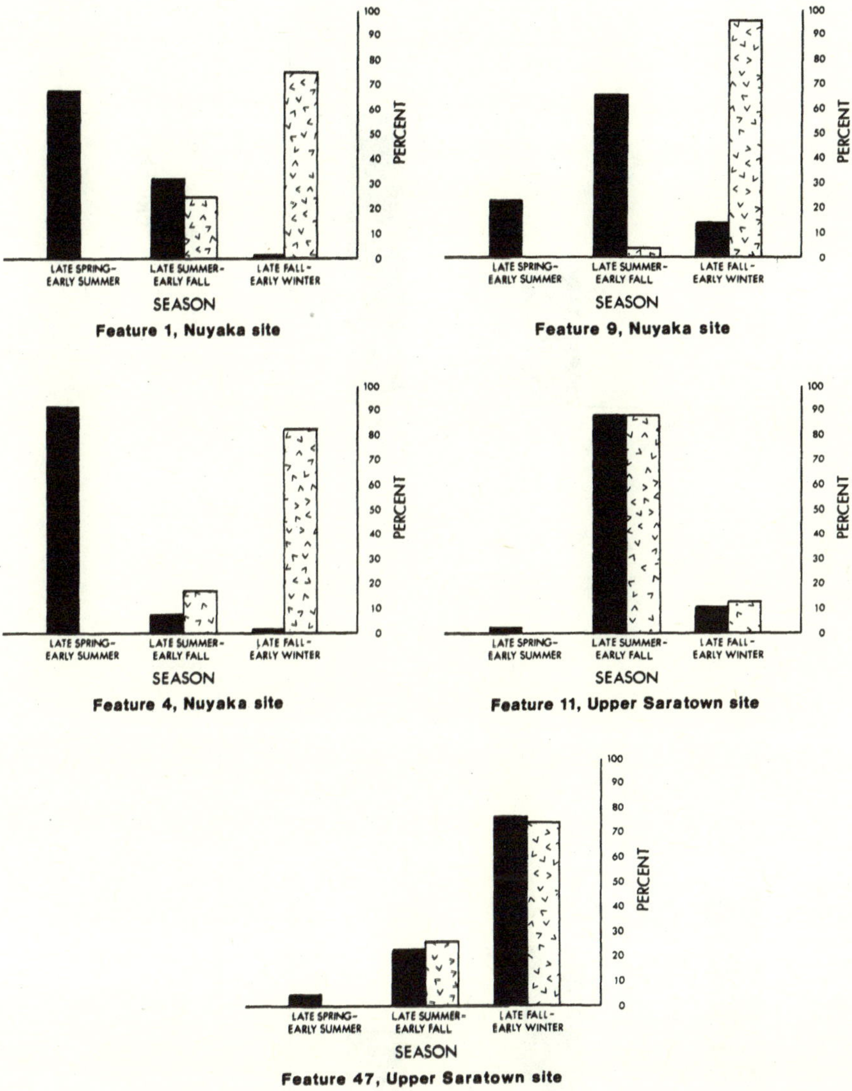

Figure 2-4. Seasonal Profiles for Archaeobotanical Remains from Borrow Pits.

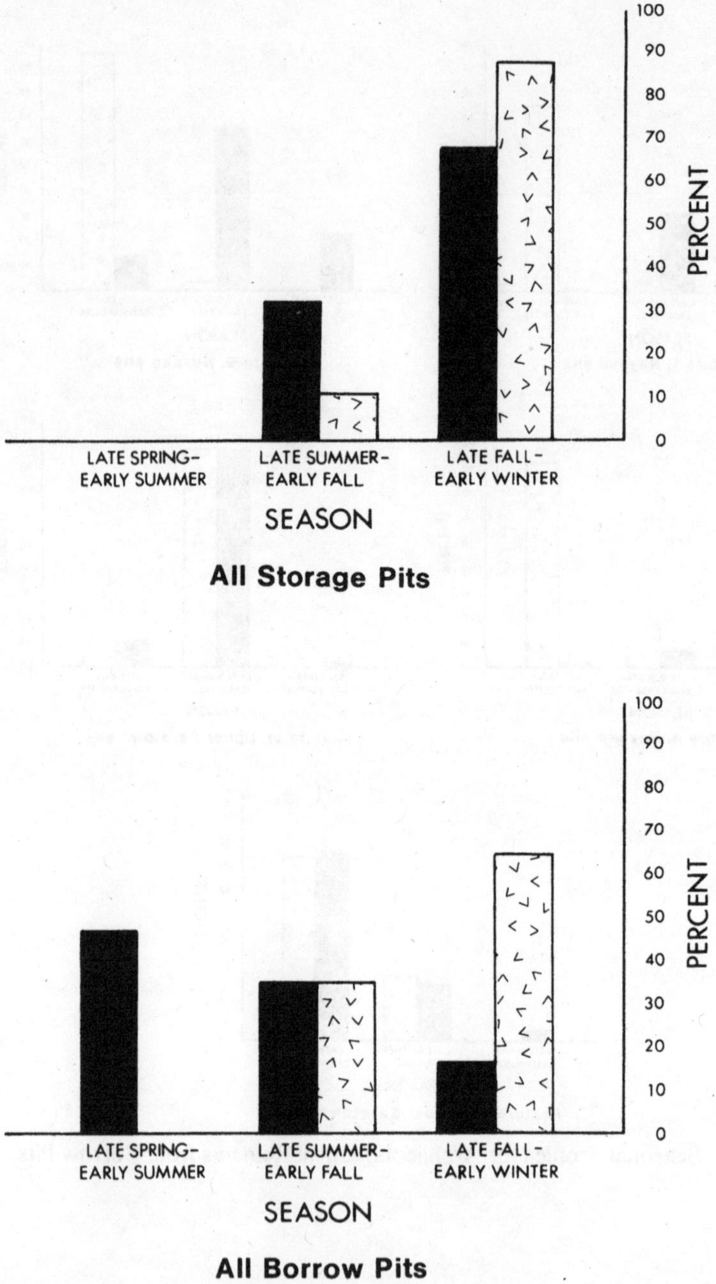

Figure 2-5. Composite Profiles for Storage and Borrow Pits.

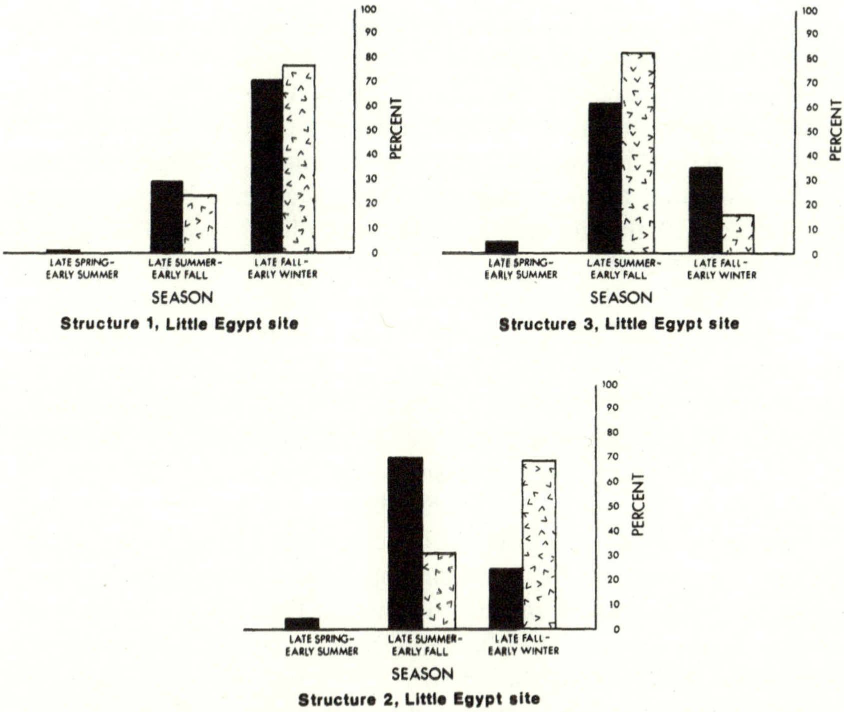

Figure 2-6. Seasonal Profiles for Archaeobotanical Remains from Structural Floors.

mains seem to represent unused plant stuffs present in the houses when they burned. The plant remains on the floor of the abandoned structure, however, can be identified as refuse that was on the floor at the time of abandonment.

Even though the plant remains from Structures 1 and 3 could not be classed as garbage, and thus differed in composition from the other remains under study, it would be useful to compare the seasonal profiles of the three floors. The seasonal profile for Structure 1, one of the burned houses, suggests a Late Fall–Early Winter destruction, probably late fall. This interpretation agrees closely with Hally's (1981:735) estimation of mid-October to mid-December. The profile of Structure 3, the other burned house, suggests destruction in the Late Summer–Early Fall interval, probably early fall. Again, this placement agrees closely with Hally's (1981:375) estimation of mid-July to mid-September. Structure

2, which showed no evidence of burning, had a Late Summer–Early Fall profile, probably late summer.

Although this archaeobotanical information from only three structural floors constitutes a very small sample, it tends to support the hypothesis that dwellings would stand a greater chance of being abandoned in warm weather and a greater chance of accidental burning in cold weather. As with the storage pits and borrow pits, the two floors (Structures 2 and 3) with the greatest percentages of Late Summer–Early Fall seeds also have the largest amounts of corn relative to nuts.

A single *hearth* (Type 4) and a single *cooking pit* (Type 5), both from the Warren Wilson site (Pisgah phase), North Carolina, were represented in the study group. One (Feature 140) was a small, circular burnt-clay depression on a house floor, and the other (Feature 57) was a medium-sized, shallow, oval depression containing burnt areas and located adjacent to a house floor (Dickens 1976:56–63). The hearth contained a rather homogeneous fill, which indicates rapid filling, whereas the larger pit contained lensed fill, which represents slower, sequential filling.

The archaeobotanical analysis revealed a Late Spring–Early Summer profile for Feature 140 (Figure 2-7), which suggests warm-period abandonment for its associated structure. The presence of approximately equal amounts of corn and nuts in the major storable food category follows the pattern already noted for pits containing large percentages of Late Spring–Early Summer seeds. The plant remains extracted from the lensed fill of Feature 57 produced the "flattest" (least seasonally specific) profile of the entire group (Figure 2-7). The probable explanation is cross-season mixing, which could have resulted from slow filling.

A single *ditch/moat* (Type 6) was included in the study (Figure 2-7). This feature (Feature 7) represented a surviving portion of a shallow ditch associated with Palisade D at the Warren Wilson site (Pisgah phase) in western North Carolina (Dickens 1976:45, 54). Although the majority of seeds (57 percent) are Late Fall–Early Winter species, some appreciable amounts of species from Late Spring–Early Summer (29 percent) and Late Summer–Early Fall (14 percent) also are present. Thus, the profile suggests a fall deposition, while also reflecting possible cross-season mixing. A rather flat profile for such a feature is predictable considering the likelihood of gradual filling.

The *postmold/wall trench* (Type 7) category also was represented by

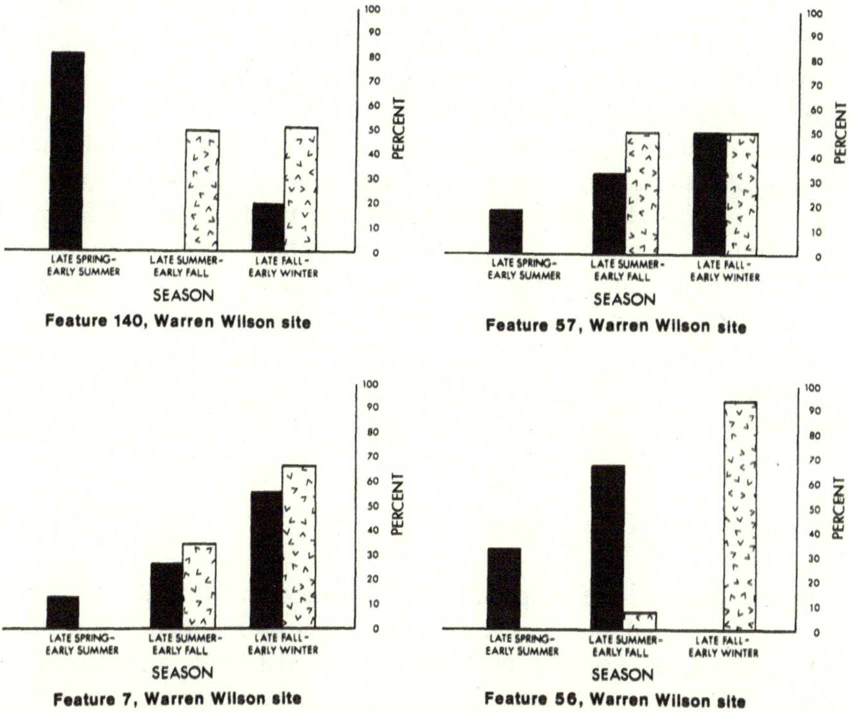

Figure 2-7. Seasonal Profiles for Archaeobotanical Remains from Selected Features at the Warren Wilson Site.

only one feature, Feature 56, at the Warren Wilson site (Figure 2-7). This feature consisted of a portion of wall trench for Palisade D (Dickens 1976:48, 56). The seeds in this feature were predominately from summer species (33 percent Late Spring–Early Summer and 67 percent Late Summer–Early Fall). A preponderance of nuts (93 percent) and lack of corn (7 percent) among the major storables, however, is inconsistent with the seed data. Nevertheless, the suggestion of summer deposition provided by the seeds supports the hypothesis of warm-month rebuilding and repair of village structures.

A single *burial pit* (Type 8), Feature 160 at the 38AN8 site (Lamar phase) in northwestern South Carolina (Wood 1981:43–44), was included in the study. This pit, which appears to be of the shaft-and-side chamber variety (Dickens 1976:103), contained three garbage-laden soil zones: (1) a zone of fill in the lower part of the pit around the skeletal remains, (2) a zone of fill in the central part of the pit, and (3) a zone of postburial slump in the upper part of the pit. The archaeobotanical analysis was by zone (Gardner 1981:216–225).

Plant remains (Figure 2-8) from the lower fill zone produced a seasonal profile indicating Late Spring–Early Summer deposition (i.e., interment). The middle zone (probably fill) also produced a Late Spring–Early Summer profile. The upper zone, undoubtedly representing postburial slump, produced a Late Fall–Early Winter profile. It is important to note that the ratio of corn to nuts shifts from the lower to upper zones. This feature provides an excellent example of the importance of separating, in recovery and analysis, fill from slump material in any feature.

Summary and Conclusions

In this study, I have proposed that pits found on late prehistoric and historic aboriginal sites in the Southeast can be grouped into formal types, that a function can be proposed for each type, and that each function resulted in ultimate abandonment and refilling within probable seasonal parameters. To test the validity of such a proposal, 22 features from six sites were grouped into formal-functional types, and hypotheses were developed concerning season of abandonment and filling for each type. Features containing household garbage, which usually indicates rapid and intentional filling, were used. Seasonality, determined from previously recorded archaeobotanical lists, was displayed as percentage "profiles."

In most cases the profiles supported the hypotheses developed for seasonality. For example, six out of seven features classed as storage pits were found to have late summer to early winter profiles, which suggests abandonment and filling at the time of the year when these pits would have been inspected for reuse as nut storage facilities. Three out of four borrow pits, on the other hand, were found to have late spring to early fall profiles, an expected finding based on an hypothesis that these pits were created during the warm months to acquire clay for architectural repairs and construction. Three other structurally related features—the floor of an abandoned house, a hearth, and a palisade wall

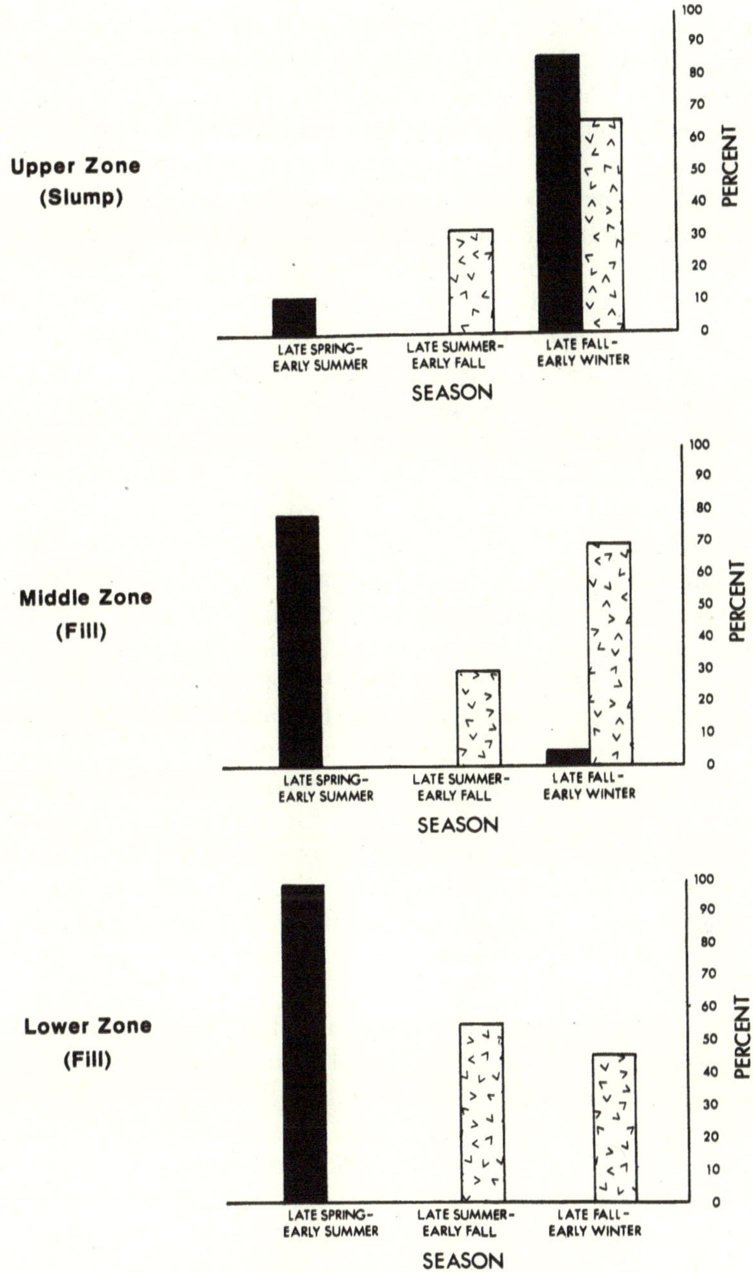

Figure 2-8. Seasonal Profiles from Three Zones of a Burial Pit.

trench—also exhibited warm-month profiles. The floors of two burned houses, on the other hand, had fall to winter profiles. A refilled cooking pit and a ditch, both of which contained evidence for long-term, sequential deposition, had less seasonally specific profiles than the other features.

Since the number of features within each type in this study is small, the seasonal patterns that seem to be present should be accepted only with caution. One should also recognize that even if the patterns are real, and are replicated in future studies, every feature within a type should not be expected to exhibit the same seasonal profile. The hypotheses are directed only to probabilities of abandonment and filling. All in all, however, the findings of this small study do suggest that archaeological features and their contents should be examined from the perspective of formation processes, rather than just in terms of their original functions or just as undifferentiated garbage receptacles—i.e., as "garbage pits."

If, as this study contends, seasonal regularity can be established for the formation of fills from various types of pits, some obvious research potentials are opened. It would aid the archaeologist in selecting features to be analyzed by specialists, so as to obtain a better cross-section of seasonal activities in a village setting. It would demonstrate, perhaps above all, that zooarchaeological and archaeobotanical data from various types of features should not be lumped if seasonal activity patterning is a primary concern. The now-classic Scovill study (Munson et al. 1971) is an especially good example of this problem. Even though the Scovill researchers excavated, analyzed, and tabulated separately the remains from each archaeological feature, and even though seasonality was a major focus of their study, the data were lumped for purposes of interpretation.

The present study also validates the need for zooarchaeological and archaeobotanical analyses of individual features and small groups of features when limitations of money and project scope do not provide for large-scale endeavors. In this regard, I have been fortunate over the years to have secured the interest of Richard Yarnell and his students in working with relatively small groups of remains. It was, in fact, the accumulation of a number of these small analyses that made the present study possible. In conclusion, therefore, Southeastern archaeologists are urged to recognize the importance of potential regularities in the formation processes of refilled pits. Excavation, recovery, analysis, and reporting of these features should be standardized to the degree necessary for intersite comparisons.

Notes

1. This paper stems in part from one of those casual yet astute observations by Joffre Coe. Some years ago, at one of the professional conferences, we were sitting together at a session on Southeastern research. The author of a paper pronounced that he was going to discuss the contents of several "garbage pits" from a particular site. Coe leaned over and whispered that there was "no such thing as a 'garbage pit' ". After the paper, he elaborated that pits were not dug to serve as garbage receptacles, but only became repositories for garbage after fulfilling their original functions. He concluded that we should not call them "garbage pits" just because they contain refuse. I hereby acknowledge that and many other such prods to my basic archaeological thinking that Joffre Coe has so exquisitely provided.

2. The range of dimensions for each feature type was determined from measurements given in a number of archaeological reports from the Southeast. They should be taken as "typical" size ranges, and not as absolute parameters.

3. Because these pits had steep, and often undercut, sides, animals that fell into them would have been trapped and eventually would have died.

4. Assignment of a species to one of the three seasons was based on personal knowledge, and reference to various botanical manuals and trailguides (e.g., Cuthbert 1948; Fernald 1950; Hall 1976; Miller 1973; Peterson 1977; Radford et al. 1964; Smith 1979).

5. Fall deposition for Feature 43 is supported further by the presence of passenger pigeon in the faunal assemblage.

3 • JACK H. WILSON, JR.

Feature Zones and Feature Fill: More Than Trash

Introduction

Time, space, and content are fundamental elements in all archaeological studies. Time and space define finite, physical parameters, while content describes the raw data—the cultural ingredient of archaeology. Archaeological information is drawn from a myriad of sources, ranging from site locations and the surrounding environmental and ecological factors, to site formation processes, to the material remains of past populations. Since content represents the "fossilized" behavioral patterns that serve as the basis for anthropological interpretations, it follows that *context* is the major determinant of the fitness and pertinence of behavioral data that comprise content.

In the study of charred plant remains from archaeological contexts, it is usually the case that feature class, such as midden, storage pit, or hearth, serves as the basic unit of analysis. It is argued here that, when feasible, a finer-grained approach to the study of plant remains may yield data higher in quality and quantity than analysis only by feature class. This proposition is examined through the analysis of a sample of plant material from the features at Upper Saratown. I try to show that feature form, function, and fill strata are not always strictly related at a site. Also, an attempt is made to evaluate some of the behavioral implications of the features and the fill they contain (see Dickens, Ward, this volume). Finally, a revised approach to the study of plant material from archaeological sites is offered.

The research endeavor providing the data used in this paper has evolved over the years into what can be termed the "Siouan Project." Its humble beginnings lie in the surveys and testing conducted by Joffre Coe and others before World War II at various Siouan sites in the North Carolina Piedmont and southern Virginia (Coe 1937; 1964:6). Almost half a century later, this work is being carried forward through the excavations by the staff and students of the Research Laboratories of Anthropology at the sites of three protohistoric and historic Sara Indian villages, referred to collectively as the Upper Saratown group (Figure 3-1).

This chapter examines the content of the features at Upper Saratown (31SKla). The refuse in these pits consists of a rich array of cultural items, including pottery; projectile points and other worked stone implements; worked antler and bone; food refuse; and European trade items, such as glass trade beads, bells, hair pieces, and brass scraps. At Upper Saratown, the features contain the residue of a variety of activities.

A number of the features, such as hearths or shallow roasting basins, contain relatively homogenous fill. Other features do not. As an example, "trash" pits, that range between two or three feet in depth and seem to have served formerly as storage pits, possess stratified and differing zones of fill. Just as the features served different purposes, their various fill zones also reflect diverse behavioral activities. The different zones are separated during excavation and in the subsequent analysis of the contents of the pit. With careful excavation and detailed analysis, it should be possible to interpret the behavioral activities that produced the combination of attributes represented in each feature fill zone. This study concentrates on the charred plant remains in the features to begin defining these behavioral activities.

The Data Base

At Upper Saratown, features are excavated following standardized procedures developed at the Research Laboratories. A feature to be excavated is first bisected in plan and one-half removed. The remaining unexcavated portion provides a profile, documenting the various zones that may be present. Excavation of each half is by depositional zones. At least a one-quart soil sample is retained from each zone within each feature. The remainder of each zone is waterscreened through 1/16th- and, more recently, 1/32nd-inch mesh screen (standard window screen) to recover the artifact material. Each zone from each half of a feature is kept separate through the entire process.

During the first four years of work at the site, 117 features were excavated following the above procedures. Twelve of these features, repre-

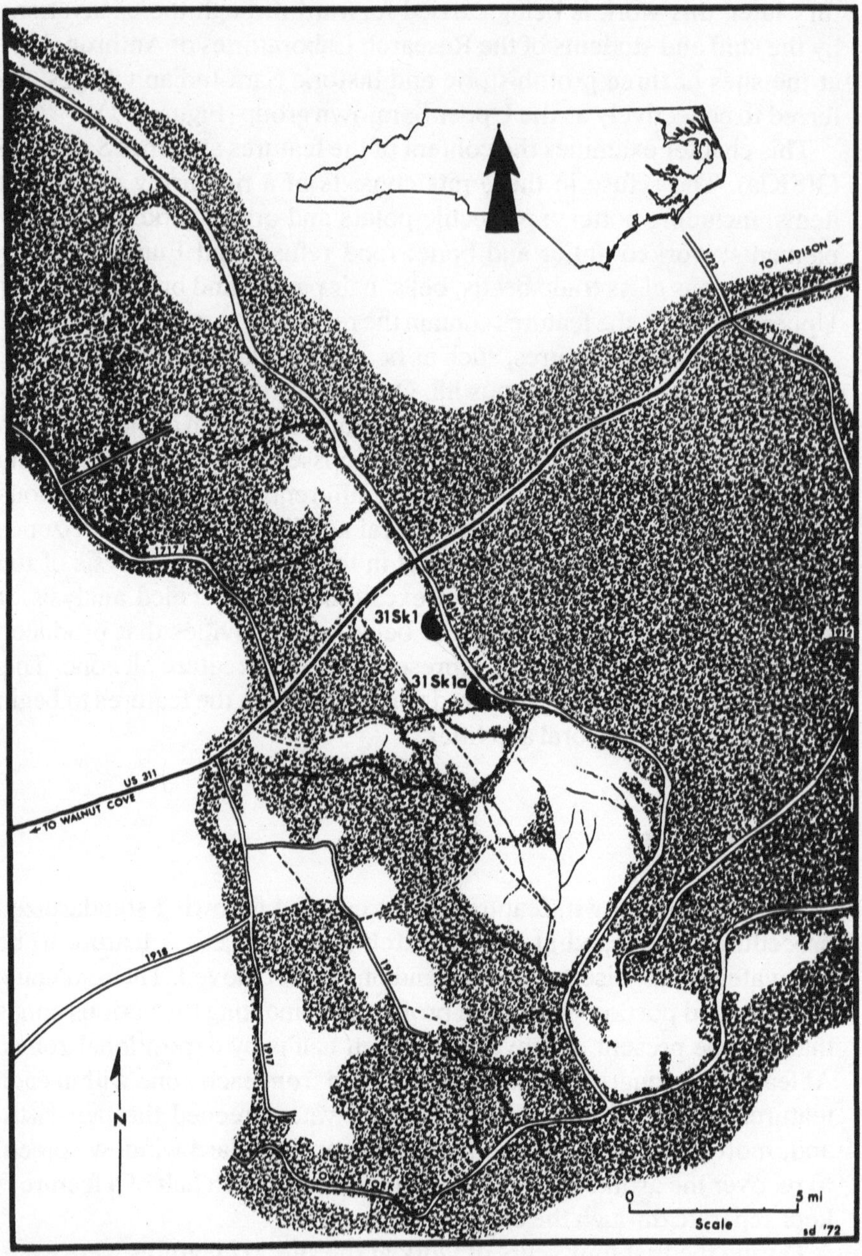

Figure 3-1. Location of Upper Saratown Site Group.

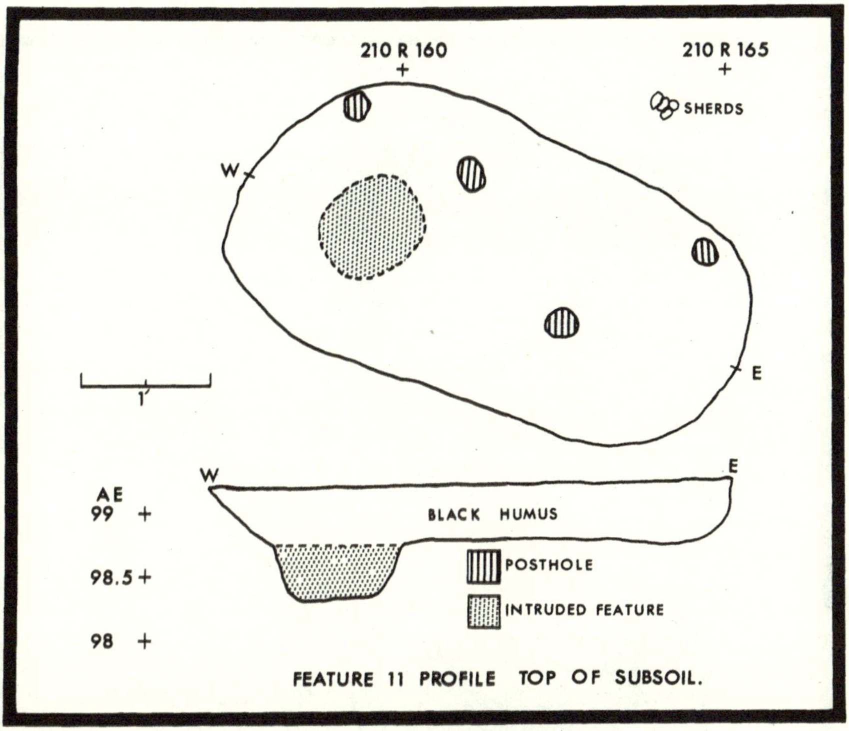

Figure 3-2. Feature 11, a Shallow Basin/Earth Oven.

senting five feature categories, were chosen for this initial study. The five categories and the number of each type of feature analyzed were as follows: five shallow basins, three storage pits, two hearths, one washout, and one slump over a burial. The five shallow basins are Features 11 (Figure 3-2), 47, 50, 52, and 111. The storage pits examined include Features 23 (Figure 3-3), 63 and 92. Features 22 and 65 comprise the hearths in the sample. The single washout is represented by Feature 60, and Feature 108 (Figure 3-4) represents slump over a burial.

Analysis of the charred botanical remains from the waterscreenings and selected soil samples from the 26 zones of fill present in these 12 features followed guidelines developed by Richard A. Yarnell. Each sample was divided into 11 portions containing particles of approximately the same size. All material that did not fall through a 2.4 mm screen was completely sorted into its various components. The quan-

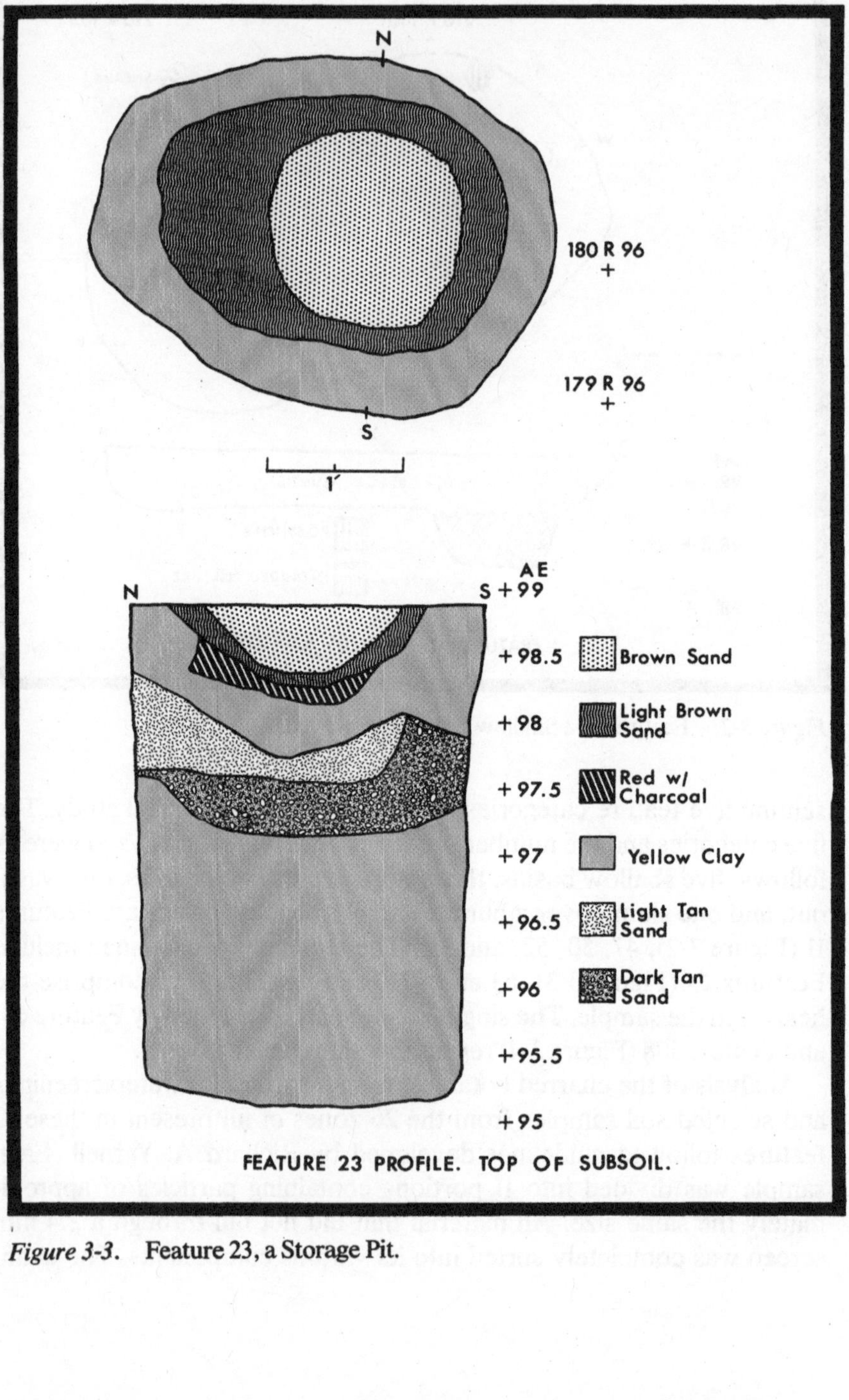

Figure 3-3. Feature 23, a Storage Pit.

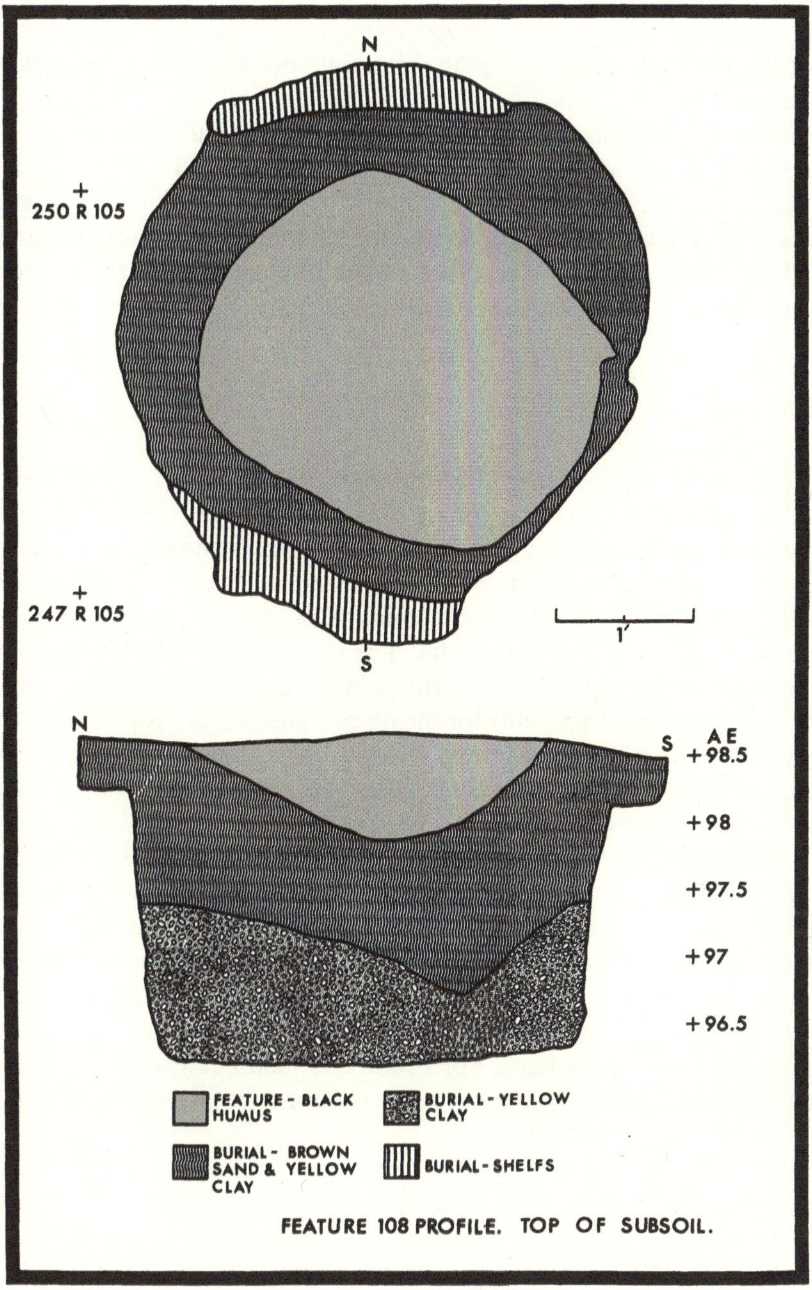

Figure 3-4. Feature 108, Fill in a Cavity Created by the Slump of a Burial.

tities of plant remains that passed through the 2.4 mm screen were checked only for seeds and plant materials not present in the larger sized subsample.

Five broad categories of identifiable charred botanical specimens were recognized during analysis. These were cultigens, nuts, fruits (here used in the general sense to include large fleshy fruits, berry fruits, aggregate fruits, and accessory fruits), herbs, and miscellaneous plant remains (such as wood charcoal). The various kinds of plant remains recovered, and their scientific names, are listed in Table 3-1.

Discussion

From the analysis of the charcoal, five distinct classes of fill were established for the 26 zones of fill identified. Tables 3-2 through 3-7 show the plant and seed remains by feature category and fill class. These classes are defined by color and fill composition. To some extent color is a function of the amount of charcoal mixed with the major soil constituent (clay, sand, etc.) of the fill. The degree to which the soil of a zone was subjected to fire also affects color, along with other factors. The soil constituent accounts for the fill composition or "feel." The five classes are black humus, white or red ash, brown loam, mottled yellow clay, and light brown/tan sand. The plant remains associated with each fill class are listed in Table 3-8 and 3-9.

The black humus class contained eight zones of fill. This category was further split into two subdivisions. A distinction could be made between those zones with relatively little plant food material and a high wood charcoal content, and those with relatively large amounts of plant food remains and relatively small quantities of wood charcoal. This distinction is illustrated in Table 3-10. In the former category were Zone 1 of Feature 63, Zones 1 and 3 of Feature 92, and Feature 60. With the exception of the zone from Feature 60, the zones of fill came from what have been called "storage pits."

The three zones of fill from Features 63 and 92 were created by material thrown into open pits. There was no evidence that they were the results of fires being built within the pit, and then being covered over. It would seem obvious, however, that these black humus zones were the remnants of fires. The large amount of wood charcoal that is the distin-

Table 3-1. Plant Remains from 31SK1a and Their Scientific Names.

CULTIGENS	
	Corn–*Zea mays* L.
	Beans–*Phaseolus vulgaris* L.
	Squash–*Cucurbita pepo* L.
	Bottlegourd–*Lagenaria siceraria* Standl.
	Sunflower–*Helianthus annus* L.
	Watermelon–*Citrullus (vulgaris) lanatus* Schrad.
	Peach–*Prunus persica* (L.) Batsch
FRUITS	
	Grapes–*Vitis* sp.
	Groundcherry–*Physalis pubescens* L.
	Hawthorn–*Crataegus rotundifolia* Moench.
	Passionflower–*Passiflora incarnata* L.
	Persimmon–*Diospyros virginiana* L.
	Plum–*Prunnus americana* Marsh.
	Bramble–*Rubus* sp.
	Blueberry (etc.)–*Vaccinium* sp.
NUTS	
	Acorn–*Quercus* sp.
	Hazelnut–*Corylus americana* Walt.
	Hickory–*Carya ovata* (Mill.) L.
	Walnut–*Juglans nigra* L.
WEEDS	
	Bedstraw–*Galium* sp.
	Copperleaf–*Acalypha virginica* L.
	Knotweed–*Polygonum* sp.
	Pokeweed–*Phytolacca americana* L.
	Tickclover–*Desmodium* sp.
GRASSES	
	Cane–*Arundinaria gigantea* Walt. or *A. tecta* Walt.
WOOD CHARCOAL	
	Chestnut–*Castanea dentata* (Marsh.) Borkh.
	Hickory–*Carya ovata* (Mill.) L.
	Oak–*Quercus* sp.
	Pine–*Pinus* sp.

guishing characteristic of these three zones amply supports this interpretation. One function of these fires was the preparation of food, most likely for consumption and not storage. The use of the fires to prepare plant foods for preservation cannot, of course, be completely rejected. Usually, however, storage preparation of plant food was accomplished

Table 3-2. Weights of Plant Remains by Zones—Shallow Basins.

	Fea. 11	Fea. 47	Feature 50			Feature 52		Feature 111		
PLANT REMAINS	BLACK HUMUS	BLACK HUMUS	BLACK BROWN	YELLOW CLAY	BROWN SAND	BLACK ORGAN.	BROWN SAND	BROWN GREY	RED GREY	WHITE GREY
Corn Kernel	0.66	2.75	0.26	0.02	0.22	0.48	—	—	0.12	0.04
Corncob	18.76	32.26	0.65	0.07	0.22	17.25	5.73	0.44	0.15	0.46
Cucurbit Rind	0.16	0.04	—	—	—	—	—	—	—	0.20
Peach Pit	5.86	6.68	—	—	—	1.00	1.68	—	0.08	0.03
Plum Pit	—	0.04	—	—	—	—	—	—	—	—
Acorn Shell	0.04	0.47	0.02	—	—	0.02	0.03	0.05	0.03	0.01
Hazelnut Shell	—	0.12	—	—	—	0.02	0.01	—	—	—
Hickory Shell	2.01	101.88	1.23	0.08	0.34	3.68	0.85	1.18	0.78	0.63
Walnut Shell	—	—	2.40	—	0.35	—	—	0.08	—	—
Subtotal	27.49	144.24	4.56	0.17	1.13	22.45	8.29	1.75	1.16	1.37
Wood Charcoal	29.12	20.42	18.01	0.54	4.59	4.08	1.49	11.44	20.20	21.01
Bark	0.81	—	—	—	—	0.02	0.02	0.02	—	—
Leaf	0.78	2.92	0.24	—	0.04	0.36	0.05	0.02	—	—
Cane	3.53	6.98	0.08	—	—	0.35	0.32	—	—	0.01
Unidentified	0.14	3.65	0.43	—	0.05	0.02	—	0.02	0.02	0.04
Subtotal	34.38	33.97	18.76	0.54	4.68	4.83	1.88	11.50	20.22	21.06
TOTAL	61.87	178.21	23.32	0.71	5.81	27.28	10.17	13.25	21.38	22.43

Table 3-3. Seed Remains by Zones—Shallow Basins.

SEEDS	Fea. 11 BLACK HUMUS	Fea. 47 BLACK HUMUS	BLACK BROWN	Feature 50 YELLOW CLAY	BROWN SAND	Feature 52 BLACK ORGAN.	BROWN SAND	BROWN GREY	Feature 111 RED GREY	WHITE GREY	TOTAL
Unidentified	3	56	21	—	1	47	2	—	1	—	131
Unidentified Legume	—	—	—	—	—	2	—	—	—	—	2
Copperleaf	—	1	—	—	—	—	—	—	—	—	1
Knotweed	—	1	—	—	—	—	—	—	—	—	1
Pokeweed	—	5	—	—	—	—	—	—	—	—	5
Tickclover	—	—	—	—	—	2	—	—	—	—	2
Grape	9	64	2	—	—	97	2	—	—	—	174
Grape Stems	—	34	—	—	—	10	1	—	—	—	45
Groundcherry	—	—	—	—	—	3	—	—	—	—	3
Hawthorn	—	2	—	—	—	—	—	—	—	1	3
Passionflower	2	4	—	—	—	1	—	—	1	1	9
Persimmon	5	12	1	—	—	—	—	—	3	8	29
Vaccinium	—	1	—	—	—	5	—	—	—	—	6
Beans	—	3	—	—	—	—	—	—	—	—	3
Bottlegourd	—	1	—	—	—	—	—	—	—	—	1
Squash	—	1	—	—	—	—	—	—	—	—	1
Watermelon	—	—	—	—	—	1	—	—	—	—	1
TOTAL	19	185	24	—	1	168	5	—	5	10	417
WEIGHT	0.25	2.67	0.04	—	*	0.83	0.02	—	0.10	0.45	4.36+

*Less than 0.01 grams.

Table 3-4. Weights of Plant Remains by Zones—Storage Pits.

	Feature 23				Feature 63				Feature 92			
PLANT REMAINS	SANDY BROWN	SANDY LIGHT	YELLOW CLAY	SAND DARK	YELLOW CLAY	BLACK HUMUS	RED/ BLACK	SAND	BLACK HUMUS	YELLOW CLAY	BLACK HUMUS	YELLOW CLAY
Corn Kernel	0.08	0.08	0.05	0.23	0.38	0.48	0.09	0.66	0.01	0.03	0.46	0.09
Corncob	0.49	—	0.05	0.08	0.47	0.70	0.24	1.86	0.09	0.08	0.42	0.02
Peach Pit	—	—	0.05	—	—	0.72	0.11	0.53	—	—	0.01	—
Acorn Shell	0.06	—	0.01	—	0.02	0.10	0.05	0.12	—	0.01	0.06	0.01
Acorn Meat	—	—	—	—	—	0.14	—	—	—	—	0.33	—
Hazelnut Shell	—	—	—	—	—	—	—	0.02	—	—	—	—
Hickory Shell	0.10	0.14	0.47	0.31	0.19	2.79	4.06	4.57	0.16	0.12	0.21	0.09
Walnut Shell	—	0.10	—	—	—	—	—	—	—	—	—	—
Subtotal	0.73	0.32	0.63	0.62	1.06	4.93	4.55	7.76	0.26	0.24	1.49	0.21
Wood Charcoal	25.32	0.38	3.32	5.19	22.49	19.54	15.00	42.98	1.92	1.54	16.29	8.76
Bark	0.03	—	0.01	0.03	0.01	0.10	—	1.07	0.11	0.01	0.25	0.01
Leaf	—	—	—	0.05	0.05	0.36	0.01	0.93	0.04	0.10	0.60	0.02
Cane	—	—	—	—	—	—	0.01	0.27	0.12	0.01	0.04	—
Unidentified	0.19	—	—	0.02	0.05	0.05	0.06	0.06	—	0.02	0.01	0.06
Subtotal	25.54	0.38	3.33	5.29	22.60	20.05	15.08	45.31	2.19	1.68	17.19	8.85
TOTAL	26.27	0.70	3.96	5.91	23.66	24.98	19.63	53.07	2.45	1.92	18.68	9.06

Table 3-5. Seed Remains by Zones–Storage Pits.

	Feature 23					Feature 63			Feature 92				
SEEDS	SANDY BROWN	SANDY LIGHT	YELLOW CLAY	SANDY DARK	YELLOW CLAY	BLACK HUMUS	RED/ BLACK	SAND	BLACK HUMUS	YELLOW CLAY	BLACK HUMUS	YELLOW CLAY	TOTAL
Unidentified	—	—	—	1	1	6	—	6	—	—	14	—	28
Galium	—	—	—	—	—	—	—	—	—	—	2	—	2
Ragweed	—	—	—	—	—	1	—	—	—	—	—	—	1
Grape	—	—	—	—	—	1	1	—	—	—	3	—	5
Passionflower	—	—	—	—	1	—	—	2	—	—	2	—	5
Persimmon	1	—	—	2	1	—	1	—	—	—	—	—	5
Rubus	—	—	—	—	—	—	—	1	—	—	—	—	1
Sunflower	—	—	—	—	—	—	—	—	—	—	1	—	1
TOTAL	1	—	—	3	3	8	2	9	—	—	22	—	48
WEIGHT	*	—	—	0.06	0.01	0.03	0.03	0.02	—	—	0.07	—	0.22+

*Less than 0.01 grams.

Table 3-6. Weights of Plant Remains by Zones—Hearths, Washout, and Slump.

PLANT REMAINS	Fea. 22 REDDISH CLAY	Fea. 65 BLACK BROWN RED	Fea. 60 BLACK GRITTY FILL	Fea. 108 BLACK HUMUS
Corn Kernel	—	0.06	0.07	1.39
Corncob	—	—	0.26	3.79
Peach Pit	—	—	2.57	1.83
Acorn Shell	0.01	—	0.01	0.80
Hazelnut Shell	—	—	—	0.02
Hickory Shell	0.02	0.56	0.21	1.57
Subtotal	0.03	0.62	3.12	9.40
Wood Charcoal	0.23	1.58	10.16	20.25
Bark	—	—	—	0.11
Leaf	—	0.34	0.10	0.24
Cane	—	—	—	0.31
Unidentified	—	0.15	0.09	0.15
Subtotal	0.23	2.07	10.35	21.06
TOTAL	0.26	2.69	13.47	30.46

Table 3-7. Seed Remains By Zones—Hearths, Washout, and Slump.

SEEDS	Fea. 22	Fea. 65	Fea. 60	Fea. 108	TOTAL
Grape	—	—	—	6	6
Persimmon	—	—	—	1	1
Rubus	—	—	—	1	1
Unidentified	—	—	—	2	2
TOTAL	—	—	—	10	10
WEIGHT	—	—	—	0.12	0.12

through drying, not burning. Nut shell, corncob, corn kernel, and peach pit would not be found in the fire remnants resulting from this activity, except in very limited quantities, since the people would not have destroyed what they wanted to preserve for future use.

Also found within the fill of Zone 1 of Feature 63 were numerous animal bone and turtle carapace fragments, which may indicate that

Table 3-8. Weights of Plant Materials by Feature Class.

COMPONENT	STORAGE PITS	SHALLOW BASINS	HEARTHS	WASH-OUT	SLUMP	TOTAL
Corn Kernel	2.64	4.55	0.06	0.07	1.39	8.71
Corncob	4.50	75.95	—	0.26	3.79	84.50
Cucurbit Rind	—	0.20	—	—	—	0.20
Peach Pit	1.42	15.33	—	2.57	1.83	21.15
Plum Pit	—	0.04	—	—	—	0.04
Acorn Shell	0.44	0.67	0.01	0.01	0.80	1.93
Acorn Meat	0.47	—	—	—	—	0.47
Hazelnut Shell	0.02	0.15	—	—	0.02	0.19
Hickory Shell	13.21	112.66	0.58	0.21	1.57	128.23
Walnut Shell	0.10	2.83	—	—	—	2.93
Wood Charcoal	162.73	130.90	1.81	10.16	20.25	325.85
Bark	1.63	0.87	—	—	0.11	2.61
Cane	0.45	11.27	—	—	0.31	12.03
"Leaf"	2.16	4.41	0.34	0.10	0.24	7.25
Unidentified	0.52	4.37	0.15	0.09	0.15	5.28
TOTAL	190.29	364.20	2.95	13.47	30.46	601.37

animal and plant foods were prepared over the same fire. This interpretation is based to some degree on speculation; just because items are found within the same fill is no guarantee that they were associated *before* they became trash. Nevertheless, the presence of plant foods in the charcoal samples from the three zones of Features 63 and 92 suggests that the fires that produced the charred remains were used in the preparation of plant food for consumption. The animal bone ancillary to Zone 1 of Feature 63 provides tenuous corroboration for this interpretation. Other activities, such as heating a structure or drying food for storage, may also have been associated with the fire(s) that produced this zone.

Feature 60, whose black humus zone was included with the above three, was a washout, shallow gully, or depression along the river bank. No seeds were found within the fill. Wood charcoal comprised the largest percentage of the charred plant remains along with some plant food charcoal. The conclusion that the fill represents the remnants of fires cannot be disputed. The presence of charred plant foods (Table 3-6), especially peach pits, supports a tentative association with cooking ac-

Table 3-9. Seeds by Feature Class.

COMPONENT	STORAGE PITS	SHALLOW BASINS	HEARTHS	WASH-OUT	SLUMP	TOTAL
Copperleaf	—	1	—	—	—	1
Galium sp.	2	—	—	—	—	2
Knotweed	—	1	—	—	—	1
Ragweed	1	—	—	—	—	1
Tickclover	—	2	—	—	—	2
Unidentified Legume	—	2	—	—	—	2
Pokeweed	—	5	—	—	—	5
Grape	5	174	—	—	6	185
Grape Stem	—	45	—	—	—	45
Groundcherry	—	3	—	—	—	3
Hawthorn	—	3	—	—	—	3
Passionflower	5	9	—	—	—	14
Persimmon	5	29	—	—	1	35
Rubus sp.	1	—	—	—	1	2
Vaccinium sp.	—	6	—	—	—	6
Beans	—	3	—	—	—	3
Bottlegourd	—	1	—	—	—	1
Squash	—	1	—	—	—	1
Sunflower	1	—	—	—	—	1
Watermelon	—	1	—	—	—	1
Unidentified	28	131	—	—	2	161
TOTAL	48	417	—	—	10	475
WEIGHT	0.22+	4.36+	—	—	0.12	4.70+

tivity. Other functions, again including heating and drying, however, cannot be ruled out. An alternative interpretation is that the fill of Feature 60 represents midden. However, when the contents of Feature 60 are compared to the amounts of animal bone, potsherds, flakes, worked stone, and daub of those zones considered to represent midden in other features (e.g., Zone 1 of Feature 23), this interpretation has to be rejected.

The other subdivision of the black humus class, made up of those zones with large amounts of plant food remains, consists of Feature 11, Feature 47, Zone 1 of Feature 52, and Feature 108. The former three features are medium-sized shallow basins, while the latter is a depression created by the slump of a burial. Animal bone was not present in great abundance within the fill from these four features. Fire-cracked

Table 3-10. Weights of Plant Remains by Zone Class.

COMPONENT	BLACK I	HUMUS II	WHITE/ RED FILL	BROWN LOAM	YELLOW CLAY	BROWN SAND	TOTAL
Corn Kernel	1.02	5.28	0.31	0.34	0.57	1.19	8.71
Corncob	1.47	72.02	0.85	1.58	0.69	7.89	84.50
Cucurbit Rind	—	0.20	—	—	—	—	0.20
Peach Pit	3.30	15.37	0.22	—	0.05	2.21	21.15
Plum Pit	—	0.04	—	—	—	—	0.04
Acorn	0.17	1.33	0.10	0.13	0.05	0.15	1.93
Acorn Meat	0.47	—	—	—	—	—	0.47
Hazelnut	—	0.16	—	—	—	0.03	0.19
Hickory	3.37	109.14	6.05	2.51	0.95	6.21	128.23
Walnut	—	—	2.40	—	—	0.53	2.93
Wood Charcoal	47.91	73.87	58.02	54.77	36.65	54.63	325.85
Bark	0.46	0.94	—	0.05	0.04	1.12	2.61
Cane	0.16	11.17	0.02	0.08	0.01	0.59	12.03
"Leaf"	1.10	4.30	0.35	0.26	0.17	1.07	7.25
Unidentified	0.15	3.96	0.27	0.64	0.13	0.13	5.28
TOTAL	59.58	297.78	68.59	60.36	39.31	75.75	601.37

rocks, however, were noted in all four. Potsherds were found in varying amounts, ranging from as many as 627 in Feature 11 to as few as 33 in Feature 52.

The most distinguishing trait of these four features is the large quantities of peach pits, nut shells, corncobs, corn kernels, and other plant foods within the fill (Tables 3-3, 3-4, 3-8, 3-9, 3-10, and 3-11). Except for Feature 108, only small amounts of wood charcoal were associated with the plant food remains. The large amounts of plant food remains, the variety of plant food remains, the relatively small quantity of wood charcoal, and the presence of fire-cracked rock and potsherds all suggest that these four features probably functioned in preparing plant foods for eating on a grand scale. John Lawson (1967) noted that "feasts" were prepared at every large village he visited on his trip through the Carolinas in the winter of 1701. Most of this journey was through the Piedmont region of North Carolina. Lawson (1967:177) also tells of feasts held each spring and fall, the former to beg for a good summer planting, the latter to give thanks for the harvest.

At these feasts, whether for a visitor such as Lawson, a neighboring

Table 3-11. Seeds by Zone Class.

COMPONENTS	BLACK I	HUMUS II	WHITE/ RED FILL	BROWN LOAM	YELLOW CLAY	BROWN SAND	TOTAL
Copperleaf	—	1	—	—	—	—	1
Galium sp.	2	—	—	—	—	—	2
Knotweed	—	1	—	—	—	—	1
Ragweed	1	—	—	—	—	—	1
Tickclover	—	2	—	—	—	—	2
Unidentified Legume	—	2	—	—	—	—	2
Pokeweed	—	5	—	—	—	—	5
Grape	4	176	1	2	—	2	185
Grape Stem	—	44	—	—	—	1	45
Groundcherry	—	3	—	—	—	—	3
Hawthorn	—	2	1	—	—	—	3
Passionflower	3	7	2	—	1	2	15
Persimmon	—	18	12	2	1	2	35
Rubus sp.	—	1	—	—	—	1	2
Vaccinium sp.	—	6	—	—	—	—	6
Beans	—	3	—	—	—	—	3
Bottlegourd	—	1	—	—	—	—	1
Squash	—	1	—	—	—	—	1
Sunflower	1	—	—	—	—	—	1
Watermelon	—	1	—	—	—	—	1
Unidentified	20	108	1	21	1	10	161
TOTAL	31	382	17	25	3	18	476
WEIGHT	0.10	3.87	0.58	0.04	0.01	0.10+	4.70+

Indian Chief, or for ceremonial purposes, large quantities of both animal and plant foods would have to be prepared at one time. The presence of nut shells, peach pits, corncobs, and corn kernels in the fill indicates that these plant foods, along with others, were being prepared for eating, not storage. It is doubtful that peaches were split open and the pits removed to facilitate storing. It is also probable that corn was not shelled prior to storage. Such activities would be expected to occur in the process of making *Quiddonies* (Lawson 1967:24) and *Rockahomine* meal (Lawson 1967:182) respectively. Likewise, the meat would not normally be extracted from hickory nuts prior to storage. Thus, it is likely that these four features and the fill they contain were the result of preparing large amounts of plant foods for eating at one point in time. Continuous use or reuse of the features was not evident, as there was no complex lensing as would have resulted from such utilization. Also, no indication of fired clay bottoms and/or sides was present to show that fires were actually built within the basins.

Despite the diverse nature of the eight zones of fill included in the black humus class, a generalization about the nature of the zones can be made. The black humus fill was the result of fires built and used for cooking, among other activities, by the Sara Indians. The subdivisions within the class may reflect other functions served by the fires producing some of the fills. Those zones of black humus fill from storage pits, for example, seem to represent fires that served in capacities other than just preparing food for eating. Also, the large amounts of wood charcoal in the black zones in trash pits indicate that the material came from hearths used over a period of time and for a variety of purposes, such as heating and drying (Tables 3-9 and 3-10).

The other division within the black humus class consists of large shallow basins. These features, in contrast to trash pits, were used over a short period of time for a specific purpose. The fill of these basins is homogeneous and appears to represent primary rather than secondary deposition. Such features may have functioned as some form of earth oven.

The second major class of zones is identified as white or red ash fill. This is only a general category, as it constitutes zones recorded in the field by such diverse descriptions as "red-black humus," "reddish grey grit," "whitish grey clay," or "reddish clay." The fill from Zone 2 of Feature 63, Zones 2 and 3 of Feature 111, Feature 22, and Feature 65 were included in this class. Features 22 and 65, identified as the prepared clay bases of hearths, contained only small amounts of any kind of charcoal (Tables 3-6 and 3-7).

In contrast, Zone 2 of Feature 63 (Tables 3-4 and 3-5) contained a quantity of wood charcoal, along with a variety of plant food remains. This zone, from a storage pit, could have been placed with the black humus class as an example of the remains from a fire used in the preparation of plant foods for cooking. However, this zone was included in the white or red ash category because of the presence of ash, which gave the fill a grey color.

The two zones from Feature 111, a reddish grey grit and a whitish grey clay fill, indicate that a small fire was built in a portion of this shallow basin. Subsequently, the basin was rapidly filled with midden. The large quantities of wood charcoal in the reddish grey grit zone, that also possessed small amounts of plant foods (Table 3-2 and 3-3), suggest that the fire was used for more than cooking plant foods. The whitish clay zone, with only a small amount of cultural material, closely resembled the prepared hearth remnants represented by Features 22 and 65.

Like the black humus class, the white or red ash fill class represents the remains of fires built by the Sara. This fill is found in prepared basins used for fires and in pits where fires were burned. The zones included in this class are the result of fires that served various functions, only one of which was preparing food for eating. The difference between this class and the first subdivision of the black humus class is primarily one of color and soil make-up.

Brown loam was the name given to the third class of fill zones. Zone 1 of Feature 23, Zone 1 of Feature 50, and Zone 1 of Feature 111 were in this class. Important characteristics include the presence of a large amount of wood charcoal, as well as a large quantity of animal bone and potsherds. Relatively small amounts of plant food remains are present (Tables 3-10 and 3-11). The contents of these zones probably represent midden that filled depressions deliberately dug, as with Features 50 and 111, or those created by the compression of fill within a pit, as in Feature 23. The former two features may have served as clay sources (borrow pits) for daub used in the construction of house walls.

The components of the brown loam class resemble the materials from the midden preserved at the Wall site (31OR11), a protohistoric village in the north central piedmont of North Carolina. This midden fill need not have been deliberately placed in the features, but could have gotten there through trampling or erosion over the course of time. A lack of lensing, however, would tend to discount the latter process.

The fourth class of fill zone is designated mottled yellow clay. Zones 3 and 5 of Feature 23, Zone 2 of Feature 50, Zones 2 and 4 of Feature 92 were included in the class. Such inclusions as animal bones, potsherds, and charcoal were intermixed with the yellow clay. The soil itself resulted from the digging of various pits (e.g., storage and burial pits) into subsoil. The clay left over from the digging became mixed with midden material present on the ground's surface. Portions of yellow clay, mixed with small amounts of midden, were then used to fill various open pits. A secondary source of refuse in the yellow clay fill would have been the fill zones surrounding the clay soil within the feature. Soil action and the excavation process are a few of the mixing mechanisms. Zone 2 of Feature 50 is an example of fill resulting from the latter process (Tables 3-2 and 3-3).

The last class of fill is light brown/tan sand. The category is represented by Zones 2, 5, and 6 of Feature 23, Zone 3 of Feature 50, Zone 3 of Feature 63, and Zone 2 of Feature 52 (Tables 3-10 and 3-11). A dichotomy within this class was noted when the content of each zone was examined. Zones 2, 5, and 6 from Feature 23 were almost devoid of any cultural material. The presence of very little charcoal was especially noticeable. The zones in Feature 23 probably represent quantities of relatively sterile sand thrown into the storage pit to fill it up. On the other hand, the sandy zones of Features 50, 52, and 63 contained a fair amount of what could best be described as midden material. This included potsherds, animal bones, wood charcoal, small amounts of plant foods, and worked stone.

The majority of the fill zones within the light brown/tan sand class were similar to the zones belonging to the brown loam midden class, except for the sandy zones in Feature 23. The distinctions between the two classes were mostly textural, and, to a lesser extent, color.

Conclusions

This short study represents an initial effort to delineate some of the behavioral patterns that are reflected in feature fill. It recognizes that the fill within archaeological features constitutes more than a homogeneous or even heterogeneous lot that can be lumped together as garbage or trash. Features had only a secondary importance for the deposit of garbage, with few, if any, pits serving a primary function as trash receptacles.

The analysis of the charred plant remains from the fill zones of selected features at Upper Saratown documents the diverse nature of the "trash" found in features. The abstraction of information from features about particular activities would seem to best be served by using data from appropriate fill zones, rather than relying solely upon feature type (see Dickens, this volume). The analysis of charred plant remains and the reconstruction of subsistence patterns can be used to illustrate the meaning of this point.

Dennell (1976:232) has proposed that there are five archaeological contexts and associated activities in which plant food remains are to be found. This model is based on work at Mesolithic sites in Bulgaria. The five types of contexts and their associated activities are as follows: for *eating* (activity), the remains are coprolites (context); for *storage*, there are facilities such as baskets, jars, or pits; for *cooking*, there are hearths or ovens; for *food preparation*, there are hearths, ovens and activity areas that show evidence of food processing; and finally, for the *miscellaneous refuse* from all the preceding activities, there is the midden.

Applying Dennell's scheme to the Upper Saratown data, the five categories are represented by only two contexts that retained their original form, hearths or ovens and midden. The original storage pits persist solely in shape, as they no longer contain the remains of the materials that were kept in them. And, none of the aboriginal above-ground structures and accompanying activity areas were preserved, because of extensive plowing and erosion.

Another consideration is that the various contexts represented at Upper Saratown have, with one exception, a high probability of having been used for more than one activity (hearths for example); or contain the residue of a myriad of behavioral activities (the midden). Earth ovens are an exception that probably can be tied to unique episodes in the lives of the Sara. These features are the only intact remains in which the original behavioral activities associated with the feature remain largely unmodified.

A major question that can now be addressed is: where does one draw the data to study subsistence behavior (see Dickens, this volume)? In the Woodland agricultural context, for example, where should one turn in the archaeological record of Upper Saratown for information concerning the plant food component of the subsistence pattern of the historic Sara? Those features identified as earth ovens would be an obvious first choice. Such features appear, however, to represent the cooking of large amounts of food at one point in time. From the charred seed remains within the fill, most of these features examined to date appear to have been in use in the fall. Data from such features and associated fill may be pertinent only to seasonally specific communal events. For insight into the everyday subsistence pattern involving plant foods, one would have to analyze the black humus fill strata from shallow trash pits or in deep storage pits. It must be kept in mind, however, that the charcoal present within these zones is the result of behavior associated with activities other than cooking. Middens represent multiple activities to an even greater degree.

To minimize the problems encountered in the study of subsistence behavior using archaeological data, both fill strata type and feature class should serve as the basis for selecting study samples, where distinctions between the two can be identified. It is obvious that other remains, including faunal material, associated with feature fill strata should be examined in conjunction with charred plant material in order to obtain a better understanding of the subsistence patterns and other behaviors that produce archaeological remains.

In contemporary archaeology, one of the most promising paths of investigation is ecological-behavioral analysis, as exemplified by the recent studies of Binford (1980), Ames (1981), and Wiessner (1982). No matter what direction is taken, however, archaeologists will continue to use inference as a primary tool in their investigations. And, context plays a primary role in the analyses and interpretations upon which inferences are based. Careful observation and interpretation of the basic relationships between inference and context are inherent in the work of Joffre Coe and those he has influenced. It is hoped that this short inquiry has illustrated the basic role played by this approach and some of its implications for future archaeological research.

4 • H. TRAWICK WARD

Social Implications of Storage and Disposal Patterns

Introduction

The complex web of interaction between environment and culture has long been a major theme of study in American archaeology. The roots of most current ecological models can be traced to Strong (1936), Steward and Seltzer (1938), Kroeber (1939), and Bennett (1943, 1946). Most of us, however, have only recently begun to look in depth at the forces that form and pattern material remains and that hold the keys to understanding cultural process (Schiffer 1972, 1976). In contrast, these concerns were forged early in Joffre Coe's career, and the recognition of activities and events that stir and shape the record in the ground has been a cornerstone of his training and teaching. Whether reflected in a detailed discourse on the effects of plow displacement or an explanation of the physical properties manifested in shaft-and-chamber burials, an appreciation of the importance of understanding site-formation processes has highlighted the "Coe style."

A reflection of this concern for formation processes has been Coe's unrelenting goal of total recovery of information from the ground. He has applied a meticulous rigor not only to the excavation of intact deposits and features but also to the retrieval of data from contexts often dismissed as hopelessly disturbed. For example, he has subjected plowzone deposits to systematic screening since 1934, when he began work at the Town Creek site, 31MG3 (see Reid, this volume). This procedure has been continued over the years and resulted in a large corpus of data from several sites.

Recently (Ward 1980), some of those plowzone data were used in a comparative spatial analysis of two late village sites, one in the northern Piedmont and the other in the Appalachian Summit area. This paper summarizes some of the results of this study and examines how plowzone data can help define the nature of cultural and natural formation processes indicative of different patterns of storage and refuse disposal.

These patterns are in turn examined to see what implications they may have in reflecting varying levels of sociopolitical complexity and culture change.

Intersite Comparisons

Upper Saratown (31SK1a) and the Warren Wilson site (31BN29) were extensively excavated under Coe's direction for several years. The summer of 1981 marked the 15th season at Warren Wilson and the 11th at Upper Saratown. The Warren Wilson site is the better known of the two because of publications by Dickens (1976, 1978, and 1979b). It represents a late prehistoric Cherokee village located in the floodplain of the Swannanoa River in Buncombe County (Figure 4-1). In many ways, Warren Wilson is typical of medium-sized villages occupied during the Pisgah phase (ca. A.D. 1100–1400) in western North Carolina.

Upper Saratown represents one of the villages probably occupied by the historic Sara Indians (Figure 4-2). It is located on the Dan River in the northern Piedmont section of Stokes County. The site, consisting of the remains of a single component village of medium size, typifies the historic Siouan occupations during the Dan River phase (Coe and Lewis 1952). Wilson (1977) has reported on plant food remains from Upper Saratown and is currently engaged in an extensive study of the Sara using archaeological as well as ethnohistoric data (see Dickens, Wilson, this volume). In many ways, the two sites reveal similar cultures, although each occupied a distinct and very different environment. There are other contrasts and it is within these contrasts that questions concerning process, change, and adaptation are posed in this paper.

Generally, the subsistence bases of the Sara and the Cherokee are the same. Both relied on a mixed agricultural economy, supplemented in varying amounts by hunting and gathering. The agricultural inventories were similar, except that the Sara supplemented native cultigens with exotics such as peaches, watermelons, muskmelons, and cucumbers. Both groups gathered hickory nuts, walnuts, hazelnuts, and acorns, as well as grapes, plums, persimmons, and various berries. Hunting, important to both groups, seems to have been used more by the Siouans. As would be expected, the Siouans also were heavily engaged in trade

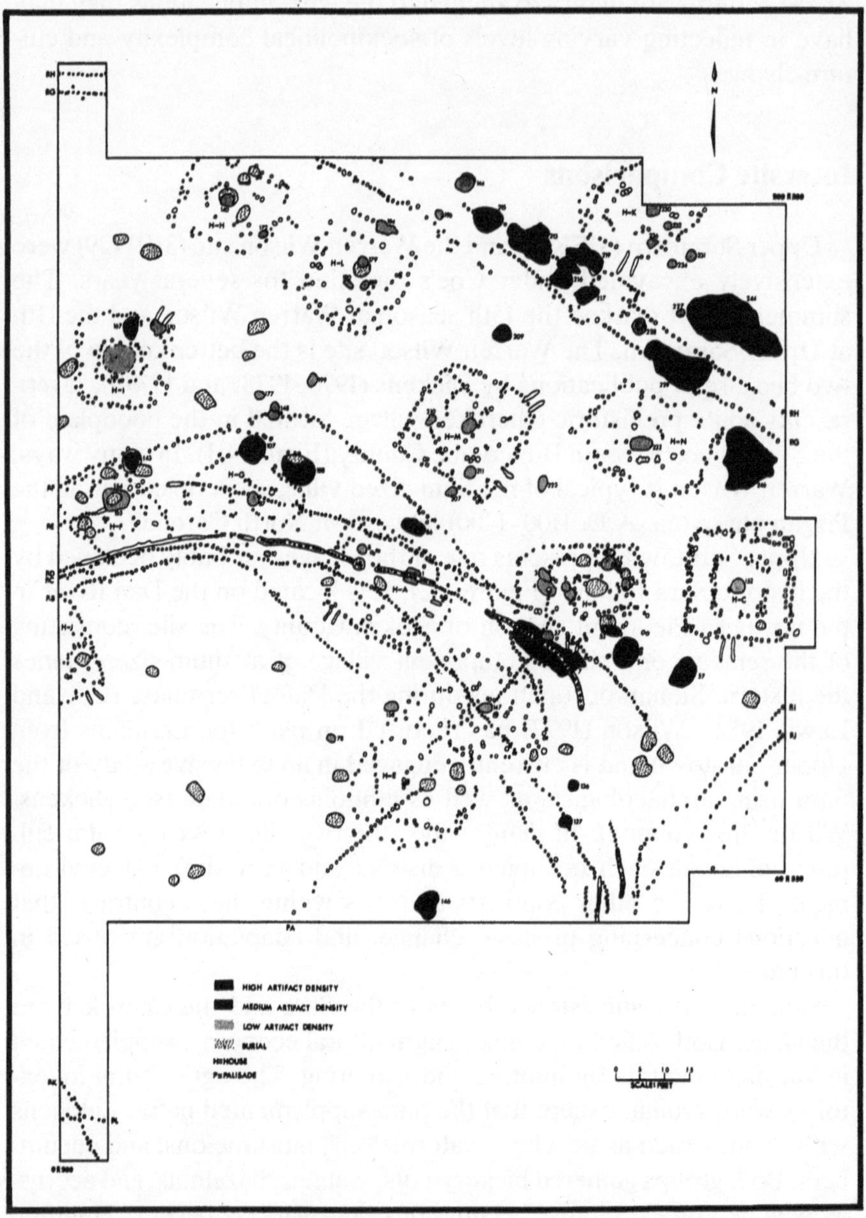

Figure 4-1. Warren Wilson Site, Plan of Features and Architecture at the Base of the Plowzone.

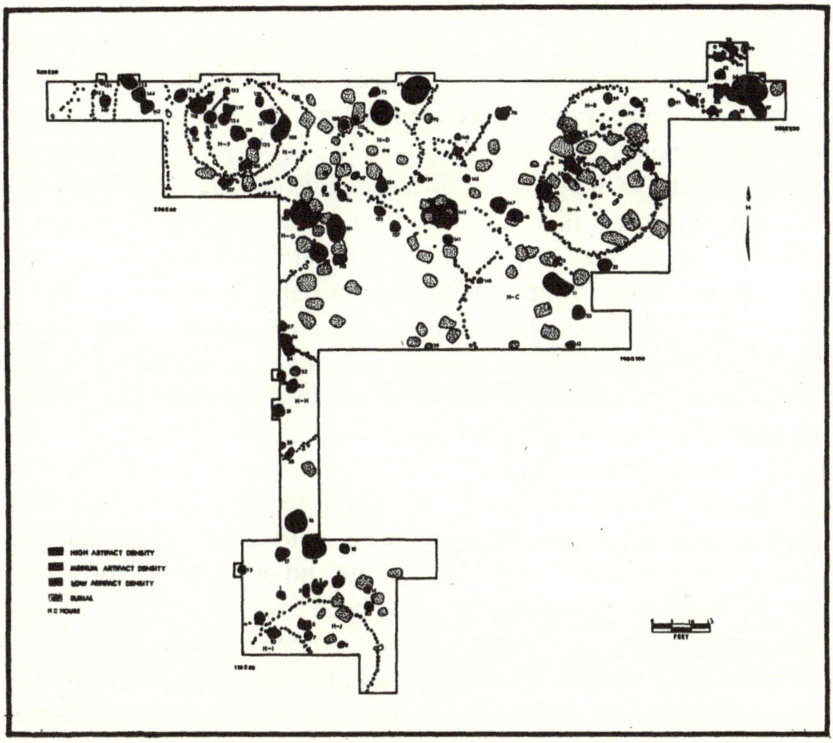

Figure 4-2. Upper Saratown, Plan of Features and Architecture at the Base of the Plowzone.

with the colonists. Archaeologically, this economic relationship for the Sara is most directly indicated by thousands of glass trade beads, compared to relatively few tools and utilitarian objects of Euro-colonial manufacture.

The Warren Wilson site and Upper Saratown are about the same size, each covering approximately three acres. They are located on well-drained alluvial soils adjacent to major rivers. In each case, the overall village plan consisted of a cluster of houses, enclosed by a palisade and arranged around a central area of light domestic activity. Although very different in shape and construction, the houses contained about the same amount of living space, approximately 400 square feet.

One of the most striking differences between the two sites is in the number of subterranean features. At the end of the 1977 field season, only 26 had been uncovered at Warren Wilson, whereas 63 pit-type facilities had been observed at Upper Saratown. Given that almost twice the area had been exposed at Warren Wilson, this difference becomes even more striking.

Characteristic of Upper Saratown are large storage pits. These features are circular in outline and range from a little over 2 feet in diameter to as much as 4.5 feet. Although the sides are usually straight, some flare outward at the bottom to produce a bell-shaped profile. Depth below the base of the plowzone varies from no more than a foot to over 4 feet. The average storage pit is around 3 feet in diameter and 3 feet deep. Another characteristic that most of these pits share is that they were refilled with refuse. This refilling usually required several dumping episodes and created a stratified, lensed fill matrix. The amounts of artifacts from these pits are high, except in the rare case where they were not recycled as garbage receptacles. Storage pits normally are found within or adjacent to houses. At the end of the 1977 field season at Upper Saratown, 39 storage pits had been excavated.

Subterranean features in general, and storage pits in particular, are rare at the Warren Wilson site. Only six pits have been identified that may have functioned in this capacity (Ward 1980:107; and see Dickens, this volume). At this site, the most distinguishing features are large ditch-like depressions usually displaying irregular outlines. They have a broad-size range, varying from 10 to 20 feet in length and from 4 to 9 feet in width. Depth is typically no more than a foot. Usually, these ditches contain a convoluted fill with large quantities of lensed village refuse. Since all these depressions coincide with the various palisades encircling the village, Dickens (this volume) has suggested they resulted from palisade maintenance, perhaps the mining of clay to replaster the walls. Regardless of their primary function, they were ultimately filled with whatever trash was handy.

Without storage pits, the inhabitants of Warren Wilson probably constructed cribs or granaries. It is well documented that such facilities were used historically by the Cherokee (Swanton 1946:380). Although no granaries have been definitely identified at Warren Wilson, there are numerous posthole clusters that may indicate their presence.

Storage and Refuse Disposals: Archaeological Correlates

The difference in storage patterns were easily recognized by comparing the two in situ site structures, i.e., the arrangements of houses, features, palisades, etc. As mentioned earlier, where there were very few pits at Warren Wilson that could have been used for storage, such pits occurred in abundance at Upper Saratown. It was, however, only after the plowzone artifact distributions for the two sites were examined that a clear picture of the differences in refuse disposal modes emerged.

The analysis of plowzone artifact distributions was originally undertaken to determine how well these distributions predicted underlying features and structures. To this end, artifact frequencies from the plowzone were compared with those from undisturbed subplowzone contexts. Ceramics, bone, unmodified flakes, and projectile points were mapped using the Computer Graphics SYMAP program. Contour, trend surface, and residual maps were compared by artifact category within each depositional context. A detailed comparison of the plowzone and in situ site structures, along with a discussion of the use of trend surface and residual mapping, can be found in Ward (1980).

During the course of this analysis, it became obvious that refuse disposal modes varied considerably, and that they determined to a large degree the extent of correspondence between the plowzone and in situ artifact distributions. And, although disposal modes varied with different artifact classes within each site, the most striking differences were between the sites.

At Warren Wilson, the majority of the artifacts from the plowzone define a pattern of secondary dumping along the various palisade lines. Ceramic sherds were most numerous and probably represent the best overall indicator of this secondary dumping (Figure 4-3a). Bone concentrations in the plowzone also peaked at points along the palisades, but because bone is fragile and rapidly disintegrates in the plowzone, it had a somewhat restricted distribution that was also spatially correlated with at least one subplowzone facility. Since this feature was also located along a palisade, the palisade-bone correlation was reinforced (compare Figures 4-1 and 4-3b). More will be said about the ability of

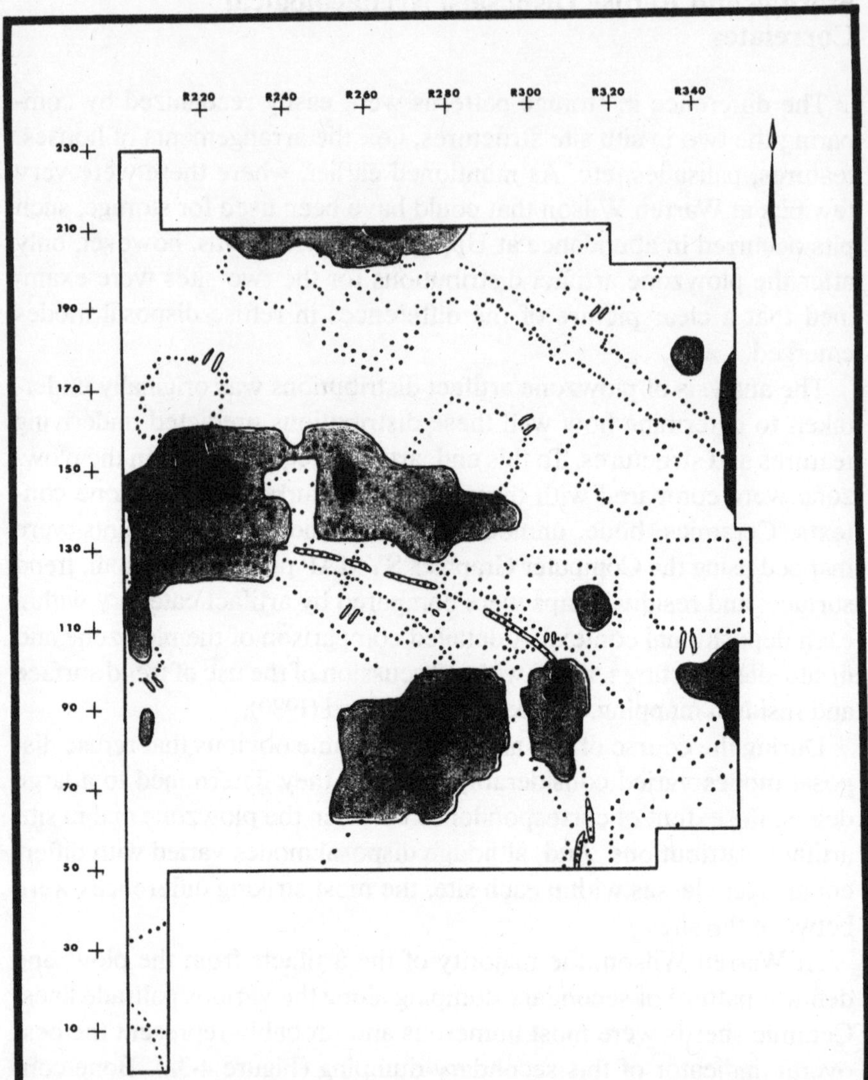

Figure 4-3A. Warren Wilson Site, Ceramic Distribution, Plowzone Residuals from a Third Order Trend Surface.

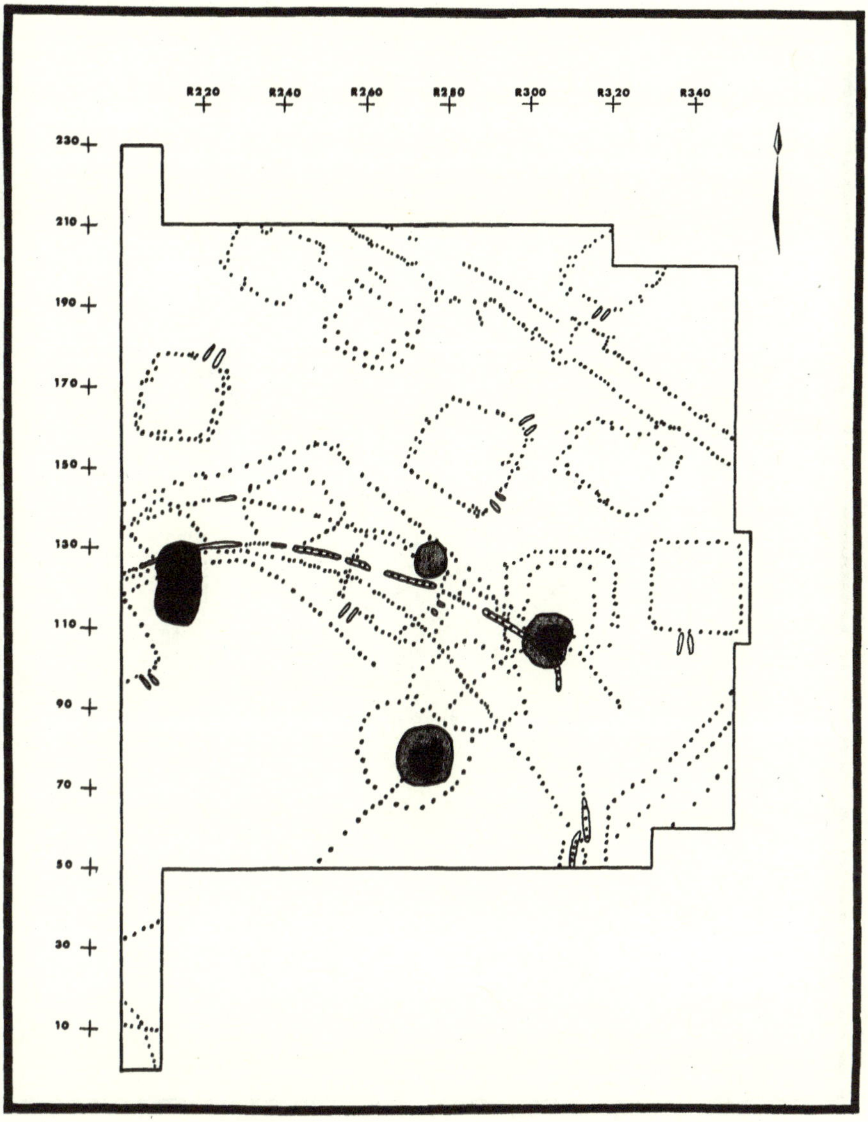

Figure 4-3B. Warren Wilson Site, Bone Distribution, Plowzone Residuals from a Third Order Trend Surface.

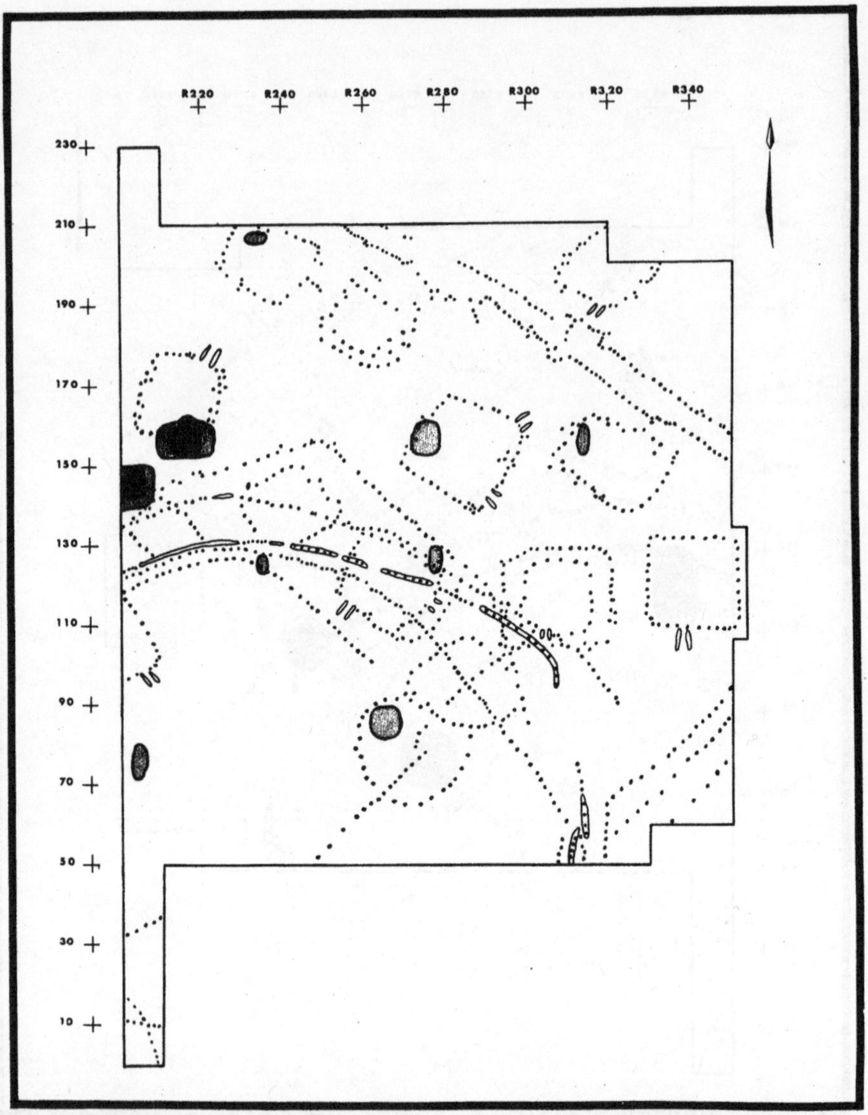

Figure 4-3C. Warren Wilson, Projectile Point Distribution, Plowzone Residuals from a Third Order Trend Surface.

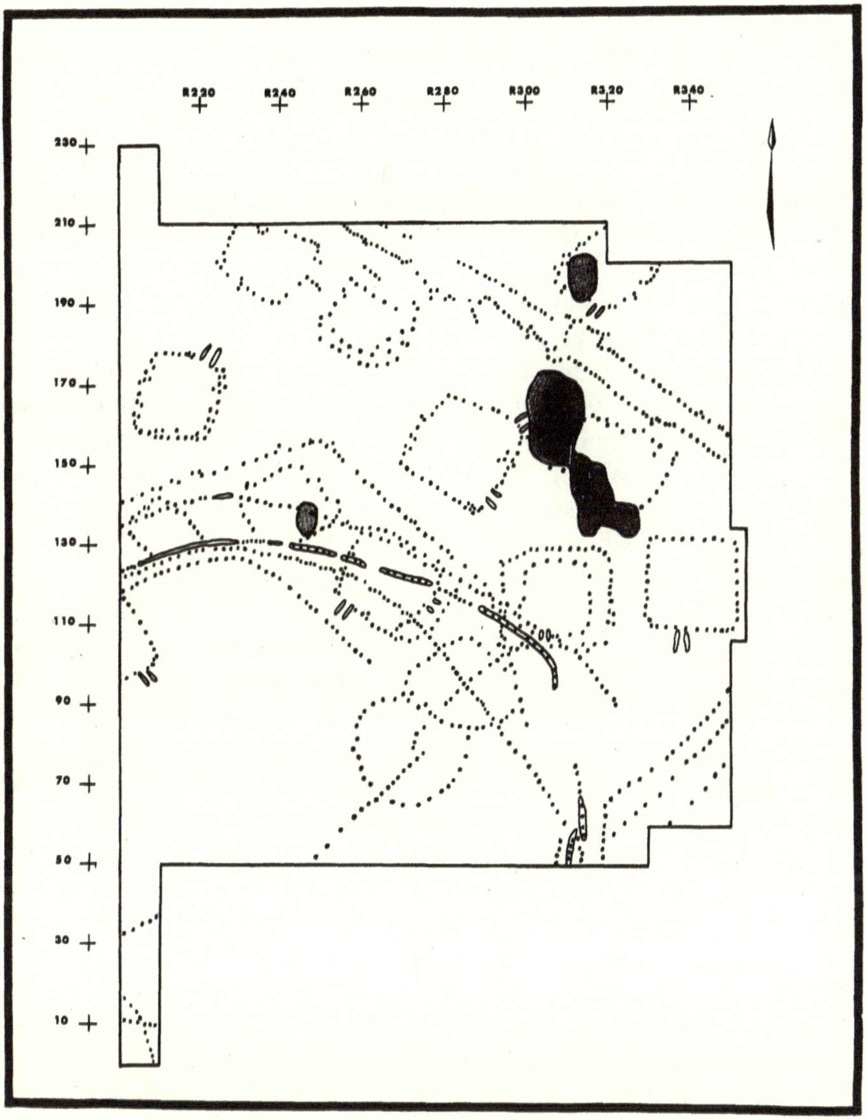

Figure 4-3D. Warren Wilson, Lithic Distribution, Plowzone Residuals from a Third Order Trend Surface.

plowzone bone to predict the presence of in situ deposits later in this discussion.

Flake debris and projectile points were more restricted in their distributions than either bone or ceramics, and both tended to reflect primary or de facto contexts. The debitage distribution clearly defined this pattern, as it was concentrated between or inside house structures located away from the areas of heavy secondary dumping along the palisades (Figure 4-3d). Apparently, lithic tool manufacture or maintenance took place around structures, and there were no concerted efforts to clean up the waste and residue. The projectile point distribution was similar, although not as clear (Figure 4-3c).

The area between the palisades, the plaza, as well as the floors of the houses themselves were apparently kept clean. This pattern is similar to that described by Binford for Hatchery West (Binford et al. 1970).

In contrast to Warren Wilson, the inhabitants of the Siouan village of Upper Saratown disposed of much of their refuse in the large, emptied storage pits which often were located within or immediately outside house structures. Because of this refuse disposal pattern, there were significant correlations between concentrations of artifacts in the plowzone and in situ site areas of heavy domestic activity (Figure 4-4). Although the contents of individual features had become swirled together by the plow and dispersed across the site, each year the surface level is lowered by successive plowings. This lowering makes it possible for fresh specimens from the tops of undisturbed features to enter the plowzone and become concentrated over or near their points of origin. This situation is somewhat analogous to a series of chimneys in close proximity where the smoke from each fans out and blends with that from its neighbor. Eventually, the puffs are inseparable in a single cloud, but fresh puffs continue to be separate and distinct. It is these "puffs" of fresh artifacts, plowed out annually, that allow one to predict fairly accurately the locations of subplowzone pits and features. This predictive acuity, however, is not even across the site.

Features and houses in the western part of the site usually were indicated by artifact concentrations in the plowzone. Features in the eastern section usually were suggested by plowzone densities, but the relationship between the plowzone and undisturbed context was not as clear here. This variation, which seems to be a consequence of plowing practices, can be seen clearly in the raw computer printout data (Ward

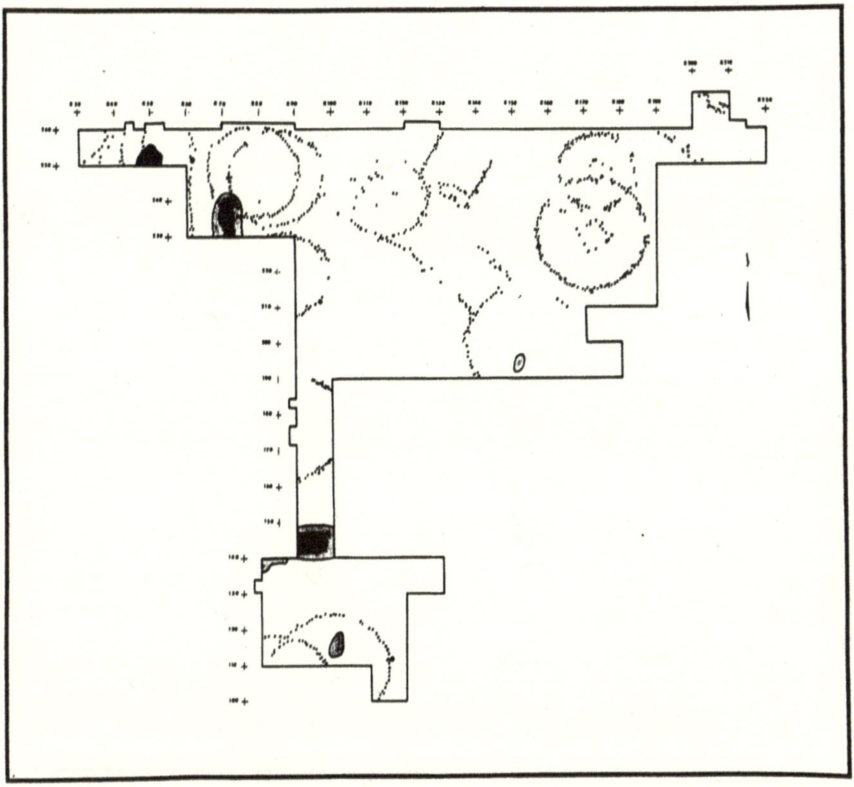

Figure 4-4A. Upper Saratown, Ceramic Distribution, Plowzone Residuals from a Third Order Trend Surface.

1980:Appendix D). The field containing the site is usually plowed in a spiral fashion beginning along the outside edge and terminating in the center. The western area of the site is oriented toward the interior of the field, and as soil is displaced toward the outer edge, the plow cuts deeper each year turning up fresh specimens from the tops of pits. In contrast, the eastern side of the site is along the edge of the field where soil is accumulating as a result of this displacement. The features here are more protected by this accumulation, and the plow is not as likely to cut into their undisturbed contents.

The refuse disposal pattern at Upper Saratown is one of secondary or de facto disposal in subsurface facilities. Sherds and bone were pe-

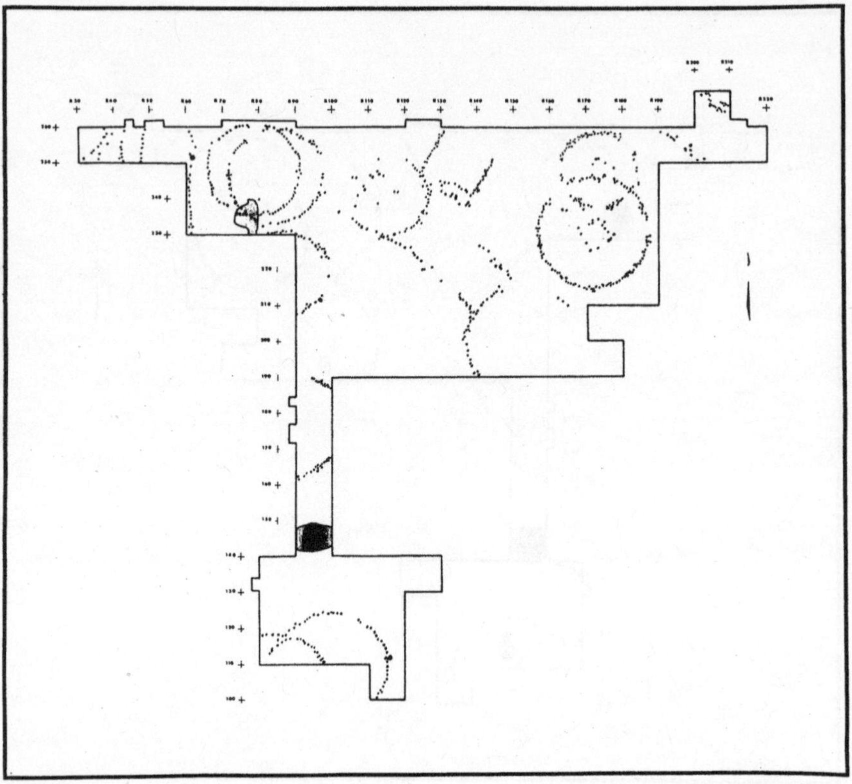

Figure 4-4B. Upper Saratown, Bone Distribution, Plowzone Residuals from a Third Order Trend Surface.

riodically cleaned up and deposited in empty storage pits, or in any convenient hole. Many small flakes and projectile points were also swept up with the other trash and represent de facto deposition. A nondeliberate disposal mode certainly applies to the small triangular projectile points since most could still be used today.

The use of subsurface storage facilities and their recycling as garbage pits stand in sharp contrast to the above-ground storage and disposal mode at Warren Wilson. In addition to the differences in storage and refuse disposal patterns, other interesting contrasts can be seen by comparing the gross artifact counts from the two sites.

The mean number of sherds per excavation unit at Warren Wilson is

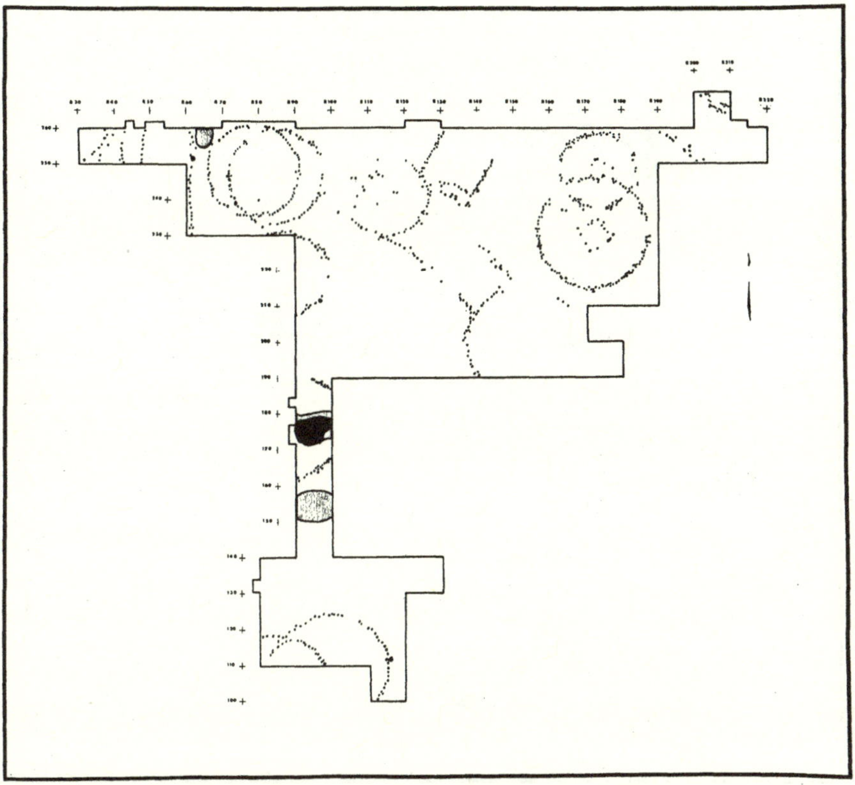

Figure 4-4C. Upper Saratown, Lithic Distribution, Plowzone Residuals from a Third Order Trend Surface.

almost three times greater than at Upper Saratown. The bone totals, on the other hand, have a similar overall density at both sites, although there is a far greater proportion of bone in features at Upper Saratown. One of the most interesting differences in gross amounts of artifacts by site are the numbers and densities of debitage and projectile points. Although twice as much area has been excavated at Warren Wilson, Upper Saratown has produced over 2,000 more flakes and 1,000 more small triangular projectile points. This difference is reflected by an average of eight projectile points and 75 flakes per square at Upper Saratown, and only four projectile points and 33 flakes per square at Warren Wilson.

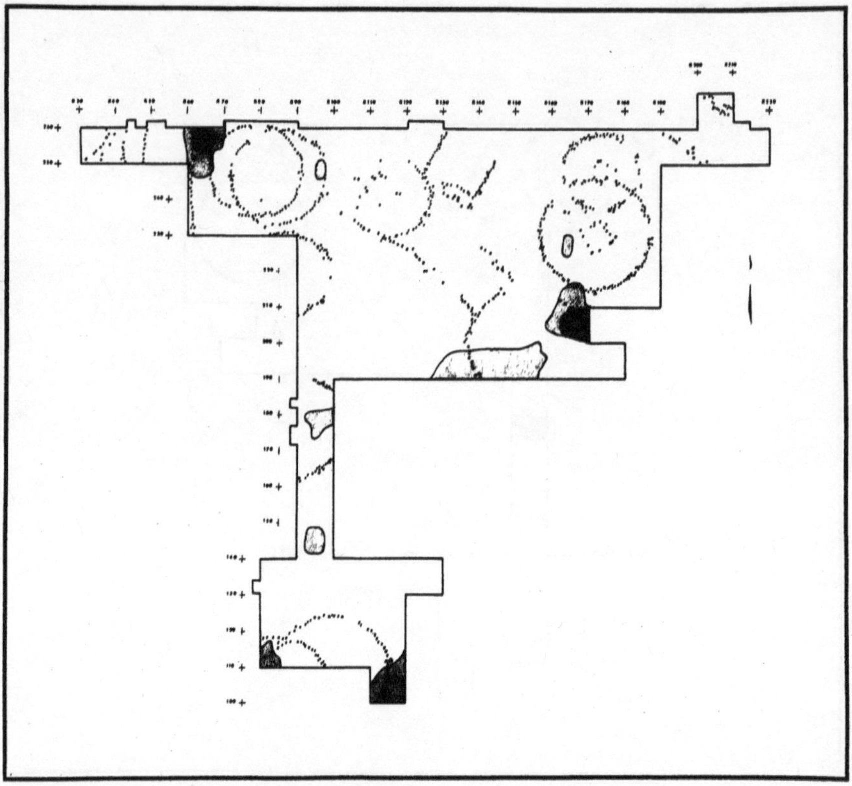

Figure 4-4D. Upper Saratown, Projectile Point Distribution, Plowzone Residuals from a Third Order Trend Surface.

The greater amount of sherds at Warren Wilson is considered to represent a more intense occupation over a longer period of time. This interpretation is supported by the fact that there is much more evidence of structural repairs and rebuilding at Warren Wilson. Variation in the amount of bone from different depositional contexts at the two sites again reflects the differences in refuse disposal patterns. The greater concentration of lithic material at Upper Saratown is probably a direct consequence of more hunting and butchering activities associated with the fur trade.

To summarize the differences between the two sites, we find that (1) at Warren Wilson surplus produce was stored in cribs, whereas at

Upper Saratown, storage took place in subterranean pits; (2) garbage was deposited in shallow depressions or on the living surface around the periphery of the village at Warren Wilson, whereas large quantities of trash were used to fill abandoned storage pits at Saratown; (3) Warren Wilson evidences a long-term occupation, whereas Upper Saratown was occupied for a relatively short time; (4) there is little evidence of use of chipped stone at Warren Wilson, whereas there was considerable evidence of its use at Upper Saratown; and (5) Warren Wilson was occupied prior to European contact, whereas trade with Europeans was well established at Upper Saratown.

Explanation and Speculation

Several explanations could be offered for the differences noted above. Originally, I viewed the use of subterranean storage by the Siouans as a direct consequence of European contact. The large number of burials at Upper Saratown (103 compared with 52 from Warren Wilson), and its short occupation span, suggest that European diseases were severely impacting the population. Systemic stresses and disequilibrium must have resulted from this decimation, as well as the other less direct effects of contact. In this destabilized sociocultural environment, I originally concluded that the pits were used as a substitute for more elaborate above ground facilities. Also, since the pits would hold less surplus than cribs, I proposed that the pits reflected a shift in socioeconomic structure from large to small units of production and consumption. This change would be in line with that expected from a group becoming heavily involved with the fur trade. Under these conditions, less emphasis was placed on agricultural production, and smaller social units began to compete to maximize economic relations with white traders.

In contrast, the cribs of the prehistoric Cherokee were thought to be indirect indicators of more surplus production, a more stable agricultural economy, and (based on ethnohistoric data) were used for the conspicuous display of goods and produce by relatively large, nonegalitarian social units. The Gentleman of Elvas states that:

> ...the difference between the houses of the lords or principal men and the others is that besides being larger they have large balconies in front and below with seats resembling benches made of canes; and round many large

> barbacoas in which they gather together the tribute paid them by their Indians, which consists of maize and deerskins and native blankets . . . (quoted in Swanton 1946:386–387).

Bartram provides an even clearer picture of the "King's granary."

> When the fruits of their labors are ripe and in fit order to gather in they all, on the same day, repair to the plantation; each gathers the produce of his own proper lot, brings it to town, and deposits it in his own crib, allotting a certain portion for the public granary, which is called the king's crib, because its contents are at his disposal, though not his private property, but considered as the tribute or free contribution of the citizens of the state, at the disposal of the king (Jones 1873:411).

In fact, these cribs described by the early explorers appear to have operated within the sociopolitical structure much like the ubiquitous yam houses so elegantly described by Malinowski during his stay with the Trobriand Islanders (Malinowski 1961). And, indeed many Southeastern Indian groups appear to have been organized into "low level" chiefdoms. The Siouans, however, are known not to have been organized into ranked societies (Swanton 1928:696). But, attempting to explain the Siouans' less complex cultural integration as a consequence of European contact and resulting systemic stress proved to be untenable, for what are now obvious reasons.

In 1981, work began on an area of Upper Saratown (31SK1) that is thought to have been occupied before the contact period. Here again were large recycled storage pits and a similar concentration of lithic tools and debris. With the obvious exception of European trade items and cultigens, the material cultural remains were not very different from those dating to the historic period. Recently, large storage pits filled with refuse have also been reported from other Late Woodland villages in southern Virginia (e.g., Egloff and Reed 1980). Therefore, the use of such facilities obviously was not in response to culture change precipitated by European contact and trade.

A modified, and still hypothetical explanation for the differences between Siouan and Cherokee refuse disposal and storage patterns is presented below. The hypothetical nature of this explanation is stressed, as there are other interpretations of equal plausibility that could be drawn from the data.

Pits are not particularly good places to store most agricultural produce, especially corn (Williams and Hill 1920:107). If, however, precautions are taken in sealing and lining them, they do seem to work, as attested by their widespread use in the Midwest, Southwest, and Plains. In these areas, pits commonly were used by semi-sedentary horticulturists who left their villages for fairly long periods of time to hunt. Mathews writes concerning the Hidatsa:

> When these Indians have harvested their crops, and before they start on their winter-hunt, they dig their *caches*, or clear out those dug in previous years . . . .Reserving a small portion of corn, dried squash, etc., for winter use, they deposit the remainder in these subterranean stor-houses, along with household utensils, and other articles of value which they wish to leave behind. They then fill up the orifices with earth, which they trample down and rake over; thus obliterating every trace of the excavation. Some *caches* are made under the floors of houses, others outside, in various parts of the village-grounds; in each case, the distance and direction from some door, post, bedstead, fire-place, or other object is noted so that the stores may be found in the return of the owners in the spring [Mathews quoted in Bushnell 1922:150].

The important thing to note in the Mathews' statement is that the pits were used not only to store goods and produce but also to hide things of value that were left behind when the village was abandoned. A similar explanation for the use of storage pits has also been reported for the Siouan speaking Oneota.

> For fear of fire, to which they are subject, they often put whatever they have that is most precious into vats and bury them in deep holes dug in their cabins . . . This gives protection not only from fire but also from the hands of thieves . . . [Kinietz quoted in McKusick 1973:38].

In fact, one of the few ethnohistoric examples of the use of storage pits in the Southeast states that they were used among the Virginia Indians to hide goods and produce (Strachey quoted in Swanton 1946:379).

Apparently, pit facilities could adequately be used to store the limited surplus food produced by semi-sedentary horticultural groups, but more importantly they were well suited for hiding this surplus when the villages were abandoned. Although their preservation potential is no doubt less than cribs, especially for corn storage, they do offer security not found in above ground facilities.

Lawson, during his 1700–1701 journey through the South Carolina and North Carolina Piedmont region, noted that villages had been vacated because of hunting activities, even in the dead of winter (Lawson 1967:34, 46). According to Mooney (1894:6), "The Siouan tribes . . . although generally cultivating the ground to a limited extent, were essentially a race of hunters."

Based on these ethnohistoric accounts and the large amount of lithic tools and debris at Upper Saratown, I propose that the Piedmont Siouans were heavily reliant on seasonal deer hunts, and that they abandoned their villages during the fall and winter in a manner similar to their Plains and Midwest cousins. This semi-sedentary, mixed agricultural–hunting economy made adopting the fur trade relatively easy since no major technological changes were required to facilitate trade with Europeans. The aboriginal economic pattern was simply continued with increased intensity. Hunting became more important, and agricultural pursuits were enhanced with the addition of European cultigens, particularly fruits that could be harvested during the spring and early summer. The storage pits were adequate for a relatively small agricultural surplus and offered a safe repository during periods when the villages were vacated. These groups possessed a tribal level of social organization, which perhaps became more familial by the creation of smaller producing and consuming social units after contact. As individual family units gained more and more social and economic autonomy, pit facilities became even more efficient for storage and caching.

In contrast, Cherokee culture developed an early reliance on intensive agriculture, and concomitantly a more stable, sedentary village life. Larger agricultural surpluses were produced and stored in above ground cribs. The sociopolitical integration of these economic conditions culminated in a ranked social structure. Much of the surplus production was controlled and redistributed by the village chief or mico. Individual skills were also pooled and centrally coordinated in large-scale cooperative techniques of production. A well organized conical clan structure developed, and specialization became increasingly important during the late prehistoric and early historic periods. In short, the Cherokee, along with the Creek, Natchez and other Southeastern groups, were organized into agriculturally based chiefdoms.

Summary

This paper has sought to demonstrate that a careful consideration of formation processes and their behavioral correlates is necessary before questions of change, adaptation, and process can be approached. Refuse disposal and storage patterns have been identified by examining artifact distributions in the plowzone and in situ site structures. Further, it has been demonstrated that disposal and storage behaviors are interrelated, and that they directly affect the configuration of plowzone artifact distributions as well as the material remains in undisturbed contexts. Finally, by viewing storage and refuse disposal behaviors as components of larger adaptive systems, an explanation of patterned variability between two sites has been suggested. Without Joffre Coe's early recognition of the importance of all the data, disturbed and undisturbed, from a site, such questions as those posed here could not have been asked, let alone attempts made to answer them.

5 • MICHAEL B. TRINKLEY

The Form and Function of South Carolina's Early Woodland Shell Rings

Introduction

One of the earliest references to the aboriginal shell rings of South Carolina and Georgia was a short letter by William McKinley in the *Smithsonian Institution Annual Report* of 1872. McKinley described three shell rings on Sapelo Island, Georgia and suggested that the "mound-circles were doubtless for councils or games." He promised that his associates would "in the course of this year, get the negroes to open the mounds" (McKinley 1873:424).

In the years following this early account, a series of both professional and amateur investigations have been conducted on shell ring sites from St. Simons Island in Georgia to the Santee River in South Carolina. The unifying thread in these investigations has been an attempt to solve the enigma of the doughnut shape and original function of the sites. The earliest references, such as McKinley's, correctly attributed the rings to aboriginal inhabitants, although the sites were interpreted as being "royal residences," "council circles," or "game courts." The large quantities of broken pottery and other refuse that were found did not alter the basically "ceremonial" nature of the posited functions of these sites (McKinley 1873:424).

There are at least 20 shell rings in South Carolina, all situated on or adjacent to tidal creeks on the outer Coastal Plain. Gradually rising sea levels have caused some sites to become isolated shell islands surrounded by marsh, although during their occupations all presumably were on higher ground. The sites consist of circular shell ridges which range from about 130 to 200 feet in diameter and two to 10 feet high (Hemmings 1970a). Distinctive of the shell rings are their clear interiors and doughnut shape. Most of the rings exhibit considerable erosion and a few evidence extensive shell removal or other damage.

Nineteen radiocarbon dates from six sites in South Carolina and Georgia place the shell rings in the second millenium B.C. with a range from 2240 ± 90 B.C. at Cannon's Point, Georgia (Marrinan 1975:48), to 935 ± 175 B.C. at Lighthouse Point, South Carolina (Trinkley 1980:192). The shell ring sites in Georgia average 350 years older than those in South Carolina. The pottery associated with these sites consists of the Stallings and Thom's Creek series (Trinkley 1976). Investigations suggest a seriation of Thom's Creek Reed Punctate, Thom's Creek Shell Punctate, Thom's Creek Finger Pinched, followed by the "last gasp" of the Thom's Creek Series, Thom's Creek Finger Impressed (see Trinkley 1980). Other artifacts associated with these Early Woodland sites include both engraved and plain bone pins, bone awls, worked antlers, sherd abraders, shell beads, whelk shell scrapers, stone projectile points, worked soapstone disks, and occasionally clay balls.

While Joffre Coe's attention has always been focused on North Carolina's prehistory, his interest in shell ring sites was aroused during a short trip to the South Carolina coast in 1964. With a local collector, Donald MackIntosh, Coe visited several sites, including the Sewee Shell Ring. This interest was further demonstrated in his support and active participation in the salvage excavations at the Lighthouse Point Shell Ring in 1976. It was also during this time that Coe examined some Thom's Creek pottery and became convinced of its close affinity with the Stallings pottery.

Previous Research

The first professional work conducted in South Carolina at a shell ring site was the 1932 excavations by Woldemar Ritter and the 1933 excavations by Warren K. Moorehead at the Chester Field Shell Ring in Beaufort County (Flannery 1943). Although at the time of the present excavation, half of the site had eroded into the Broad River, the remaining portion of the ring suggested a diameter of about 180 feet. The plan drawings and field notes of Ritter (on file at the Charleston Museum, Charleston, S.C.) indicate that 883 square feet of shell midden and ring interior were excavated and a quantity of artifacts collected (probably without sifting the fill).

Ritter's excavations followed no recognizable grid, although the stratigraphy was carefully recorded in drawings and in a daily log. Levels consisted "mainly of shell and some food bones," sand lenses, periwinkle shell pockets, burnt sand and ash, and a light yellowish undisturbed sand. The profiles revealed banding of the various levels, and shell clusters that followed a conical contour. Moorehead and Ritter found features within the shell midden described as containing "hard lump[s] of ashes" (square D-1) (Ritter's field notes, on file at the Charleston Museum, Charleston, S.C.). A large number of periwinkle concentrations were also found in the ring-shaped midden. Features were reported from the ring interior, although there is little information on these pits in the field notes. One feature is described as a "fire pit" and the other as a "small shell midden" (Flannery 1943:150). All of the excavation units within the ring interior were described as containing few remains, whereas pottery, stone tools, and animal bones were said to be abundant within the shell midden.

Flannery (1943:151) suggests that the Chester Field ring was a permanent village, "the level space enclosed by the mound [ring] evidently having been reserved for the dwellings." Implicit in this statement was a failure to recognize the crushing and banding of the shell midden which had been illustrated to some degree in Ritter's profiles. There is nothing in Flannery's discussion or in Ritter's field notes to suggest occupation within the ring area; in fact, the investigators consistently noted an absence of cultural materials or disturbances.

Work conducted only a few years later by Antonio Waring and Lewis Larson (1968) at the Sapelo Island Shell Ring in Georgia revealed at least six "shallow, basin-shaped pits" intruding into the yellow sand under the shell ring (Waring and Larson 1968:271). These pits were 1.0 to 1.5 feet in diameter and 0.7 feet deep and contained midden fill or cemented masses of shell and ash. Pits and ash deposits were also observed in the profiles. Waring and Larson bisected one edge of the ring with an irregularly shaped excavation, of about 1,325 square feet, to sample the ring and ring interior.

The most significant outcome of this research was the assessment of site formation processes and function. Waring and Larson (1968:273) state that the shell ring

> was composed of occupational midden in primary position which was deposited as the result of habitation sites located on the ring. . . . It would seem very likely that the shell ring was the site of many small habitations. The

> occupants apparently piled the rapidly accumulating shell beside their small dwellings; later they moved, and the new shell was then piled on the former habitation site. . . . The area in the center of the ring was sterile of refuse except for that which had washed down from the encircling midden.

This exemplary analysis, however, soon was forgotten. In 1965, William Edwards began excavation at the Sewee Shell Ring in Charleston County, South Carolina. This ring is incomplete on its southeastern side, probably because of historic shell removal, and is associated with a small subsidiary midden or shell ridge about 30 feet to the east of the ring. Using clam rakes and both hand sorting and water screening as recovery techniques, Edwards excavated nine or ten five-foot squares (Edwards 1965). Although he expected to find the remains of house structures, Edwards was unable to firmly document any postholes. He delimited three periwinkle concentrations and two pits containing charcoal and shell refuse. Little more data were contained in his discussion of the profiles, with problems of site interpretation being attributed to the small test units.

Based on the faulty assumptions that the sea level had been falling since 2000 B.C. (rather than gradually rising; cf. Colquhoun et al. 1981), and that the ring had been constructed as an incomplete circle, Edwards hypothesized that the site functioned as a fish trap. He proposed that originally the site had been built from scavenged shell, and that later it actually was lived on while it functioned as a weir. The careful orientation of the ring opening, according to Edwards (1965:38), "was reasoned out by an especially observant and intelligent individual, who perhaps reported to the group that instructions had been super-naturally transmitted in a dream."

A less speculative analysis was provided by Alan Calmes in his brief report on excavations at the Sea Pines Shell Ring and the Skull Creek Shell Rings in Beaufort County, South Carolina. As at the Chester Field Ring, both Stallings and Thom's Creek series pottery were found. Once again, however, the investigator attempted to "test" the sites using isolated five- and 10-foot square units. At the Sea Pines Shell Ring, a single five-foot square was excavated adjacent to an old trench bisecting the ring. The stratigraphy suggested "that the top of the [occupied] ridge was constantly being leveled off as it gained in height, causing secondary interior ridges or piles down the slopes" (Calmes 1967:8). The Skull Creek Shell Rings, consisting of two superimposed rings, were tested with 175 square feet of excavations. Postholes were discovered within the ring midden and discrete features were found in the ring interiors. Within the smaller ring were found postholes and a "pit filled with shell," while a "pit with hard, concretion like, material" was found in the central area of the larger ring. Despite Calmes' emphasis on pottery, he noted that the excavations "displayed distinct stratigraphic lines running through the oyster shell. . . . indicat[ing] piling over a very long period of time. Large portions of the shell are loosely packed unbroken shell, while thin bands of crushed shell, charcoal and potsherds form tops of piles. . . . " (Calmes 1967:10).

By the time that E. Thomas Hemmings (1970a and 1970b) began excavations at the larger of the two Fig Island Shell Rings in Charleston County, South Carolina, there had been sufficient work to suggest that the Early Woodland shell rings were habitation sites that needed excavation using large units. Hemmings' investigations, however, consisted of the same bisecting trench excavation technique that had been characteristic of the early 1900s. His profile drawings indicated only a naturally weathered and crushed humus zone overlying loosely packed oyster shell, which in turn overlay sterile yellow sand. Slump was noted at each end of the trench and several possible features were indicated in the profiles, although no interior features or postholes were discovered (notes on file at the Institute of Archeology and Anthropology, U. S. C.).

The failure to find evidence of occupation was attributed to the fact that "[t]he interior area is wet just beneath the surface, and is covered by salt water during highest tides" (Hemmings 1970a:6). In a discussion of previous research, Hemmings (1970a:4) notes that "[h]earths, crushed shell floors and heavily concentrated organic lenses have been interpreted as evidence of habitation on the rim summits, but these features are not always apparent or well defined." The final assessment was that the excavations "did little to resolve the question of use" of the shell rings (Hemmings 1970b:9).

More recently, Rochelle Marrinan (1975) has excavated a total of about 1,850 square feet of midden and outlying marsh at two shell rings in Georgia. One of the major problems Marrinan chose to investigate was the function of the rings. The "utilization of large, adjacent excavation units" was thought to be the most direct and efficient means of understanding midden deposition (Marrinan 1975:24). Unfortunately, as it turned out, none of the excavations was larger than approximately 10 by 20 feet, with the result that while Marrinan determined that the middens were "purposeful accumulations" she could offer no functional hypotheses on the process of ring deposition (Marrinan 1975:117).

Thus, for over 40 years, archaeologists have struggled with the enigma of the shell rings. This failure to break the puzzle of shell ring function and settlement type seems to be attributable to the data collection techniques. Previous researchers attempted to answer subsistence and settlement questions by excavating either random squares (Moorehead and Ritter at Chester Field, Edwards at Sewee, Calmes at Skull Creek and Sea Pines, and Marrinan at Cannon's Point) or by bisecting the site with trenches (Waring and Larson at Sapelo, and Hemmings at Fig Island). Trenching confines observations to a narrow dimension and hampers the detection of artifact and feature patterns. While dispersed test units may give a statistically unbiased view of a site, the method has failings similar to (and probably worse than) the trenching technique. Block unit excavations, on the other hand, are an expedient method of obtaining information on subsurface features, site patterning, and intrasite patterning. Larger block units than were used by Marrinan, however, must be employed for this technique to be successful.

Investigation at the Lighthouse Point and Stratton Place Shell Rings

Excavations were conducted by the author at the Lighthouse Shell Ring in 1976 and 1979 and at the Stratton Place Shell Ring in 1979. Both sites are located in South Carolina. Investigations at Lighthouse Point were funded partly by the National Science Foundation, while the excavations at Stratton Place were accomplished largely through a College of Charleston archaeology field school. A total of 2,250 square feet were excavated at Lighthouse Point (Figure 5-1) and 1,500 square feet at Stratton Place (Figure 5-2). The preliminary work at Lighthouse Point provided data on two midden areas covering a total of 1,100 square feet (Figures 5-3 and 5-4), one area of interior ring edge (500 square feet), one area of exterior ring edge (400 square feet), and two areas of ring interior (250 square feet). At Stratton Place, emphasis was placed on the investigation of the shell ring interior, with 1,300 square feet (about

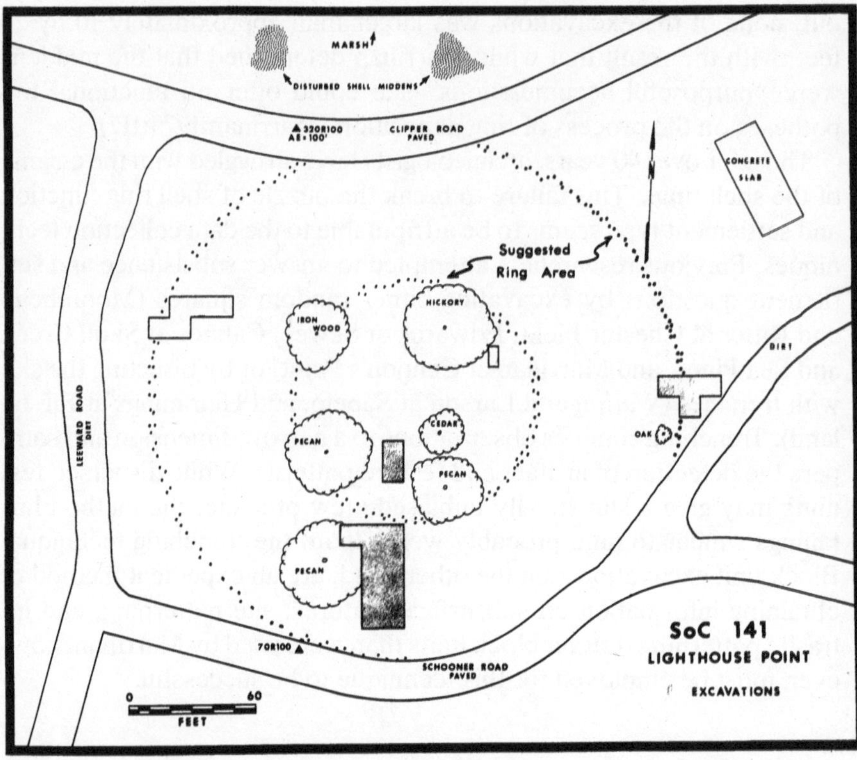

Figure 5-1. Lighthouse Point Shell Ring, Charleston County, South Carolina.

one-quarter of the total interior area) excavated. An additional 200 square feet were excavated outside the ring. Through the use of large conterminous excavation units, soil chemistry analyses, and the excavation of a number of features, it was possible to detect intrasite patterns at Lighthouse Point, and to verify their existence at Stratton Place.

Comparisons of the data from these two shell ring sites with those from other excavated sites suggest that whereas all shell rings are similar, they are not identical. The similarities, however, easily outweigh the differences, and at the level of intrasite patterning the sites appear to have four activity areas: (1) the exterior edge of the midden, (2) the shell midden ring, (3) the interior edge of the ring, and (4) the interior of the ring.

Excavation on the east edge of Lighthouse Point identified the ex-

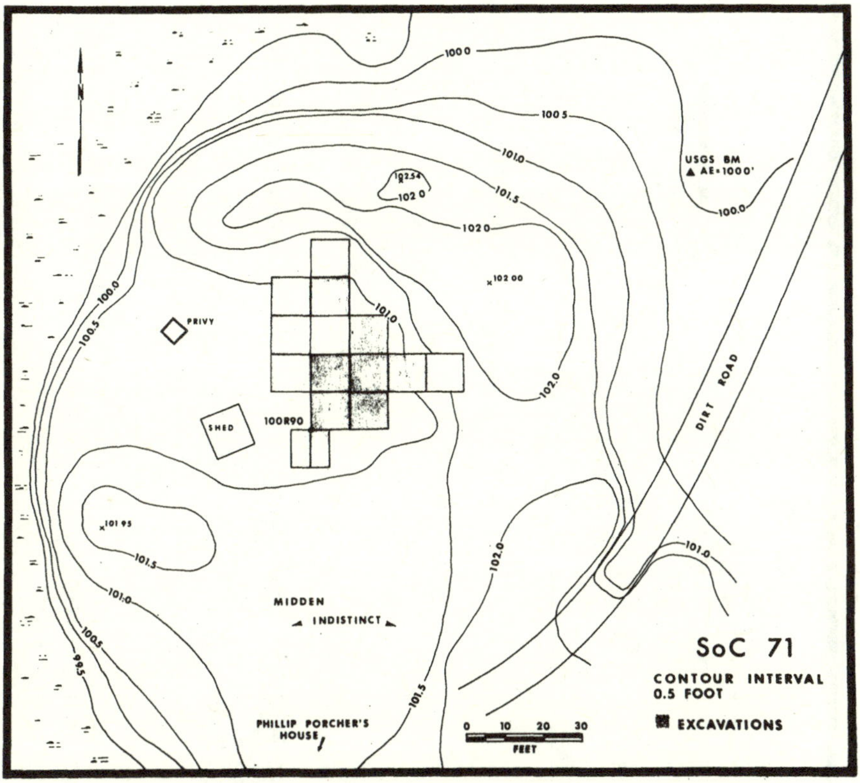

Figure 5-2. Stratton Place Shell Ring, Charleston County, South Carolina.

terior edge of the ring in the eastern corner of the N200 profile, with the western edge of the ring tentatively identified in square 220R40. Excavation of a block unit on the southern edge of the site revealed that the site margin was under a paved road, and that squares 80R140–150 actually began in the interior edge of the ring. Evidence of plowing in the area east of the midden was identified, and this recent plowzone was removed to search for possible exterior features or postholes. Although there was no evidence of structures, a large quantity of pottery was found along the outside edge of the ring. The ratio of large (over one inch in diameter) sherds from the interior of the ring to the midden to the exterior is 1:1.6:2 (N = 8,066), whereas the ratio of small sherds is 1:1.6:2.8 (N = 18,675). The larger number of sherds in the ring midden

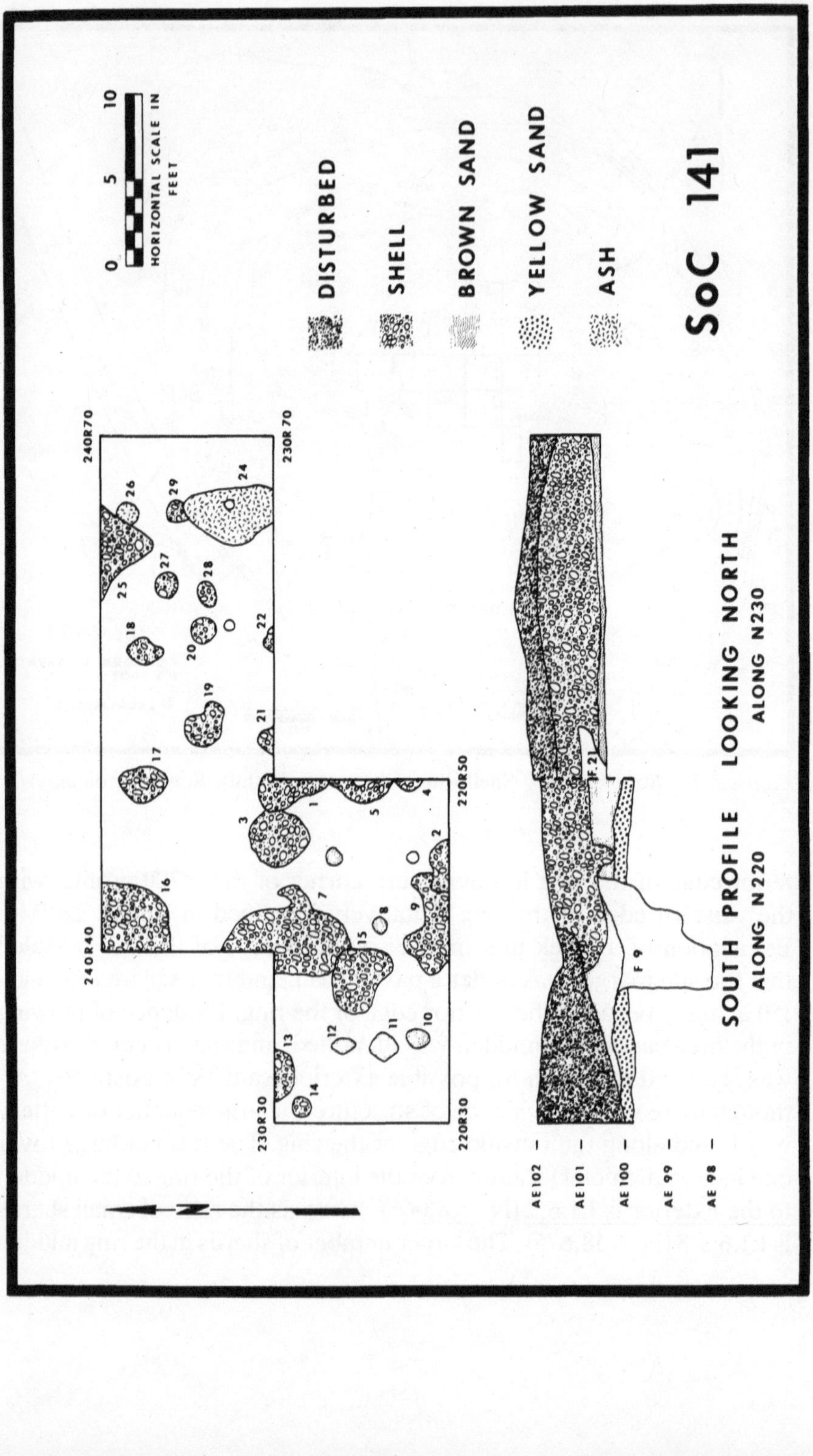

Figure 5-3. Plan View of the 1976 Excavations at Lighthouse Point.

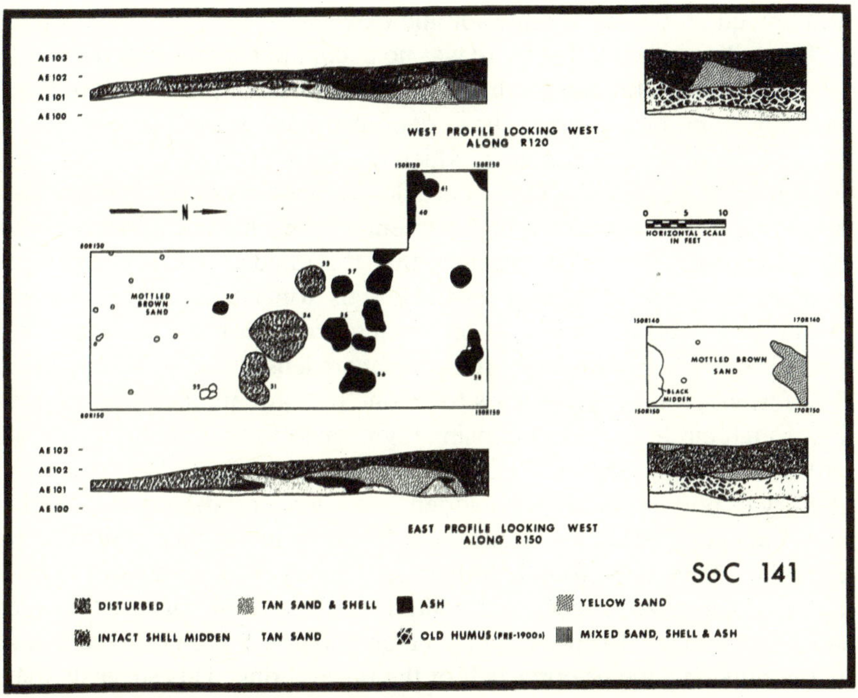

Figure 5-4. Plan View of the 1979 Excavations at Lighthouse Point.

than the exterior probably resulted from gradual expansion outward of the midden and the occasional flattening of the existing midden. Garbage apparently was deposited just over the edge of the shell ring. The occurrence of pottery and shell refuse, however, quickly drops at 20 feet from the ring, and, based on surface examination of several recently cleared house lots, virtually no aboriginal remains are found 50 to 100 feet from the ring.

Soil chemicals provide another source of data for differentiating activity areas at shell ring sites (see Trinkley and Ward 1978; Trinkley 1980). The soil pH at Lighthouse Point rises from exterior readings of about 7.6 to highs of about 8.2 under the midden, and gradually falls to a low of 7.6 in the interior of the ring. Analyses of nitrogen in the soil reveal a slight rise in the midden area, with a subsequent reduction in the readings in the interior. Lighthouse Point soils show a dramatic increase in phosphorus and phosphate within the midden area of the ring, and low quantities on the interior and exterior.

These data indicate that there was no occupation on the exterior edge of the midden, although there was some disposal of garbage down the exterior slope of the ring. These data also have suggested extensive occupation of the midden area, which has high levels of soil chemicals indicative of human use. Grain particle size analysis of the midden soil reveals that the midden has high percentages of silt and clay with a low percentage of sand. This suggests that the midden soil is comprised primarily of wind-blown particles and humus from intentional deposition.

The ring itself is composed of varying proportions of shell, animal bone, pottery, soil, and other artifacts that are lensed and highly crushed. The formation process appears to be one of house middens, deposited in a rough circle, gradually closing together to form a continuous ring of varying height and width. As previously mentioned, there is a high density of pottery within the midden and a concentration of soil chemicals indicative of human occupation. It is only in the shell midden that coprolites have been found, with 36 specimens recovered from Lighthouse Point. Size, shape, and content (Callen 1963) suggest that the stools are human. Twenty-eight (78 percent) of the coprolites were found in the outside edge or outer half of the posited ring. This suggests that a particular part of the site was preferred for defecation, perhaps for reasons of modesty, sanitation, or odor.

Under the midden were found large shell pits, several feet in diameter and several feet in depth, filled with crushed and lensed shell, sand and charcoal, and large quantities of bones. Sometimes only the bottom portions of these pits, characterized by a brown stain and almost sterile fill, were found. The upper portion, which blended into the shell midden, was indistinct during excavation. Several of the shallow basins reported by Waring and Larson (1968:271) may represent similar features. To a large extent, the shell midden probably was the result of these pits gradually blending together. These shell pits, with their quantity of unburnt shell, charcoal, and frequent lensing, suggest shellfish steaming, with the fire partially smothered to make an earth oven and with the shellfish added to the top and perhaps covered. Fish and reptiles also may have been prepared in this manner. Similar small pits, filled solely with periwinkle shells, suggest steam cooking of snails. The fire, in an oxygen-limited atmosphere, would produce charcoal, not ash, and the shells would be heated, not burnt. The removal of the shellfish, and their apparent later return to the pit as garbage, would account for the crushed and broken shell zones mixed with the sand (Figures 5-5 and 5-6). The bottom brown sand zone represents leaching and mixing by the Indians during the digging process. These pits were used several times and may have been enlarged in the later uses.

Postholes are abundant under the ring midden (see Figures 5-3 and 5-4) and are 0.4 to 0.8 feet in diameter. Only those posts which penetrated the subsoil have been identified, although similar posts are suspected to have existed in the midden zone as well. Several exhibit a mold within the hole and two evidence burning of the post. Although no structures have been identified, many of the posts are sufficiently large to be structural members and others may represent lean-tos, hide tanning racks, or other lightweight supports.

Distinct from the ring midden is the interior edge of the shell. In this area of the Lighthouse Point ring, concentrations of soil chemicals have been observed, as well as a pit type different from the steaming pits found in the midden. These pits are filled with quantities of hardened ash, burnt shell, and fishbone (Figure 5-7). A quantity of partially articulated fish bones are found embedded in the hardened ash, suggesting that skeletons, stripped of flesh, were thrown into these pits. The ash and burnt shell indicate hot fires that fully oxidized the wood. The pits evidence a thick ash lens overlying a thicker zone of mixed ash lumps and sand. Occasionally, burnt red sand is observed at the bottom or on the sides of the pit. These pits were used for the roasting of mammal and fish meats and may also have functioned to provide heat during the winter. Moorehead and Ritter (notes on file, Charleston Museum, Charleston, S.C.) found such a pit on the interior edge of the Chester Field Shell Ring. Waring and Larson (1968:271) also mention ash pits at Sapelo, although they do not provide information on either the nature of the pits or their locations in the ring.

Pottery is still abundant on the interior edge of the ring, although postholes are fewer than under the ring. On the basis of the abundance of pottery, the concentration of soil chemicals, and the hot-fire cooking pits, the interior edge appears to represent a "non-habitation activity area." Whereas the postholes and garbage buildup suggest occupation in the ring area, the interior edge was used for food preparation and possibly other activities.

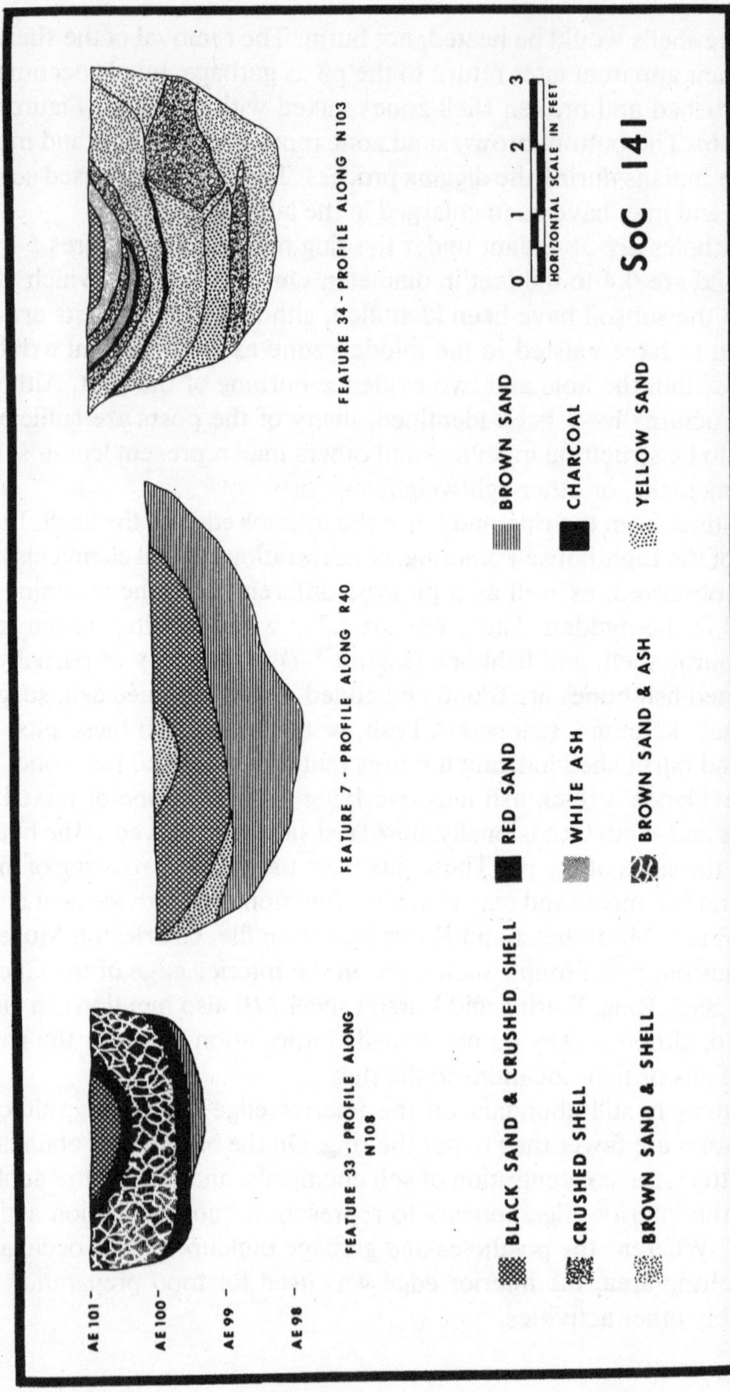

Figure 5-5. Typical Feature Profiles from Lighthouse Point.

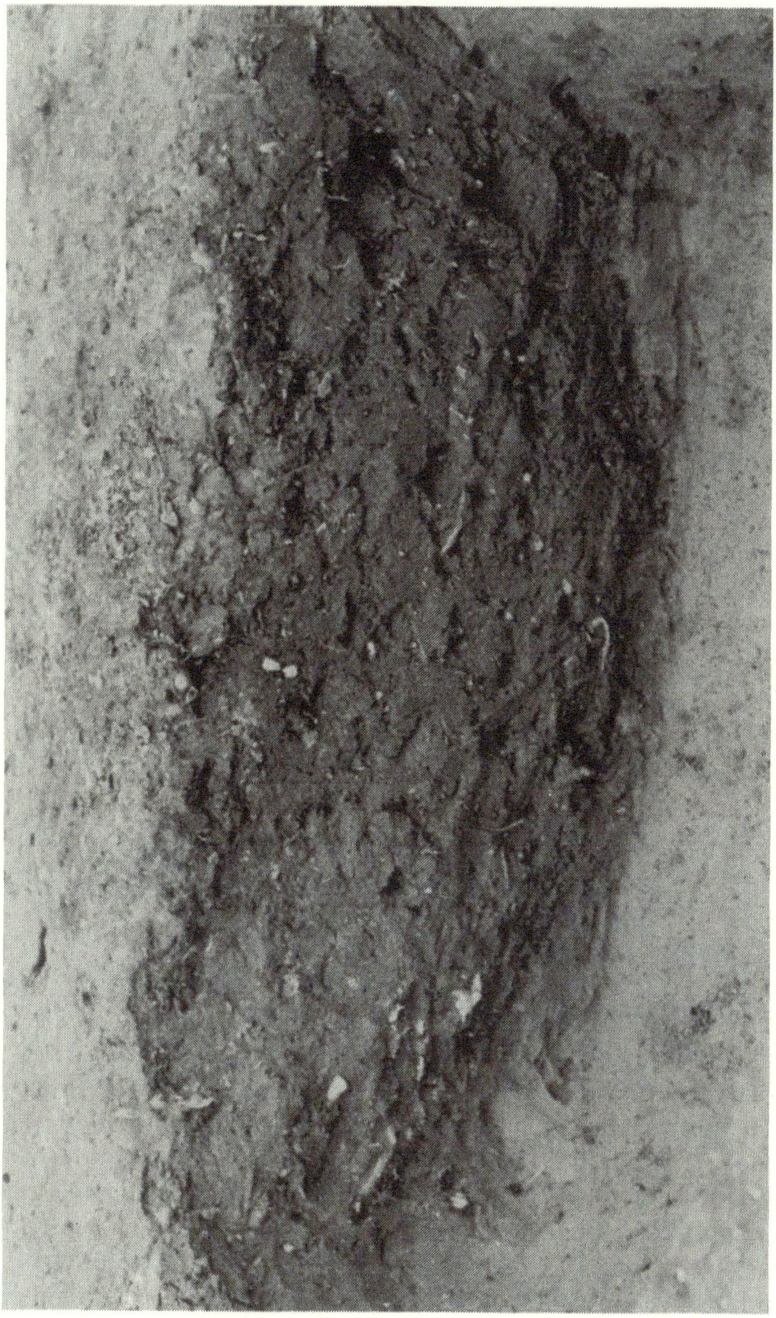

Figure 5-6. Feature 33, South Half Excavated, View to the North.

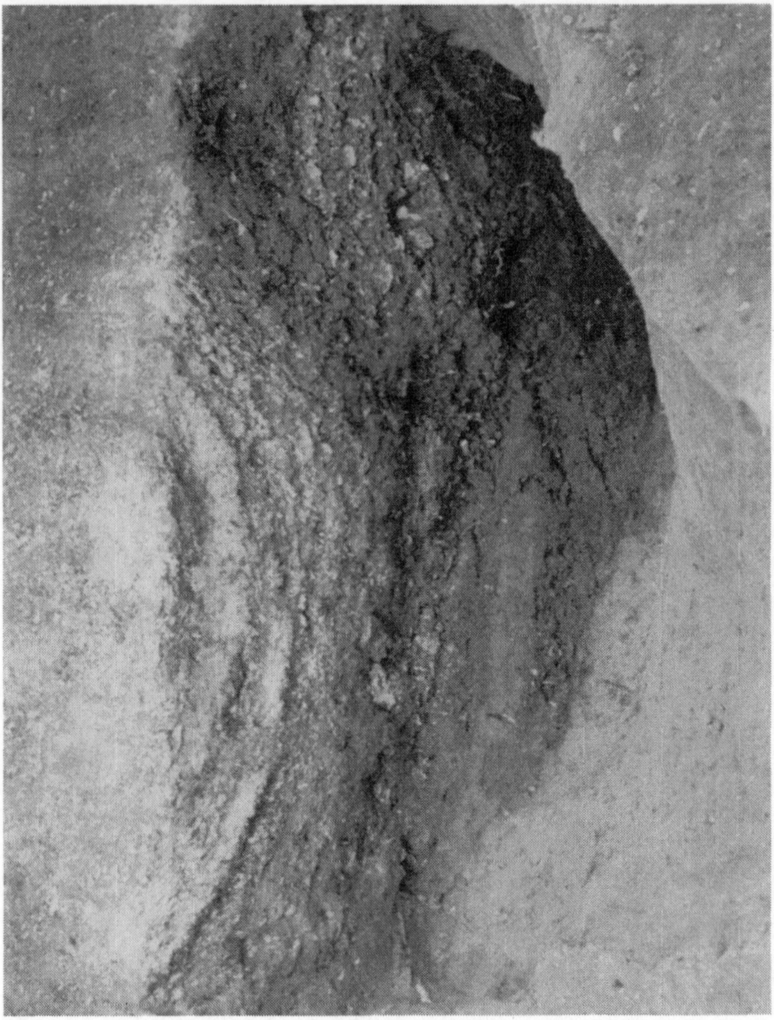

Figure 5-7. Feature 34, South Half Excavated, View to the North.

During excavation at Lighthouse Point and particularly at Stratton Place it was discovered that sherd density, although relatively great around the edges, fell off rapidly in the interior. This is not, however, to imply that the interior lacks all evidence of aboriginal activity, since some pottery is found in the interior of the ring. Sherds from the interior are, however, greatly fragmented.

The low levels of soil chemicals in the ring interior reflect limited occupational activities in that portion of the site. Excavations at the Stratton Place Shell Ring identified a prering humus of brown-to-gray sand overlying a lighter tan-to-white sterile sand. The old humus gradually diminished toward the center of the site, probably the result of a combination of phenomena, including leaching, extensive aboriginal use of the center which broke up and mixed the humus, and a failure of aboriginal use to replenish the organic content of the soil. Toward the ring midden this zone gets thicker, partly because of an area of soil accumulation within the ring. These data support the idea that the ring interior was kept relatively clean and that it was used for activities other than refuse disposal or habitation. Based on the fragmentation of the pottery and the depth to which it was pushed in the soil by pedestrian traffic, it appears that the interior was used.

The few features found within the shell rings are small and difficult to interpret. Two pits were found at Lighthouse Point, and the one excavated was filled with homogeneous brown-black sand and a number of sherds. A single feature, consisting of a shallow, oval pit, was identified within the interior of the Stratton Place ring. The pit contained a small quantity of pottery, a few flecks of charcoal, crushed shell, and a single mammal tooth. There was no evidence of burning or discoloration of the shell or the surrounding sand matrix. These pits, with no obvious function, are distinct from any other features identified at the sites. Although both Flannery (1943:150) and Calmes (1967) report pits within the ring interior, few data are provided by either investigator. Ritter's field notes from Chester Field, however, stress the "sterile" nature of the interior area.

The data from Lighthouse Point and Stratton Place indicate that the shell rings were gradually formed habitation sites, with occupation taking place on the rings. The rings were formed from kitchen refuse, particularly shellfish and animal bone. Large steaming pits and postholes are found in the midden areas, whereas roasting pits are found on the edges of the rings. The relatively clear interiors appear to function as areas of communal activity. It may be that too much emphasis has been placed on a presumed concern by the aborigines to keep the interior clean. It is probable that no special effort was required to prevent the spread of garbage into a homogeneous pile. There is evidence that broken pottery was probably unintentionally distributed in the ring center and that some activity fragmented these remains and forced them into the sand.

Fundamentally, the circular shape of the shell rings may be related to the egalitarian nature of Early Woodland societies, where a circular clustering of habitations would promote communication and social interaction. Circular settlements, with a central area reserved for group activities, are common in the ethnographic literature of the Southeast. Whereas recent investigations have significantly contributed to a clearer understanding of the organization and function of shell ring sites, many questions still are unresolved.

6 · ALEXANDER H. MORRISON II

A New Way of Looking at Old Holes: Methods for Excavating and Interpreting Timber Structures

Introduction

Timber molds and their construction holes are among the features encountered most frequently on archaeological sites in the eastern United States. While sometimes enigmatic, or even bothersome, they present the archaeologist with an important body of useful information. Their spatial relationships often indicate a site's architectural components, e.g., buildings, fencelines, and palisades. Their stratigraphic relationships, to each other and to other features, can be used to develop a relative chronology for a site, and artifacts from them may provide even more precise temporal control. But, the utility of this information is directly dependent upon the methods by which it is obtained.

Early archaeologists emphasized vertical trenching in their excavations of middens, burial mounds, and temple mounds. With this technique, it was very difficult to observe timber molds and holes. By the 1930s, horizontal stripping became a common practice, and sites were excavated in stratigraphic levels whenever possible. This method permitted archaeologists to observe, record, and excavate postmolds, wall trenches, and palisade lines, thus making it possible to delineate structures, determine the sequence in which they were built, and ascertain their cultural affiliations (Webb 1938; Lewis and Kneberg 1946).

Excavations by Joffre Coe in the 1960s and 1970s continued the techniques begun earlier and greatly improved them. After the surface of a stratum was exposed, cultural features were carefully recorded in plan, and an attempt always was made to note their stratigraphic relationships (e.g., Egloff 1971; Dickens 1976; Keel 1976). Whenever possible, features were cleaned out before the square in which they occurred was excavated deeper. When this could not be done, postmolds were not excavated until subsoil was reached. But in every case, an attempt was made to keep artifacts from intrusive molds separate from older ones, and care was taken to preserve and record in profile the shape of the original cavity and the stratigraphic relationships observed in plan. By carefully working with plan drawings and the excavation data, it often was possible to determine the postmold pattern of individual, closely superimposed building phases (e.g., Egloff 1971:62–67).

The gradual emergence of historical archaeology in the United States produced a blending and modification of techniques borrowed from American and British prehistorians. This has resulted in a distinctive approach to the excavation and interpretation of sites of the Colonial and later periods (Harrington 1952:343). Most familiar is the technique of retaining balks between squares. These unexcavated sections preserve examples of the stratigraphy of all four sides of a square during excavation. This emphasis on the observation of stratigraphy also resulted in the sectioning of features, including postmolds and postholes, so that their fills could be studied and drawn (Noël Hume 1969:77–84, 136). This method served adequately on eighteenth-century domestic sites that had substantial masonry foundations and relatively few timber molds.

Problem

Recent work on seventeenth-century English sites in the Chesapeake area (Figure 6-1) has demonstrated the need to change excavation approaches. Intensive excavations at sites along the James, York, and Potomac rivers in Virginia and in St. Mary's City, Maryland, have shown that timber foundations were the norm, and masonry foundations rare (Buchannan and Heite 1971; Kelso 1975, 1976; Outlaw 1978; Noël Hume 1979; Neiman 1980). Even on sites with masonry foundations, post-in-the-ground construction generally was used for outbuildings, additions, and repairs (Barka 1979; Keeler 1978).

The documentary evidence corroborates this field observation. In a sample of 22 dwellings built between 1648 and 1674, Garry Stone has found that none had masonry foundations, and only one had a brick chimney. These structures ranged in size from 15 by 10 feet to 40 by 25 feet, and in value from 200 to 3,500 pounds of tobacco (with one extraordinary specimen valued at 20,000 pounds). Six of these houses

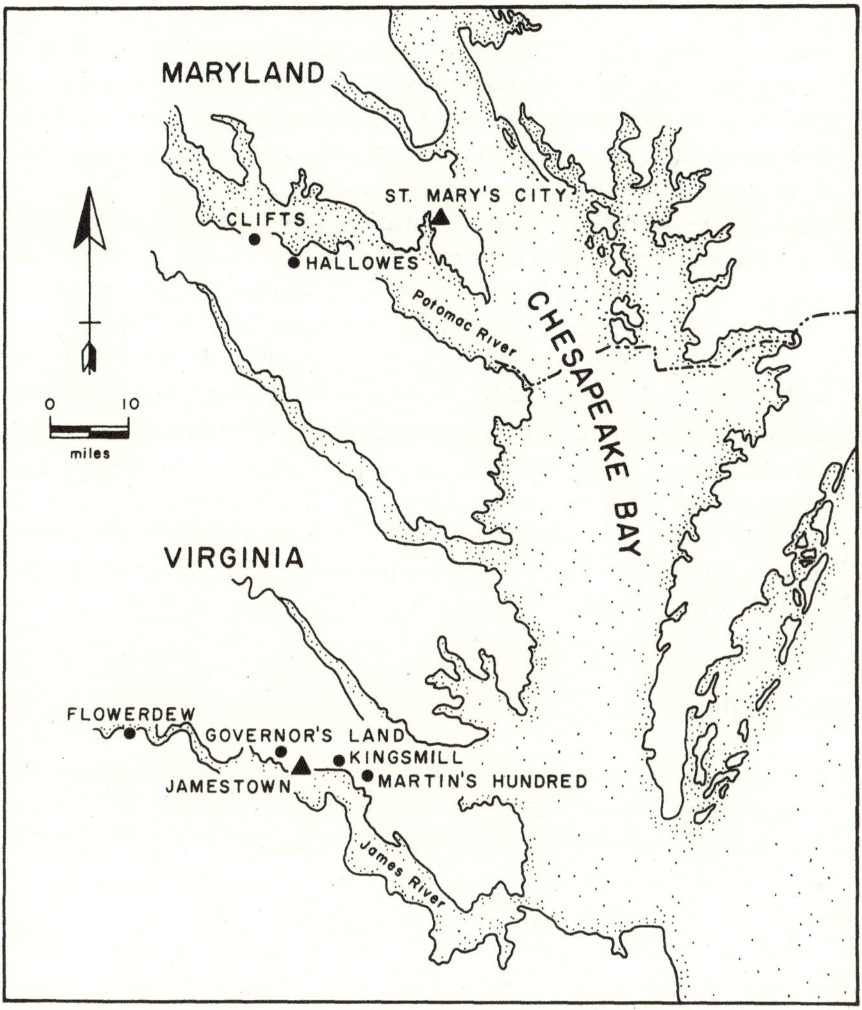

Figure 6-1. Map of the Chesapeake Area with Selected Seventeenth-Century Archaeological Sites.

were built for gentlemen, and the rest were built for ordinary planters and leaseholders (Stone 1982:Table 5-1). It is clear that seventeenth-century English colonists, at all social and economic levels, preferred timber foundations, probably because they were cheaper to build than masonry foundations.

Except for structures that were box-framed on ground-laid sills, these buildings were constructed with earthfast, vertical timbers. The archaeological evidence of post-in-the-ground construction consists of a multitude of postmolds and postholes. In St. Mary's City, the site of Maryland's first settlement and seventeenth-century capital, difficulties were encountered in measuring and analyzing buildings whose structural features were excavated at different times. In addition, postmold information often was poorly preserved at the feature surface. Scavengers in search of building materials, as well as rodents, roots, and pothunters, frequently had converted the tops of timber molds into craters. The best timber data are recovered from the bottom half of a postmold (Figure 6-2). These factors have led to a change from the traditional approach of planning and sectioning individual features as they are encountered, to a more systematic dissection of timber molds and holes as components of a single structure. In order to adequately analyze and interpret post-in-the-ground structures, it is necessary to excavate all of their timbers more or less simultaneously and to replan them (Stone 1978; Morrison 1979).

Methods

The methods now used in St. Mary's City for excavating timber structures have been modified over several field seasons. They involve the simultaneous excavation of timber molds and holes in horizontal slices, while compiling their vertical cross-sections in incremental segments.

The plowzone is stripped from the entire structure following standard archaeological procedures. Balks are retained along the major and minor axes of the structure only if unplowed strata are present and they are needed for vertical control. Overall photographs are taken of the structure after the plowzone is removed. Plan drawings are then made of all features in each square. The axis, along which the cross-section of each timber mold and its hole will be drawn, is determined, and its ends are marked with nails to facilitate subsequent recording. The locations of the nails are recorded on the plan drawings. In general, these features are sectioned along their long axes, but one pair of timbers may be sectioned in the opposite direction as a control.

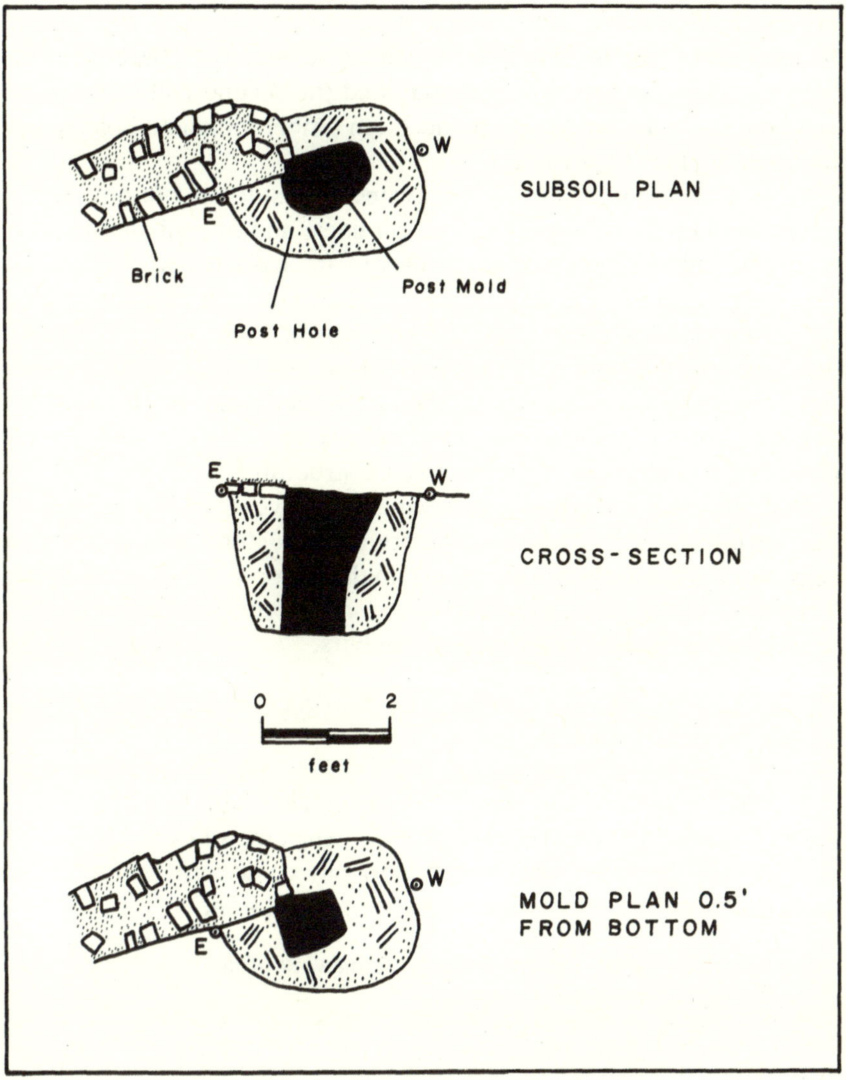

Figure 6-2. Southeast Corner Post, van Sweringen Outbuilding.

Each postmold is probed or cored to determine its approximate depth below the feature surface. One-half of each mold, and then one-half of the hole fill, is excavated to a depth of 0.25 to 0.5 feet above the bottom. Materials from the mold are provenienced separately from those of the hole fill. The cross-section is drawn, and the second half of the mold and hole is excavated to this point. Each timber mold and hole is then redrawn in plan (Figure 6-2).

With all associated features excavated almost to the bottom, strings are positioned along approximate wall lines, and overall and diagonal timber-to-timber dimensions are measured. If the diagonals are not equal, the corner angles of the structure are determined with a transit set over the string intersections. Then the first half of each mold and hole is excavated to the bottom. From one transit station, the bottom elevations of all associated molds and holes are measured. Each cross-section is completed, and the remainder of each feature is excavated. Overall photographs are taken of the completed structure.

Discretion must be used in following the above procedures. Features that intrude, or are intruded by, the primary structural features must be segregated from them and excavated in their proper stratigraphic order. The excavator must be prepared to record information observed prior to redrawing the plans of structural timbers.

Construction Types

Use of this method can provide archaeologists with much more than a set of precise dimensions and plan drawings for an excavated structure. At least four types of construction may be discerned from timber mold and hole patterns recorded in the ground (Stone 1978:1):

1. Structures nailed together around a framework of individually hole-set posts that extended to the plates.
2. Box-framed structures on continuous sills supported by short, individually hole-set posts (blocks).
3. Structures with preassembled tie-beam pairs erected in carefully excavated holes.
4. Structures with preassembled sidewalls erected as a unit in carefully excavated holes.

Types 3 and 4 are illustrated in Figure 6-3. It is likely that these different

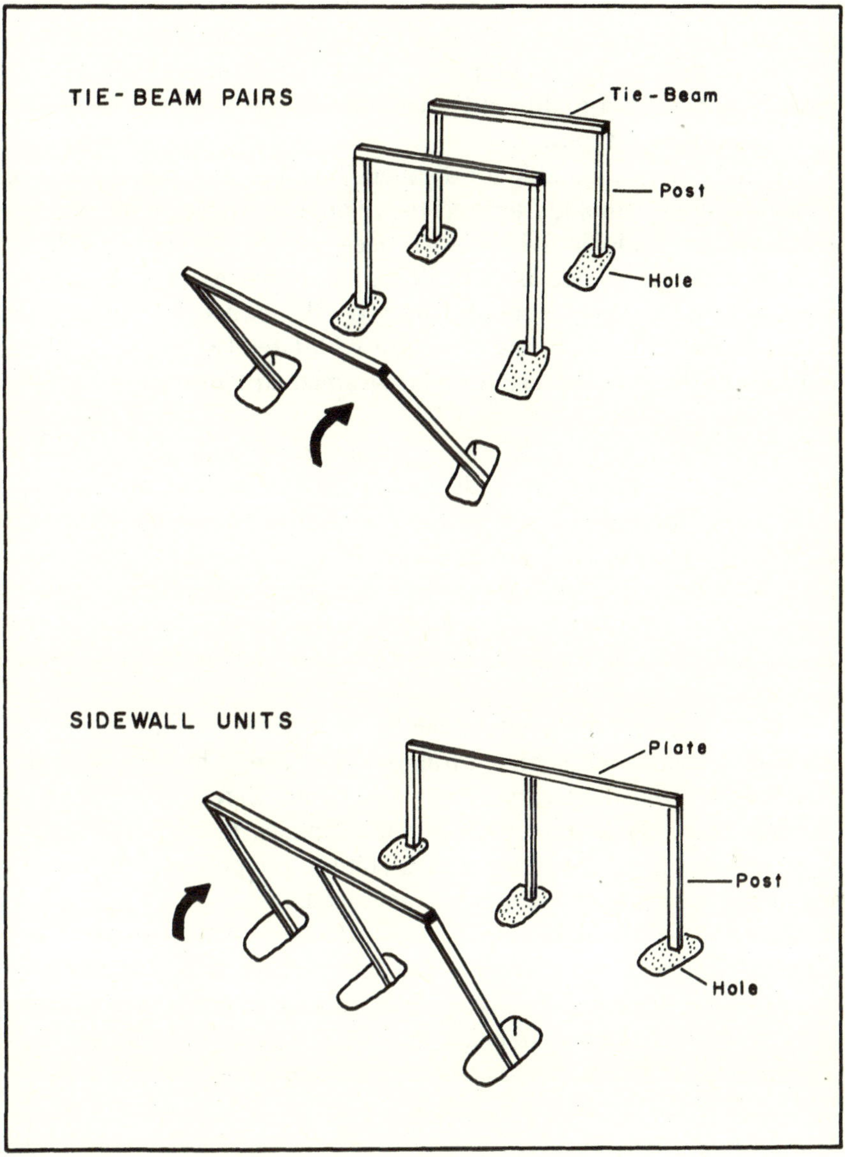

Figure 6-3. Methods of Raising Preassembled Frames.

construction techniques produced characteristic timber mold and hole patterns that can be determined from careful archaeology. The basic premise is that the more completely framed structures (3 and 4) leave more regular timber molds and holes. Several variables can be used to infer construction types.

The most useful variable for distinguishing between individually set posts and preassembled frames is the relative elevation of the bottoms of the timber molds. Individual posts need not be set at the same depth; their tops can be leveled as the building is assembled. Also, these posts need not be set very deeply in the ground, because the subsequent house frame will supply the structure with lateral stability. Similarly, the tops of the short blocks for a box-framed structure can be leveled as the sills are attached (Stone 1978:2).

Preassembled frames are erected most easily if uniform-length posts are set in holes of approximately equal bottom elevations. This assures level plates for the erection of the roof frame. Minor corrections in bottom elevations can be made after the frame has been propped in place by shimming a post up or scooping a hole deeper. If unacceptable variations in depth are discovered before the frame is raised, the necessary holes can be partially backfilled before setting the posts (Stone 1978:2).

It is not known how much variability in the bottoms of postmolds is compatible with preassembled frames. The current hypothesis is that postmold bottoms that vary by no more than 0.25 feet in elevation are uniform and indicative of preassembled frames. If the bottom elevations are measured from one transit station, the potential for error in making this determination can be minimized.

The shape of the hole also is useful in distinguishing between individually set posts and preassembled frames. Square or circular holes usually have vertical sides that might bind the timbers of preassembled units as they are tipped into place, thus suggesting individually set posts. Rectangular or subrectangular holes facilitate excavation of a deeper hole and provide more working space when erecting long timbers. This type of hole suggests structural posts of preassembled frames (Stone 1978:8).

When dealing with rectangular holes, the relationship of their long axes to the structure's ridge (building length) is useful in determining which type of preassembled frame was raised. Holes whose axes are parallel to the structure's ridge suggest the raising of tie-beam pairs, whereas holes with axes perpendicular to the ridge suggest sidewalls erected as a unit. This information in plan often is corroborated in cross-section. Profiles of the long axes of the holes frequently show them to be sloped or stepped in the direction in which the wall was raised, with each post having come to rest near the far side of the hole at its deepest point.

Single variables are unlikely to be diagnostic of a particular type of construction. However, if postmolds and their construction holes exhibit similarities by sidewalls or tie-beam pairs (as discussed above), a use of preassembled frames usually can be inferred. If they vary from hole to hole, it is likely that construction was with individually set posts (Stone 1978:8).

Archaeological Evidence

Some timber structures pose questions that cannot be answered until more information is obtained from extant buildings. Nevertheless, sufficient archaeological data have been recovered to illustrate all four types of construction discussed above.

At the Governor's Land Archaeological District in Virginia, excavations have revealed a series of seventeenth-century sites with post-in-the-ground structures. There were four such buildings at the Maine site (ca. 1620–1630). These shared several characteristics: the postmolds of each varied greatly in size, shape, and depth. Within each structure, the postmolds varied by a foot or more in their bottom elevations. None of the posts was set deeper than two feet into the ground, and most were much more shallow. These characteristics suggest that the structures were framed around individually set posts that extended to the plates (Outlaw 1978:13–46).

Structure 1 was the largest of the buildings at the Maine site. Its posts defined a structure with maximum exterior dimensions of 24 by 22 feet. A series of interior postmolds, with an associated concentration of daub fragments, indicated the probable location of a chimney. These details, and several nearby pits filled with domestic refuse, suggest that the structure was a dwelling. The other buildings were unheated and approximately half the size of Structure 1. They appear to be associated and may have been used for storage purposes (Outlaw 1978:19–24, 44).

The Clifts Plantation (ca. 1670–1730) on the grounds of Stratford Hall in Westmoreland County, Virginia is much more complex and was occupied for a longer period of time than the Maine site. Excavation at the Clifts site revealed the remains of the plantation house, two quarters, several other outbuildings, cemetery, palisade, and numerous fencelines (Neiman 1980:31). Although the structures at the Clifts site present an assortment of post-in-the-ground construction techniques, only one will be discussed here.

The plantation house at the Clifts site initially consisted of a 41 by 18.5-foot principal core, separated into two rooms by a central hearth. Several original additions were attached to this core. The core was constructed in two units—three eastern bays and a western cross-passage. The three eastern bays consisted of four transverse pairs of posts that were set on approximately 10-foot centers. Seven of the eight original postmolds had been destoyed by subsequent repairs. The holes for these original timbers were rectangular in plan and approximately twice as long as they were wide. The long axes of these holes paralleled the ridge of the building. When the bottom elevations for each pair of holes were compared, they were found to vary by only 0.1 feet. These two characteristics suggest that this section of the plantation house was erected in tie-beam pairs. Rather than sloping in the direction in which the pairs were raised, each hole had a long, flat bottom that may have permitted longitudinal adjustments as the precut plates were fitted to the tie-beams. It is interesting to note that the pairs of postholes at the ends of this 30-foot section of the house were approximately half a foot deeper than the two in the middle. This seems to emphasize the structural independence of this part of the house, which may have needed additional lateral stability (Neiman 1980:42–43).

The rest of the central core was framed in a less substantial manner. Although the method by which it was raised is unclear, stratigraphic evidence does indicate that it was built after the eastern portion was erected. Of the additions to the core, at least two (the back room and the porch entry) were erected in tie-beam pairs (Neiman 1980:47–49).

The remaining construction types can be illustrated with examples from the van Sweringen site (ca. 1675–1745) in St. Mary's City, Maryland. Excavations conducted by the St. Mary's City Commission have revealed a large dwelling, a small cellar with an associated post-in-the-ground structure, a larger outbuilding, and a number of fencelines. These buildings and features are thought to be on the one-acre lot owned by Gerret van Sweringen and his heirs well into the eighteenth century (Morrison 1980).

The dwelling (Figure 6-4) was a rambling, L-shaped building with approximate exterior dimensions of 60 by 40 feet. Although excavation of this structure is not complete, work to date has focused on the northwestern room thought to have been the kitchen. This room went through three major building phases. Initially, the room was 15.5 by 17 feet, with an exterior chimney. The posts of the south wall were set in holes. On the north side, a brick wall enclosed a cooling pit 1.65 feet deep. Three posts set in this brickwork framed the north wall of the kitchen. Apparently this room was poorly built, and it was soon replaced.

In the second phase (ca. 1690), the room was demolished and reconstructed; only the chimney foundation was reused. It is unclear how the south wall, adjacent to another room, was assembled. The north wall appears to have been raised as a unit. Three postholes were dug, two of which intruded through the builder's trench of the earlier brick wall and extended 0.9 feet below its bottom. The third hole relocated the room's northwest corner some four feet north of the chimney base. These three holes, and the timbers set in them, shared several similarities. The holes were rectangular and measured approximately 4 by 3 feet. Their long axes were perpendicular to the ridge of the room, and in cross-section they sloped or were stepped from the north side. The postmolds were located near the south side of each hole. Transit elevations of the bottoms of the three molds varied by only 0.19 feet, which makes it likely that this wall was erected as a preassembled sidewall unit. Also during this phase, the cooling pit was filled and a brick floor was laid over it. The new dimensions of the room, including the chimney, were 18.5 by 21 feet. During the second quarter of the eighteenth century, the north wall was reinforced by posts set through the brick floor. By this time, the structure probably ceased to be used for domestic purposes.

Fifty feet east of the dwelling, a one-room outbuilding (ca. 1700), with an exterior chimney, was excavated (Figure 6-5). Four principal timbers were set in holes at its corners. One shallow intermediate post was set approximately in the center of the south side; evidence of others may have been destroyed by plowing. Three of the corner posts were approximately square, and the fourth was rectangular. All of the holes

Figure 6-4. The van Sweringen Dwelling in St. Mary's City, Maryland.

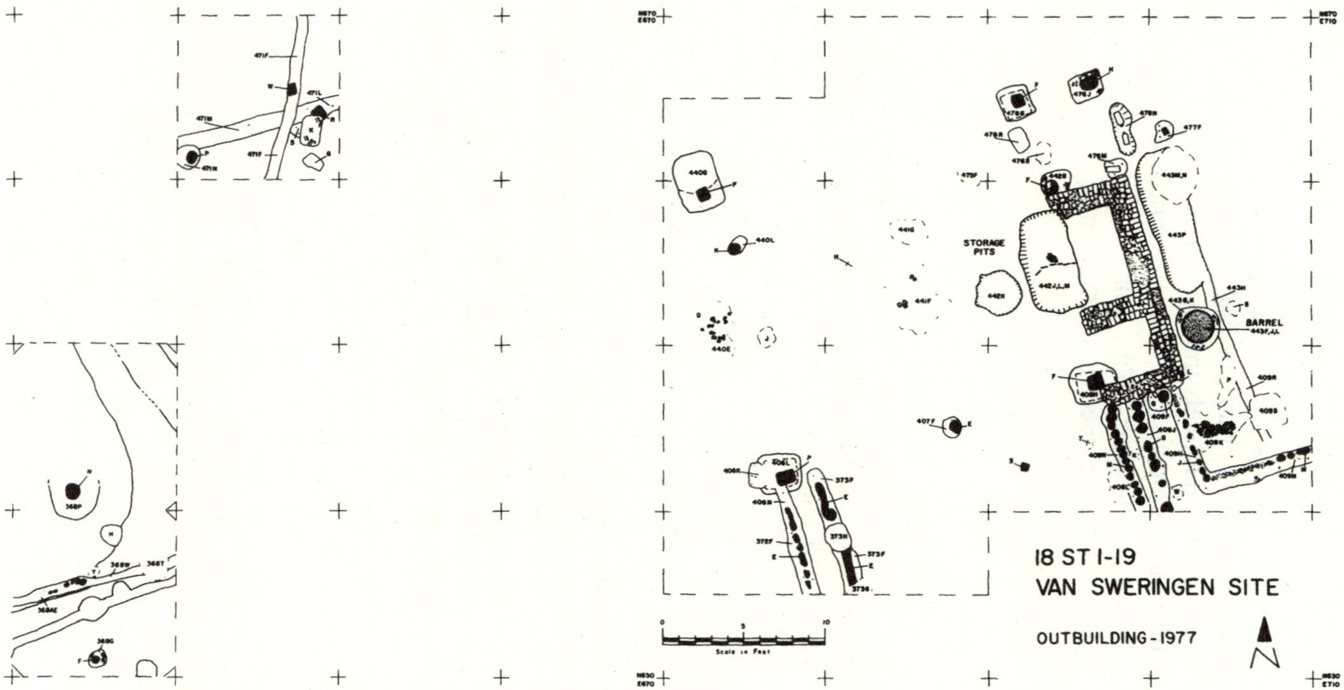

Figure 6-5. The van Sweringen Outbuilding in St. Mary's City, Maryland.

were moderately deep (2.5 feet or greater) and had nearly vertical sides. The bottom elevations of the corner postmolds varied by as much as 0.6 feet. From this evidence, it is likely that the van Sweringen outbuilding was box-framed on continuous sills that were supported mainly by four, short blocks set in the corner holes. Smaller intermediate posts, set in shallow holes, may have helped support the sills.

Conclusions

The study of architecture is more than an end in itself. Structures are among the largest artifacts through which the past can be investigated. In the Chesapeake area, changes in architecture seem to reflect the gradual growth of a stable social order from a frontier society.

The above examples serve to illustrate four types of post-in-the-ground construction common in the Chesapeake during the seventeenth century. Although archaeological information on this period is just now emerging, there is a sufficiently large sample of excavated sites, supplemented by data from extant structures and documentary sources, to permit tentative conclusions.

English colonists in the Chesapeake area quickly learned that frontier wages made the construction of fully framed houses extremely expensive, while temporary, European-style structures rapidly decayed. By combining old building traditions with the rich timber resources of the New World, Chesapeake carpenters developed an inexpensive, modular structure that was suited to any domestic or agricultural function (Carson et al. 1981:138; Stone 1982:150–151).

The settlers' new ecological niche provided an abundant supply of free-riving, old growth hardwood. Thinly riven clapboards were used to cover the walls and roofs of these structures, and riven scantlings were used in their wall and roof frames. Riving reduced construction costs because it was faster than sawing, and it produced strong members that were thin and light in weight. These lightweight elements were fastened by nailed, lap joints, reducing the number of costly mortise-and-tenon joints. By taking advantage of these factors, Chesapeake carpenters produced inexpensive buildings despite high wages (Stone 1982:241–243).

Architectural historians think that the Colonial Chesapeake area experienced three stages of building construction. In the first stage, huts provided temporary shelter until something more permanent could be built. These huts were followed quickly by impermanent, earthfast buildings that were weatherproof, inexpensive, and easy to build. They were used for a variety of purposes and, as housing, proved to be an acceptable alternative to the fully framed or brick buildings achieved by only a few Chesapeake colonists in the third stage (Carson et al. 1981:148).

The impermanent, earthfast buildings are represented by the four construction types discussed in this essay. Structures framed around individually hole-set posts are considered to be the most primitive of the four types. The development of preassembled frames simplified layout and construction, and buildings with preassembled tie-beam pairs or sidewalls set in holes were widespread during the seventeenth century (Carson et al. 1981:148–153).

Raising structures in tie-beam pairs is the earlier technique. Tie-beam pairs were easier to raise because they were shorter and lighter than sidewall units. This technique was used frequently on early or frontier sites where labor was limited. Although easy to raise, these frames were tedious to assemble into a structure because of the number of units that had to be spaced and aligned accurately. Raising sidewalls was simpler work because only two frames had to be raised. But because sidewalls were larger and heavier, this method required more neighbors than were available in earlier periods (Stone 1982:261–265).

Despite a noticeable number of bricklayers by the 1670s, impermanent, timber foundations continued in common use. Toward the end of the seventeenth century, box-framed structures became increasingly common. Because their sills were raised above the ground on short, hole-set blocks, they were as protected from rot as sills on masonry foundations. Box-framed houses were widespread during the eighteenth century, relegating preassembled, post-in-the-ground frames to outbuildings and barns (Carson et al. 1981:153; Stone 1982:288–293).

The persistence of impermanent building techniques seems to be related to a variety of social, economic, and demographic factors. The economy of the Colonial Chesapeake area was based on a single cash crop—tobacco. The cultivation of tobacco was unusually labor intensive, and the profits it returned were directly proportional to the quantity grown. As quickly as capital could be raised, it was spent on more labor and improvements to the farmstead, rather than on better housing. In addition, the mortality rate, was high among immigrants to the area, and they had no guarantee that accumulated wealth would be passed on to their heirs. It may have seemed better to put profits back into production, or spend them on material goods, than to build things to last. Impermanent dwellings were not replaced until the economic base became diversified and the population stable (Carson et al. 1981:168–178).

Our understanding of the archaeological record can be no better than the quality of the data on which it is based. The technique of simultaneously excavating and replanning structural features is offered as a systematic method of dissecting timber buildings. Joffre Coe's insistence upon meticulous excavation is as applicable to historical archaeologists as to prehistorians. If standardized field methods are adopted and applied rigorously, the analysis of archaeological sites will be enhanced. In addition, comparisons between sites can be made with greater confidence, and explanations and interpretations can be built upon firmer foundations.

Acknowledgments

Special thanks are due Garry Stone for his advice and assistance in the preparation of this essay. He first demonstrated to Chesapeake archaeologists the need and utility of a systematic approach to earthfast structures. Henry Miller and Michael Smolek also offered valuable comments, and Chinh Hoang assisted in drafting Figure 6-4.

Section II

Intersite Comparisons and Regional Chronology

7 • JEFFERSON CHAPMAN

Archaeology and the Archaic Period in the Southern Ridge-and-Valley Province

Introduction

Twenty-five years ago the evidence for the Archaic culture period in eastern Tennessee was considered rare, and remnant Paleoindian populations were even postulated to have had contact with Early Woodland period cultures. Elsewhere in the eastern United States, however, researchers were beginning to document a long sequence of Archaic period complexes. Influenced by these data, the latter view was gradually modified, but it was not until 1973 that the magnitude of the Archaic period remains was realized. Although "state of the art" papers in archaeology may be viewed as passé or provincial by some theoretically oriented scholars, they provide the data upon which their behavioral inquiries are based. The following paper summarizes some of the significant work conducted recently in the southern Ridge-and-Valley Province and focuses specifically on the lower Little Tennessee River Valley. The culture sequences, artifact assemblages, and settlement and subsistence patterns typical of this valley are proposed to be similar to those of the larger southern Ridge-and-Valley Province.

The Study Area

The geographical focus of this survey is the southern section of the Ridge-and-Valley physiographic province, comprising portions of southwest Virginia, east Tennessee, and northwest Georgia (Figure 7-1). The Ridge-and-Valley Province extends for 1,200 miles, from the St. Lawrence Valley on the north to the Gulf Coastal Plain on the south (Fenneman 1938). The valley ranges in width from 14 to 80 miles and is characterized by northeast-southwest trending mountain ridges.

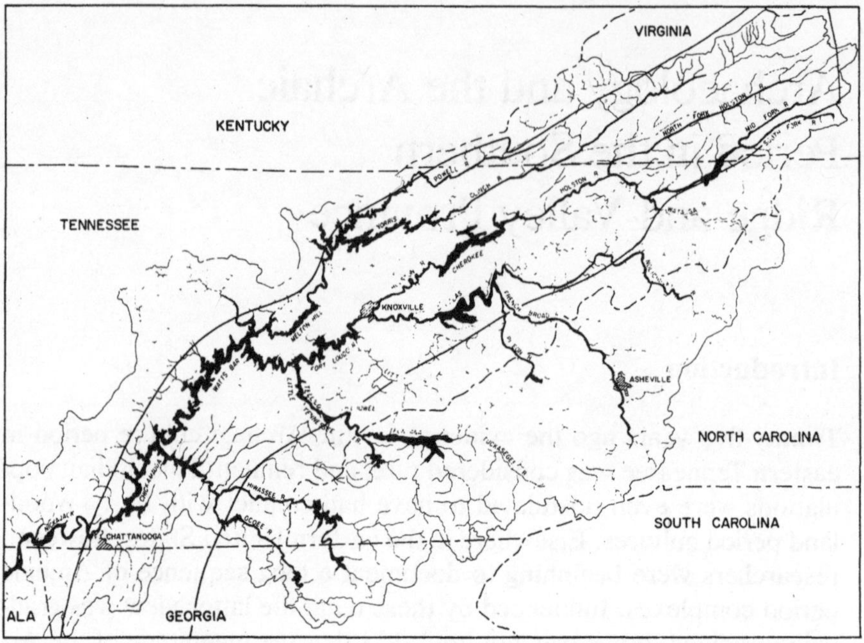

Figure 7-1. The Upper Tennessee River Drainage and Southern Ridge-and-Valley Province.

The northern boundary of the southern section of the province is the divide between the New and the Tennessee rivers. In this section, the valley floor is generally flat below Knoxville but steepens progressively as one moves toward the New River divide. To the east and west, the Blue Ridge and Piedmont provinces and the Cumberland Plateau form clear, abrupt boundaries. Within this section, the major streams trend longitudinally until the Tennessee River breaks out west of Chattanooga and flows west through a gorge onto the Cumberland Plateau. The waters of the Tennessee River are derived from the Powell, Clinch, Holston, Nolichucky, and French Broad rivers; major streams draining the Blue Ridge Province that intersect these waters are the Watauga, French Broad, Pigeon, Little Tennessee, and Hiwassee rivers. All of these drainages provided aboriginal passageways to the north and east (cf. Myer 1928).

The region is characterized by a temperate, deciduous forest, and is situated toward the eastern edge of the mixed mesophytic forest and adjacent to the oak-chestnut forest of the Blue Ridge Province (Shelford 1963). The valley has a humid, mesothermal climate characterized by a definite seasonal rhythm. Precipitation averages 40 to 60 inches per year and the growing season ranges from 170 to over 200 days.

Although the Coosa River drainage continues the southwestern trend of the Ridge-and-Valley Province through northwest Georgia and into central Alabama, this paper establishes an arbitrary boundary at the divide between the Tennessee and Coosa rivers.

Archaeological Research and the Concept of an Archaic

Considerable archaeological activity was focused on the southern Ridge-and-Valley Province in the nineteenth and twentieth centuries. In the 1880s, archaeologists from the Bureau of American Ethnology of the Smithsonian Institution investigated over 100 mounds in East Tennessee (Holmes 1884; Thomas 1894). Traveling in the steamboat "Gopher," C. B. Moore excavated archaeological sites along the Tennessee River between 1914 and 1915, extending his investigations upstream as far as Knoxville (Moore 1915). The first to recognize a cultural sequence based on assemblage differences as well as stratigraphy in this area was M. R. Harrington, who excavated at Bussell Island at the mouth of the Little Tennessee River and elsewhere in the southern Ridge-and-Valley in 1919 (Harrington 1922).

The year 1933 was a momentous one for Southeastern archaeology. With the inauguration of the Civil Works Administration, money was allocated for archaeological fieldwork in affected project areas. The Tennessee Valley Authority was founded the same year, and its reservoir construction activities have greatly shaped the scope of archaeological research in the Tennessee River Valley to the present. In 1934, recognizing that "the construction of dams and the consequent flooding of large areas adjacent to such construction would destroy all records of prehistoric occupation and forever prevent future archaeological investigation of such inundated areas" (Webb 1938:1), the first of a series of reservoir archaeological salvage projects was begun in the Norris Basin on the Clinch River. In the same year, a Division of Anthropology was established at the University of Tennessee, with T. M. N. Lewis as its head. The creation of the Works Progress Administration in 1936 brought a resurgence of large-scale fieldwork; in a six-year period, excavations were conducted in the Pickwick (Webb and DeJarnette 1942), Guntersville (Webb and Wilder 1951), Chickamauga (Lewis and Kneberg 1941, 1946), Kentucky (Lewis and Kneberg 1947; Lewis and Lewis 1961), Watts Bar (Field records, Frank H. McClung Museum, Knoxville,Tennessee), and Douglas (Field records, Frank H. McClung Museum, Knoxville,Tennessee) reservoirs. The enormous volume of material and interpretations generated by these investigations have influenced archaeological research in the Southeast since. The recognition and definition of an Archaic stage went hand-in-hand with these excavations.

In the Norris Basin report, Webb (1938:364) suggested the presence of an earlier culture based on data from cave sites: "At least the occupancy of caves of this region by a people of quite primitive type seems demonstrated. It is assumed that this occupancy antedated that of the village-building people, since the cave dwellers had rather crude artifacts characteristic of their cultural level, and later evidences of development are not found in the caves." Although not so designated, the concept of Shell Mound Archaic began to emerge from work in the Wheeler Basin (Webb 1939:180): "The author is convinced that a spear throwing, hunting, and fishing people who made no pottery and used no bows and arrows, laid down the great shell midden at the base of the mound site Lu°86."

By the early 1940s, investigation in the Pickwick (Webb and DeJarnette 1942) and Kentucky (Lewis and Kneberg 1947; Lewis and Lewis 1961) basins, and along the Green River (Webb 1946) in Kentucky, had established an Archaic "pattern." Later, Lewis and Kneberg were led to conclude that little or no Archaic occupation had occurred in the eastern Tennessee Valley (Lewis and Kneberg 1941, 1946; Kneberg 1952). Faced with the presence of fluted points and Candy Creek type points (a Hardaway-Dalton variant, cf. Roberts 1977) within an Early Woodland ceramic assemblage at the Camp Creek (40GN1) and Candy Creek (40BY14) sites, Lewis and Kneberg (1955; 1957:20; Lewis 1956) concluded that "the meager evidence of Archaic culture in eastern Tennessee suggests that Paleoindians remained undisturbed in that area until the advent of Woodland peoples around 1000 B.C. or perhaps even earlier." Meanwhile on the North Carolina Piedmont Joffre Coe (1951,

1952) was reporting deeply stratified Archaic occupations that would later serve to define an Archaic sequence for much of the eastern United States.

By the later 1950s and early 1960s, the concept of the Archaic period, or stage, had come of age. Regional (Lewis and Kneberg 1959; Witthoft 1959) and pan-eastern (Caldwell 1958; Byers 1959) syntheses were developed, and radiocarbon dates provided time depth for the sequences. The seminal work on Archaic period cultures, however, was Joffre Coe's (1964) *The Formative Cultures of the Carolina Piedmont*. In this research, Coe not only established a well-documented temporal sequence of cultural complexes but he proposed several principles that continue to guide archaeological research. He developed a model for buried site location, a set of excavation methods, and a series of temporal changes in projectile point form. He further suggested that given their derivation from good stratigraphic context, the recognized projectile point forms could be used as temporal markers for the building of chronologies as well as for establishing the time of occupation of sites represented only by surface collections. Broyles' (1966, 1971) work at the St. Albans site in West Virginia (46KA27) confirmed Coe's sequence. In the southern Ridge-and-Valley, found relatively devoid of Archaic period sites by researchers in the 1940s and early 1950s, evidence for the Archaic became more obvious.

In the 1960s and 1970s, archaeologists began to encounter buried Archaic components during archaeological mitigation activities. The depth below ground surface, project time constraints, and commitments to later components situated above the Archaic strata, however, permitted only limited investigation. Just outside the southern Ridge-and-Valley area, Faulkner and Graham (1965, 1966a, 1966b) recorded buried Archaic period components at four sites in the Nickajack Reservoir on the Tennessee River. To these researchers, the discovery of deeply buried strata containing Archaic materials was one of the most important discoveries made in the reservoir, and they were led to reflect: "While it is gratifying to be able to briefly discuss this early culture phase in the eastern valley, it is with a sad note that we ponder what deeply buried layers have been overlooked in other portions of the valley" (Faulkner and Graham 1966a:120). Later, at the I-75 bridge across Watts Bar Reservoir, McCollough and Faulkner (1973; McCollough 1973) excavated two Late Archaic living floors. Thus, as Coe had already demonstrated for the Piedmont, it was becoming evident that much of the data pertaining to the Archaic lay buried in the alluvial sediments of river terraces over much of the Southeast.

Investigations in the Lower Little Tennessee River Valley

In 1967, the Tennessee Valley Authority began construction of the Tellico Dam at the confluence of the Little Tennessee and Tennessee rivers. Finally, in 1979, after many delays, the reservoir was impounded, flooding approximately 14,000 acres of the lower Little Tennessee and Tellico rivers (Figure 7-2). Between 1967 and 1982, under contracts with TVA and the National Park Service, the University of Tennessee's Department of Anthropology and the Tennessee Division of Archaeology conducted extensive archaeological research within the pool area and on TVA-owned lands adjacent to the reservoir. One of the research objectives of the Tellico Archaeological Project was to locate and excavate stratified Archaic period sites; it was not, however, until 1973 that the first such site was found on Rose Island (40MR44) (Chapman 1975a).

Over the next four years more sites were discovered through backhoe testing, and excavations were conducted at eight buried, stratified Archaic sites: Icehouse Bottom (40MR23) (Chapman 1977), Harrison Branch (40MR21) (Chapman 1977), Patrick (40MR40) (Chapman 1977), Calloway Island (40MR41) (Chapman 1979), Howard (40MR66) (Chapman 1979), Bacon Farm (40LD35) (Chapman 1978), Iddins (40LD38) (Chapman 1981), Bacon Bend (40MR25) (Chapman 1981). In addition, a deep-testing survey in 1976 located 60 buried sites, and the survey results suggested that buried sites were present within most of the first terraces.

The data base for the Archaic period generated by the above excavations is virtually unparalleled in the eastern United States. Excavations at these sites and test excavations at a number of others yielded close to 250,000 lithic artifacts from undisturbed Archaic contexts. Although the majority of these artifacts is debitage (92 percent), a large and diverse assemblage of lithic implements also was recovered. Analyses of these collections have permitted researchers to begin address-

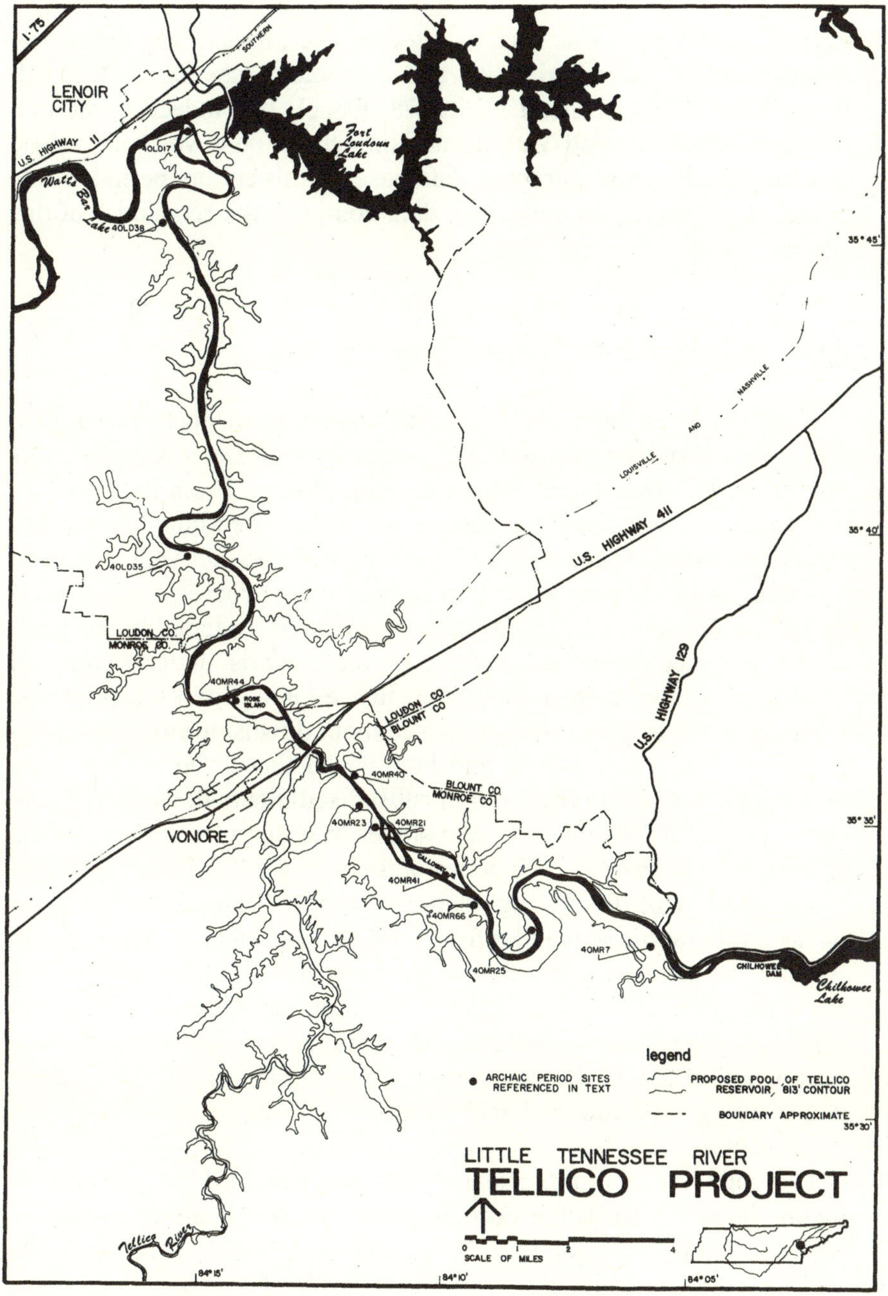

Figure 7-2. Tellico Project Area.

ing behavioral questions such as intersite and intrasite variability, site function, assemblage variability, and technology (see Davis, this volume; Davis 1980a; Kimball 1976, 1978, 1980b). It is indeed ironic that the southern Ridge-and-Valley, once thought to be devoid of Archaic remains, has become a primary data base for this culture period. Some observations based on these new data comprise the remainder of this chapter.

Archaic Period Site Preservation

A pattern of sedimentation, apparently applicable to much of the Ridge-and-Valley Province, has been developed by Paul Delcourt (1980a) for data from the lower Little Tennessee River Valley. From 1979 surveys and backhoe trench profiles, Delcourt has identified nine Quaternary alluvial terraces. These surfaces were created through valley incision by the Little Tennessee River in response to the progressive downcutting of the Tennessee River. Quaternary glacial/interstadial cycles modulated the mechanical production of rock debris under periglacial conditions on mid to high elevations in the Great Smoky Mountains, which resulted in the reworking of sediment downslope and valley aggradation during late glacial and interglacial times. During the early Holocene, increased precipitation caused sediments derived from the exposed rock debris on mountain slopes to accumulate rapidly in the valleys, thus forming a thick series of first terraces (Delcourt 1980b).

The rapidity of this T1 aggradation is verified by radiocarbon dates on the stratigraphic sequences from Icehouse Bottom and Bacon Farm. At both sites, waterlogged organic layers in gleyed, coarse sands were encountered at 20 to 22 feet below ground surface; these deposits dated essentially the same in radiocarbon years as the first Early Archaic occupation of the T1 situated 10 feet above. By about 500 B.C., aggradation was greatly reduced and the floodplain was within a few feet of its present surface.

The implications of this phenomenon are twofold: First, the odds of finding in situ Paleoindian occupations in the floodplain are reduced. The T2 is too old (32,330 + 2720 − 4140 C-14 yr B.P., 31,230 + 1550–1930 C-14 yr B.P. [Chapman 1978]; 27,595 ± 980 C-14 yr B.P. [GX-7724]), and the T1 may be too young. Whereas remnant channel bars containing Paleoindian occupation may be buried within the T1, they will be difficult to locate and a greater possibility exists that the energetics of the early T1 deposition have destroyed earlier late glacial occupations. Second, one could expect Archaic period sites to be buried in the T1 sediments throughout much of the southern Ridge-and-Valley, although stream gradient and valley width probably will regulate preservation (a factor in the upper reaches of the Clinch, Powell, Holston, French Broad, and Nolichucky rivers).

Chronology

The divisions of the Archaic period as identified for the lower Little Tennessee River Valley, and as proposed for the southern (and middle) Ridge-and-Valley, are presented in Table 7-1. The basic divisions of Early, Middle, and Late have been in use for some time and in most studies follow Griffin's (1967) synthesis. As more data accumulate, these divisions are becoming less distinct, as are the criteria used to distinguish them. The subdivisions within these periods have been variously called "complexes" (Coe 1964), "traditions" and "phases" (Lewis and Kneberg 1959; Chapman 1975a, 1976b), or "temporal units" (Kimball 1980a). In most cases, these subdivisions are based on stratigraphic separation of distinct projectile point forms, which have consistently been the most sensitive time markers for the Archaic period (cf. Coe 1964).

Archaic Period Precursors

The evidence for Dalton and Clovis occupations is represented by isolated finds through the southern Ridge-and-Valley. In the lower Little Tennessee River Valley, Dalton and Clovis points occasionally have been recovered from T1, older alluvial terraces, and upland contexts, but on none of these could a distinct occupation area be recognized. Undoubtedly, the record has been affected by the dynamics of early Holocene alluviation; based on negative evidence, however, it is possible to propose that the region was less densely populated than the plateau and basin to the west. At least three early sites have been located elsewhere in the region: LeCroy site (40HA43) (Lewis and Kne-

Table 7-1. Archaeological Cultural Periods and Phases/Temporal Units in the Lower Little Tennessee River Valley as Identified through Archaeological Excavations.

Culture Period	Phases/Temporal Units	Date Range	Diagnostic Artifact	Excavated Components
PALEOINDIAN	Clovis	11000–8500 B.C. (?)	Clovis Fluted PP/K	Isolated finds
ARCHAIC				
Transitional	Dalton	8500–8000 B.C. (?)	Dalton PP/K	Isolated finds
Early	Lower Kirk	8000–7300 B.C.	Lower Kirk Corner Notched PP/K Varieties	Icehouse Bottom[1]
	Upper Kirk	7400–6800 B.C.	Upper Kirk Corner Notched PP/K Varieties	Icehouse Bottom,[1] Bacon Farm,[2] Rose Island,[3] Patrick,[4] Calloway Island[5]
	St. Albans	6900–6500 B.C.	St. Albans Side Notched PP/K	Icehouse Bottom,[1] Bacon Farm,[2] Rose Island,[3] Patrick,[4] Calloway Island[5]
	LeCroy	6500–5800 B.C.	LeCroy Bifurcated Stem PP/K	Icehouse Bottom,[1] Bacon Farm,[2] Rose Island,[3] Patrick,[4] Calloway Island[5]
	Kanawha	6100–5800 B.C.	Kanawha Stemmed PP/K	Icehouse Bottom,[1] Bacon Farm,[2] Rose Island,[3] Patrick[4]
Middle	Kirk Stemmed	6000–5800 B.C.	Kirk Stemmed PP/K	Bacon Farm,[2] Rose Island,[3] Howard,[6] Citico,[7] Calloway Island[5]
	Stanly	5800–5500 B.C.	Stanly Stemmed Variety PP/K	Icehouse Bottom,[1] Calloway Island,[5] Howard,[6] Citico[7] (40MR7)
	Morrow Mountain	5500–5000 B.C.	Morrow Mountain I & II Stemmed PP/K	Icehouse Bottom,[1] Calloway Island,[5] Howard[6]
	Guilford	5000–4000 B.C. (?)	Guilford Lanceolate PP/K	Isolated finds
	Undesignated	4500–3000 B.C. (?)	Sykes PP/K	Isolated finds
Late	Savannah River	3000–1800 B.C.	Savannah River Stemmed PP/K	Bacon Bend,[9] Isolated finds
	Iddins	1800–1200 B.C.	Iddins Undifferentiated Stemmed PP/K	Iddins,[10] Patrick,[11] Harrison Branch[12]

[1]Chapman 1977 [2]Chapman 1978 [3]Chapman 1975b [4]Chapman 1977 [5]Chapman 1979 [6]Chapman 1979 [7]Chapman and Newman 1979 [8]Chapman 1977 [9]Chapman 1981 [10]Chapman 1981 [11]Schroedl 1978 [12]Schroedl 1975

berg 1955, 1956), Webster site (40KN49) (Cobb n.d.), and Camp Creek site (40GN1) (Lewis and Kneberg 1957). Unfortunately, the stratigraphic relationship of the Paleoindian/Dalton components to the Early Archaic components at these sites has not been determined.

Early Archaic

The earliest in situ occupations identified in the region are associated with Kirk Corner Notched and Palmer (Coe 1964) projectile points. These components have been divided into Lower and Upper Kirk on the basis of stratigraphy and morphological distinctions in the projectile points (cf. Kimball 1976, 1978). Lower Kirk was identified in Strata M–O at the Icehouse Bottom site (Chapman 1977), and apparently represents the earliest example of corner-notched points in the area. Based on a sample of 240 corner-notched points from the Upper Kirk horizons at Bacon Farm and Icehouse Bottom (Chapman 1977, 1978), a considerable range of execution existed at any one time; hence, the term Kirk Corner Notched "Cluster" (Chapman 1975a) is retained. Although we lack a comparable Paleoindian assemblage from the valley, the Kirk Corner Notched lithic assemblage appears to share with earlier assemblages in other areas many elements, including blades, formalized end scrapers, and a number of cutting and scraping implements manufactured on blades and flakes. Because of the preservation variables discussed above, it is not known whether there is a shift in settlement pattern or in population density. The possibility of Paleoindian/Early Archaic continuity is proposed by Gardner (1974) from the Flint Run complex in the middle part of Ridge-and-Valley Province.

Manos and metates, which traditionally have been associated with the Archaic, were recovered at residential bases and presumably were used in processing wild plant foods (see below). Celts, manufactured by bifacial percussion and then ground to varying degrees, were recovered from three sites. Because of the time and effort expended in their manufacture, these artifacts probably were used until exhausted or destroyed, thus infrequently entering the archaeological record. The idea that the appearance of corner notched points marks the advent of the spear thrower (cf. Gardner 1974), with concomitant changes in hunting strategies, is not supported by our research. The atlatl weight, though not a necessary accompaniment to the atlatl, does not appear in the archaeological record until around 6000 B.C.

A generalized Archaic settlement pattern is established early (whether it differs from Paleoindian is not known). Probable residential bases, such as Bussell Island (40LD17), Bacon Farm, Rose Island, Patrick, Icehouse Bottom, and Calloway Island, are situated in areas of maximum microenvironmental diversity and/or adjacent to lithic sources. Close to these sites are riverine resources, sloughs, backwaters, creeks, broad floodplains, valley slopes, and uplands. These base sites, in turn, probably articulated with a number of field camps elsewhere on the floodplain and in the uplands. Movement (or exchange) beyond a single valley, such as the Little Tennessee River Valley, is reflected in nonlocal cherts having been employed especially in projectile point manufacture. Bass (1977) in his survey within the Great Smoky Mountains recovered Early Archaic points made from Ridge-and-Valley cherts, which suggests pan-regional exploitation of this resource.

The Bifurcate Tradition (Chapman 1975b) emerged around 6700 B.C. and is divided, based on projectile point morphology, into the St. Albans, LeCroy, and Kanawha phases (the McCorkle Stemmed type [Broyles 1971] is now viewed as a large variant of the St. Albans Side Notched type [Broyles 1966]). A short span of time between Upper Kirk and LeCroy may be reflected in the combination of corner notching and basal notching in the St. Albans Side Notched type. Although they share many elements with the preceding Kirk lithic assemblage, the bifurcate assemblages are characterized by less formalized end scrapers, an increase in bipolar tools, and a reduction in the amount of unifacial tools.

Middle Archaic

The division between Early and Middle Archaic, set at around 6000 B.C., is marked by the appearance of atlatl weights, netsinkers, and the use of quartz, quartzite, and slate in addition to chert. Diagnostic projectile points, in use for the first thousand years, include the Kirk Stemmed (Coe 1964), Stanly Stemmed (Coe 1964), and Morrow Mountain I Stemmed (Coe 1964) types. Based on the Little Tennessee River Valley data for the period between ca. 4500–3000 B.C., pronounced floodplain sites (with assumed residential base or multiple re-use) are missing from the archaeological record. Several explanations are possible: there was a shift in the settlement system that has made it difficult for us to recognize the sites of this period (for example, populations may have become more dispersed, resulting in less obvious sites that have not been excavated to date because of the strategies of opportunism and artifact maximization that have guided salvage archaeology); the archaeological remains were more subject to erosion by natural forces since terrace aggradation had slowed (see above), with many sites being destroyed; or the shift in settlement resulted in a partial depopulation and restricted exploitation of the lower Tennessee River Valley. Whether a similar lack of sites exists throughout the southern Ridge-and-Valley is not known. However, it is known that the area was not totally abandoned, since small numbers of projectile points similar to the types Guilford Lanceolate (Coe 1964) and Sykes (Lewis and Lewis 1961) have been found.

Such a gap in the record raises the old question of an Altithermal and its potential impact on aboriginal cultures (cf. Lewis and Kneberg 1959; Lewis and Lewis 1961; Reeves 1973). Recent pollen and plant macrofossil analyses of sediment cores from two sites on the eastern Highland Rim of Middle Tennessee do suggest a warming and drying trend between 6000 and 3000 B.C. (Delcourt 1979; Delcourt and Delcourt 1979, 1980). What impact this might have had on the environment of the lower Little Tennessee River Valley (e.g., availability of traditional plant and animal resources) is presently unknown (further analyses of pollen samples from the valley by Paul and Hazel Delcourt and Patricia Cridlebaugh should provide significant new information). It cannot be discounted, however, that by 5000 B.C. there were some alterations in aboriginal adaptive strategies. Since virtually no components of the period 5000–2500 B.C. have been excavated, cultural remains as well as paleobotanical data are lacking which would be (cf. Chapman and Shea 1977, 1981) sufficient to assess the causes of these changes.

Late Archaic

The Late Archaic period in the Middle South has long been considered synonymous with the exploitation of freshwater shellfish. The vast shell "mounds" and middens of the middle and western Tennessee River Valley, the Green River Valley of Kentucky, and the middle Savannah River of Georgia (Moore 1915; Claflin 1931; Webb 1939, 1946; Webb and DeJarnette 1942; Lewis and Lewis 1961) came to typify this culture period (cf. Lewis and Kneberg 1959). The absence of these large middens north of Chattanooga was a compelling reason for discounting any significant Archaic period occupation of the eastern Tennessee River Valley. Although there is indeed a lack of shell remains (cf. Chapman 1981), it now appears that Late Archaic sites are widespread and frequent in the region. Unfortunately, only limited excavations of Late Archaic sites in the southern Ridge-and-Valley have occurred (McCollough and Faulkner 1973; Chapman 1981); diagnostic projectile points and rock-filled fire pits, however, are ubiquitous in the floodplain deposits.

Evidence from the Little Tennessee River Valley tends to support McCollough's (1973) observation that there is a near continuous linear distribution of the remains of discrete domestic units along the banks of the major drainages in the eastern Tennessee River Valley, a phenomenon that is probably also true for the Early and Middle Archaic. Although the archaeological evidence is very scanty, it is postulated that there were locations at which a number of social groups would gather at certain times. The pronounced midden and feature density at the Iddins site (Chapman 1981), for example, suggests a diversity of activities to be found at a residential base. The site was situated at the end of a long series of shoals, an ideal location for collecting fish (e.g., suckers) during the spring. Unfortunately, it is not known if Iddins is typical.

The probable emergence of an exchange network in eastern North America by the Late Archaic period has been addressed by a number of writers (Caldwell 1958; Winters 1968; Brose 1979; Goad 1980). Based upon the apparent involvement of the Middle Woodland people at Icehouse Bottom in the "Hopewell Interaction Sphere," I have proposed elsewhere (Chapman 1973; Chapman and Keel 1979) that these exchange networks in the southern Ridge-and-Valley had earlier origins. Of significance in the movement of goods and ideas throughout the Southeast was a network of Indian trails, well documented for the historic period (Myer 1928). At that time, the southern Ridge-and-Valley was linked to a north-south route by the Tennessee, Ohio, and Great Lakes trails, the Great Indian Warpath, and the Clinch River and Cumberland Gap Trail, while east-west trails included the Catawba Trail, the East-and-West Trail, and Rutherford's War Trace.

Whether copper and marine shell reached the southern Ridge-and-Valley during the Late Archaic period is unknown (cf. Goad 1980). There is, however, abundant evidence of exchange and movement of lithic materials between the valley and western North and South Carolina. Soapstone bowls are the best evidence of this exchange. Implements manufactured from Carolina slates, and occasionally from exotic minerals such as olivine, reflect a rudimentary exchange system and a movement of people that increased in complexity and composition in subsequent periods.

The appearance of cucurbits in the lower Little Tennessee River Valley may be related to this early interaction. Carbonized *Cucurbita pepo* dated to the third millennium B.C. at the Bacon Bend site is among the earliest of these remains in eastern North America (Chapman and Shea 1977, 1981; Chomko and Crawford 1978; Kay et al. 1980). This cultigen was supplemented by a second domesticate, sunflower *(Helianthus annus)*, by 900 B.C. (Brewer 1973). The archaeobotanical record for the Archaic period in the lower Little Tennessee River Valley is extensive and provides both subsistence and paleoenvironmental data (Chapman and Shea 1977, 1981); on the other hand, bone preservation in the valley is poor and with the exception of a few calcined fragments, faunal data are lacking. A narrow spectrum of plant foods appear in the paleobotanical samples from Early and Middle Archaic contexts, the most important of which are hickory nuts (*Carya* sp.) and acorns (*Quercus* sp.), with the frequency of herbaceous seeds so low that they probably were insignificant in the diet. In the Late Archaic samples there is an increase in walnut (*Juglans* sp.) and the appearance of relatively large amounts of chenopodium (*Chenopodium* sp.) and maygrass (*Phalaris caroliniana*). Wood charcoal types suggest a mixed deciduous forest with an increase, beginning in Late Archaic times, of second growth species such as pine and cedar, perhaps reflecting the increasing impact of humans on the vegetation.

Faulkner and Graham (1966a) have employed the term "Terminal Archaic" for the Archaic unit just prior to the Woodland period (ca. 1200–600 B.C.). The Terminal Archaic lithic assemblage includes forms that continue into the Early Woodland period. The fiber tempered Wheeler series ceramics, that appear in the middle Tennessee River

Valley by 1000 B.C., scarcely penetrate the southern Ridge-and-Valley. Instead, ceramics may have entered the region from the northeast around 900 B.C., diffusing southward among the Terminal Archaic inhabitants (Lafferty 1978).

Summary and Conclusions

In the last 20 years, we have learned a great deal about the Archaic period in the southern Ridge-and-Valley Province. If the number of sites recorded in the lower Little Tennessee River Valley is any reflection of the distribution of sites throughout the region, there was far more Archaic exploitation of this area than researchers once thought. Recent research has, however, achieved more than just demonstrating the presence of Archaic sites. First, the research has established a sound regional chronology and has identified a series of temporally diagnostic artifacts. In addition to achieving this primary archaeological objective, other anthropological and methodological questions have been addressed.

Building on the work of Joffre Coe, a methodology has been refined for locating and excavating buried sites in this area and other parts of the Southeast, probably the greatest source of objects and data pertaining to the cultures of the Archaic period. Furthermore, investigations in the Little Tennessee River Valley have recovered artifact samples from a number of localities within a single valley, thus permitting researchers to address intersite and intrasite patterning and settlement variability in a restricted universe. Past comparative work has been with data from widely separate contexts that probably represent quite different adaptive strategies. Finally, the recovery of assemblages from sealed stratigraphic contexts has permitted interpretations not only of site variability, but also of site function and trends in lithic technology. Studies of these floodplain assemblages have allowed the ubiquitous lithic scatter in the adjacent uplands to be integrated into systemic context with greater confidence (see Canouts and Goodyear, this volume).

Future excavations of stratified floodplain sites should focus less on the vertical sequence of cultures, as was achieved in the past by block excavations into the richest portion of a site. Until a large area of a buried Kirk Corner Notched stratum, for example, is exposed and assemblage patterning identified, it will never be known to what extent earlier glimpses of these strata reflect the reality of artifact patterning. What, for example, occurred at site peripheries, areas seldom excavated because of their low artifact yields? Is intersite variability a product of the cultures involved or of excavation units placed at different locations on two sites? Small marginal sites need to be excavated, since they may preserve better the occupational patterning that would have been obscured by multiple re-use at the large residential base camps. Finally, more work needs to be done in the analysis of artifact assemblages, to transcend the focus on formal types and to address the morphology, wear patterns, and distributional patterning of all the constituent elements.

Although the concept of the Archaic has probably not changed much from Webb's "spear throwing, hunting and fishing people who made no pottery," we are now learning about the diversity of local adaptive responses by these people. More importantly, we are now beginning to address behavioral questions with hard data that should lead to a better understanding of this eight-millennia span of Southeastern prehistory.

Acknowledgments

Fieldwork and analysis associated with the University of Tennessee, Department of Anthropology, Tellico Archaeological Project were conducted under a series of contracts with the Tennessee Valley Authority, the National Park Service, and the Heritage Conservation and Recreation Service. Additional funds were made available from the National Geographic Society, and corporate and individual donors. The assistance and cooperation of these agencies and individuals are greatly appreciated. I also wish to thank Larry Kimball and R. P. Stephen Davis, Jr., for their comments on the manuscript.

8 • R. P. STEPHEN DAVIS, JR.

Intersite Assemblage Variability in the Lower Little Tennessee River Valley:

EXPLORING EXTINCT SETTLEMENT SYSTEMS THROUGH PROBABILISTIC SAMPLING

Introduction

The following paper discusses the results of two probabilistic surveys in valley and upland zones of Tellico Reservoir in southeastern Tennessee. Data are analyzed using multivariate statistical techniques to assess intersite assemblage variability. Regularities in assemblage variability are interpreted within the context of contemporary theory of hunter-gatherer subsistence systems and evaluated along spatial and temporal dimensions. The survey methods developed and described herein reflect the deep concern with data comparability which Joffre Coe impressed upon his students. It is argued, largely through example, that probabilistic survey in the heavily vegetated Southeast *can* yield useful data for addressing substantive behavioral questions if the survey design seeks to provide comparable and representative samples. The controlled surface collection of systematically plowed, areally extensive sampling units is suggested as one method for generating such data.

Recognizing the need to generate data relevant to the study of the total cultural-environmental system, a probabilistic "non-site" sampling design was developed and implemented for the lower Little Tennessee River Valley (Davis et al. 1980). Two phases of fieldwork have been completed, and these provide data for comparative analyses of archaeological resources within both upland and valley geomorphological zones. Sampling methods and the implications of the probabilistic survey are discussed below, and a preliminary analysis which examines the potential of the derived data for studying prehistoric settlement systems is presented. Specifically, the goals of the analysis are: to determine if it is possible to recognize distinct, functionally interpretable archaeological settlement types within the project area; and to determine the kind(s) of correlation among site function (as reflected by assemblage variability), settlement location, and temporal affinity for the data set. This analysis, which should be considered strictly exploratory since all of the data for the survey sample are not yet available, seeks only to examine or develop one method for detecting and interpreting patterned variability within the archaeological record.

Methods and Assumptions

The survey methods used within the Tellico Project are based on probability sampling theory (Cochran 1977) and are directed toward sampling units of geographical space rather than the actual population of archaeological sites (Thomas 1975). The purpose of this kind of survey is to obtain random samples of artifacts from a survey area where the population of archaeological sites and the distribution of artifacts are unknown. These samples then can be used to assess artifact assemblage variability within the survey area and to test hypotheses about aboriginal land use along functional, temporal, and spatial dimensions. The specific sampling procedures have been presented elsewhere (Davis 1980a, 1980b) and are only summarized here.

Although archaeologists are ultimately concerned with the dynamics and evolution of cultural systems, their database represents only a sample of artifacts from the *residue* of those systems. Cowgill (1970) has discussed the implications of this dilemma as it relates to archaeological sampling and has defined four hierarchical system states: (1) population of human behavior (the set of human behavior that is governed by cultural rules or norms and that defines the settlement system); (2) physical consequences population (the physical consequences, residues or otherwise, of events that comprise the elements of the settlement system); (3) physical finds population (the residue of the physical consequences that remains following cultural and natural transformations); and (4) physical finds sample (the portion of the physical finds population which is recovered archaeologically, excluding those materials that are not recovered because of methodological limitations or systematic bias). The anthropological goal of the Tellico probabilistic survey was to develop reliable parameter estimates that describe certain patterns of extinct human behavior; however, due to the fragmentary and incomplete condition of archaeological data, these estimates are necessarily derived from a physical finds sample.

Several working assumptions precede the following analysis. These assumptions relate both to the behavioral implications of the survey data set and to our ability to make valid inferences about that set. These assumptions are outlined below:

(1) A patterned behavioral response to the environment of a region will be reflected by variability in archaeological site distribution and content. The distribution and assemblage composition of archaeological sites can therefore be used to define the residual pattern of an extinct settlement system.

(2) A sample of artifacts from a site or region, given that the sample size is sufficiently large, can be used to obtain unbiased parameter estimates for the population of artifacts if the sample is obtained in a systematic manner (following a random sampling design).

(3) A technique of archaeological survey that employs systematic plowing at an archaeological site (or any defined sampling unit) will expose a collection of artifacts which reflects the entire artifact assemblage occurring within the plowzone. These artifacts will be representative of the entire site provided that dissimilar archaeological deposits do not extend beneath the base of the plowzone. Features truncated by the plow should be adequately represented within the plowzone if feature fill is nonstratified and homogeneous (see Dickens, Wilson, this volume). This assumption is supported by recent investigations at "plowzone" sites within Tellico Reservoir (Davis 1981); however, the reliability of small artifact samples to predict adequately the frequency occurrence of "rare" artifact classes must be questioned in light of the effects of attenuation (Cowgill 1970).

(4) The spatial distribution of artifacts occurring at the surface following plowing will reflect a site's (or sampling unit's) structure, though probably at a much lower degree of resolution than exists within undisturbed deposits (e.g., Binford et al. 1970). This assumption is also partly supported by preliminary analyses of Tellico survey data (Davis 1981). (For a different opinion on this issue see Ward, this volume.) The primary implication of this assumption is that an assemblage of artifacts recovered from a spatially discrete locus should reflect certain activi-

ties performed there (i.e., specific kinds of tool manufacture and use). The term *assemblage* as used throughout this paper refers simply to the collection of artifacts from a specific location (i.e., sampling unit).

(5) For purposes of the present analysis, it is assumed that a surface artifact assemblage will reflect at least a partial set of activities performed at a site. Artifacts from a multicomponent site are necessarily treated as a single assemblage.

The following analysis is based on data from two probabilistic surveys conducted within a 13,700-acre area inundated by Tellico Reservoir and within a 2,700-acre upland tract situated adjacent to the reservoir (Figure 8-1). The "below pool" survey area was subdivided and sampled as four separate sampling domains (Table 8-1). A total of 164 sampling units was examined, which included 100 units from the below pool zone (sampling fraction = .015) and 64 units from the upland tract, designated Area II (sampling fraction = .05). Approximately 74 percent, or 121 units, produced artifacts indicative of aboriginal occupation. These are treated below as single site samples. The specific sampling procedures used for both surveys are summarized as follows:

(1) An imaginary 300 by 300-foot grid was imposed on the survey area (see Davis 1980a). A predetermined number of units was then selected using a random digit table.

(2) The sampling units were located in the field and staked, bush-hogged (if needed), and then plowed to a depth of approximately 1.0 feet. Plowing was performed to create uniform collecting surfaces for all of the sampling units and to eliminate survey problems resulting from poor surface visibility. The pattern of plowing is illustrated in Figure 8-2. This provided representative coverage of the entire sampling unit.

(3) After a sufficient amount of rainfall, a controlled surface collection was made of each unit. Artifacts were collected in 20 by 20-foot and 20 by 40-foot units for the below pool sample and 10 by 10-foot units for the Area II sample. All visible artifacts, including fire-cracked rock, were collected.

Settlement Pattern Recognition Model

Analysis of the probabilistic survey data was undertaken to examine the spatial, temporal, and assemblage variability within the study area.

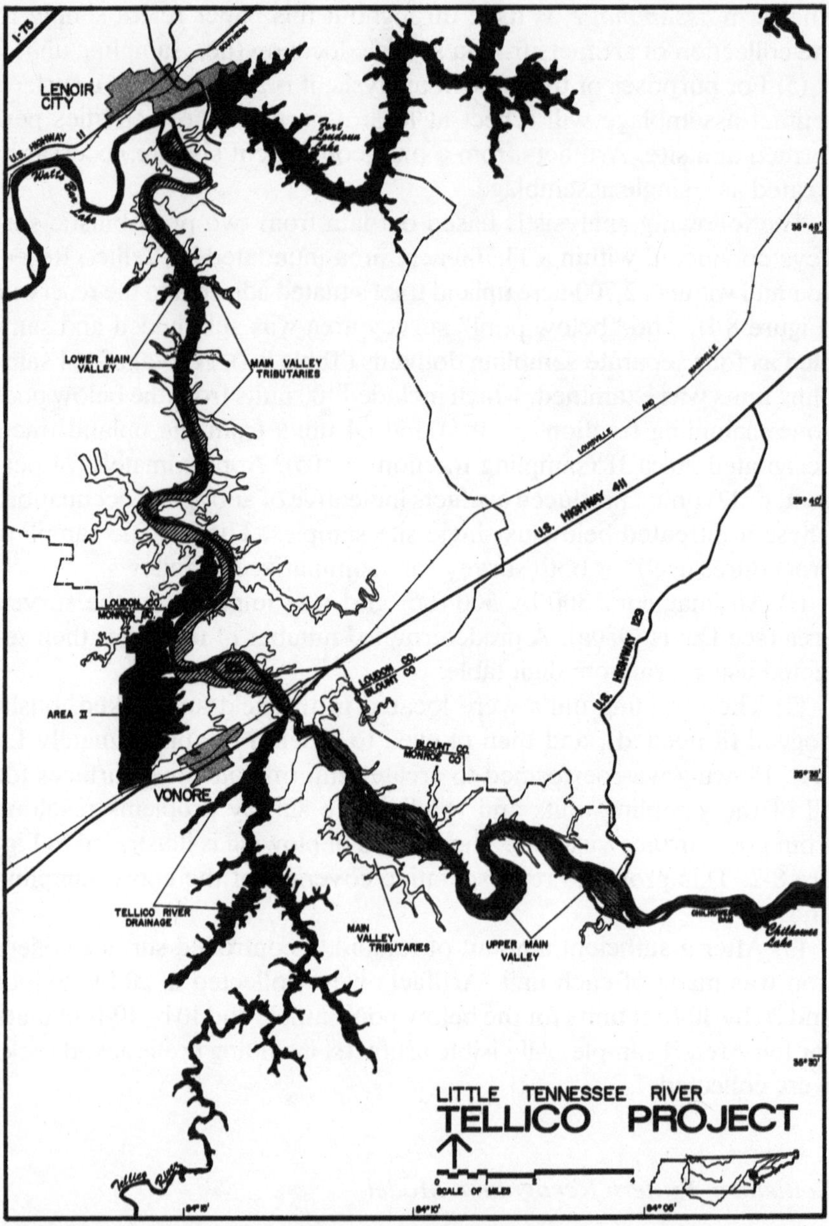

Figure 8-1. Map of Tellico Reservoir Showing the Sampling Domains Used in the Study.

Table 8-1. Summary of Sampling Domains Used in the Analysis.

Sampling Domain	Sample Size	No. of Units With Material	Description
Lower Main Valley	18	15	The alluvial terraces of the lower Little Tennessee River Valley between Tellico Dam and the mouth of Tellico River. The valley is generally narrow (ca. 0.3 miles wide) and terraces are well drained.
Upper Main Valley	20	20	The alluvial terraces of the lower Little Tennessee River Valley between the mouth of Tellico River and Citico Creek. The terrace systems in this domain are extensive and have resulted in a wide valley floor (i.e., up to 1.3 miles in width). Terraces are generally well drained.
Main Valley Tributaries	43	27	All nonalluvial terrace lands inundated by Tellico Reservoir, excluding Tellico River drainage. This domain includes much of the valley slopes and minor portions of the adjacent uplands at the lower end of the reservoir.
Tellico River Drainage	19	18	All inundated lands along Tellico River. This domain includes tributary valleys and slopes in addition to the Tellico River Valley. Much of this area lies within a geomorphological zone of deeply dissected knobs.
Area II	64	41	A 2700-acre upland tract adjacent to Tellico Reservoir. The surface of this domain can be characterized as "rolling" and karst topographic features such as sinkholes and underground streams predominate.

Figure 8-2. View of a Typical Sampling Unit Following Controlled Plowing.

Steps involved in this analysis included: (1) organization of the data into meaningful classes representing discrete activities, based upon blank and working edge attributes of the lithic artifacts; (2) determination of the assemblage relative frequency breakdowns by activity group for each sampling unit; (3) examination of interassemblage structure through factor analysis and the reduction of initial activity groups into a smaller number of new, uncorrelated (i.e., orthogonal statistically) groups; (4) calculation of a new set of values (i.e., factor scores) for these new groups for each sampling unit; (5) use of cluster analysis to combine empirically similar units from the scores for the independent dimensions (i.e., factors); (6) establishment of intuitively meaningful sampling unit classes using the results of Step 5 and based upon contemporary theory of hunter-gatherer settlement systems; and (7) examination of the distribution of sampling unit classes along both spatial and temporal dimensions in order to recognize patterns of interassemblage variability within the study area.

Artifact Analysis

A sample of 18,486 lithic artifacts, 789 ceramic artifacts, and 22,478 fire-cracked rock was collected during the below pool survey; the Area II sample is comprised of only 357 lithic artifacts and two fire-cracked rocks. All lithic artifacts were analyzed along mineralogical, technological, functional, and formal-stylistic dimensions (Kimball 1980b). Specific information used for this study included blank attributes (related to method of manufacture) and working edge attributes (indicative of probable primary function), as well as the necessary formal-stylistic attributes of projectile points and certain other implements in order to classify them into temporally specific types. Ceramic artifacts were analyzed along technological, morphological, and stylistic dimensions, with an emphasis on paste and surface-treatment attributes. These artifacts were used as temporal indicators following a model for Tellico developed by Kimball and Baden (1980a).

Following the measurement and classification of recovered artifacts, the data were organized into activity groups (Table 8-2). The activity groups defined for this study are derived from Kimball and Baden (1980b) and represent intuitive groupings of blank and working edge attributes that reflect specific activities related to lithic resource procurement, tool manufacture, or tool use. Activity interpretation is inferred from microwear analyses conducted elsewhere (Keeley 1980), ethnoarchaeology and ethnographic analogy, and recent Tellico lithic analyses (Bass 1979). Detailed high magnification microwear analysis of tool edges has yet to be undertaken to confirm these interpretations for the Tellico data. Because most lithic artifacts can possess multiple working edge attribute states in addition to a singular blank attribute state (e.g., an end scraper and graver on a bifacial thinning flake), the frequency of artifacts representing all activity groups at a sampling unit usually exceeds the total number of artifacts. Activity group frequencies for each unit constitute the basic data used in all subsequent analyses. Although the absence of archaeological remains within a unit is important in the interpretation of site patterning, initial analysis is oriented toward recognizing the structure of the observed artifact collection; consequently, "empty" sampling units are temporarily omitted from the study.

Table 8-2. Definition of Activity Groups Based Upon Artifact Blank and Working Edge Classification.

Activity Group	Blank Categories[1]	Working Edge Categories
Chert Acquisition (CHERT)	Chert nodule	Tested nodule
Primary Reduction Debitage (PRIMARY)	Primary Flake Shatter fragment Amorphous core Core rejuvenation flake	
Bifacial Debitage (BIFACIAL)	Biface Preform Bifacial thinning flake	
Bipolar Debitage (BIPOLAR)	Bipolar flake Preform Bifacial thinning flake	
Blade Debitage (BLADE)	Blade Blade Core	
Hearth Use (HEARTH)	Fire-cracked rock	
Architecture (ARCH)	Daub	
Cutting (CUT)		Side scraper Retouched edge Utilized edge Knife
Nonlithic Tool Manufacture (NLTM)		Drill Graver Spokeshave Denticulate
Pièce Esquillée (PE)		Piece Esquillee
Plant Food Processing (PLANT)		Mano Milling stone Pestle Nutting stone
Heavy Butchering (HBUTCH)		Chopper Chopper/scraper
Fishing (FISH)		Netsinker
Cooking (COOK)	Steatite bowl frag. Ceramic vessel frag.	
Hunting (HUNT)		Projectile point (except when Blank = Preform)
Hide working (HW)		End scraper Perforator
Woodworking (WW)		Celt Axe Chisel
Flintknapping (KNAP)		Hammerstone Pitted cobble Abrader
Personal Adornment/ Ceremonial		Utilized mineral (hematite) Ear spool Pendant Smoking pipe

[1]includes ceramic artifact categories.

Statistical Analysis of Assemblages

Principal Component Analysis

Initial multivariate analysis of the survey data consisted of an R-type principal component analysis (SPSS Principal factoring without interation: PA1, with VARIMAX rotation) to examine the data structure and to create a reduced number of source variables, or factors, for further analysis (Rummel 1967). Prior to analysis activity group frequencies were transformed into proportional, or relative frequency, values for each sampling unit. Bartlett's (1950) chi-square test was used to test the statistical significance of the correlation matrix ($|R| = .0007119$). This test rejected the null hypothesis of no significant difference ($p<.01$) between the correlation matrix and an identity matrix.

The rotated principal component analysis resulted in a nine factor solution, and all factors with an associated eigenvalue of less than 1.0 were eliminated (Table 8-3). These factors represent uncorrelated (orthogonal) patterns of activity group covariance. Examination of the factor loading matrix suggests that all factors can be interpreted in terms of more general activity sets following contemporary models of prehistoric lithic technology and subsistence activity organization. These loadings range in value from 0 to ± 1 and can be read simply as the correlation of a variable with the definition of a particular factor.

The behavioral interpretations of the factor solution suggest that most of the variability within the data set can be explained by four general kinds of activities: (1) hunting and related activities of meat and hide processing (Factors 1, 3, 7, and 9); (2) lithic raw material procurement, reduction, and tool manufacture (Factors 4, 6, and 8); (3) specialized procurement and processing of vegetal and aquatic resources (Factor 5); and (4) activities related to the maintenance of long-term habitation camps (Factor 2). Based on these results it should be possible to define functionally discrete assemblage categories through the differential importance of these factors at individual sampling units.

Definition of Expected Settlement Types

Two generalized models of hunter-gatherer settlement systems, with expected archaeological correlates, have been proposed by Binford (1980)

Table 8-3. VARIMAX Rotated Factor Loading Matrix Based Upon 121 Surface Assemblages.[1]

Variable (Activity Group)	Factor 1	2	3	4	5	6	7	8	9	
Chert Acquisition	.01	−.06	.01	.08	.00	−.09	−.05	.74	.00	
Primary Reduction	.02	−.24	.02	.89	−.07	.01	.11	.00	−.09	
Bifacial Reduction	.17	−.46	.11	−.33	−.21	−.41	.37	−.36	−.20	
Bipolar Reduction	−.10	−.15	−.10	−.33	−.16	.05	.21	.60	−.07	
Blade Manufacture	.81	.05	−.01	.12	.02	.03	−.06	.07	.03	
Hearth Use	−.14	.71	−.12	−.18	.33	.36	.05	−.06	.03	
Architecture	.00	.67	.00	−.03	−.18	−.08	.02	−.06	.01	
Cutting	.85	−.16	−.02	−.02	−.02	.05	.10	−.08	−.06	
Nonlithic Tool Manufacture	.84	−.04	−.01	−.10	−.02	−.05	.03	−.04	.00	
Pièce Esquillée	−.02	−.08	.86	.03	−.03	.00	.04	−.04	−.01	
Plant Food Processing	.00	.07	.03	−.02	.67	−.05	−.03	.03	.02	
Heavy Butchering	−.02	−.08	−.01	−.06	−.03	−.03	.03	−.03	.98	
Fishing	−.02	−.13	−.06	−.02	.68	.00	.09	−.09	−.05	
Cooking	.02	.62	.00	.00	−.09	−.11	−.03	−.04	.00	
Hunting	−.07	−.19	−.06	−.14	−.09	−.05	−.93	−.06	−.05	
Hide Working	−.03	.00	.87	−.03	.00	.00	.01	.00	.00	
Woodworking	−.09	.01	−.12	.30	−.09	−.35	.11	−.16	.05	
Flintknapping	.00	−.11	−.04	.05	−.15	.83	.10	−.16	−.02	
Personal Adornment	−.06	.40	−.03	−.07	.08	.00	.15	−.02	−.08	
% total variance	11.4	10.0	8.2	6.3	6.2	6.1	6.0	5.9	5.4	/ 65.5
% common variance	17.4	15.3	12.5	9.6	9.5	9.3	9.2	9.0	8.2	/100.0

[1]Underlined factor loadings were determined to be significantly different from 0 with $p \leq .001$, following criteria proposed by Cliff and Hamburger (1967).

for forager and collector economies. Forager economies are generally typified by seasonal residential moves among a series of critical resources and lack of dependence upon storage technology. Collector economies, on the other hand, tend to focus upon logistical strategies employing seasonal storage of certain resources. Such strategies allow a group to exploit, simultaneously, two or more spatially segregated critical resources. Agriculturally based subsistence systems, which also involve the procurement of wild food resources, are considered here to represent specialized collector economies. From present knowledge regarding prehistoric subsistence strategies in the interior Southeast (Swanton 1946), Binford's (1980) model for collector strategies would appear to have heuristic value in interpreting archaeological resource variability in the survey area. The occurrence of possible storage facilities for all major cultural periods represented in the Tellico area (Early Archaic to Late Mississippian) suggests that all known prehistoric occupants within the study area were potentially engaged in logistical strategies involving seasonal storage of certain resources. However, it should be pointed out that explanations of how these facilities functioned are lacking.

Five specific site types are recognized for collector subsistence economies (Binford 1980:10): residential base, field camp (a temporary encampment for a specialized task group), location (a locality where extractive tasks were carried out), station (an observational location such as hunting stand), and cache (a temporary field storage facility). Archaeological visibility for the latter two types is considered to be extremely low given the likely co-occurrence of other activities at these sites (Binford 1980:12); consequently, these two types are not used in the present analysis. Following Binford's (1980) generalizations regarding Nunamuit subsistence strategies, we would expect *residential bases* to be characterized by assemblages reflecting a wide range of diverse activities and including evidence of extended habitation. *Field camps*, on the other hand, might contain evidence of extended occupation (i.e., fire-cracked rock), but should reflect a limited range of activities related to hunting and initial meat processing. Finally, *locations* should be represented archaeologically as assemblages that contain artifacts from one or a few related activities and probably from a single event. Because locations are activity specific, a wide range of diverse sites may be contained within this category; however, it is suspected that most such sites within the study area result from hunting-related activities. Whereas residential bases may be expected to be correlated with specific environmental resources (level and well-drained ground, permanent water source, etc.), locations and possibly field camps should be more randomly dispersed across the landscape, particularly those sites resulting from hunters' encounters with game. These expectations are, of course, based on the assumption that previous and subsequent use of the same site have not obscured the pattern.

Cluster Analysis

Following factor analysis, a factor score matrix was generated for the data set. These scores were then used as primary data to group "similar" sampling units. Specifically, a hierarchical cluster analysis (SAS CLUSTER procedure) was used to determine like clusters of assemblages (Johnson 1967). The decision of where to truncate the hierarchical groupings was based upon a Scree-test (see Cattell 1965). This procedure resulted in a 17 cluster solution summarized in Table 8-4. The large number of retained clusters, including seven sampling units that failed to cluster with any other units, is indicative of substantial heterogeneity within the data, or of idiosyncratic activities. Despite this variability, three general classes of assemblages can be recognized, based on expectations discussed above. The combining of the 17 clusters into three classes followed a careful examination of factor score means for each cluster. The three assemblage classes are evaluated below.

Clusters 1, 7, 8, and 12 possess high mean scores for factors indicative of relative site permanence, and therefore are interpreted as residential bases. Specifically, most of these clusters have high scores for Factors 2 and 5, which are interpreted as measures of site maintenance and specialized processing/procurement.

Clusters 2 and 16 are interpreted as field camps or overnight hunting camps. This interpretation is based on the relative importance of tool manufacturing activities (Factors 2, 4, and 7) reflected in these assemblages. An examination of the original artifact frequencies also indicates the occurrence of cutting, hunting, and hide-working implements.

Finally, 11 clusters are interpreted as locations. The majority of these represent probable loci of hunting-related activities. Clusters 5, 13, 14, 15, and 17 are interpreted as butchering loci, and Cluster 6 assemblages, which consist of isolated projectile point finds, are interpreted as kill or encounter loci. Sampling units grouped into Clusters 3, 4, and 10 consist almost solely of small samples of lithic debitage and may represent kill-butchering locations; however, this interpretation is purely speculative.

Table 8-4. Summary and Interpretation of Cluster Analysis Results Based Upon Factor Scores.

Cluster	No. of SU's	Important Factors[1]		Category	Interpretation
1	44	2,6,5,7	(+)	Residential Base	Extended habitation camp
		1,4,3	(−)		
2	25	4,7	(+)	Field Camp	Overnight hunting camp
		2,6,5,9,3	(−)		
3	7	4,8,6	(+)	Location	Lithic reduction locus
		2,1,5,3,9	(−)		
4	13	7	(+)	Location	Lithic reduction locus
		4,2,8,6,5,9,3	(−)		
5	3	3	(+)	Location	Butchering locus
		2,5	(−)		
6	5	7,2,8,1	(−)	Location	Kill locus
7	2	5,8	(+)	Residential Base	Extended habitation camp (?)
8	9	2	(+)	Residential Base	Extended habitation camp
		5,8,6,3	(−)		
9	1	4	(+)	Location	Woodworking locus
		6	(−)		
10	4	8	(+)	Location	Lithic reduction locus
		4,2,5,1,3,9	(−)		
11	1	8	(+)	Location	Chert procurement locus
12	2	5	(+)	Residential Base	Specialized habitation camp
13	1	1	(+)	Location	Butchering locus
14	1	1	(+)	Location	Butchering locus
15	1	3	(+)	Location	Butchering locus
16	1	6	(+)	Field Camp	Overnight hunting camp
17	1	9	(+)	Location	Butchering locus

[1]Factors are listed in order of importance. Mean sources for these factors are significantly different from 0 at $p \leq .05$ (using Student's t-test). Factors with *highest* scores are indicated for clusters represented by only one sampling unit.

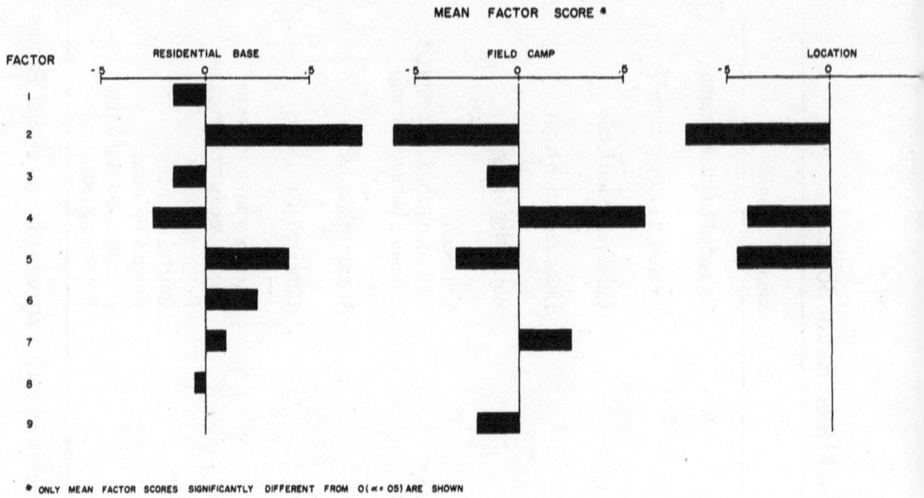

Figure 8-3. Summary of Factor Scores by Assemblage Category.

Clusters 9 and 11 represent single assemblages that are not related to hunting activities; instead, they indicate woodworking (i.e., the isolated occurrence of a celt fragment) and lithic procurement (i.e., the occurrence of tested chert nodules) activities. Both of these clusters are classified as locations.

The relative importance of the nine factors to the three assemblage categories defined above is shown graphically in Figure 8-3. In addition, the original activity group data used in the factor analysis are summarized by category in Figure 8-4. To conclude the discussion of the cluster analysis, specific observations can be made about the resulting assemblage categorizations. First, assemblages interpreted as residential bases are collectively made up of artifacts representing all recognized activity groups. This pattern is dominated by a high proportion of fire-cracked rock (suggesting hearth use) and a more moderate proportion of primary and bifacial reduction debitage. Second, sampling units identified as field camps contain relatively large amounts of primary and bifacial reduction debitage, and lesser amounts of fire-cracked rock and cutting implements. Other implement categories are either rare or absent, which suggests a limited range of activities for these units. Third, the collective assemblage pattern for locations is dominated by a high proportion of hunting implements and bifacial debitage.

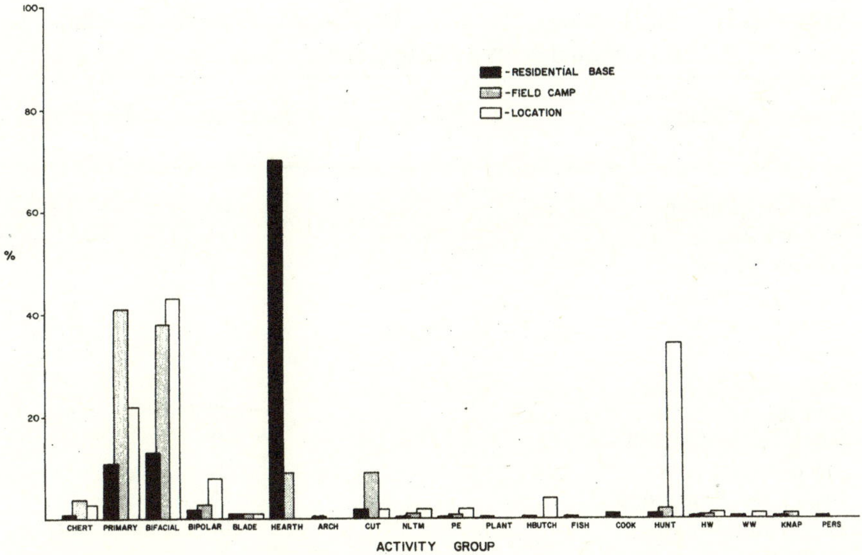

Figure 8-4. Distribution of Activity Group Percentages Among the Three Assemblage Categories.

In addition, primary lithic reduction and several other tool categories associated with hunting activities (specifically, meat processing and weapon maintenance) are also represented. All of these assemblages appear to be the result of specific tasks and are probably not products of redundant activity.

Discriminant Analysis

Discriminant analysis was undertaken to measure the "uniqueness" of the three assemblage categories intuitively defined from the cluster analysis results and to classify additional sites identified by nonprobabilistic survey within Area II by assemblage category. Because of the paucity of temporally diagnostic artifacts from field camps and locations (most of which are situated in Area II), it was necessary to use additional nonprobabilistic samples from Area II to evaluate temporal patterning for these assemblage categories. The discriminant analysis, based on the original relative frequency data instead of factor scores,

Table 8-5. Standardized Canonical Discriminant Function Coefficients for Original Activity Group Data.

Variable (Activity Group)	Function 1	Function 2
Chert Acquisition	.09	1.33
Primary Reduction	.34	2.75
Bifacial Reduction	.41	3.79
Bipolar Reduction	.18	2.26
Blade Manufacture	.16	.52
Hearth Use	1.25	2.16
Architecture	−.05	.04
Cutting	−.29	−.41
Nonlithic Tool Manufacture	.05	.51
Pièce Esquillée	.01	1.19
Plant Food Processing	−.06	.01
Heavy Butchering	.07	1.48
Fishing	.31	.22
Cooking	.25	.31
Hunting	.14	3.19
Hide Working	−.04	−.19
Woodworking	−.03	.67
Flintknapping	−.18	−.01
Personal Adornment	.26	.05
Eigenvalue	6.79	.42
% Variance	94.15	5.85

utilized an SPSS stepwise discriminant procedure (Wilk's method) with proportional prior probabilities and tolerance = .001 (Tatsuoka 1971). The discriminant functions were then applied to the original relative frequency data to predict the group membership of these assemblages. Almost 86 percent of these assemblages were correctly classified by this procedure (Tables 8-5 and 8-6). Most residential base assemblages were correctly classified but several misclassifications occurred with both field camps and locations. This suggests that while residential base assemblages are distinct from both field camps and locations, there is a certain degree of overlap for these latter two categories. This situation is expected since both categories represent a limited range of partly similar activities. A bivariate plot of all probabilistic samples based upon

Table 8-6. Classification Results of the Discriminant Analysis Using Relative Frequency Data.

Assemblage Category	No. of Cases	Residential Base n	Residential Base %	Field Camp n	Field Camp %	Location n	Location %
Residential Base	57	55	96.5	2	3.5	0	.0
Field Camp	26	1	3.8	19	73.1	6	23.1
Location	38	0	.0	8	21.1	30	78.9
Unclassified Area II Sites	129	0	.0	39	30.2	90	69.8

Predicted Group Membership: Residential Base, Field Camp, Location.

85.95% of "grouped" cases were correctly classified.

discriminant-function scores is presented in Figure 8-5. The three tight clusters of location assemblages are a result of small sample size and represent (from top to bottom) isolated projectile points, bifacial thinning flakes, and primary flakes.

Following the construction of discriminant functions and evaluation of their classificatory power, 129 nonprobabilistic site samples from Area II were classified as either field camps or locations. These data will be used later in discussions of temporal variability.

Spatial Variability

Following the functional classification of the survey sample through multivariate analysis, assemblage variability was examined along spatial and temporal dimensions. As stated earlier, the probabilistic sample was obtained from five separate domains. These sampling domains are generally representative of discrete classes of similar landforms (Table 8-1) and therefore constitute a legitimate basis for assessing spatial differences in assemblage occurrence. Moreover, since these samples were obtained by random sampling, population parameter estimates can be derived for each domain. Parameter estimates were calculated in the following manner. First, sampling units from each domain were placed into one of four categories (i.e., three assemblage categories, or a fourth

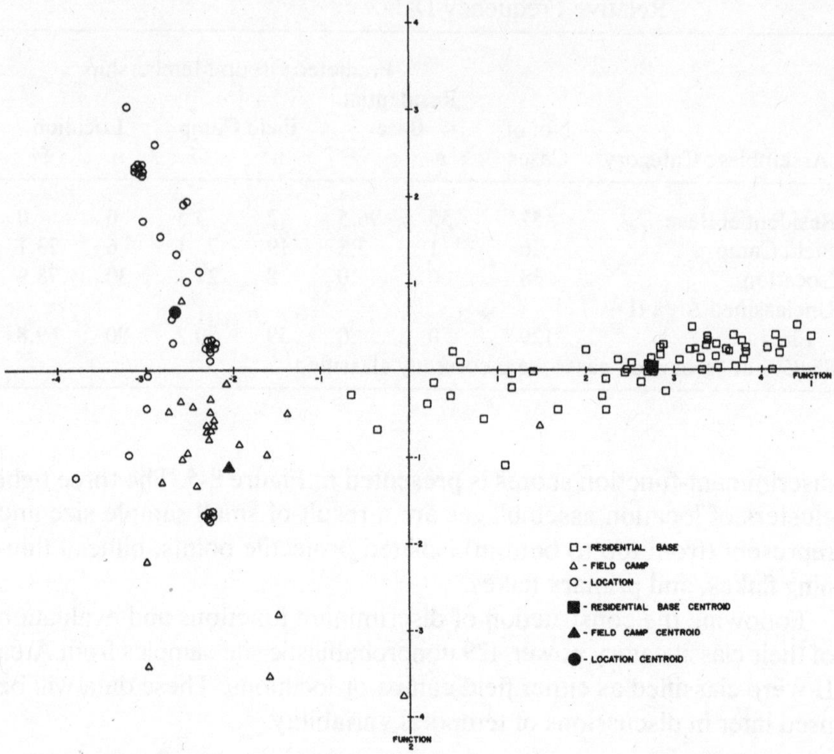

Figure 8-5. Bivariate Plot of All Probabilistic Samples Based upon Discriminant Function Scores.

category containing units which failed to produce archaeological material). Next, the relative frequency of each category was calculated. These measures represent unbiased estimates of the population proportions. Finally, 90 percent confidence intervals were calculated for each estimator following Cochran (1977:57–59). Confidence interval contrasts are presented in Figure 8-6.

Examination of confidence intervals indicates patterned spatial variability of archaeological assemblages within the survey area. The Lower Main Valley, Upper Main Valley, and Tellico River Drainage domains produced the highest proportions of residential bases, while the Main

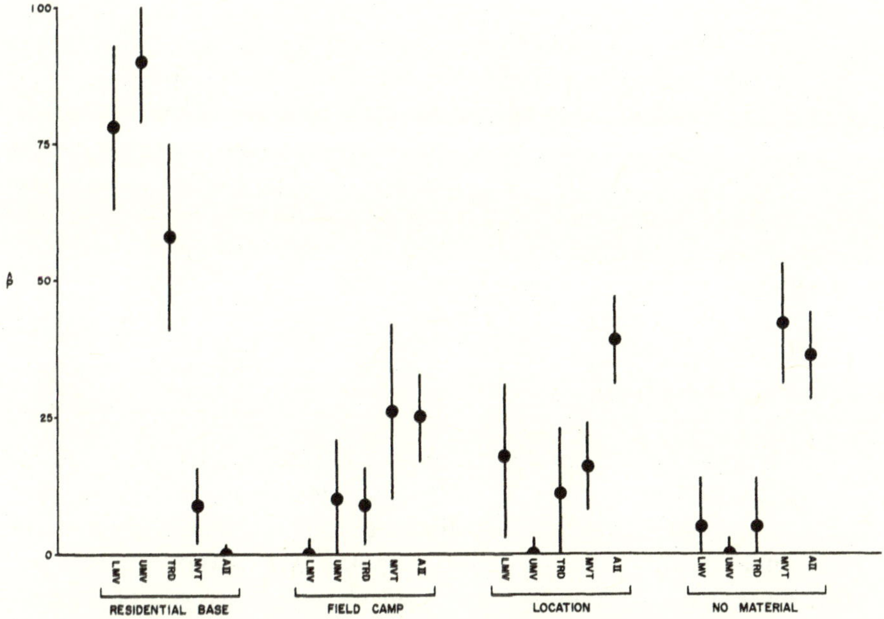

Figure 8-6. Comparisons of 90 Percent Confidence Intervals for Assemblage Categories by Sampling Domains.

Valley Tributaries and Area II samples yielded very few such assemblages. It is apparent from these results that residential bases are strongly correlated with the Little Tennessee River and Tellico River valleys. Although the confidence intervals for field camps overlap and therefore are not significantly different (in a statistical sense), there is an apparent tendency for such assemblages to occur in greater proportions within the Main Valley Tributaries and Area II domains. The occurrence of field camps within the Little Tennessee River and Tellico River valleys is obviously overshadowed by the predominance of residential bases in those areas. Locations occur in all sampling domains except the Upper Main Valley; however, such assemblages are proportionately rare in all but Area II. Approximately 40 percent of all units within this domain were classified as locations. Finally, few sampling units within the valley domains failed to produce archaeological material, in marked contrast to the two upland domains (Main Valley Tributaries and Area II) which produced numerous "empty" units. These results suggest a differential use of valley and upland zones, with upland land use being comprised of specific (but sporadic) activity leaving little in the way of preservable archaeological remains. The close relationship between field camp and location assemblages, as reflected in the discriminant analysis, is supported by the similar spatial distributions for these two assemblage categories. This can tentatively be postulated to represent functionally related manifestations of upland-oriented hunting pursuits. The spatial distribution of individual units classified into the three assemblage categories is shown in Figure 8-7.

Temporal Variability

Assessment of temporal patterning within the data set was examined from two perspectives. First, a chi-square test of association was performed to assess the null hypothesis that assemblage categories are randomly associated with major temporal periods (no temporal patterning exists). Second, variability in the co-occurrence of different temporal units within individual assemblages was examined to assess settlement pattern stability and redundancy in site occupation. Temporal assignment of assemblages is based on the occurrence of traditional, temporally diagnostic indicators (e.g., stylistically distinct projectile points and ceramic artifacts). This method obviously has problems since such artifacts seldom occur in sufficient quantities to preclude the coexistence of other unidentified temporal units. Because of the paucity of diagnostic artifacts from Area II units, 129 sites identified by nonprobabilistic survey were added to the sample. These sites were classified by assemblage category during the discriminant analysis. Previous analysis of the Area II nonprobabilistic sample suggests that it is representative of the population of archaeological sites within this domain with respect to the kinds of activities represented (Davis 1981).

The chi-square test was performed on a 3 by 3 contingency table, namely, assemblage category by major temporal period (Archaic, Woodland, and Mississippian). This test produced a significant statistic of $X^2 = 27.21$ (x^2 9.49 df 4 $p<.05$). Examination of individual cell values (not presented) shows that both Archaic residential bases and Woodland locations are substantially under-represented in the sample. The

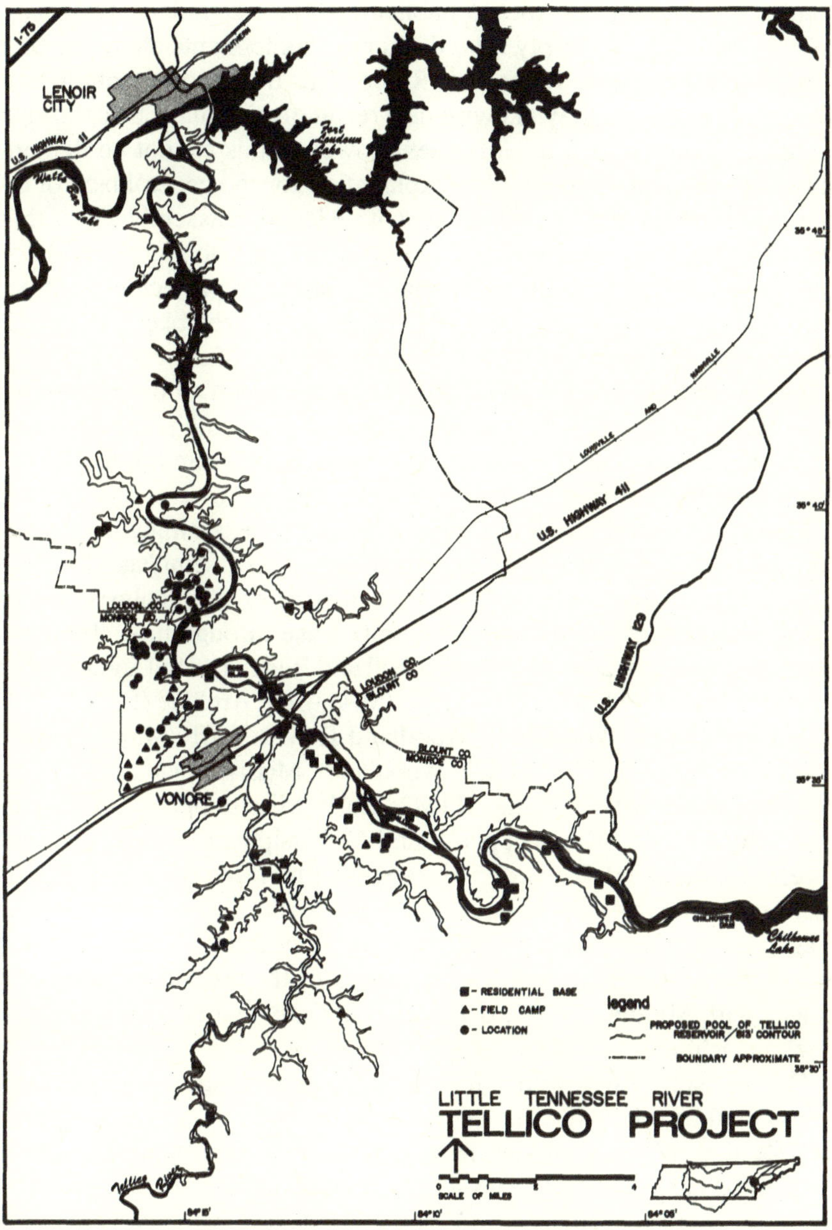

Figure 8-7. Map of Tellico Reservoir Showing the Spatial Distribution of Sampling Units by Assemblage Category.

infrequent occurrence of Archaic residential bases is probably explained by the fact that the probabilistic surface sample is systematically biased against deeply buried Archaic components along the first terrace of the Little Tennessee River. The under-representation of Woodland locations may likewise be a result of systematic bias through failure to identify such assemblages; however, this cannot be demonstrated at present. One possible explanation for the general lack of diagnostic Woodland projectile points within location assemblages is that Woodland hunting strategies (as they relate to specific tool use and discard) may not result in the same rate or pattern of projectile point occurrence observed for Archaic and Mississippian assemblages (Kimball, personal communication 1980). Certainly, the use of a weapon such as a spear with a removable foreshaft, versus the use of a bow and arrow, has direct implications for the proportion of projectile points that can be expected to occur within an assemblage and the kind of toolkit associated with hunting activities.

Finally, temporal variability was analyzed by examining the co-occurrence of temporally diagnostic indicators within assemblages for each assemblage category (Table 8-7). The purpose of this analysis was to assess patterns of site (or sampling unit) reuse through time. Ten temporal units were used following Kimball and Baden (1980a) and include: Early Archaic (EA), Middle Archaic (MA), Late Archaic (LA), Woodland I (W1: Early Woodland), Woodland II (W2: Early/Middle Woodland), Woodland III (W3: Middle Woodland), Mississippian I (M1: Early Mississippian), Mississippian II (M2: Early Mississippian), Mississippian III (M3: Late Mississippian), and Mississippian IV (M4: Historic Overhill Cherokee). The cell values shown in Table 8-7 are single directional comparisons that indicate the proportion of assemblages with diagnostic artifacts representing specific temporal unit pairs. For example, the value of the MA-LA cell indicates the proportion of assemblages with Middle Archaic diagnostic artifacts that also contain Late Archaic artifacts.

Comparison of cell values for the three assemblage categories suggests considerable variability, part of which is probably a result of small sample size. Whereas moderate to high values were obtained for most residential base cells, the majority of the cell values for field camps and locations were extremely low. Residential bases display considerable redundancy in site occupation. This suggests that the criteria for resi-

Table 8-7. Matrices for Each Assemblage Category Showing the Proportion (p) of Assemblages with Specific Temporal Unit Combinations: (n = the Number of Assemblages with Temporally Diagnostic Artifacts).

Residential Base

	EA n=13	MA n=19	LA n=19	W1 n=9	W2 n=13	W3 n=16	M1 n=3	M2 n=5	M3 n=7	M4 n=16
EA	1.00									
MA	.77	1.00								
LA	.62	.53	1.00							
W1	.08	.21	.32	1.00						
W2	.31	.37	.37	.67	1.00					
W3	.38	.21	.42	.56	.54	1.00				
M1	.00	.05	.11	.00	.08	.13	1.00			
M2	.15	.11	.11	.11	.38	.13	.33	1.00		
M3	.08	.11	.32	.22	.23	.19	.00	.20	1.00	
M4	.15	.26	.42	.67	.62	.50	1.00	.60	.57	1.00

Field Camp

	EA n=12	MA n=7	LA n=6	W1 n=0	W2 n=3	W3 n=1	M1 n=0	M2 n=2	M3 n=3	M4 n=0
EA	1.00									
MA	.58	1.00								
LA	.42	.71	1.00							
W1	.00	.00	.00	1.00						
W2	.08	.29	.33	.00	1.00					
W3	.08	.14	.17	.00	.00	1.00				
M1	.00	.00	.00	.00	.00	.00	1.00			
M2	.08	.14	.17	.00	.00	.00	.00	1.00		
M3	.17	.14	.17	.00	.00	.00	.00	.00	1.00	
M4	.00	.00	.00	.00	.00	.00	.00	.00	.00	1.00

Location

	EA n=18	MA n=8	LA n=6	W1 n=0	W2 n=2	W3 n=1	M1 n=0	M2 n=0	M3 n=7	M4 n=0
EA	1.00									
MA	.17	1.00								
LA		.00	1.00			.11				
W1	.00	.00	.00	1.00						
W2	.06	.00	.00	.00	1.00					
W3	.06	.13	.00	.00	.00	1.00				
M1	.00	.00	.00	.00	.00	.00	1.00			
M2	.00	.00	.00	.00	.00	.00	.00	1.00		
M3	.06	.00	.00	.00	.00	.00	.00	.00	1.00	
M4	.00	.00	.00	.00	.00	.00	.00	.00	.00	1.00

dence selection was generally the same for all temporal units. However, a closer examination of the residential base matrix indicates some noticeable exceptions to this generalization. The occurrence of high cell values (i.e., > .50) for all Archaic period and Woodland period combinations stands in marked contrast to the generally low values for Mississippian period comparisons. Part of this pattern may be due to the relatively small number of assemblages that yielded diagnostic Mississippian (specifically, M1 to M3) material. There is, however, some evidence to suggest a possible shift in settlement orientation after the Woodland period. The fact that very few Mississippian occupations (except M4) were identified by the probabilistic survey may indicate a settlement pattern distinct from earlier patterns. Although such a shift could be related to a greater reliance on agriculture and increased settlement nucleation, this remains to be demonstrated. Finally, the last Mississippian temporal unit, identified historically as Overhill Cherokee, shows a consistently high incidence of Woodland and Mississippian site reuse.

Two observations can be made regarding field camps and locations. First, a high proportion of field camp assemblages yielded evidence of multiple Archaic occupations. However, following the Archaic period no temporally contiguous units are represented within any assemblages. Although sample size may again be a problem, this situation could reflect a shift in hunting strategies during the Woodland period. The second observation concerns the lack of multicomponent assemblages within both field camp and location categories. This pattern, when compared with the one observed earlier for residential base assemblages, suggests that activities represented by field camps and locations were not constrained by the same external factors that affected residence location. Put another way, the spatial location of hunting-related activities is directly dependent upon the behavioral patterns of game (principally deer) and therefore is only indirectly controlled by factors such as topography and hydrology.

Conclusions

The primary purposes of the preceding analysis have been to explore variability within survey data generated through probabilistic sampling and to consider the implications of these data for settlement studies. As a result of this analysis, three general conclusions can be presented. First, there is patterned variability within the data that can be interpreted within the context of contemporary theory of collector subsistence systems. The analyzed assemblages represent a range of activity sets which generally match our expectations of the major settlement types within such systems. Second, assemblage categories representing the archaeological correlates of these settlement types are differentially distributed among the five sampling domains used in the study, indicating differential land use (and resource extraction) patterns. Finally, regularities in temporal variability were observed among the three assemblage categories, some of which support earlier functional interpretations of these categories. However, the number of diagnostic indicators for the Woodland and Mississippian periods is insufficient to make valid comparisons between specific temporal units.

This study represents only a starting point in the analysis of settlement systems within the study area. A final phase of probabilistic sampling is well underway, and when completed, will produce survey coverage for almost 34,000 acres of contiguous lands along the lower Little Tennessee River. At that time, all data derived through sampling will be analyzed to develop a model of aboriginal settlement systems. The results of the preceding analysis, while admittedly short of this goal, demonstrate the applicability of the probability-based sample for addressing settlement questions. Future study along these lines should produce a better understanding of the nature and dynamics of prehistoric settlement systems and land use within the lower Little Tennessee River Valley.

Acknowledgments

Funding for all fieldwork and analyses described herein was provided by the Tennessee Valley Authority under contracts TV53015A, TV52982A, and TV56255A. Earlier drafts of this paper were read by William O. Autry, William Baden, Jefferson Chapman, Larry R. Kimball, Gipsie Ranney, and Gerald F. Schroedl. Their many helpful comments are greatly appreciated.

9 • VELETTA CANOUTS AND ALBERT C. GOODYEAR III

Lithic Scatters in the South Carolina Piedmont

Introduction

Until recently, numerous lithic biface and flake scatters, occurring on the eroded ridgetops and ridgeslopes of the South Carolina Piedmont uplands, were virtually ignored by professional archaeologists who saw in them limited research potential. These sites are usually shallow, plowed, and eroded; a large number are multicomponent; the assemblages are dominated by bifaces manufactured primarily of quartz; and they are utterly ubiquitous, found throughout the entire interriverine areas of the Piedmont. Consequently, there is a tendency to regard these sites as a single class of remains which are analytically intractable. Owing to the research done in the context of cultural resource management (CRM) studies, more site integrity and structural variability have now been identified. Researchers are beginning to focus on the human activities responsible for the creation of these sites and the underlying processes responsible for the formation of such an homogenized, redundant archaeological pattern. This chapter reviews the approaches and results of recent investigations in the South Carolina Piedmont.

Previous Considerations of Upland Lithic Scatters

In the late 1940s, Joffre Coe (1964:6) recognized that the mixing of temporally sensitive artifacts recovered from surface collections on North Carolina Piedmont sites thwarted his attempts to identify and order chronologically archaeological complexes. As Coe (1964:8) himself noted, the lithic artifacts he first associated with Badin pottery were subsequently dated 5,000 years earlier, based on his classic stratigraphic analysis of preceramic and ceramic assemblages excavated from deeply buried sites along the Yadkin-Pee Dee drainage (Coe 1964:121). This cultural sequence, which is applicable regionally (e.g., Tippitt and Marquardt 1982), shows these shallow, mixed upland sites to have been variously occupied over the past 10,000 years.

Unlike the metavolcanic and other metasedimentary rock identified by Coe (1964) in the North Carolina Piedmont assemblages, quartz dominates the lithic assemblages found in the Piedmont of Georgia and South Carolina. Caldwell (1954), excavating at the Lake Springs site on the Savannah River, isolated what he called the Old Quartz Industry in a preceramic, alluvially sealed deposit. He then assigned the very noticeable quartz-bearing sites eroding from the clay hills to this same complex (Caldwell 1958:9). The excavation of one of these small hilltop sites in Georgia confirmed the presence of ovate blades and the absence of "heavy-duty" stone tools in what was described as an "Old Quartz" assemblage (Dickens 1964). The shallow, relatively undisturbed artifact remains at the site suggested its use as a seasonal, short-term hunting camp of Early and Middle Archaic peoples (Dickens 1964:46). Dickens' (1964) work at Stone Mountain is noteworthy in that it appears to be the first effort to understand the structure of these sites through excavation.

Artifact cross-dating using Coe's chronological sequence indicates that the quartz ovate bifaces no doubt correlate with the Morrow Mountain and probably Guilford phases of the Middle Archaic period, but quartz also predominates as a raw material in all earlier and later assemblages, thus denying any classificatory utility of the Old Quartz Industry (Goodyear et al. 1979:108).

With a few notable exceptions (e.g., Kelly 1972), later investigators chose to concentrate on the river valleys and coasts, ascribing low occupation densities or a near absence of human settlement in the hinterlands or Piedmont uplands (Stoltman 1972, 1974; Turnbaugh 1975). In the past ten years, CRM studies undertaken in the South Carolina Piedmont have contributed to a total of over one thousand documented prehistoric sites (cf. Taylor 1979). Every phase within every period is represented (South Carolina Statewide Archaeological Site Inventory Files). It is important that these numerous lithic scatters be analyzed and understood, and especially so, given that the upland portion of the Piedmont constitutes at least 90 percent of the land surface and probably contains more than 90 percent of the archaeological sites, estimated to number in the thousands, even tens of thousands.

The burst of CRM studies, beginning in the 1970s, increased archaeological activities in "marginal" areas throughout the country (Goodyear et al. 1978). Supposedly nonresearchable sites came under fresh scrutiny, and governmental agencies publicly acknowledged the research potential of sites which were both "difficult to study" and "unprepossessing in form" (Talmage et al. 1977:12). In the absence of preexisting, relevant research goals, the challenges of how and what to study have been faced and individually met by the authors, working in the Southwest (e.g., Canouts 1977b; Goodyear 1977), the Midwest (Goodyear 1974, 1957b; Canouts et al. 1977), and in the Southeast, where Goodyear (1975a) designed a state highway program (then under the auspices of the Institute of Archeology and Anthropology) to incorporate data from small, limited activity sites into a comprehensive research framework (House and Ballenger 1976; Canouts 1976; Cable et al. 1978; House and Wogaman 1978; Goodyear et al. 1979).

Site Patterns and the Issue of Site Integrity

Present research efforts have been directed toward elucidating the processes that may be contributing to broadly shared site patterns: multicomponent, low artifact density, shallow deposits dominated by a quartz biface industry. These characteristics, which seem so redundant from site to site, are of interest to archaeologists modeling: (1) the relationships of limited activity sites in the context of larger subsistence-settlement systems; (2) the use of local and nonlocal sources of raw material; and (3) long-term exploitative strategies as evidenced through site reoccupation. Both intra- and intersite variability along these dimensions is now emerging for the first time from research in the South Carolina Piedmont. Although a number of different investigators are working in the Piedmont, the remainder of this discussion will rely heavily on survey data generated by the Institute of Archeology and Anthropology because collection methods, biases, and analytical strategies are thought to be comparable and because the studies were designed to advance systematically and to build upon one another (Goodyear 1975a; Canouts 1977a).

The Piedmont Environment

Physiographically, the Piedmont is part of the Central and Southern Appalachians, forming a distinct province that stretches continuously

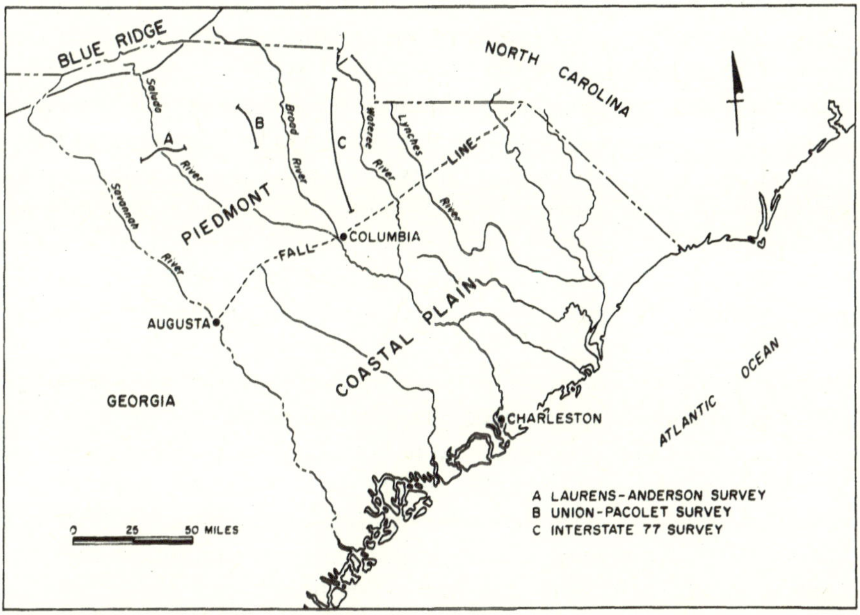

Figure 9-1. The Piedmont Study Area in South Carolina, and the Location of Survey Data Bases.

from central Alabama to New Jersey. The Piedmont is a peneplain, or perhaps a series of peneplains, exhibiting dissection and degradation mainly from fluvial processes. The landscape is described as "rolling," since practically all land surfaces are either hillside, hilltop, or valley bottom, with no sharp breaks separating these categories (Fenneman 1938:131). Because of the comparatively steep gradients of the Piedmont drainages, streams tend to cut vertically rather than laterally, resulting in narrow river valleys and floodplains (Garner 1974:297–299).

One of the striking features of the Piedmont environment is the regularity in the distribution of drainage systems (Figure 9-1). Along the Atlantic Slope, the major southeasterly flowing drainages occur at roughly equal distances from one another. This uniformity is attributable to the fact that there is a general homogeneity in the strengths of the underlying rocks such that drainage patterns are not strongly controlled by differential resistance (Fenneman 1938:123). Lithologically, the Piedmont is composed of crystalline igneous and metamorphic rocks overlain by a deep red clay soil mantle (Spencer 1965:480).

Today, a mosaic of soil types supports an oak-pine vegetation (Braun 1950). The native (pre-European) vegetation has not been well described. Oaks and hickories are thought to have been dominant under conditions prior to the massive land clearings beginning in the eighteenth century (Küchler 1964; Trimble 1974). Modern descriptions have utilized mature forest tracts thought to be representative of the precolonial vegetation (Oosting 1942; Whitehead and Barghoorn 1962), as well as historical records, to reconstruct probable proportions of hardwood and pines on major soil types (Nelson 1957). Although considerable edaphic variability is indicated, in any locality in the Piedmont the drier, elevated ridgetops support different species and compositions of species than the cooler, more mesic bottomlands, ravines, and coves (Whitehead and Barghoorn 1962:349; Oosting 1942).

The fauna of the Piedmont need not be recapitulated here except to say that this region is included within the oak-hickory zone of the Southern Temperate Deciduous Forest Biome as classified by Shelford (1963). Beyond the economically important terrestrial mammals typically found in prehistoric sites in the Southeast, such as white-tailed deer, turkey, raccoon, squirrel, and oppossum (Parmalee 1962), the southern Piedmont also possessed significant quantities of anadromous fish that migrated seasonally up certain of the Piedmont rivers (Rostlund 1952:73–74; Logan 1859:75–76). Although the relationship between sea level rise, alteration of river gradients, and the time in the Holocene during which anadromous fish such as shad and sturgeon first began penetrating the Piedmont river systems is not yet known, it seems reasonable that at least by Late Archaic times (3000–2000 B.C.) such fish were present (Turnbaugh 1975:59).

In the foregoing discussion, the Piedmont environment has been described as it is known from the historic and modern periods. Work by palynologists in the Coastal Plain (e.g., Whitehead 1965; Watts 1971, 1980) and the Southern Appalachians (e.g., Watts 1970; 1975) indicates that substantial changes took place from the late Pleistocene to the Holocene, as well as important minor changes during the Holocene. From the beginning of the Holocene (ca. 8000 B.C.), it is clear, however, that the basic modern biota of the Piedmont was essentially in place (Watts 1970, 1975, 1980).

Limited Activity Sites

Sites located in the interriverine Piedmont (Goodyear et al. 1979:131–145) appear to be geographically extensive and to show little assemblage diversity. Such sites have been widely interpreted as limited or specialized activity sites that represent resource exploitation or other distinct functions. Nearly all investigators working in the Piedmont have related these sites to activities involving hunting, nut gathering, and procuring of lithic raw materials (Goodyear et al. 1979:147–178).

Leaving aside for a moment the problem of assemblage integrity, the assemblages at these sites appear to be composed primarily of flakes and bifaces that represent various stages of manufacture, use, resharpening, breakage, and discard (Table 9-1). There is concern about the horizontal and vertical disturbance vectors, such as slope wash, tree throw, soil cracking, and plowing (Canouts 1976), and even artifact removal by amateur collectors (Charles 1981). However, examination of the assemblages reveals a range of artifact size and condition, from small thinning flakes to whole, as well as broken and exhausted, bifaces. In other words, the contents appear to be essentially intact with no major lacunae.

Evidence of subsurface structural remains is virtually nonexistent for these sites, a situation that cannot be assigned real meaning until more sites are excavated. No features were found at Windy Ridge (House and Wogaman 1978), although undisturbed soils may have been present. Features have been reported, however, from a plowed site on a knoll overlooking Rabon Creek (Wood and Gresham 1980).

The most productive strategy thus far employed for discerning structural patterning has been the intrasite spatial analysis of surface collections. Definite diachronic, and probably synchronic, occupation patterns have been elucidated using computer graphic programs (such as SYMAP) to graph surface data. Mapping the surface collection from the Stoddard site, for example, showed Middle Archaic bifaces located in different areas of the site from the Late Archaic bifaces (Goodyear et al. 1979:77–87, Figures 9–12). At the Windy Ridge site, excavated material from the plowzone and just beneath it showed different spatial distributions of raw materials across the site and definite clustering of quartz Morrow Mountain points with quartz debitage, defining possible activity areas (House and Wogaman 1978:112–125, Figures 19–24).

Table 9-1. Frequency Distribution of Artifacts Recovered from South Carolina Piedmont Lithic Scatter Sites.

Artifact Categories	L/A[1] n=165	I-77[2] n=61	U/P[3] n=24	Total n=250	%
Debitage					
Chunks	6,378	348	643	7,369	
Other Flakes	7,324	739	69	8,132	
Thinning Flakes	8,485	510	647	9,642	
Subtotal	22,187	1,597	1,359	25,143	90
Flake Cores	410	26	8	444	2
Flake Tools	163	18	0	181	.6
Unifacial Tools	84	9	15	108	.4
Bifaces					
Points	617	35	19	671	
Preforms	227	—	6	233	
Blanks	666	70	—	736	
Undifferentitated	—	65	27	92	
Subtotal	1,510	170	52	1,732	6
Other Stone Artifacts					
Ground Stone	14[4]	—	—		
Hammerstone	—	1	—	15	
Chipped Stone	17	7	14	38	
Subtotal	31	8	14	53	.2
Pottery	216	5	3	224	.8
TOTAL	24,601	1,833	1,451	27,885	100.0

Key: 1 Laurens-Anderson survey (Goodyear et al. 1979)
2 I-77 survey (House and Ballenger 1976)
3 Union-Pacolet survey (Cable et al. 1978)
4 minimum occurrence
n number of archaeological loci

Artifact assemblages have been used in conjunction with locational variables to indicate functional differences between maintenance and extractive components of larger settlement-subsistence systems (Binford and Binford 1966). At the present time, there is no obvious spatial patterning in site location (Goodyear et al. 1979:255–261; House and Ballenger 1976:168–171; Taylor and Smith 1978:368–387; White and Goodyear 1981). Furthermore no large-scale correlations between site location and assemblage composition were found in a catchment study involving Rank 3 drainages and bottomlands and the number of Rank 1 and 2 drainages (House and Ballenger 1976:109–114).

Biotic Extraction. Although there is environmental variation in the interriverine Piedmont, the variants tend to be repeated at very close intervals, which produces a spatially homogenized picture when viewed at a large scale. For example, Goodyear et al. (1979:45–75) plotted a random-sampling vector through an arbitrary region surrounding their highway survey corridor. Although the results were used for the purpose of evaluating the sampling biases, they were also interesting from the standpoint of environmental redundancy. Five variables were analyzed: elevation, slope, slope orientation, drainage rank, and types of landforms intersected. The highway corridor constituted a statistically random sample of these environmental variables, except that of elevation.

In a uniform environment, slight differences in topography or productivity may eventually be shown to relate to site location. It is interesting to note, in this regard, that site frequency along the Laurens-Anderson route (Figure 9-1) appeared to increase at the major watershed divides (Goodyear et al. 1979:59). There, broad ridgetops bound natural catchment areas. These flat ridgetops are also easily travelled. Modern agricultural uses of these areas would also tend to increase site visibility, however. In another survey study, several interlocking site variables were compared against modern soil productivity rankings (Cable et al. 1978:24–38). The density of sites, the number and diversity of tools, and the number of multicomponent sites increased with greater soil productivity; site size did not. Although today's soil rankings probably still measure relative productivity, severe slope erosion has resulted in lower productivity ratings for slopes than for level ground. It remains to be seen, therefore, whether this correlation reflects productivity or topographic variables.

The natural productivity of temperate forests follows seasonal and yearly cycles of resource occurrence and abundance. Seasonality has been inferred from the biface assemblage at these sites. The biotic resource structure may be characterized as exploitable plant products (sap, berries, seeds, fruits, nuts, tubers, and greens) that become available seasonally; anadromous fish; and animals whose diets reflect seasonality but whose mobility crosscuts microenvironments. Within seasons, the major distributional differences probably relate to moisture, soil productivity, and ground disturbances or successional mosaics brought about by storms, fires, and floods.

The most important upland resources are acorns and hickory nuts, and white-tailed deer and other animals that are known to forage for nuts (e.g., turkeys and squirrels). The seasonal hypothesis emphasizes the maximized hunting potential of deer in the fall when mast is produced and when the deer are most vulnerable (Smith 1975; Canouts 1971; Swanton 1922). Because chipped-stone tools are not used effectively to process nuts, the assemblages have been directly associated with animal butchering, primarily of white-tailed deer.

Lithic Extraction. Tool manufacture and tool use relate to distinct spheres of technological activity. However, the problem of separating these two patterns in the archaeological record can be confounding when the two co-occur. Different stages of biface reduction are recognizable in the debris categories, as are the preliminary blanks and preforms which are subsequently fashioned into bifaces. Quite often thinning flakes can be distinguished from resharpening flakes during laboratory analysis. What is unclear is whether tool manufacture, use, and discard happened serially, at the same location, or whether the events were separated in time and space.

In order to determine if different sites reflected different phases of tool manufacture versus tool use, an early stage reduction index (number of chunks and other flakes/number of thinning flakes) and a biface discard index (number of biface and biface fragments/number of other flakes) were devised by House and Ballenger (1976:96–98) to characterize site assemblages. The results of the early stage reduction formula were not especially successful in distinguishing site activities. This may have resulted from the fact that the predominant raw material, quartz, was so ubiquitous that it did not "behave" like quarried material in Gould's (1977) sense of "quarried" (House and Ballenger 1976:99).

Quartz is widely distributed and was extensively used in the manufacture of bifaces through time (Table 2, from House and Ballenger 1976; Cable et al. 1978; Taylor and Smith 1978; Goodyear et al. 1979). The fact that quartz appears predominant in the soil, showing as a poor quality quartz residuum in the field, may give the false impression of abundance. Much of this rock has been exposed by erosion. The grade of quartz being worked was suitable for the production of well formed and precisely resharpened bifaces, and higher quality, milky white or translucent deposits might well have been selected. But in a relative sense, the fact that quartz is widely available is not an issue. The metamorphic rocks of the Kings Mountain, Charlotte, Carolina Slàte, and Inner Piedmont belts all contain quartzite and quartz in exposed beds and veins, in conglomerate formations, and as quartz pebbles (Overstreet and Bell 1965). On the Laurens-Anderson survey (Goodyear et al. 1979), quartz outcrops were observed at estimated intervals of one-and-a-half kilometers. Over half manifested quarrying activities.

The location of quartz outcrops becomes critical to the explication of both the expedient and the curated use of quartz. Quartz appears to be less highly curated than other metamorphic rocks, although the technological measures based on narrow, thin flakes of bifacial retouch (House and Ballenger 1976:130–133) are difficult to record on quartz materials. While its availability and low transport cost relative to its distribution and processing might suggest that tools were used and discarded on-site, the production of hafted, quartz bifaces suggests a certain time expenditure involved in manufacture as well as curation by edge and tip maintenance.

Goodyear (Goodyear et al. 1979:166–167) performed a factor analysis of three debitage classes (chunks, other flakes, and biface thinning flakes) and four core classes (points and point fragments, preforms, biface blanks, and flake cores) in order to analyze the same site formation problem involving tool manufacture and tool use. In the initial run, all debitage and core variables dominated the single resulting factor, with debitage accounting for most of the variance. However, hafted bifaces, preforms, and blanks seemed to separate. A subsequently imposed two-factor solution ordered the biface classes on the second factor leaving the debitage classes and the flake cores on the first. An obvious interpretation is that debitage was left at the locus of production while the biface classes were moved together through the settlement system. Flake cores, which showed an affinity with debitage, appear to be an "expedient" artifact class, one that "behaves" like debitage.

Although quartz dominates the assemblages, other local materials (e.g., rhyolite, argillite, and other metavolcanic and metasedimentary rocks) and nonlocal cherts from the Atlantic coast and the western Appalachian foothills were used in the manufacture of tools. The ratios changed significantly during the Early Archaic and the Late Archaic (Table 9-2). This pattern is clearly regional (Goodyear et al. 1979) and

Table 9-2. Frequency Distribution of Quartz and Nonquartz, Temporally Diagnostic, Hafted Bifaces.

BIFACE TYPE	QUARTZ	OTHER	TOTAL
Dalton	7 ((87.5%)	1 (12.5%)	8
Hardaway (Hardaway Blade, Hardaway-Dalton, and Hardaway Side Notched)	5 (100.0%)	0 (0.0%)	5
Palmer Corner Notched	59 (74.7%)	20 (25.3%)	79
Kirk (Kirk Corner Notched, Kirk Stemmed, and Kirk Serrated)	10 (35.7%)	18 (64.3%)	28
Stanly Stemmed	2 (33.3%)	4 (66.7%)	6
Morrow Mountain I and II Stemmed	244 (95.7%)	11 (4.3%)	255
Guilford Lanceolate	104 (96.3%)	4 (3.7%)	108
Savannah River Stemmed	83 (52.9%)	74 (47.1%)	157
Otarre Stemmed	4 (57.1%)	3 (42.9%)	7
Swannanoa Stemmed	14 (93.3%)	1 (6.7%)	15
Yadkin Large Triangular	50 (89.3%)	6 (10.7%)	56
Woodland Stemmed	2 (100.0%)	0 (0.0%)	2
Mississippian Triangular	15 (83.3%)	3 (16.7%)	18
Unidentified	225 (79.5%)	58 (20.5%)	283
TOTAL	824 (80.2%)	203 (19.8%)	1027

is well reflected in the Piedmont in the stratified riverine deposits at Gregg Shoals, where the Early Archaic reflects greater use of nonlocal cryptocrystalline materials, and the Late Archaic greater use of nonquartz, local materials (Tippitt and Marquardt 1982).

Site Reoccupation

Upland sites are heavily reoccupied. For example, comparison of four temporal components, Palmer, Morrow Mountain, Guilford, and Early Woodland, shows a three-to-one ratio of multicomponent to single component sites (Goodyear et al. 1979:175). Although the frequency for upland sites is exceedingly high, this ratio is still somewhat surprising given the apparent uniformity of the upland landscape and thus its potential for widely dispersed occupations. Coe's (1964) observation of spatially associated assemblages such as Guilford and Badin, while proving temporally incorrect, does suggest either some long-lived locational strategy or a common advantage found in a number of different logistical strategies.

Site discovery advantages also accrue from the shallow, disturbed deposits. Under these conditions, it may be assumed that there is an equal probability of detecting early and late temporal components, given site-discovery constraints. With a large enough sample over a large region, their frequency may be represented proportionally.

The Laurens-Anderson interriverine survey data were used to compare site reoccupation through time based on the frequencies, by temporal period, of single component sites and of sites with the component of the preceding phase present (Goodyear et al. 1979:169–178). Despite probable sampling biases, the results show distinct locational breaks (Goodyear et al. 1979: Figure 17). The first locational break, based on a pairwise comparison of the Palmer, Morrow Mountain, Guilford, and Early Woodland sites, occurred between the Morrow Mountain and Guilford sites. A chi-square analysis indicates that significantly fewer activities took place on completely new locations in the Guilford phase as compared to the Morrow Mountain phase. The Palmer and Morrow Mountain ratios, which are similar to each other, are quite dissimilar to the Guilford and Early Woodland ratios, which are also quite similar to each other. Thus, over the past 6,000 to 7,000 years, new landforms were not being utilized in the interriverine zone. However, the degree to which settlement patterns conformed to those of preceding periods did change during this time. In the Late Archaic period, another major break occurred in upland site locations. Of the 10 Savannah River sites, only four were located on the possible 20 Guilford sites. Of the seven Otarre sites, only three were located on the Savannah River sites. Not only are there fewer sites recorded in the interriverine zone between 3000 to 800 B.C., but there are also significant geographic shifts. Searching for other locational continuities and breaks in site reoccupation could prove productive.

Conclusions

To this point, the approach has been essentially descriptive and exploratory. Archaeological patterning has been elucidated in several aspects: the predominant use of quartz for hafted bifaces throughout prehistory, albeit with significant variation through time in the use of nonquartz lithic raw materials; the continued use of hafted bifaces and few other formal tools; spatial patterning on the intra- and intersite level with suggestions of patterning through time in each; and interesting trends in the patterns of site reoccupation. No doubt, further intra- and intersite variability will become manifested as greater research potential and site integrity are realized in upland scatters. Broader issues still remain, however, regarding the shared patterning.

Site characteristics show strong modal tendencies in material output, site location and frequency, and assemblage composition throughout the Holocene. Although certainly variability can be found within these data, there are impressive archaeological redundancies at the regional level related to (1) a basic suite of upland resources, (2) the use of hafted bifaces in their exploitation, and (3) the ready availability of quartz for solving tool-replacement problems. Future research must link, at different geographical scales, the organizational levels of adaptive systems to an archaeological record that represents thousands of years of evolving logistical and occupational strategies.

Whether artifact types or entire assemblages are chosen to measure diversity, neither reveals much variation in the artifact content of these sites at the present level of analysis. Even if the site assemblages resulted from a number of use episodes, whereby few artifacts accumulating over a long period of time ultimately achieve a threshold of archaeological site visibility, the assemblages appear to indicate functionally repetitive site use. Whatever task or variety of tasks was performed, the resulting debris exhibits similar "signatures" after a passage of time (Binford 1982:17).

Still recognizable intra- and interregional differences are apparent during the Early Archaic and Late Archaic periods. For example, the pronounced use of Coastal Plain cherts by Paleoindian and Early Archaic groups for curated utilitarian tools, such as hafted bifaces and scrapers, suggests a lithic signature of interregional mobility (Binford 1979; Goodyear et al. 1979:198–199). By the Late Archaic period, there is enough site and assemblage diversity to differentiate riverine and interriverine sites (White and Goodyear 1981; Goodyear et al. 1979). Whether or not the combined resource structure of the riverine and interriverine Piedmont was capable of supporting year-round inhabitants during the Late Archaic period is yet to be resolved. Certainly, the increased use of local, nonquartz lithic material suggests intensive exploitation of Piedmont resources.

The intervening Middle Archaic period is not well differentiated. The pronounced reliance on quartz during the Morrow Mountain and Guilford phases (Table 9-2) may indicate either a change in raw material procurement strategies resulting from a major reorganization in land use strategies, which still incorporated the Coastal Plain and Piedmont, or possible year-round occupation of the Piedmont. While archaeological data are limited, compositional variability in assemblages relative to location (riverine or interriverine) and raw material appears minimal. Despite "over-wintering" problems encountered in temperate forests, the repetitive resource structure and milder climate of the southern Piedmont may have decreased the number of functionally distinct or logistically distinct use areas. At this time, no one has proposed year-round exploitation of the uplands, away from the major river valleys, although the resource structure may not necessarily prohibit such a pattern. At the same time, no one has proposed a level of organizational complexity that would emphasize differences between major river valleys and uplands in the Middle Archaic, although such a plan has been hypothesized for the Late Archaic (cf. Turnbaugh 1975).

Future investigators of upland sites must effect broad scale spatial analyses comparable to the temporal analyses that have followed the excavation of deeply stratified sites. Both endeavors are necessary for a total understanding of Piedmont prehistory. Future researchers must concentrate on surviving upland contexts, i.e., the regional or geographic distributions of artifacts and/or environmental resources, not only within, but across physiographic provinces; and intrasite structural relationships that recognize different depositional episodes on originally exposed occupational surfaces, as well as on deflated archaeological surfaces (Binford 1982:16–17).

The issue is not the existence of distributional or spatial patterns, but the scale and meaning of such patterns. To that end, arguments must be introduced that effectively distinguish functional associations of items and features from their combinations due to site transformation processes that have been aggravated in the Piedmont by overexploitative Euro-American land practices. Furthermore, virtually untapped data sets, which include such mundane residue as fire-cracked rock and lithic debitage, must be given analytical consideration.

In sum, these upland lithic scatters are proving amenable to a number of investigative approaches. However, it is doubtful that any theoretical or methodological breakthrough by itself will lead to full understanding of upland sites. The challenge of the Piedmont is no different from the rest of archaeology. We must begin with questions relevant to the record at hand, and then derive appropriate methods to aid in their investigation.

10 • BILLY L. OLIVER

Tradition and Typology: Basic Elements of the Carolina Projectile Point Sequence

Introduction

Artifact types provide an organizational tool that allows archaeologists to " . . . group specimens into bodies which have demonstrable meaning in terms of behavior patterns" (Krieger 1944:272). Type has been variously defined as "a demonstrable clustering of attributes observed among specimens of a given class of phenomena" (Binford 1963:194), and as "a set of somewhat variable attributes which can be observed to occur together in the majority of cases . . . in such a way as to permit comparison" (Deetz 1967:51). Numerous archaeologists have suggested that types represent the idealized form of an object from the perspective of the craftsman (Deetz 1967; Krieger 1944; Taylor 1948; Smith 1976). Deetz (1967:51) refers to this as a "mental template," where the form of an object represents a close facsimile of the template, and variation in form is accounted for by variance in the ideas which produce them. In a similar manner, Smith (1976:70) states that "natural" types represent "real and functional things in the minds of the prehistoric men, women, and children who made them." In contrast to the perspectives of Deetz (1967) and Smith (1976), other archaeologists (e.g., Rouse 1972; Spaulding 1960) suggest that collections of artifacts may be described in terms of modes or diagnostic attribute sets, and that type represents a nonrandom clustering of attributes observed in a class of artifacts. In this sense, a type may represent the concept of the manufacturer, functional variability, the nature of the resource material, or all of the above.

For the purposes of this paper, a type is considered to be a cluster of both discrete and continuous attributes within a group of specimens; similar types are separated by demonstrable morphological, technological, and stratigraphic factors, and not, as is often the case, upon analytical or taxonomic convenience (cf. Krieger 1944:272).

Continuum and Technological Discontinuity

We should consider that the manufacture of an artifact represents the transmission of appropriate knowledge from one generation to another. The knowledge of how to manufacture, what are the most suitable resource materials, where to locate and procure the necessary resource materials, and what are the appropriate uses of the product is passed from generation to generation in such a way that a particular form of projectile point, knife, or axe is considered appropriate (cf. Deetz 1967:46). A tradition, therefore, represents a behavioral pattern shared by a group of people and passed from generation to generation as a part of the socialization process. Therefore, "an archaeological tradition is a primarily temporal continuity represented by persistent configurations in single technologies or other systems of related forms" (Willey and Phillips 1958:37). Each projectile point should exhibit slight differences in manufacture as replication of the "ideal form" progresses from generation to generation. Even though the first specimen produced in a lithic tradition may differ greatly from the last, if a large enough sample of specimens were observed, the thread of continuity would become clearly visible.

This concept of a technological tradition has, thus far, emphasized temporal processes, yet the spatial aspects effecting change also should be considered. Groups sharing a common technological heritage and occupying a relatively restricted geographical area over a considerable period of time may be identified with a specific "regional tradition" (cf. Willey and Phillips 1958:36–37), and should exhibit similar tool types. Shared behavioral patterns of what constitutes the correct form for a projectile point will be reinforced by proximity and intercommunication. Other groups sharing this same technological heritage, but occupying a different geographical area over a lengthy period of time, may be expected to retain basic elements of the tradition, although differences from the former will increase through time.

A technological tradition, therefore, is defined on the basis of the recognition of a continuum in which certain elements, traits, or attributes persist over a considerable period of time within a relatively restricted geographical area. Recognizing technological continuity through time and across space also allows the archaeologist to identify technological discontinuities in the interpretation of processes of culture change. Only with the aid of precise definitions, perceptions of morphological, temporal and spatial relationships with known types, and large numbers of specimens associated with substantiated time-space contexts can we recognize the discontinuity of intrusive technological elements. Hypotheses derived from this concept may be tested, and the limits of their utility in terms of prediction and/or control may be established and, subsequently, replaced by hypotheses of greater utility.

Following the work of Coe (1964), a continuum of stemmed projectile point manufacture, referred to as the "Piedmont Tradition," can be recognized (Oliver 1981). This tradition of projectile point manufacture, based on current stratigraphic, typological, and attribute data, appears to begin during the Paleoindian period (ca. 10,000 B.C.), continues through the Archaic period, and abruptly terminates during the early ceramic period (ca. 500 B.C.). At this time, it is replaced by an intrusive triangular point tradition. A continuum of triangular manufacture is then recognizable stratigraphically and typologically well into historic times.

The Piedmont Tradition

The Piedmont Tradition of lithic manufacture appears to begin as a regionalized technological modification of Paleoindian projectile point style. Many of the oldest projectile points recovered from excavated contexts in North Carolina have facial fluting or thinning, which " . . . in cases where the side-notches or basal portions were missing, . . . could be mistaken for fluted points of the Paleo-Indian period" (Coe 1964:120). The earliest of these point types (Figure 10-1a), identified as the Hardaway Blade (Coe 1964:64), is consistently recovered from the lowest depths of the Hardaway site (31ST4). At Hardaway, the Hardaway Blade is associated with a distinctive unifacial side-scraper (Figure 10-2a), which is morphologically identical to those found at many sites traditionally recognized as Paleoindian (Coe 1981, personal communication).

Since fluted Clovis-like points have been recovered from disturbed

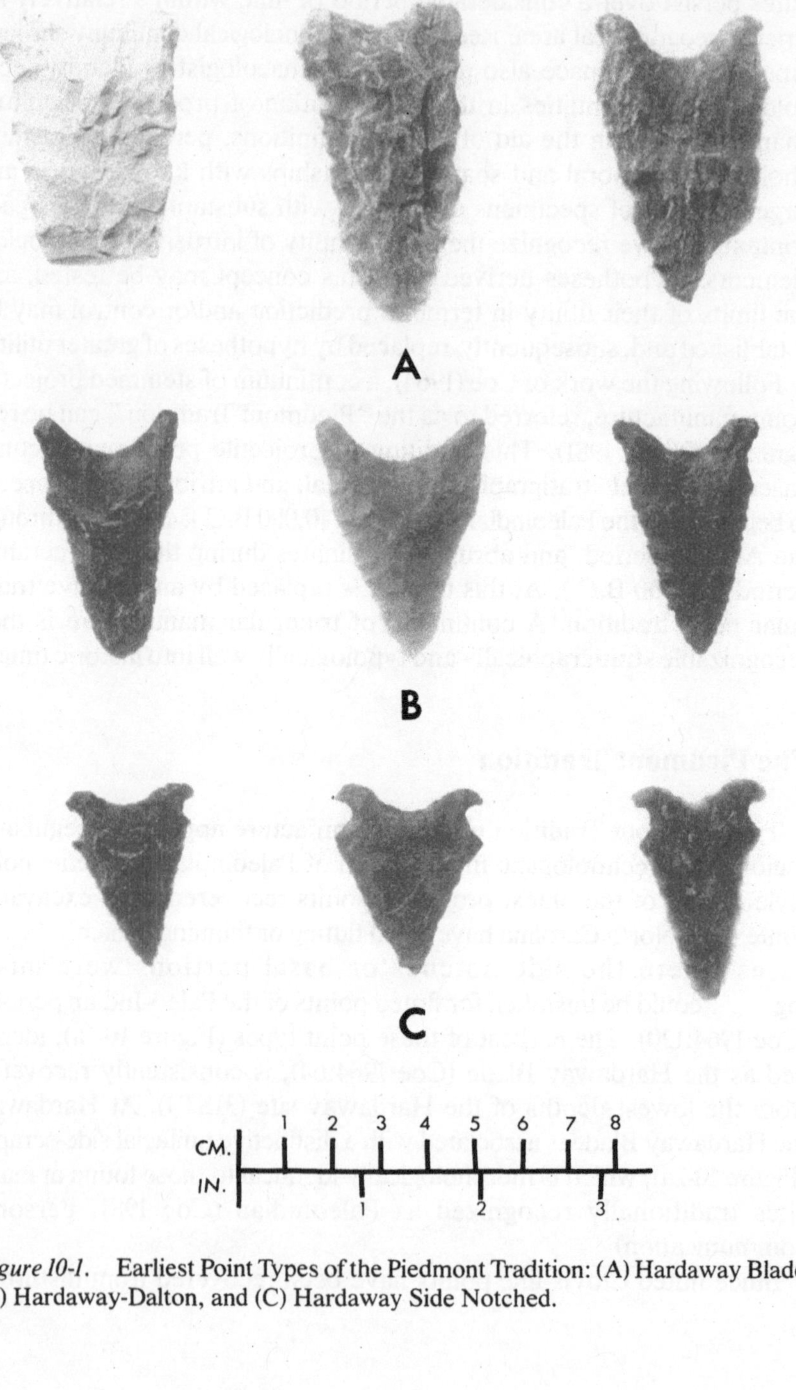

Figure 10-1. Earliest Point Types of the Piedmont Tradition: (A) Hardaway Blade, (B) Hardaway-Dalton, and (C) Hardaway Side Notched.

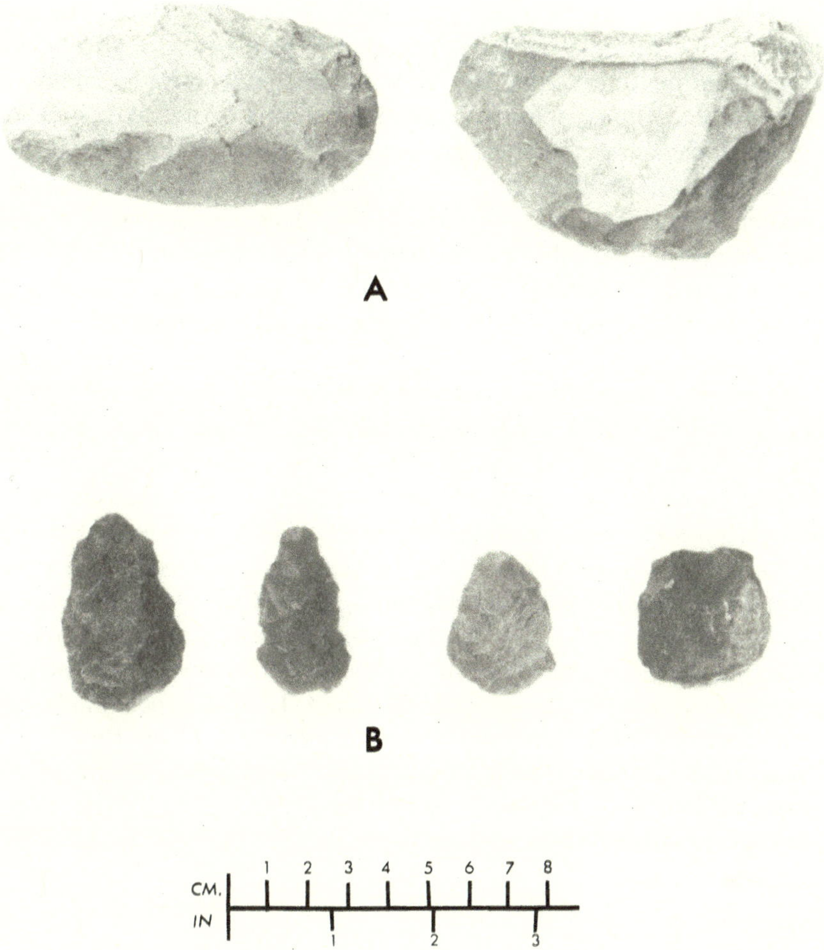

Figure 10-2. Characteristic Scrapers of the Hardaway and Palmer Complexes: (A) Hardaway Side-Scraper, and (B) Palmer Scraper.

contexts at the Hardaway site (Coe 1964:120), and because the Hardaway scraper complex is typically Paleoindian, the Hardaway Blade may reflect an early change in adaptive strategy for the southern Piedmont region. This possibility is strengthened by continued diminution of point size through time as the Hardaway Blade evolved into the Hardaway-Dalton (Figure 10-1b), the Hardaway-Dalton evolved (Figure 10-1c) into the Hardaway Side Notched (Coe 1964:67), and the Hardaway Side Notched evolved into the Palmer Corner-Notched type (Figure 10-3a). It is interesting to note that many Hardaway points have facial fluting, and that one Palmer point was reworked from a Clovis-like point. Although unifacial side-scrapers are associated with the Hardaway types, (Figure 10-2a), small, snub-nosed end-scrapers characterize the succeeding Palmer complex (Figure 10-2b). This characteristic Palmer scraper, morphologically similar to those recovered from many late Paleoindian sites, and the Palmer point type distinguish the Palmer complex from the preceding Hardaway complex (cf. Coe 1964:122).

In a large sample of projectile points, one can easily recognize the progression of the Hardaway Side-Notched into the Palmer Corner-Notched type. Although size is generally quite comparable between the two, the side-notches of the Hardaway type evolved into narrow, U-shaped corner-notches in the Palmer type. Although bases continued to be ground in the Palmer type, the bases seldom exhibited any degree of concavity. Straight, thoroughly ground bases are one of the most characteristic attributes of the Palmer type (Coe 1964:67), and it seems likely that emphasis placed on the extent of basal grinding may have led to the development of the straight base of the Palmer from the concave base of the Hardaway Side-Notched. In both types, blades are small and triangular, generally with straight lateral edges. Bevelling is occasionally found in the Hardaway types, but occurs more frequently in the Palmer type. Palmer Corner-Notched blades often exhibit deep serrations, which appear to have been made at the conclusion of production (Coe 1964:67).

The Piedmont Tradition of lithic manufacture continued as the Palmer Corner-Notched evolved (Figure 10-3b) into the Kirk Corner-Notched type (Coe 1964:69–70). At this time, there is a notable increase in the size of projectile points, which may be related to an increased emphasis on percussion flaking as the primary method of manufacture. Whereas Palmer points show considerable pressure flaking, this technique was used on Kirk Corner-Notched points only to shape edges, notches, and serrations (Coe 1964:67–70). The large triangular blades of the Kirk type were begun with broad, shallow percussion flakes, edges were shaped by pressure flaking and finished with deep serrations. Bases were not ground and corner-notches gradually became broader and less pronounced as the Kirk Corner Notched evolved (Figure 10-3c) into

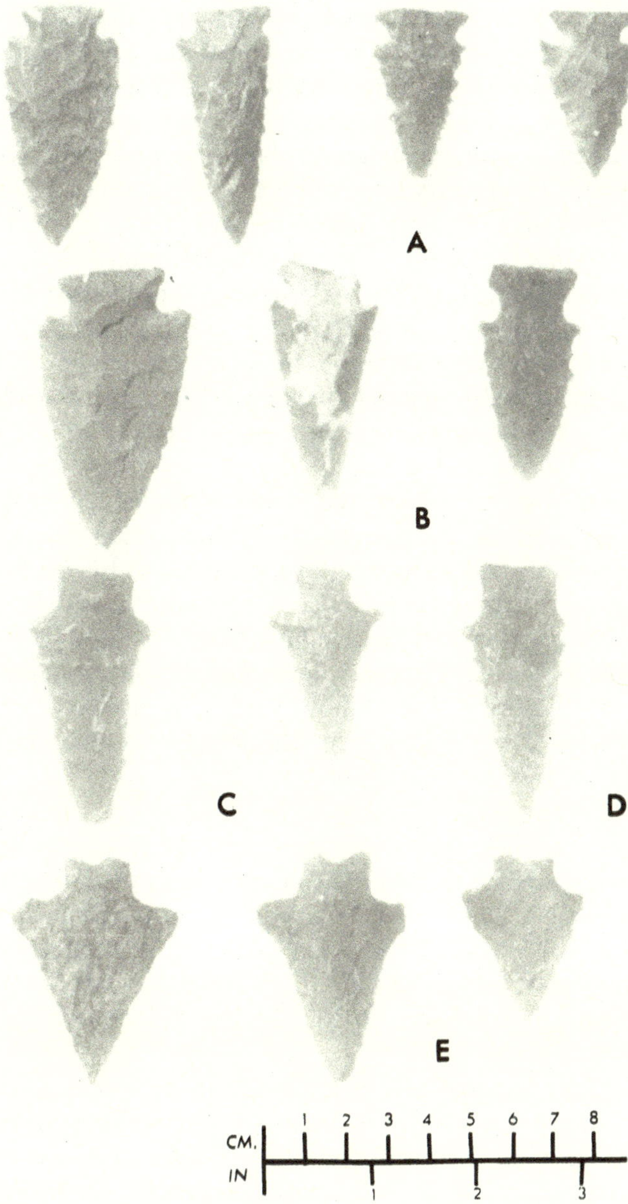

Figure 10-3. Late Paleoindian and Early Archaic Projectile Point Types of the Piedmont Tradition: (A) Palmer Corner Notched, (B) Kirk Corner Notched, (C) Kirk Stemmed, (D) Kirk Serrated, and (E) Stanly Stemmed.

the Kirk Stemmed type (Coe 1964:70). The blade was made narrower, bevelling was decreased, and deep serrations were continued as the broad notches of the Kirk Stemmed were changed into the straight, nearly square stem (Figure 10-3d) of the Kirk Serrated type (Coe 1964: 70–72).

Coe's (1964:70) original estimate of the age of the Kirk type projectile points as 6000–5000 B.C. appears to have been somewhat conservative. Recent investigations in eastern Tennessee have identified deeply buried Kirk components that consistently date to between 7500 and 6700 B.C. (Chapman 1977:21, 123–124), and investigations in West Virginia (Broyles 1971) and Virginia (Gardner 1974; Benthall 1978) provide dates of about 7800 B.C. for what appear to be Kirk components. This growing body of data strongly suggests greater antiquity for the Kirk, Palmer, and Hardaway complexes than previously had been acknowledged.

The Kirk Serrated type evolved into the Stanly Stemmed type (Figure 10-3e) as the straight, square stem of the Kirk Serrated became smaller and developed a shallow incurvature of the base. Blades became broader and more triangular in shape (Coe 1964:35). Although bases were thinned, there was no basal grinding. True bifurcated points are infrequent in the Piedmont. They are more numerous in the mountainous western part of North Carolina, however, and appear to represent a divergent outgrowth of the Kirk type. This interpretation recently has been elaborated on by Chapman (1975b).

The larger points of the Stanly Stemmed type blend with the smaller points of the succeeding Savannah River Stemmed type (Figure 10-4), and although no stratigraphic evidence of an intermediate type between the Stanly and Savannah River types has been identified, Benthall's (1978) Cedar Creek type (ca. 3780 B.C.) may represent this transition both stratigraphically and typologically. It is hoped that future work will provide much needed information on this Middle-to-Late Archaic development.

The Savannah River Stemmed type (Figure 10-4) represents a departure from the general trend of the Piedmont Tradition types to decrease in size through time. The shift to larger, broader, and heavier projectile points may again reflect an emphasis on percussion flaking as the primary method of manufacture, but also may indicate a technological modification to a particular type of spear or spear-thrower.

Figure 10-4. Savannah River Stemmed Projectile Points.

Experimental results indicate that broad, heavy projectiles, when attached to spears between 5 and 7 feet in length, will considerably increase the distance of a throw without greatly affecting accuracy (Van Buren 1974:30–31).

If, because of increasing population densities during the Archaic, forests became more open, plant foods would have become more abundant and habitats beneficial to a variety of game species (e.g., deer, bear, turkey, rabbit, and squirrel) would have increased. As these open forest areas were expanded through the activities of man, changes in hunting strategy may have been required. For example, greater distance between the hunter and the hunted would have altered the effectiveness of projectile trajectory, velocity, and accuracy. The Savannah River Stemmed projectile point, therefore, because of its increased size and weight, may represent a technological modification to provide greater throwing distance without loss of velocity or accuracy.

Coe (1964:123–124) proposed a "discontinuity" between the Savannah River Stemmed and large triangular points (Badin and Vincent types) in the Carolina Piedmont sequence. Although recent analysis indicates a minor continuation of stemmed points into the early ceramic period in the Piedmont Province, they continued to be made for a much longer time in the Blue Ridge Province (Oliver 1981).

In both the Piedmont and Blue Ridge provinces, the Savannah River Stemmed type evolved into a Small Savannah River Stemmed type (South 1959:153–157; Oliver 1981:181–183) as overall size decreased and blades became more triangular (Figure 10-5). In many ways, the Small Savannah River type may be considered a variety of the Savannah River Stemmed. However, since the small version is consistently found in the upper portions of the Savannah River zone at a number of stratified North Carolina sites (e.g., Doerschuk, Warren Wilson, Gaston, and Gashes Creek), it appears to be a temporal marker for the latter part of the Late Archaic Savannah River phase.

The Small Savannah River Stemmed evolved into the Gypsy Stemmed type (Oliver 1981:188–189) (Figure 10-6), as size continued to decrease, and resource materials became more diverse. Craftsmanship often appears quite crude, and in some instances may be related to the increased diversity and differential qualities of resource materials. At Piedmont sites (e.g., Doerschuk, Gaston, and Thelma) the Gypsy Stemmed is found in early ceramic zones (Badin and Vincent phases),

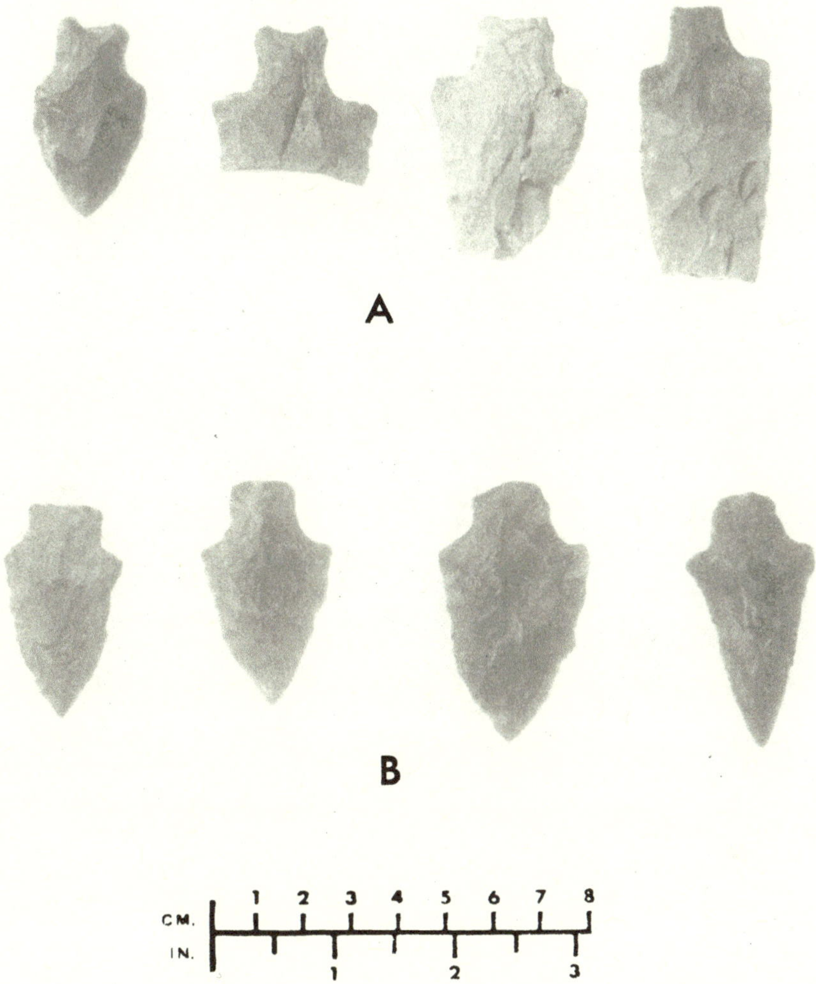

Figure 10-5. Small Savannah River Stemmed Projectile Points: (A) Doerschuk Site, and (B) Warren Wilson Site.

where it is associated with cord- and fabric-marked ceramics and large triangular projectile points (Badin and Vincent types). At the Warren Wilson site, situated in the Blue Ridge Province, the Gypsy Stemmed is again identified within the early ceramic zone (Swannanoa phase),

Figure 10-6. Gypsy Stemmed Projectile Points.

Figure 10-7. Swannanoa Stemmed Projectile Points.

which has cord- and fabric-marked ceramics and large triangular projectile points (Garden Creek and Transylvania types). These points are also associated with soapstone sherds and a similar stemmed point identified by Keel (1976:196–198) as Swannanoa Stemmed (Figure 10-7). The Swannanoa Stemmed type, which appears to be a lineal descendant of the Gypsy Stemmed, represents the terminal expression of the Piedmont Tradition of lithic manufacture. In both the Piedmont and Blue Ridge provinces, a continuum of triangular point manufacture begins after the initial appearance of triangular points during the early ceramic period. Stemmed points are no longer present, and technological discontinuity is evinced stratigraphically.

Assuming that the early ceramic phases (Badin, Vincent, and Swannanoa) are roughly equivalent in time, a comparison of the frequencies of stemmed points to large triangular points at sites in each province reveals an important difference. In the Piedmont sites, 95.1 percent (n = 143) of the points recovered from early ceramic zones are of the large triangular type, while at the Warren Wilson site in the Blue Ridge Province, only 5.4 percent (n = 130) are large triangular points.

The high frequency of triangular points within the early ceramic zones at the Piedmont sites and the low frequency of similar types in the Blue Ridge Province seem to indicate an earlier introduction to, and quite rapid acceptance of, the triangular point technology by Piedmont groups. Similarly, the higher frequency of Gypsy Stemmed and Swannanoa Stemmed points at Warren Wilson suggests a longer continuation of the Piedmont Tradition in that area. These relative frequencies and distributions suggest an hypothesis. Assuming that the triangular point technology was diffused from the Northeast, since earlier occurrences of triangular points are found there (e.g., Ritchie 1969:32–34, 216; Tuck 1978:35), somewhat later introductions of the triangular point type should occur in areas south of North Carolina. These southern areas should also exhibit longer continuations of their traditional lithic technology. Conversely, areas to the north of North Carolina should evince an earlier introduction of the triangular point type. This perspective does not imply a flood-like diffusion, but rather a meandering diffusion along preexisting networks of communication and exchange.

Some support for this hypothesis is found in the work of Claflin (1931) and Bullen and Greene (1970) at Stallings Island, Georgia. Claflin (1931:38) observed that only four triangular projectile points were identified from the hundreds he found, and noted that "the dearth of this type of point is interesting, due to the fact that it is a common form throughout the Savannah River Valley." Of the nearly 200 points recovered by Bullen and Greene (1970:15), only one was triangular, a very small point that probably was associated with a much later occupation. In both investigations, the overwhelming majority of points recovered appears to be variations of the Savannah River, Small Savannah River, and Gypsy Stemmed types, which occur in a stratigraphic and typological continuum similar to that in North Carolina.

One may reasonably assume that the termination of the Piedmont Tradition, the appearance of the triangular point type, and the subsequent stratigraphic continuum of triangular point manufacture signal the introduction of the bow-and-arrow in the Southern Piedmont. It cannot be stated with certainty that there is a one-to-one correspondence of triangular points and use of the bow-and-arrow, yet one can document historic usage of small triangular points hafted on arrows at the Coweeta Creek site (31MA34) in Macon County, North Carolina, the stratigraphic evolution of small triangular points from larger forms (see Coe 1964:110–111, 119, 124), the absence of atlatl weights and stemmed points after the appearance of triangular points during the early ceramic period (Coe 1964:123–124), and the earlier appearance of triangular points in the Northeast (Ritchie 1969:32–34, 216; Tuck 1978:35) and in the Arctic Denbigh complex (Griffin 1966:286). These observations suggest that points of the Piedmont Tradition and triangular points represent different but co-occurring technologies within the same stratigraphic contexts in North Carolina, that the Piedmont Tradition terminates during the early ceramic period, and that the introduction of triangular points begins a new continuum of development.

Conclusions

The Piedmont Tradition (Figure 10-8) represents a lineal development of projectile point manufacture, which was passed from generation to generation in such a way that certain basic attributes persisted through time within a restricted geographical area. This tradition of manufacture, which emphasized stemmed points, appears to have begun as a regionalized technological modification of preexisting Paleoindian styles and developed through time until it was abruptly replaced by a triangular point technology during the early ceramic period. A continuum of triangular point manufacture is then recognized well into historic times.

A relationship between time, space, and context is necessary if one expects to go beyond categorization and provide meaningful behavioral interpretations. To extract meaning from projectile point types requires the recognition of traditions of lithic manufacture. The exact meaning of any particular projectile point is forever lost, but by viewing projectile points as products of a continuum of development, archaeologists may yet " . . . extract meaning from the cold, hard stones of reality" (Coe 1975:232).

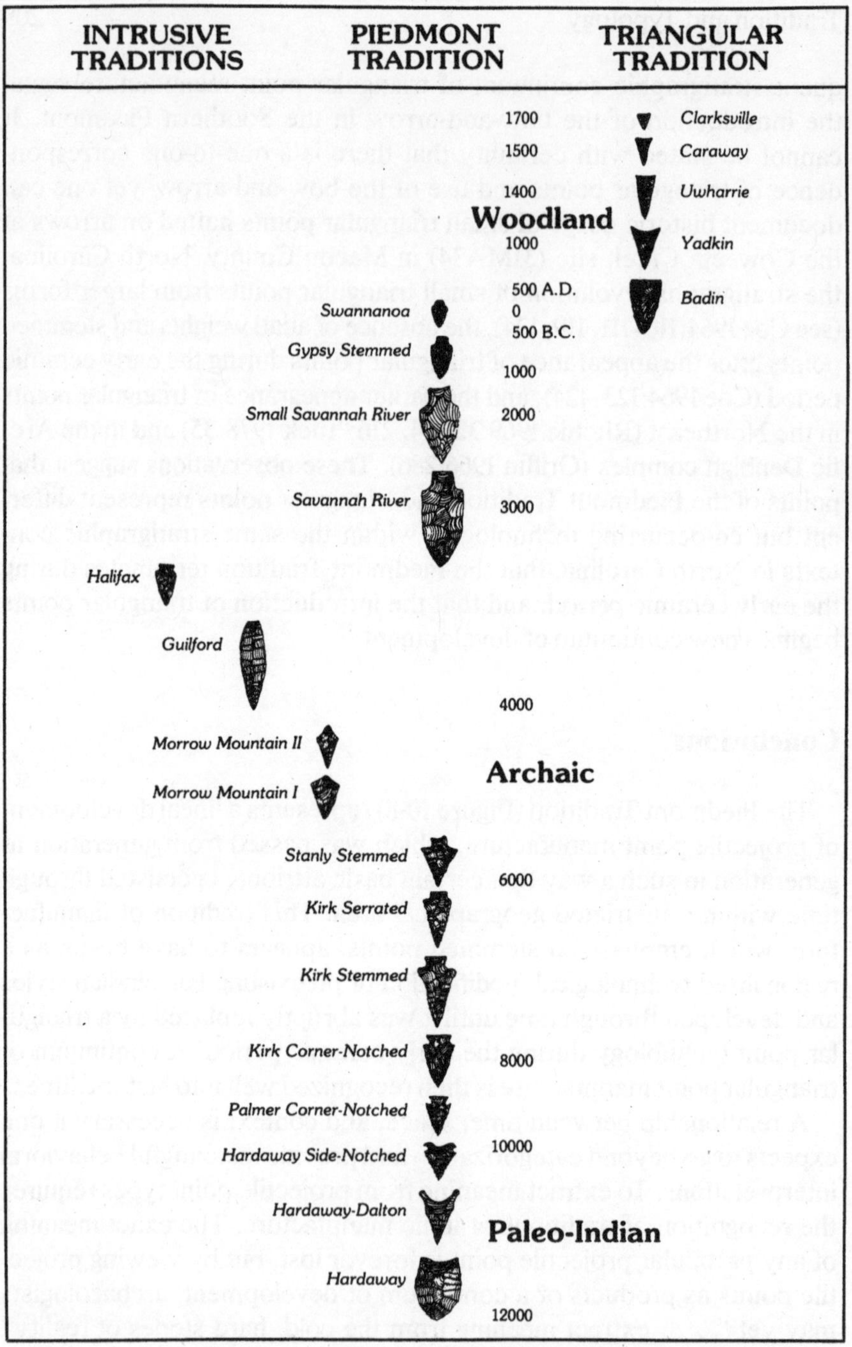

Figure 10-8. Projectile Point Traditions of the Piedmont and Blue Ridge Provinces.

Acknowledgments

I have no adequate means to demonstrate my deep gratitude for all Joffre Coe has taught me, and the patience he has shown during my "formative" years. Perhaps the contents of this discussion will reflect a mixture of his teachings and my own thoughts. I sincerely believe that Joffre Coe wants all his students to "stand on their own two feet" in the field of archaeology, to refine old ideas, and yet to develop new perspectives that will be meaningful and based on firm foundations. I could not ask for better instruction than that which he has provided.

11 · KIT W. WESLER

Model and Sequence in the Maryland Archaic

Introduction

The Archaic period in Maryland has not been a major interest of archaeologists in the eastern United States. Three decades ago, Schmitt (1952) had very few data on which to draw in presenting a pre-Woodland chronology of the Chesapeake region. In the years since, a body of indigenous and comparative data has accrued. Although these data may not be sufficient to provide definitive answers to questions of Archaic cultural development, they at least suggest profitable directions and valuable perspectives in which research might be conducted.

Much of the recent work in Maryland has been pursued within the framework of contract archaeology, and has favored survey far more than excavation. As a result, working models have emphasized settlement patterns, geared toward the practicalities of predicting site locations. More generally, the perspective has been one of exploring the relationships of humans to their environments.

In evaluating current models of Archaic lifeways, one encounters problems with existing reconstructions of paleoenvironment and cultural chronology. Data for approaching both problems in Maryland show important gaps, and critical evaluation of the evidence must continue to be a fundamental concern. This chapter attempts to summarize current views on environmental change and cultural sequences in Maryland, and to suggest the roles of inference and analogy in the construction of models applicable to Archaic subsistence and settlement.

Paleoenvironmental Reconstruction

Recent models of cultural development in Maryland have had an important basis in increasingly thorough reconstructions of past environments. The major emphases have been on the changing climate of

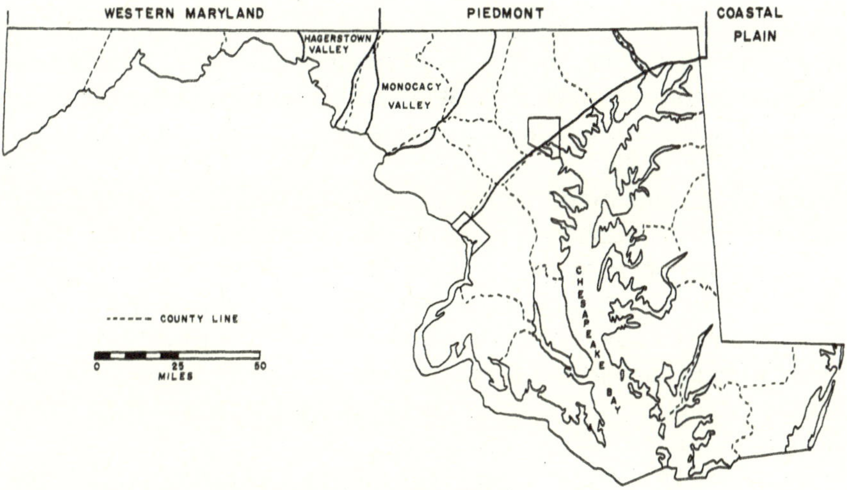

Figure 11-1. Geographic Provinces of Maryland.

the Pleistocene and Holocene, especially as expressed in the character of the vegetation, and on the regional geomorphology as affected by the formation of the Chesapeake Bay (Figure 11-1). Both problems are highly complex, but a growing body of data allows continual refinement of environmental reconstruction and of inferences about the ecology of prehistoric populations.

Relict drainage patterns lying under present Chesapeake Bay (Schubel and Zabawa 1972) demonstrate that, during the low sea stands of the Wisconsin and previous glaciations, the central coastal plain of Maryland was occupied by a broad valley of the ancestral Susquehanna River. By analogy with the Delaware, the mouth of the ancient Susquehanna was a tidal estuary by 8000 B.C. (Kraft 1976). Data reported by Kraft (1976; Kraft and John 1978) on local relative sea level rise in the Delaware Bay may be applied in general to the Chesapeake, although core borings from the mouth of the latter indicate that tectonic warping would have resulted in local variation (Harrison et al. 1965).

Since the Susquehanna River must have maintained an open channel to the Atlantic Ocean, sea level rise gradually would have inundated the river valley. The exact timing of this process is still in doubt, and studies currently underway on Patuxent River cores (Wayne Clark, personal communication 1979) will be very informative. The rapidity of sea level rise before 3000 B.C. (Kraft 1976), however, implies that biotic communities may not have stabilized until after that date. Radiocarbon dates on shell middens in the upper Chesapeake suggest aboriginal use of oysters soon after 4000 B.C. (Wilke and Thompson 1974), though the reported data leave the cultural associations of these dates unclear. It may be inferred that oysters would have been available progressively earlier toward the mouth of the bay. On the Atlantic Coast, shoreline and barrier reef morphology probably was much like that of today (Kraft 1976), leaving open the possibility of quite early exploitation of oyster beds. But the steep walls of the lower river valley (Hack 1957), which suggest a shore morphology much like that of the present upper bay, along with the rapidity of marine transgression, probably prevented the stabilization of marsh environments until the Late Archaic (cf. Newman and Rusnak 1965).

Thus, though continued inundation has resulted in further transgression of shorelines, the broad patterns of estuarine and marshland environments probably settled into their modern relationships during the Late Archaic period. The most thorough study of past environments in the Middle Atlantic is by Carbone (1976). His focus is the Shenandoah Valley, but he discusses comparative data from elsewhere in the region. His use of the square-wave model (Wendland and Bryson 1974) is open to argument (cf. Watts 1979), but his general scheme is applicable to the western portions of Maryland.

Briefly, Carbone (1976) suggests that the area had a full-glacial environment until about 10,700 B.C. Other investigators agree that the vegetation was characterized by an open forest-parkland, "marked by stands of spruce, . . . mingled with dwarf shrubs, especially dwarf birch, and by wet meadows with tall herbs. Probably some local stands of more obviously tundra-like vegetation were also present" (Watts 1979:460). During the late glacial period, this mosaic pattern continued, with open tundra areas reduced by encroachment of a boreal spruce-pine woodland (Carbone 1976). Coastal areas (Figure 11-1) probably contained a similar open and mixed vegetation during the glacial period (Carbone 1976).

In the mountain regions (Figure 11-1), Carbone (1976) proposes a "mesic stage" lasting from about 6200 to 3000 B.C. Watts (1979) suggests a "Hypsithermal" interval at about the same time. The pollen samples are characterized by maxima in the percentages of hemlock, followed by oak. The major aspect of these forests is dominance by oak (Carbone 1976). A subsequent "xeric stage," lasting until about 1200 B.C., saw a rise in hickory, though oak was still dominant in the early part of the period (Carbone 1976). Chestnut, slowest of the major species to migrate northward, was present by the beginning of this period (Watts 1979).

Comparable data for the piedmont of Virginia or Maryland do not exist, and pollen samples from farther north are difficult to apply here due to early tundra conditions (e.g., Martin 1958). Nor is it evident that rising sea level had much influence on piedmont or western environments. It is likely that the inundation of the Chesapeake Bay was felt in changing stream gradients, flow characteristics, and water tables. However, interior coastal plain swamps, such as Zekiah, may have been little affected by sea levels (Hack 1957:828). Further data are needed to interpret these areas.

There are a number of pollen sequences from the Middle Atlantic coastal plain (Owens et al. 1974; Florer 1972; Harrison et al. 1965; Whitehead 1972; Watts 1979), and Edwards and Merrill (1977) have provided a chronological scheme for climatic change. Spruce declined toward the end of the glacial period, and sometime between 8000 and 7000 B.C. there was a sharp increase in oak. Since about 7000 B.C., all of the pollen sequences, except where local edaphic factors in the formation of Dismal Swamp interfere (Whitehead 1972), demonstrate remarkable consistency in the oak-dominated forest cover. An early maximum of hemlock can be discerned, then a modern oak-hickory forest becomes established and is maintained until major disruption by recent human activity. Microenvironmental variation undoubtedly accompanied changes in precipitation, temperature gradients, and water tables, but an oak-hickory forest assemblage appears to persist in the uplands of the coastal plain after perhaps 6000 B.C.

Boreal fauna were present during the late glacial period, but data on paleofaunal assemblages are few. The most diverse assemblage comes from Saltville, Virginia, where a number of extinct megafauna were recovered (Ray et al. 1967). Mastodon are known from several sites, including the continental shelf (Whitmore et al. 1967; Dreimanis 1968; Guilday and Berman 1969). Carbone (1976) suggests that an essentially modern fauna was present by 7300 B.C.

In broad patterns, these environmental sequences set the background for studies of human paleoecology. Microenvironmental variation has yet to be reconstructed in detail for most areas, as the range of data with which Carbone approached the Shenandoah Valley is not duplicated from coastal plain or piedmont settings. One important element that is quite clear, however, is the inundation of early sites in the lower Susquehanna drainage, perhaps severely biasing the data base until at least the Late Archaic. Comparison of environmental and cultural chronologies is necessary for the interpretation of current models of the Archaic period.

Cultural Chronology

The cultural chronology of the Paleoindian and Archaic periods in Maryland is largely based on those of nearby regions, particularly the typological sequences of projectile point styles established to the north and south. Few stratified sites have been excavated and fully reported around the Chesapeake Bay, so that morphological similarities and chronological estimates of diagnostic projectile point styles are the primary dating tool. In essence, these are analogies, and controlled data from the local region are badly needed to add precision to Maryland studies.

The major effect of this lack of local, controlled samples is a proliferation of type names, often incompletely referenced or described. Type names are borrowed from sequences as far away as Oklahoma, or they are simply invented, and the result is grand confusion (see Oliver, this volume).

In large part, the problem is similar to that which Wobst (1978) has called "the tyranny of the ethnographic record." Wobst suggests that archaeologists, like ethnographers, tend to create bounded culture areas by working in widely separated localities. We tend to establish centralizing typologies to which specimens from other areas are cursorily compared. In areas between those with established sequences, type definitions may be applied without appreciation for stylistic continua; thus variation may be misunderstood, and an "in-between" area may be seen as a boundary or a zone of mixture, even of ecological competition, instead of a geographical transition.

Maryland is just such a nether region, where researchers are forced

Table 11-1. Schematic Summary of a Postulated Cultural and Environmental Sequence for Maryland.

Years B.C.	Period	Environment: mountains	Environment: coastal plain	Marker projectile points
1,000				Dry Brook
		Xeric—		
2,000	LATE	rise in		Holmes
		hickory	oak-	
3,000	ARCHAIC	----------------------	hickory	Vernon
		Mesic/	forest	
4,000	————————	Hypsithermal:		Piscataway
		oak		Morrow
5,000	MIDDLE	dominance,		Mountain
	ARCHAIC	early hem-	----------------------	
6,000	————————	lock max.	maximum in	Guilford
		----------------------	hemlock,	
7,000	EARLY	encroaching	spruce declining	Stanly
	ARCHAIC	boreal	----------------------	Bifurcates
8,000	————————	forest,	open	Kirk
		some open	spruce-pine	Palmer
9,000	PALEO-	tundra	forest	Hardaway Side-
	INDIAN			notched
10,000				Hardaway-
				Dalton
11,000		----------------------	----------------------	Mid-Paleo
		Full glacial:		Clovis
		spruce parkland		

to use Coe's (1964) sequence from North Carolina and Ritchie's (1961, 1969) sequence from New York, and others, as investigators search farther afield for "types" similar to their local specimens. A model based on stylistic and spatial continuity, which included variability within a type, would permit the construction of a single basic sequence. Table 11-1 presents a distilled projectile point sequence for coastal and piedmont Maryland. The sequence is tentative, and must be applied cautiously to western Maryland.

The Paleoindian, Early Archaic, and Middle Archaic sequences are based on Coe's (1964) pioneering work in piedmont North Carolina, as confirmed and refined for areas closer to Maryland by Broyles (1971) at St. Albans and Gardner (1974) at the Flint Run Complex. Later types are drawn from descriptions by Stephenson (1963) and Kinsey (1972). Only the Holmes type (Gardner 1976:35–36) has not been described fully in the published literature. This point is closely related to Ritchie's (1961) Bare Island and Poplar Island types, and Stephenson's (1963) Bare Island and Clagett complexes. Use of the Holmes type is tentative, pending formal description.

Space limitations preclude a full explanation of the reasoning behind this particular sequence. Such a discussion will need to be presented elsewhere (Wesler in press). The sequence in Table 11-1, however, will serve as a consistent scheme on which to focus the following discussion, as well as a proposal for a more coherent model for general consideration.

Models

Recent work in the Middle Atlantic region has emphasized models of subsistence and settlement patterns. Most of the data have resulted from survey work in an environmental/ecological perspective, and reporting of recovered materials is steadily improving. There are several problems, however, inherent in attempts to construct "subsistence-settlement" models, especially when the data base consists overwhelmingly of surface collections.

A settlement model requires spatial data, particularly on the distribution of sites at local and regional scales. Difficulties arise in Maryland from the loss of shoreline and river-bank sites through erosion, floodplain aggradation, historic construction, and, on a grand scale in the coastal plain, the inundation of the lower Susquehanna drainage. Especially for the Archaic period, we must be wary that settlement patterns inferred from distributions of known sites may be truncated upland constructs.

Furthermore, emphasis on diachronic settlement models has led to attempts to establish "phases" of short duration, generally based on particular styles of projectile points. These chronological schemes, of course, can only be as good as the typologies. As noted above, there has been a tendency to merge regional sequences, without critical discussion of the implications or of working definitions of the typology employed (e.g., Hoffman and Foss 1980). In the absence of a reliable chronology, the assignment of surface sites to temporal positions of short duration is uncertain, and the use of sites so "dated" to construct "settlement patterns" for each "phase" may be quite misleading.

Again, since many of the models are largely based on surface sites, the "subsistence" aspect of the hypotheses often relies on tenuous inference. Reports on ethnobotanical remains from Maryland sites of the Archaic period are scarce, and are exemplified by Ayers' (1972) note of the presence of charred hickory shell in a piedmont site. As a consequence, much subsistence modeling is predicated on inference based on the environmental situation of a single site. It is hoped that ethnobotanical and faunal remains will be forthcoming to provide badly needed direct evidence of prehistoric subsistence practices.

On a general level, valuable insights into Paleoindian and Archaic ecological orientations already are beginning to emerge. Although fluted points are still predominantly isolated surface finds, they tend to cluster in characteristic situations. On the Delmarva coastal plain, Thomas (1974, 1976) has noted that Paleoindian sites tend to be associated with ponds and sinks, or otherwise poorly drained areas likely to have been water sources in the early post-Pleistocene. Paleoindian sites in New Jersey are similarly associated with pingos (Cavallo 1979). Of the three Paleoindian sites in Delaware that have yielded more than isolated projectile points, one is near a swamp, but the other two are near jasper quarries (Thomas 1976).

The importance of cryptocrystalline lithic sources has been a prime focus of Gardner's work (1974, 1978, 1980a, 1980b). He suggests that Paleoindian groups were oriented to quarry areas, outcrops of suitable rock in the Blue Ridge and deposits of cryptocrystalline cobbles in the coastal plain. "Away from these outcrops, reported sites and projectile points drop off markedly" (Gardner 1980a:4). He postulates a nomadic round in which groups return regularly to the quarry from the hunting hinterland (Gardner 1974).

The thin scatter of fluted projectile points and the analogy of Eastern Clovis to the western model, where groups seem to have been adapted to the hunting of migratory herd animals, has led to a general assumption of free-ranging nomadism for eastern Paleoindians. Gardner (1974,

1980a, 1980b) reasonably suggests that this characterization is less suitable for groups in the southeastern woodlands, who may have been more locally oriented than has often been suspected. In the north, Paleoindian groups may well have been geared to hunting caribou herds, but further south, where forests were heavier, they probably were adapted to a relatively generalized foraging pattern, with an emphasis on hunting forest game (Gardner 1980b:21; cf. Brose 1978:729).

Gardner (1974) proposes that his Flint Run complex represents a continuity of the Palmer and Kirk phase adaptive patterns from those of the Paleoindians. In part, this is based on continued preference for cryptocrystalline lithics, which he infers would maintain the postulated focus on quarry areas. Such sites as Hardaway (Coe 1964) clearly support continuities from the Paleoindian well into the Middle Archaic.

Data from eastern Tennessee also demonstrate continuity of ethnobotanical and artifactual assemblages from Kirk to bifurcate levels. At Rose Island, Chapman (1975) performed flotation on soil samples. From the Early Archaic zones, he reports hickory and acorn shells in large proportion, with small amounts of butternut shell and honey locust seed. These data, as well as those from the Shawnee-Minisink site in the Delaware Valley (Kauffman and Dent 1978), indicate very early exploitation of vegetable foods.

Chapman (1975b) also points out that the four known large sites of the bifurcate tradition, including the St. Albans and Rose Island sites, are found on alluvial terraces. Kavanagh (1980) reports a site on the Monocacy River that produced nine St. Albans points, a high enough number to suggest that this site was another base camp. Based on this evidence, Chapman has revised the general model held by most archaeologists that Early Archaic sites are located in upland settings (see Chapman, this volume). If Gardner's thesis of continuity from Paleoindian to Archaic holds, then a terrace-oriented base camp pattern can be pushed backwards in time. In his Potomac River (inner coastal plain) sample, Gardner (1978) notes that the number of Early Archaic sites diminishes with distance from the river, but it is not clear whether this trend is a function of his cobble-quarry model, Chapman's river terrace model, or simply site preservation factors. Stewart (1980), working in the Hagerstown Valley, finds that his Paleoindian materials were recovered in floodplain, alluvial fan, and low terrace settings, especially near soils that indicate swampy conditions in the early post-Pleistocene.

A reasonable model for Paleoindian and early Early Archaic patterns, then, should integrate Gardner's suggestion of generalized foraging with a hunting emphasis and Chapman's model of base camps in riverine settings. Cryptocrystalline materials do seem to have been preferred by Paleoindian and Early Archaic groups in the Chesapeake area, at least into Kirk times, and intimate knowledge of these resources may be inferred. There is no apparent reason why only a central quarry should have been known to each group; the concentration of materials around quarries may represent long-term nodes of activity rather than foci of restricted localities. Base camps in riverine settings may have been the other main focus of activities, where hunting and foraging resources would have been most plentiful. Gardner's (1980b) recent term, "Primary Open Forest Efficiency," with its inherent reference to Caldwell's (1958) original formulation, seems quite apt.

By the late Early Archaic period, marked by the bifurcate tradition, the open forest would have been shifting toward a more deciduous association in the mountains, and approaching the modern forest types in the coastal plain. Concurrently, as Gardner (1978) has noted, there was a lesser emphasis on cryptocrystalline lithic materials, and thus on quarries, in favor of more locally available materials such as quartzite. Stewart (1980) proposes a shift to rhyolite in the Hagerstown Valley. In North Carolina, Coe (1964) finds an increase in quarry blanks beginning in the Kirk levels and continuing in later phases, which would also imply progressively less reliance on settlement near quarries.

This trend continues into the Middle Archaic, in which period Gardner (1978, 1980a) notes use of a greater diversity of lithic materials, many locally available. In the Hagerstown Valley, Stewart (1980) has evidence for a continuing rise in the use of rhyolite, and infers an increase in the exploitation of Blue Ridge microenvironments. Data from this area and from the Monocacy Valley of the western piedmont (Kavanagh 1980) indicate a trend away from the main rivers, with more sites on smaller streams. This would imply exploitation of more varied settings, perhaps with more seasonality, larger populations, or both. Stewart (1980) has noted specifically a lack of Middle Archaic base camps in the Hagerstown Valley, which could again be the result of burial of sites by alluvial deposition. On the inner coastal plain, Gardner's (1978) data suggest that the focus of activity was the edges of inland swamps such as Zekiah, with transitory camps in the uplands. This may be a continuation of early patterns, since an association of Paleoindian sites with swampy areas has been noted already in the Hagerstown Valley (Stewart 1980) and the Delmarva Peninsula (Thomas 1976).

Direct evidence of Middle Archaic subsistence practices is sadly lacking in Maryland. In North Carolina, Coe (1964:80) noted the occurrence of a slab mortar in the Stanly level at Doerschuk, probable evidence for the processing of vegetable foods. Chapman (1977) found that walnut shells first appeared in the Stanly levels in the Tellico sites, as did net sinkers, both suggesting increasing diversity of food sources.

These data argue for an increase in generalized foraging during the Middle Archaic, with campsites scattered more widely and with new foodstuffs incorporated into the diet. Gardner has proposed that this was an adaptation to the deciduous forest environment, which, with a relatively warm climate, would have provided a more diverse natural food supply, though perhaps concurrent forest closure would have reduced deer and elk populations. He offers the term "Primary Closed Forest Efficiency" (1980b) to denote a closely adapted lifeway much like that suggested by Caldwell (1958).

The trend toward forest closure may have continued into the Late Archaic, perhaps reaching mature deciduous forest conditions at a later date in the mountains than on the coastal plain. At the same time, the rise of sea level was slowing, and estuarine and perhaps marshland environments would have been stabilized. By the time of the Broadspear tradition, in most of the coastal and piedmont areas of the Middle Atlantic, there seems to have been an orientation to riverine and estuarine resources, a trend similar to the development of the "Shellmound Archaic" on the Savannah River (Claflin 1931; Fairbanks 1942). Carbon-14 dates on shell mounds in Kent County, Maryland range from 3615 ± 65 to 185 ± 70 B.C. (Wilke and Thompson 1974), or from Late Archaic into Early Woodland.

Late Archaic sites are widely scattered across the Delmarva Peninsula, implying a diverse exploitive strategy (Thomas 1976). Gardner (1978) reports finding Late Archaic materials near the larger streams, with transient camps across the uplands. Fishing implements are noteworthy in the Upper Delaware assemblages, and Kinsey (1975) proposes a generalized foraging pattern with a riverine emphasis through the Late Archaic.

This riverine and estuarine emphasis continued toward the end of the Archaic period. In Delaware, sites with Broadspear and Fishtail associations tend to be larger than earlier sites, and there is a shift to river valleys and especially to the lower reaches of major streams for the largest sites (Thomas 1974, 1976). Larger sites with longer occupation and a river-edge focus also mark the Fishtail tradition sites in the Upper Delaware Valley (Kinsey 1975). Custer (1978) has suggested a climatic change leading to the exploitation of fish runs. He cites as evidence an interpretation of certain posthole patterns as fish-drying racks, suggestions of use of Broadspears as harpoons (Turnbaugh 1975), and an absence of netsinkers in Broadspear sites. The latter, however, is inconsistent with Kinsey's (1972) artifact list, Ritchie's (1969:159) data for the Frost Island phase, and Witthoft's (1953) initial definition of the Broadspear phase. More important, a shift to riverine settings in general, and an earlier Late Archaic tool kit designed for fishing in the Upper Delaware Valley (Kinsey 1975) and New York (Ritchie 1969), suggest that the trend toward emphasis on aquatic resources was already in progress in the northern Middle Atlantic area.

Although most of Ayers' (1972) sites in the Potomac piedmont are on islands and river terraces, he reports a few rock shelters and upland sites. In the Hagerstown Valley, floodplains and low terraces of the larger streams yield evidence of the most intense utilization, though sites are also found on low-order streams and high terraces (Stewart 1980). Although along the Monocacy River, earlier Late Archaic sites show a diversity of locations, a tendency for location near the river is evident during Broadspear and especially during Fishtail times (Kavanagh 1980). Concentration in river zones probably indicates increased exploitation of fish and river mussels, though direct evidence is lacking. Again, Gardner (1980b) suggests a term to describe this ecological orientation, "Primary Riverine-Estuarine Efficiency."

Gardner's terms are deliberate echoes of Caldwell's (1958) original formulation. Caldwell saw a long-term adaptation to local environments, including riverine resources, which culminated in the Late Archaic. To him, the Archaic period was a long process of adjustment, the effect of which was "the establishment of primary forest efficiency" (Caldwell 1958:71). Gardner's (1980b) terms, however, reflect a more detailed understanding of past environments, and a postulate that effective adaptation was the rule throughout the Archaic period. Although cultural development of the period still may be viewed as a continuum, it now seems to represent a set of trends which maintained, rather than produced, adaptive efficiency. At all times, then, local populations took advantage of many foods and other natural resources as they were available. Environmental change from spruce-parkland at the end of the Pleistocene, to closed, oak-dominated forest cover, to relative stabilization of productive riverine and estuarine habitats, was reflected in cultural development from primary open forest, to primary closed forest, to primary riverine–estuarine efficiencies (Gardner 1980b). These may be seen as the overriding trends of the Archaic period prehistory of Maryland, as reflected in material-cultural traditions which have yet to be explored thoroughly in their local manifestations.

Conclusions

This paper has attempted to summarize current perspectives and available data on the Archaic period in Maryland prehistory. It also has made evident large gaps in the data base, and thus in the models by which the data are synthesized. The major thesis presented here is that the projectile point type sequence for Maryland can be simplified and standardized, at least as a working model, and that acceptance of such a scheme can replace the inconsistent use of analogy that resulted in an ill-explained dichotomy between two postulated traditions. Maryland, thus, can be placed in a continuum of material culture, rather than in either a border area or a zone of overlap between regions.

It must be emphasized, however, that the specific type sequence presented is tentative, and should be refined or revised as more data become available. At present, far too much of the evidence comes from surface collections, and the few excavated data from potentially unmixed contexts are either incompletely published or the results of limited tests. Reliance on surface data has created problems of interpretation in almost all aspects of present syntheses of the Archaic period in Maryland. Without controlled samples, projectile point (and other artifact) types have been created without a full understanding of variation within the populations, which in turn has handicapped morphological comparison. Without controlled contexts and demonstrable associations with independently dated materials, chronology must remain approximate and rely on typological analogy.

The definition of archaeological complexes has also been retarded in the Maryland Archaic. Coe's (1964:6, 8) discussion of his revised views on the Guilford and Badin complexes is germane to any assessment of surface assemblages, for example Wright's (1959) Kuykendahl complex in the Upper Potomac region. Like the Kuykendahl focus, and like most sites from which the Maryland data still come, the Badin and Guilford foci were based on surface collections. "It was assumed that, if a significant number of traits were found to occur together on a series of sites, then they were probably the physical remains of the activities of a particular group of people of a particular period of time" (Coe 1964:6).

Although Coe did define the Badin focus on this basis, he noted at the time that the definition was based on "typological seriation of surface collections, and this evidence will have to be verified by controlled excavations" (Coe 1952:302). A glance at his illustration for the Badin focus (1952:Figure 163) will identify over half a dozen types of projectile points, plus atlatl weights and ceramics. This "focus" clearly contained materials dating from the Early Archaic to the Early Woodland periods. Later, controlled excavations demonstrated the "mythical" nature of the focus, providing "irrefutable evidence that those recurring complexes of traits were in reality the remains of recurring occupations on those sites by the same sequence of people" (Coe 1964:6).

Deflation of upland (even locally high) sites due to erosion will mix components inextricably, and will keep all materials on or near the surface. Further, as Coe (1964:6) noted, "it would be unrealistic to assume that any of these sites were occupied only once during the 10,000 years with which we are concerned." The result is that the cultural association of artifacts in surface collections may be assumed only with the most exacting comparison to complexes defined from excavated, unmixed contexts. If components cannot be isolated, questions of associations of subsistence tool assemblages, for instance, and thus of the range of exploitive techniques of any group, cannot be explored with confidence.

Distributions of known sites are basic to the generation of settlement models, but these too must be approached with caution. Here again, the fact that most of the known sites are represented by surface collections raises problems. Until artifact assemblages are defined from controlled contexts, researchers must take care to distinguish between component and projectile point distributions.

Site typologies are generally based on site size, and the quantity and variety of materials collected. A site bearing a projectile point and two flakes, for example, may be classified as a hunting camp of the period indicated by the point style. Another site, with three points, two dozen flakes, a few utilized flakes or cores, and perhaps a ground stone fragment, may be interpreted as a longer-term encampment. But how is the site to be interpreted if the three points represent three different styles? Are the co-occurring artifacts primarily associated with one point—and if so, which?—with the others representing small hunting camps? Or do the three points represent three roughly equivalent components of the three stylistic periods? This problem of comparability of mixed components in surface sites has yet to be considered fully. (Possible prior collection by persons unknown, of course, raises still other problems.)

Low-lying areas, especially floodplains, present the opposite situation from site deflation. Investigators must allow for missing sites, for instance those obscured by river-valley deposition or inundation; in the latter case, analogy to environmental situations similar to those now inundated may be the only recourse. In the former, multicomponent but stratified sites may be represented on the surface only by the most recent occupation. Although researchers generally seem to be aware of this problem, an efficient method of inventorying and sampling most such sites has yet to be developed. Here, components identified by marker types, such as projectile points, may be missing rather that misemphasized.

Further, diachronic models of settlement pattern based on sites placed in time by projectile points are only as good as the point typology. Where a marker type is ill-defined, uncertainly identified, or dubiously dated, settlement models of the sequential periods may be badly skewed. A proposed "settlement pattern" of the Late Archaic in a given river valley, for example, may be biased if one of the marker types utilized should actually be placed in the Early Woodland, and the model for the latter period will be equally skewed by the absence of a number of sites belonging in it. The settlement models discussed in the body of this paper reflect this problem at least to the extent of the substantial uncertainties of the typology.

Finally, excavated data will be invaluable in any study of site formation processes and biases. A general understanding of deposition (and disturbance) processes must be refined for each region and each site, for a detailed evaluation of associations. Coe's (1964:6–8) warning against taking simple proximity of artifacts, even in the ground, "as *prima facie* evidence that they were functionally related," is still valid. The more limited the excavation, the more limited will be the evidence with which problems of site formation and integrity of association may be addressed.

Direct evidence of subsistence resources, in the forms of floral and faunal remains, also must be found in demonstrable associations as well as in deposits conducive to their preservation. Current suggestions of subsistence practices rely largely on data from outside Maryland, and on the locations of sites within reconstructed environments. The effectiveness of the latter method is limited. Although it is true that an understanding of the range of resources available to a prehistoric population is valuable, direct evidence of the choices made by prehistoric groups is also crucial to reconstruction of exploitive strategies.

The main body of this paper has illustrated, simply by the frequency with which extra-Maryland data were invoked, the heavy role of interregional analogy in current models of the Maryland Archaic. As research continues in Maryland, more emphasis must be placed on extensive excavation that will produce data by which direct evidence of subsistence practices may proceed (see Chapman, this volume). Controlled contextual data both within sites and across the region will be necessary to address typological, spatial, and chronological problems, to refine and extend current ideas of settlement patterning and environmental orientations, and to explore even more difficult questions about the relationships among material culture, cultural ecology, and the nature of Eastern Archaic societies. It is already evident that a much broader data base is available now than in 1952, when Schmitt presented the Archaic chronology of the Middle Atlantic states. Current research is refining approaches to archaeological data, and the potential for more thorough understanding of the Archaic record in Maryland is only beginning to be realized.

Acknowledgments

This paper was drafted while I was on the staff of the Maryland Historical Trust, whose resources were indispensable. For many hours of valuable conversation and for comments on the draft, I would like to thank Wayne E. Clark, Alvin Luckenbach, and L. Daniel Myers. Comments from Roy Dickens, H. Trawick Ward, and Kenneth Carstens, were also appreciated, as was the typing of the manuscript by Charlotte Hayes. Any critical insight that may be evident in this paper is due largely to training by Dr. Joffre L. Coe. Of course, all responsibility for content is my own.

12 • KEITH T. EGLOFF

Spheres of Cultural Interaction across the Coastal Plain of Virginia in the Woodland Period

Introduction

Research in eastern Virginia has revealed that ceramic variability across the Coastal Plain conforms, in general, to specific environmental provinces and reflects spheres of cultural interaction. Interaction spheres reflect the transmission of information by increased societal contact, expanded rates of innovation, and changes in the distribution patterns of material culture (Caldwell 1964; Dickens 1980). The purpose of this paper is to assess the meaning of patterned ceramic variability from the combined perspective of the environment, ethnography, and material culture.

Eastern Virginia can be divided into three physiographic provinces: the Estuarine Coastal Plain, Interior Coastal Plain, and Piedmont. Environmental studies have illustrated the uniqueness of each province, while ethnographic evidence has illustrated their cultural distinctiveness. Ceramic variability and distribution across eastern Virginia suggest the presence of culture areas conforming to the three provinces, with corresponding spheres of interaction within and between them.

Environment

Eastern Virginia's three physiographic provinces (Figure 12-1) exhibit environmental factors that conditioned and stabilized aboriginal culture. The Estuarine Coastal Plain encompasses an area beginning east of the freshwater-saltwater transition and extending to the Atlantic Ocean. The freshwater-saltwater transition is a hard-to-define zone of declining water salinity that fluctuated throughout late prehistoric times in response to both sea level rise and seasonal wet and dry periods. For this

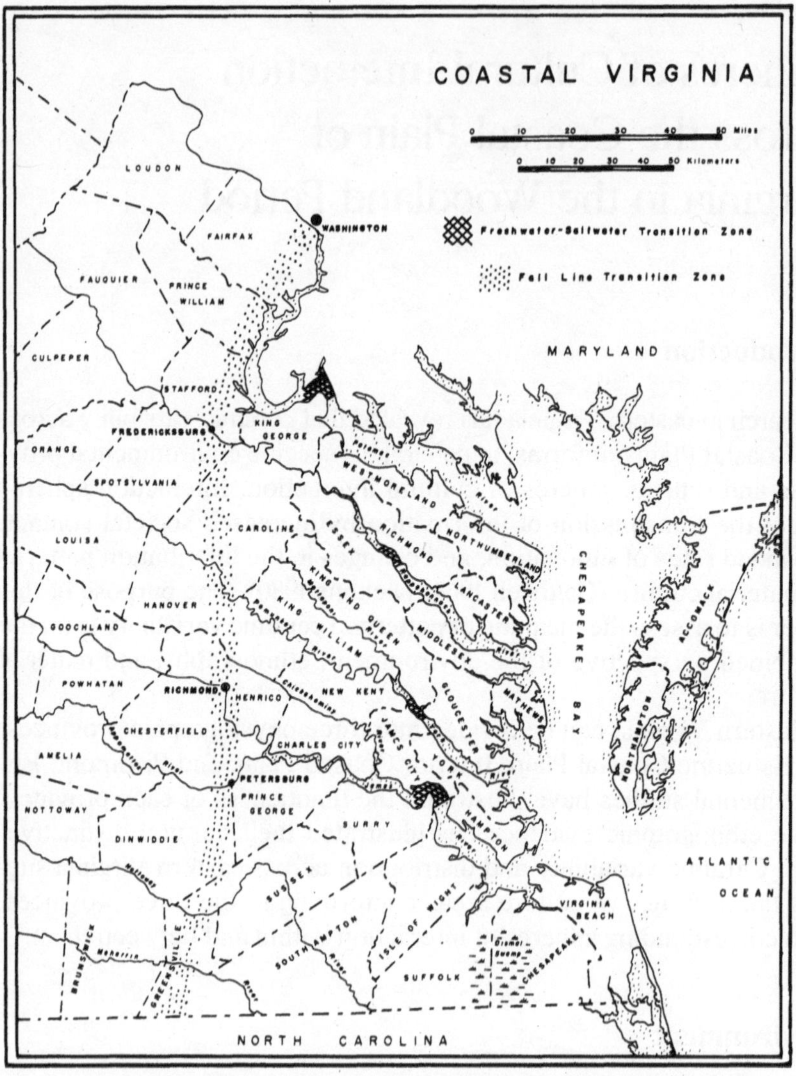

Figure 12-1. **Physiographic Provinces and Counties of Eastern Virginia.**

study the transition is defined by the present limit of the distribution of oysters. The majority of the Estuarine Coastal Plain soils are unconsolidated sediments, usually less than 30 feet in elevation. The Interior Coastal Plain extends from west of the freshwater-saltwater transition and the Dismal Swamp to the fall line. The nearly level to sloping soils of this area have formed in unconsolidated sediments greater than 30 feet in elevation. The gently rolling Piedmont is divided from the Interior Coastal Plain by the fall line transition, another vague zone straddling the fall line. The Piedmont soils are clayey, shallow, and typically less fertile than the soils of the Interior Coastal Plain.

Recently, environmental studies of eastern Virginia have suggested that the Interior Coastal Plain offers more floral and faunal diversity, and a larger biomass more desirable to humans, than either the Piedmont or Estuarine Coastal Plain. Research by Turner (1976:82), based in part on earlier work by Binford (1964), concluded that the best area for exploiting the widest range of fauna occurs in the Interior Coastal Plain in the vicinity of the freshwater-saltwater transition. Work in the fall line transition (Egloff 1980) along the Appomattox River has revealed significant vegetational and wildlife diversity, especially in that portion adjacent to the Interior Coastal Plain.

Carville Earle (1979), an historian of seventeenth-century Chesapeake, demonstrated a close relationship between environment, disease, and mortality in colonial Virginia. He observed that early settlements located in or east of the freshwater-saltwater transition, notably Jamestown, were more susceptible to epidemics of typhoid, dysentery, and salt poisoning, promoted by the unclean, salty water of the hot, dry summers, than were settlements further inland near abundant sources of freshwater. This suggests that large, permanent prehistoric villages would have been more successfully located in the Interior Coastal Plain near permanent freshwater sources.

Ethnographic Evidence

Studies of early historic accounts of the piedmont Siouan, coastal Algonquian, and interior coastal plain Iroquoian groups demonstrate cultural distinctiveness for people living in the three physiographic provinces. Turner (1976:111), for example, pointed out that the center of the Algonquian Powhatan Chiefdom (the six districts traditionally most closely aligned with Powhatan and inherited from his ancestors) were located in the Interior Coastal Plain along the upper reaches of the James and York rivers. Algonquian speaking groups to the north between the Rappahannock and Potomac rivers and on the Eastern Shore did not participate as fully, if at all, in the chiefdom, whereas a group to the south, the Chesapeaks, were brought into the chiefdom by conquest (Feest 1978). Culturally, the coastal Algonquian peoples were quite distinct from the Manahoac, Monacon, and Occaneechi Siouan groups living in the Piedmont along the Rappahannock, James, and Roanoke rivers.

Population estimates calculated by Turner (1976:164) for seven subregions within the Powhatan Chiefdom demonstrate that the largest districts were located in the Interior Coastal Plain. The two Interior Coastal Plain subregions have estimated population densities of 97 persons per 40 square miles, while the five subregions in the Estuarine Coastal Plain have estimates of 64 persons per 40 square miles. The estimated population density of 79 persons per 40 square miles for the entire coastal plain Algonquian is in stark contrast to the estimate by Kroeber (1939:145) of 9 individuals per 40 square miles for the piedmont Siouan. Recently, however, Ubelaker (1976) has suggested that Kroeber's rather conservative estimates be increased. At European contact, the Nottoway and Meherrin Iroquoian groups lived along the rivers that bear their names. Significantly, in response to seventeenth-century colonial expansion, the Nottaway and Meherrin moved east, not west as might be expected, and concentrated their settlements in a region east of the fall line transition, probably to take advantage of the environmentally richer Interior Coastal Plain (Boyce 1978).

In general, evidence from environmental data and historical accounts indicates that the Interior Coastal Plain of Virginia had more resource diversity and a larger biomass more desirable to humans, and higher population estimates than either the Estuarine Coastal Plain or Piedmont. Furthermore, the Interior Coastal Plain contained groups traditionally and, in some cases, culturally distinct from groups in both the Estuarine Coastal Plain and Piedmont.

Ceramics

This study focuses on describing the patterned ceramic variability across the Coastal Plain of Virginia. The ceramics suggest that by the Middle Woodland period there existed: (1) the piedmont and coastal cultural dichotomy described by Captain John Smith in 1607; (2) a Circum-Chesapeake Bay cultural interaction sphere within coastal Virginia, Maryland, and Delaware; and (3) groups inhabiting the Interior Coastal Plain that were distinct from those of the Piedmont and Estuarine Coastal Plain.

Marcey Creek Ware

The attributes of Marcey Creek Ware, dated 1200–800 B.C., are soapstone temper, rectanguloid or round flat bases with protruding basal heels, lug handles, shallow forms, hand modeling, and plain vessel surfaces with basal sherds often bearing impressions of an open-weave matting (Manson 1948). This ware is widely distributed, but in small quantities especially to the south, across the entire Coastal Plain, and is closely related to the later soapstone-tempered, coiled, and cord-marked Seldon Island Ware (Slattery 1946). A ware closely related to Marcey Creek, except for temper, is Bushnell Plain (radiocarbon dated 1110 B.C. ± 60) found in Westmoreland County (Waselkov 1982). Its temper is composed of crushed schist with occasional clay, fiber, and soapstone inclusions.

Croaker Landing Ware

The plain and cord-marked Croaker Landing Ware, when compared to the Marcey Creek and Seldon Island wares, has identical attributes, except that it contains clay temper (Egloff 1979). Sherds found on sites along the Chickahominy River in New Kent County exhibit both clay-and-soapstone particles (McCary 1976), a composite temper also noted by Painter (1970) in sherds from the Dismal Swamp area. This ware probably is contemporary with the Marcey Creek and Seldon Island wares, although its distribution is concentrated in the southern Coastal

Plain (New Kent and York counties, and the cities of Suffolk and Chesapeake).

Accokeek Ware

Accokeek Ware has a sand and crushed quartz tempered conoidal body with a cord-marked surface treatment. Accokeek Net Impressed is a minority type (Stephenson 1963). The accepted temporal range for this ware in the Potomac River Valley is 800–300 B.C., which overlaps with the Popes Creek Ware, dated 500 B.C.–A.D. 200 (McNett 1975). Its known distribution in the Coastal Plain is from the Potomac River south to the James.

Popes Creek Ware

Popes Creek Ware is identified by its medium sand temper, conoidal bases, interior scoring, and knotted-net surface treatment. Popes Creek Cord Marked is a minority type (Stephenson 1963). The ware is found throughout the Coastal Plain north of the James River.

Stony Creek Ware

Stony Creek Ware has a medium sand temper, conoidal bases, and surfaces treated with a wide wicker-fabric, cord, or knotted-net (Binford 1964). In North Carolina, pottery similar to the Stony Creek Ware collected from the Roanoke Rapids Basin was referred to as the Vincent and Clements wares (Coe 1964). Recently the Vincent and Clements wares have been assigned to the Early and Middle Woodland periods (Phelps 1980). Stony Creek Ware is restricted to the Coastal Plain south of the James River.

Prince George Ware

Prince George Ware is noted for its pebble temper and a row of widely spaced finger pinchings or reed punctations below the vertical rim (Evans 1955). The surface treatment of the ware is a wide wicker-fabric, cord, or knotted-net. The ware appears to have developed in the Interior Coastal Plain of central Virginia, and probably dates 400 B.C.–A.D. 200 (Egloff 1980).

Mockley Ware

The shell-tempered Mockley Ware has cord, knotted-net, and plain surface treatments, and dates A.D. 200–900 (Barka and McCary 1976, Griffith and Artusy 1977). Later rims occasionally exhibit cross-hatched or diagonally incised lines (Opperman 1980). This ware, found on the Eastern Shore and throughout the Coastal Plain, except in Dinwiddie and Greensville counties, is uncharacteristically widespread and homogeneous from Delaware to southern Virginia.

Hercules Ware

Hercules Ware, with 30–60 percent of its contorted paste made up of a crushed-granite or gneiss temper, has medium wicker-fabric and cord surface treatments. It lacks decoration. Chronologically, it has been placed before the Townsend Ware of the Late Woodland period, thus making it late Middle Woodland (Smith 1971). Its general distribution is restricted to a region south of the James River in the Interior Coastal Plain and Fall Line transition.

Townsend Ware

The shell-tempered Townsend Ware, first defined in Delaware (Blaker 1950), is found throughout the Eastern Shore and Coastal Plain except in Dinwiddie and Greensville counties. The ware has a fine wicker-fabric surface treatment and is commonly decorated below the rim with incised bands, chevrons, cross-hatching, punctations, and possible cord designs. In Virginia, the ware has been dated A.D. 945–1590 (Outlaw 1978; MacCord 1965). In the Estuarine Coastal Plain of northern North Carolina, the fabric-marked Colington Ware (Phelps 1981), dated A.D. 800 to European contact, is comparable to the Townsend Ware.

Cashie Ware

Cashie Ware, with wicker-fabric, simple-stamped, and plain surface treatments, has slightly angular to rounded quartz pebbles for temper (Phelps 1980). The ware, dated A.D. 1150–1425, has occasional incisions, punctations, and folded rims. Cashie Ware, distributed throughout the Interior Coastal Plain of northwestern North Carolina, also occurs in Virginia in Greensville, Southampton, and Sussex counties.

Gaston Ware

Gaston Ware, composed primarily of one type, simple-stamped, has crushed-quartz temper, and folded and decorated rims. The ware was dated by Coe (1964:119) in the Roanoke Rapids Basin as post A.D. 1700. Similar pottery is found along the Fall Line transition and Interior Coastal Plain in Chesterfield, Charles City, and Prince George counties, and occasionally as far north as Henrico and Hanover counties (C. Hodges 1979).

Potomac Creek Ware

Potomac Creek Ware, with cord-marked and plain surface treatments, has angular quartz and/or sand temper in a clayey, compact paste. The ware, dated A.D. 1300–1650, is decorated with cord impressions placed horizontally, vertically, or criss-crossed about a thickened rim. The ware is found mainly in the Interior Coastal Plain in Caroline, Essex, Fairfax, King George, Prince William, Stafford, and Westmoreland counties (Clark 1980).

Roanoke Ware

The shell-tempered Roanoke Ware has a simple-stamped surface treatment, and its only form of decoration is lip notching made with a thong wrapped paddle. This ware, found near the bottom of a ditch around the original Fort Raleigh in North Carolina, and excavated from a pit containing mixed Colonial and Indian artifacts at the trading post of Kicotan, in Hampton, Virginia, dates from the latter part of the Late Woodland period into the Historic period (Blaker 1952; Harrington 1948). Roanoke Ware is distributed along the Estuarine Coastal Plain in Gloucester, James City, King and Queen, Prince George, and York counties, and the cities of Hampton and Virginia Beach.

Courtland Ware

Courtland Ware, found in Southampton County and dated A.D. 1660–1750, contains a combination of aboriginal and European traits (Binford 1964). The plain and burnished shallow bowls, plates, and small mugs are made from a fine-textured clayey paste.

Camden Ware

The untempered Camden Ware, placed A.D. 1660, has plain-surfaced bowls with flattened bases (MacCord 1969). The ware is distributed in the Interior Coastal Plain. along the Rappahannock River in Caroline, Essex, and Westmoreland counties.

Colono Ware

Shell-tempered, plain-surfaced Colono Ware, dated A.D. 1680 to well into the nineteenth century, has vessels patterned after European wares, including bowls, jars, plates, chamber pots, pipkins, and porringers (Noël Hume 1962; M. Hodges 1980). Some of the plain earthenware, especially when found on plantation sites, probably was produced by black slaves (Ferguson 1980). The ware is found mainly in the Estuarine Coastal Plain, in Charles City, Gloucester, James City, King William, Lancaster, New Kent, Northumberland, Richmond, Southampton, and York counties. Occasionally sherds have been noted in the Interior Coastal Plain, in Caroline, Hanover, and Prince George counties. A ware that is closely related, but predates Colono Ware is Yeocomico found in Westmoreland and Northumberland counties (Potter 1982). This plain, scraped, and cord-marked shell-tempered ceramic dates from A.D. 1510 to 1690.

Ceramic Trends in Coastal Virginia

A ware is defined by a combination of attributes. The distribution of a ware through time and space may reflect cultural interaction. Furthermore, by examining attribute trends that traverse ware definitions, it may be possible to clarify the nature of the interaction between cultures.

Early Woodland Period (1200 to 500 B.C.)

Early ceramic vessels, 1200–800 B.C., reminiscent of carved soapstone vessels, are quite diverse through time and space, which probably reflects a period of experimentation in manufacture. When examined closely, these ceramics exhibit an unexpected amount of variation in temper (soapstone, soapstone-and-clay, clay, sand, shell, and schist), surface treatment (plain and cord-marked surfaces, and open-weave mat impressions on bases), vessel shape (rectanguloid and rounded flat bases), and method of manufacture (modeled and coiled). Sand- or small particle-tempered, cord-marked coiled vessels with conical bases (Accokeek and Stony Creek wares) became the overwhelming choice by 800 B.C. and continued to be popular until 300 B.C.

Middle Woodland Period (500 B.C. to A.D. 900)

In the Middle Woodland period cord-marked vessels remained in common use, with the addition of net-impressed surfaces and a wide wicker-fabric surface treatment (probably introduced from the southern Piedmont). Only in the southern and central Coastal Plain did these three surface treatments overlap, forming the Stony Creek and Prince George wares. North of the James River, the predominant ceramic was net-impressed Popes Creek Ware.

Shell tempering, probably introduced into the Chesapeake Bay area as early as 600 B.C. (Painter 1977), became very popular, lasting 2,500 years. It extended inland as far as the Fall Line, but seldom beyond. The shell-tempered Mockley Ware with net- and cord-impressed surfaces was popular throughout the Circum-Chesapeake Bay area north of the James River in the period A.D. 200–900.

The Middle Woodland trend of including large particles in the paste was exaggerated in the unique pebble-tempered, punctate-decorated Prince George Ware. Significantly, this ware, dated to the first half of the Middle Woodland period, appears to have originated and remained predominately in the Interior Coastal Plain of central Virginia.

The crushed granite- and gneiss-tempered Hercules Ware is also restricted to the Interior Coastal Plain, but in an area mainly south of the James River. Its moderately wide wicker-fabric and cord impressions, and lack of decoration, suggest a temporal placement in the last half of the Middle Woodland period.

Divisions of ceramic distribution in the Coastal Plain by the beginning of the Middle Woodland period suggest an elaborate interplay of spheres of cultural interaction. The Popes Creek and Mockley wares, rare in the Piedmont, predominated in the Coastal Plain along and north of the James River, indicating that the piedmont and coastal cultural dichotomy described by Captain John Smith existed by the Middle Woodland period. Furthermore, the Prince George and Hercules wares suggest that groups distinct from those on the Piedmont and Estuarine Coastal Plain had developed within the Interior Coastal Plain of central and southern Virginia by the Middle Woodland period.

Late Woodland Period (A.D. 900 to 1520)

The Coastal Plain phenomenon of shell tempering continued into and during the Late Woodland period in the fine wicker fabric-impressed, incised, and punctated Townsend Ware. In a few Interior Coastal Plain counties south of the James River, the granule-tempered Cashie Ware with fabric, simple-stamped, and plain surface impressions had greater expression.

A major influence from the south, which appeared in the latter stage of the Late Woodland period, was simple stamping. The shell-tempered Roanoke Ware occurs along the Estuarine Coastal Plain, whereas the granule-tempered Gaston Ware is found along the Fall Line transition and Interior Coastal Plain. Simple-stamping became popular, and was still predominant at some sites in the southern Coastal Plain at the time of European contact.

The northern Interior Coastal Plain of Virginia felt the influence of the Potomac Creek Ware during the last half of the Late Woodland period. Its ceramic traits included granule temper, cord-impressed and decorated surfaces, and thickened rims.

Although incising and punctating were used rarely on late Mockley Ware, surface decorations became popular on coastal ceramics during the Late Woodland period. Incising and punctation were common on the Townsend Ware, but the Roanoke Ware, normally associated with the Townsend Ware in the Estuarine Coastal Plain of southern Virginia, lacked surface decoration except for rim notching. Rim thickening, pinching, and cord decorations, attributes derived from the Piedmont, became common on the granule-tempered Gaston, Cashie, and Potomac Creek wares, all found in the Fall Line transition and Interior Coastal Plain.

In the Late Woodland period, ceramic distributions are remarkably similar to those described for the Middle Woodland period. Townsend Ware, more widespread than the earlier Mockley Ware, occurred rarely in the Piedmont but more extensively in the Interior Coastal Plain south of the James River. Significantly, the evolution of Mockley to Townsend was rather uniform throughout the Circum-Chesapeake Bay region, suggesting the interaction of groups possessing a common culture. As might be expected, the Interior Coastal Plain contained its own unique array of ceramic traits, which demonstrate interaction with the Piedmont and Estuarine Coastal Plain.

Protohistoric and Historic Periods (A.D. 1520 to 1800s)

Early European contact, followed by the arrival of Englishmen at Jamestown in A.D. 1607, heralded a dramatic change in Indian ceramics throughout the Coastal Plain of Virginia (Potter 1982). Traditional ceramic attributes, such as conical bases, impressed surface treatments, incised and punctated surface decorations, and thickened rims, gradually disappeared during the seventeenth century. Plain-surfaced pottery, patterned after European (or African) vessels became overwhelmingly preferred by the eighteenth century. On the Pamunkey Indian Reservation, similar vessels were made into the twentieth century (Stern 1951). As expected, historic Indian wares found in the Estuarine Coastal Plain and along the James and York rivers into the Interior

Coastal Plain, were shell-tempered, while the Courtland and Camden wares, with no temper, were common in the Interior Coastal Plain.

Conclusions

On examining eastern Virginia, one finds that the floral and faunal resources of the Interior Coastal Plain were more abundant and diverse, resulting in a larger biomass more desirable to humans. Higher populations, estimated from ethnographic data, have been proposed for the Interior Coastal Plain.

Patterned ceramic distribution across eastern Virginia suggests that distinct ceramic areas conformed to physiographical provinces, with spheres of cultural interaction within and between these areas. The distribution of the Mockley and Townsend ceramics suggests that the piedmont and coastal cultural dichotomy described by Captain John Smith in 1607 existed by the Middle Woodland period, perhaps by A.D. 200 (Holland 1966). Furthermore, the Mockley and Townsend ceramics found north of and along the James River, are similar to ceramics found in Delaware and Maryland, and suggest a Circum-Chesapeake Bay cultural interaction sphere (Wright 1973). Ceramics found south of the James River—Hercules, Cashie, Gaston, and Roanoke wares—are most closely related to wares found along the rivers that flow into the Albemarle Sound in North Carolina.

Why would wares, theoretically reflecting interaction between groups of people, conform to physiographic provinces? Kroeber (1939) once theorized that without external influences cultures are inclined to change slowly once they have adjusted to a particular environment. They are predisposed to spread over the whole of the natural area in which their structure was formed, before expanding to a different environment. Kroeber presented the coastal Algonquian and the piedmont Siouan of Virginia in 1607 as the clearest coincidence of natural and native culture area boundaries to be found in North America. Recent work has explained the development of Piedmont segmented societies and the Coastal Plain ranked societies within the framework of differences in the structure of the physiographic provinces (Mouer 1981).

Present evidence indicates that the Interior Coastal Plain was distinct from the Piedmont and Estuarine Coastal Plain not only in population density, culture, and tradition, but also in the distribution of ceramic wares. In the Middle Woodland period, Prince George Ware originated and remained within the Interior Coastal Plain. Later, in the Middle Woodland period, Hercules Ware spread across the Interior Coastal Plain and Fall Line transition south of the James River. Cashie and Gaston wares were found in the same province by the Late Woodland period. Similarly, in the last half of the Late Woodland period, Potomac Creek Ware was dispersed across the Interior Coastal Plain and Fall Line transition in the region between the Potomac and Mattaponi rivers.

From the movement of Estuarine Coastal Plain wares (i.e., Mockley, Townsend, and Roanoke) and Piedmont ceramic traits (i.e., large particle temper, thickened rims, pinching, and cord decorations) into the Interior Coastal Plain, one might hypothesize that societal contact (trade, marriage, warfare, etc.) in eastern Virginia took place predominately in the Interior Coastal Plain. Perhaps the appealing resources of this area coupled with its strategic location caused more intensive cultural interaction.

Acknowledgments

The writer is especially grateful to Stephen Potter, David Phelps, Daniel Mouer, Charles Hodges, Mary Ellen Norrisey Hodges, Keith Bott, and E. Randolph Turner for sharing their ceramic knowledge and lending their professional aid and support.

13 • JOHN A. WALTHALL

Early Hopewellian Ceremonial Encampments in the South Appalachian Highlands

Introduction

The appearance of Hopewell traits over the Southeast has traditionally been treated as a synchronic phenomenon. However, as better chronological data have been obtained from Middle Woodland components, a developmental sequence has emerged, marked by both early and late horizon styles. James B. Griffin (Griffin et al. 1970; Griffin 1979), William Sears (1962), and other researchers have noted that marker artifacts for early Hopewell interaction include copper panpipes and earspools, obsidian implements, platform pipes, and prismatic blades manufactured from Flint Ridge chalcedony and other exotic northern cherts. Among later horizon markers are reel-shape copper gorgets, steatite elbow pipes, and large animal effigy pipes (Walthall 1980:107).

Numerous radiocarbon dates from mounds containing such artifacts have confirmed this relative sequence. Sites with earlier horizon markers consistently date between A.D. 1 and 200; sites with later artifact styles temporally cluster in the period A.D. 200–500. Although numerous mounds that date to one of these early or late Middle Woodland subperiods have been excavated, few contemporary habitation sites have been examined. Five such habitation sites have recently been reported in the South Appalachian region. All appear to have major components that date to the early Middle Woodland period. Summary descriptions of each of these sites are given below. Subsequently, a discussion and an interpretive treatment concerning their function and relationship to Hopewell ritual systems are offered.

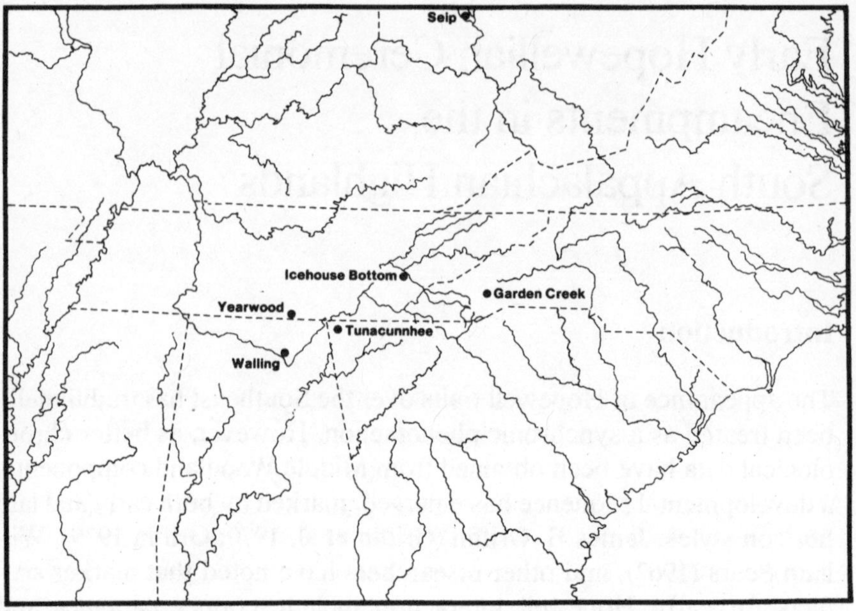

Figure 13-1. Map of the South Appalachian Region Showing the Location of Sites Discussed in the Text.

Sites

Walling, Madison County, Alabama

The Walling site, situated near the confluence of the Flint and Tennessee rivers in northern Alabama (Figure 13-1) was excavated in 1939 by WPA archaeologists. The results of these investigations were being compiled for publication when the outbreak of World War II terminated the regional archaeological program. The cultural materials and records from this site were later studied and reported by Walthall (1973).

The excavation of the Walling habitation area was somewhat fortuitous. The actual focus of the investigation was a substructure platform mound located on the southwestern portion of the 2.5-acre habitation area. The mound, which was found to contain four stages of construction and both round and rectangular structure patterns, had been erected over a thin midden .4–.5 feet in depth. Extant records do not allow precise cultural affiliation of the levels of mound construction. The upper two levels contained shell-tempered sherds, demonstrating that at least these final caps had been built by Mississippian peoples. The lower two levels, including both structure patterns, and the middle zone contained only Middle Woodland ceramics and lithic materials. One trench excavated into the midden yielded an arc of postholes which was not traced.

Lithic materials recovered from the midden include medium triangular projectile points, biface blades, a few scrapers, and various knife forms. Uniface blades, some of prismatic form, were present in this lithic sample, which had clearly been "high graded" by discarding most of the debitage. Of particular note was the presence of Copena greenstone celts and spades, artifacts extremely rare outside mound context. Similar artifacts were recovered in an associated Copena burial mound located nearby (Walthall 1973:422).

The ceramic sample from Walling was composed of some 1,090 sherds. Of these, 80 percent were limestone tempered while the remainder was primarily composed of sand- or grog-tempered sherds. The limestone-tempered sample consisted of 51 percent plain, 25 percent cord marked, 10 percent simple stamped, and 67 percent check stamped. Incised, punctated, and complicated-stamped sherds formed less than 1 percent of the total. The Walling ceramic collection also included a significant amount of exotic types. Among these were 19 limestone-tempered rocker-stamped sherds. Only one other such sherd has ever been found at the scores of sites investigated in the middle Tennessee Valley. A distinctive sand-tempered ware was composed of plain, simple-stamped, check-stamped, cord-marked, and incised sherds. The micaceous paste of these sherds points to an eastern, "over the mountain" source area, likely northern Georgia or western North Carolina. Two grog-tempered sherds were of special note, one was the base of tetrapodal vessel, the other a zoned rocker-stamped body sherd identified as Marksville Stamped, variety Manny (Jenkins 1979:179). Tetrapodal supports were represented in each temper group. Complete bases indicate that these were miniature to small tetrapodal jars.

Yearwood, Lincoln County, Tennessee

The Yearwood site, situated on a terrace remnant above the Elk River, was excavated by Brian Butler in 1975. Butler's (1977; 1979) reports on this site indicate that Yearwood was a multicomponent site with a major Middle Woodland occupation covering about 2.5 acres. The use of heavy machinery to strip away this topsoil allowed maximum spatial exposure of this habitation area. Butler (1979:151) has reported that 14 structure patterns were found, all associated with the Middle Woodland component. A rectangular single-post construction was most common, but oval and semicircular, open-sided shelters were also present. No superposition or rebuilding of these structures was noted. This observation, and the presence of only a light midden and few pit features (40), led Butler (1979:152) to postulate a brief single-phase occupation with the majority (if not all) of the structures being contemporaneous.

Nine burials and a crematory basin were also found at Yearwood. The burial sample consisted of four redeposited cremations, three extended flesh burials, one disarticulated infant burial, and one probable bundle burial. The crematory basin was exposed in an area 262 feet to the southwest of the structures. This feature, which measured 9.2 feet by 6.6 feet, was a shallow rectangular pit with a flat bottom. The walls and sides of the pit were heavily fired.

The cultural materials recovered at Yearwood include ceramics, medium triangular projectile points, cores and prismatic blades, copper earspools, galena, and mica. Some of the prismatic blades were manufactured of Flint Ridge (Ohio) chalcedony. The ceramic sample was composed largely of limestone-tempered sherds. Major surface treatments are cord marked (54 percent), plain (32 percent) and check stamped (8 percent). The major vessel form was the small tetrapodal jar. A variety of exotic ceramics was also recovered. These include 37 rocker-stamped sherds (representing as many as 12 vessels), one grog-tempered rocker-dentate stamped Marksville-like sherd, and a collection of micaceous sand-tempered pottery. Finish and decorative treatments on this latter series are rocker stamped, simple stamped, complicated stamped, incised-and-punctated, and plain.

A series of five radiocarbon dates places the Middle Woodland component at Yearwood into the first century A.D. (Butler 1979:155). Analysis of the seasonal data recovered suggests the Middle Woodland components at Yearwood was a warm weather, late summer or early fall occupation. Extensive surveys in the Elk and nearby Duck River drainage areas have resulted in the discovery of a number of Middle Woodland villages and campsites. None of these sites has produced a ceramic assemblage like that found by Butler at Yearwood. However, Yearwood is located only a few miles from the headwaters of the Flint River some 40 miles upstream from the Walling site.

Tunacunnhee, Dade County, Georgia

The Tunacunnhee mounds and habitation area are located in Lookout Valley on the eastern edge of the Appalachian Plateau in extreme northwestern Georgia. The site was excavated by the University of Georgia and has been reported by Richard Jeffries (1976, 1979). The Tunacunnhee locality contains four Middle Woodland burial mounds built partially or entirely of local limestone. Burial types found within these structures include extended and flexed burials, secondary burials, and cremations.

An extraordinary amount of cultural material was found in association with these burials. Among these artifacts are numerous copper panpipes, earspools, and breastplates, mica, platform pipes, and bear canines (Jeffries 1976:21–30). No pottery vessels were found in direct association with the burials. However, on the northern edge of Mound C, a cache consisting of two vessels was found. Both of these vessels were small tetrapodal jars, one plain and one simple stamped. A radiocarbon sample from Mound C yielded a date of A.D. 150 ± 95 (UGa-ML-8) (Jeffries 1979:164).

The habitation area at Tunacunnhee was located some 600 feet to the southwest of the mound group and was only partially excavated. Two structure patterns were exposed. One of these features was an oval to subrectangular structure measuring 10.2 feet in diameter. The second structure, which was partially excavated, was substantially larger and was also oval to rectangular in shape. Other features found included a number of pits, one stone filled.

A sample of 523 sherds was recovered from the habitation area: 66 percent of these were limestone tempered and 34 percent were sand tempered. There were three major finish treatments, plain (53 percent), cord marked (28 percent), and simple stamped (19 percent). The major vessel form represented was the flat-bottomed jar commonly with tetrapodal appendages. Lithic materials included medium triangular projectile points, bifacial knives, and prismatic blades. Such blades were recovered both from the mounds and in the habitation area. One of the prismatic blades found in Mound C has been identified as Flint Ridge (Ohio) chalcedony (Jeffries 1976:30).

The nature of the ceramic assemblage found at the Tunacunnhee habitation area caused some controversy. Extensive surveys and excavation in northern Georgia (Wauchope 1966) indicate that a regional village dating to the early portion of the Middle Woodland period should yield a sand-tempered ceramic assemblage consisting of plain, check-stamped, and simple-stamped wares. The ceramic sample at Tunacunnhee with its high percentage of nonlocal limestone-tempered sherds does not neatly fit into the established ceramic sequence. A subsequent survey of the Lookout Valley area conducted by Jeffries resulted in the discovery of 30 other Woodland sites (1979:169). However, only Tunacunnhee was associated with a mound group. The only site that contained a ceramic collection similar to that at Tunacunnhee was found in an area nearby and is now considered a part of the Tunacunnhee locality.

Garden Creek, Haywood County, North Carolina

University of North Carolina archaeological investigations of sites in the Appalachian Summit region resulted in the excavation of the Garden Creek site between 1965 and 1967 (Keel 1976). Garden Creek, situated on the east bank of the Pigeon River, is a multicomponent site with three mounds and associated habitation areas.

The investigations of the Middle Woodland component at Garden Creek were concentrated in the area of Mound 2. This mound proved to be a substructured platform constructed in two stages. The primary mound formed a platform 43 by 62 feet in diameter and 1.7 feet high. A mantle of midden soil was later added to form a second platform. Mound 2 at Garden Creek represents one of the earliest well-documented platform mounds in the Southeast, although recent evaluations of other sites in the region indicate that such pre-Mississippian mounds are much more common than previously thought (e.g., Dickens 1975; Hally 1975).

The material culture of the Middle Woodland Connesstee component from Mound 2 at Garden Creek includes local and exotic ceramics, medium triangular projectile points, celts, gorgets, and cut deer mandibles. A Hopewellian-derived assemblage associated with the Connesstee occupation consisted of prismatic blades, polyhedral cores, cache blades, sheet copper, copper plates, a copper pin, human and animal ceramic figurines, and stamped ceramics. The prismatic blades were made from black or gray Tennessee chert, quartz crystal, and Flint Ridge (Ohio) chalcedony.

The Connesstee ceramic series is tempered with micaceous sand. Major finish types include simple stamped (42 percent), cord marked (21 percent), plain (22 percent), and check stamped (13 percent). Complicated-stamped and incised or punctated sherds totaled less than 1 percent of the collection. The small tetrapodal jar was a major vessel form. Some 92 limestone-tempered sherds representing numerous individual vessels were recovered. These sherds are likely derived from the Tennessee River drainage area to the west. Surface treatments similar to those found on the Connesstee pottery were noted. A second exotic ceramic series found at Garden Creek has been classified by Keel (1976:118–119) as Ohio Hopewell. The 100 specimens in this sample consisted of sherds decorated with dentate rocker stamping (66 percent), plain rocker stamping, simple stamping, and crosshatching.

Chapman and Keel (1979:161) have suggested that a principal element in Hopewell trade with the Appalachians was mica. Extensive deposits of mica are found in western North Carolina in the vicinity of Garden Creek. This region may also have been a major source for other Hopewell raw materials such as steatite, copper, and greenstone.

Icehouse Bottom, Monroe County, Tennessee

Icehouse Bottom has been investigated by University of Tennessee field parties under the direction of Jefferson Chapman (1973). This multicomponent habitation site is located on a large alluvial bottom along the Little Tennessee River in the mountains of extreme eastern Tennessee. Middle Woodland materials have been found over an area of 3.5 acres. A number of unexcavated conical mounds have been discovered on nearby ridge tops. Stratum II, the major Middle Woodland occupation level, was found to contain numerous postholes and pits. The most common feature was a small globular fire pit.

Cultural materials recovered from this Middle Woodland component include local limestone-tempered pottery, sand-tempered Connestee ceramics, medium triangular projectile points, cut mica, and prismatic blades and cores. Major surface finishes on both limestone- and sand-tempered ceramics (from Unit A) were plain (52 percent), simple stamped (31 percent), and cord marked (8 percent). Minority types include check stamped, complicated stamped, and incised. Small tetrapodal vessels were common to both temper groups. Hopewell-derived artifacts, such as Flint Ridge (Ohio) chalcedony prismatic blades, rocker-stamped sherds, and cross-hatched rims, were found.

Chapman and Keel (1979:159) note that extensive surveys conducted in the Little Tennessee Valley have failed to locate any other sites similar to Icehouse Bottom and are convinced that this type of Middle Woodland habitation site is unique in the area. While a number of radiocarbon dates, ranging from A.D. 170 to 605, have been obtained on materials from Icehouse Bottom, two dates, A.D. 170 ± 110 (UGa-1880) and A.D. 270 ± 80 (UGa-1882) indicate that the Hopewell-related component there is at least partially contemporaneous with the other South Appalachian sites discussed.

Discussion

The five sites described above share a number of characteristics that clearly distinguish them from other South Appalachian Middle Woodland habitation sites. Where these components are not masked by later settlement, the lack of structure superposition and rebuilding and the presence of only thin midden deposits indicate occupations of brief duration. Site size is consistently small, ranging from 2.5 to 3.8 acres. All of these sites exhibit evidence of having mortuary activities conducted on them or in close proximity to them. Four are situated near known burial mounds.

Human skeletal material recovered from these sites or from nearby burial mounds indicate elaborate mortuary treatment including defleshing and cremation.

Each site exhibits evidence of a range of activities related to the preparation of food, especially meat. Structure patterns, ranging from rectangular to circular in shape, were exposed at the sites having extensive excavation. Postholes and arcs of postholes were found at sites less extensively excavated.

Prismatic blades, some of Flint Ridge chalcedony, were recovered at each site. Prismatic blades are extremely rare in the South Appalachian region and their occurrence in numbers at these sites is significant. Blades of Flint Ridge lithic material have been recovered at no other sites in the region.

The ceramic assemblages from these sites are very similar in both surface treatment and vessel form. All of these sites have collections typified by high percentages of cord-marked and/or simple-stamped sherds. Extant chronologies for the various subregions where each of these sites is located indicate that after A.D. 200 check-stamped and complicated-stamped wares increase in frequency while simple stamping declines and disappears. The small percentages of check-stamped sherds and the absence or near absence of complicated-stamped sherds strongly indicate a chronological placement of these components in the first two centuries A.D. Radiocarbon dates support this interpretation. A major vessel form at these sites is the small tetrapodal jar. Such vessels are rarely found in numbers on other Middle Woodland habitation sites within the South Appalachian region.

In summation, these five sites exhibit a number of shared distinctive traits that set them apart from contemporary village sites. Sites with comparable assemblages are absent or rare in adjacent regions. A survey of extant Middle Woodland literature indicates that the only sites with fully comparable assemblages are found to the north. These northern sites are the Ohio Hopewell ceremonial centers.

Ohio Hopewell

The ceramic materials recovered from the major Ohio Hopewell centers have been the subject of an extensive study by Prufer (1968), who has described three ceramic series. The indigenous pottery, the Scioto series, is composed of two finish types, cord-marked and plain ware. Although the most common temper material used in the production of Scioto pottery is grit, limestone and grog tempering are occasionally recognized. The remaining two series have foreign origins. The Hopewell series is characterized by a basic plain ware decorated with a variety of rocker-stamping techniques and by incising. These decorative techniques appear to be related to the Lower Mississippi Valley Marksville ceramics and the Illinois Valley Hopewell ware. Grit and limestone are major temper materials. Vessels of this series are typically small to miniature bowls and jars with slightly rounded to flattened bases.

The third type of ceramics found at Ohio Hopewell sites has been named the Southeastern series. This assemblage is composed of grit-, sand-, or limestone-tempered, small to miniature, globular jars with tetrapodal bases (Figure 13-2). Simple stamping, the most common surface treatment, has two varieties (Prufer 1968). One variety, apparently related to northern Georgia Mossy Oak Simple Stamped, was produced with a paddle carved with multiple thin lines and overall has the appearance of brushing. Keel (1976) believes that some of this stamping actually grades into a brushed treatment. This latter subvariety has been referred to as simple stamped/brushed (Chapman 1973; Keel 1976). The second variety recognized by Prufer (1968) was produced with a paddle upon which regularly spaced wide lines were carved. Both varieties have been reported at all five of the South Appalachian sites described in this paper. Consideration of the total Ohio Southeastern stamped assemblage yields the following percentage of surface treatments:

Simple Stamped	Check Stamped	Complicated Stamped
73 percent	25 percent	2 percent

The Southeastern series varies in frequency from 1 percent of the total ceramic collection at Tremper to 54 percent at Russell Brown Mound 2. This latter structure has been radiocarbon dated A.D. 90 ± 90 (UCLA-245). The complicated-stamped vessels represented in the Southeastern series were found at only two sites, Seip (11 sherds) and Turner (2 sherds). Two other finish treatments, cord-marked and plain ware, have been added to the Southeastern series by Prufer (1968:14) on the basis of temper (sand) or because these surface treatments were noted on tetrapodal supports.

In general, the Ohio Hopewell ceramics are dominated by the Scioto series. Major surface treatments for the entire Ohio Hopewell collection, in descending order of frequence are: cord marked, plain, simple stamped, rocker stamped, and check stamped. Comparisons of the Ohio

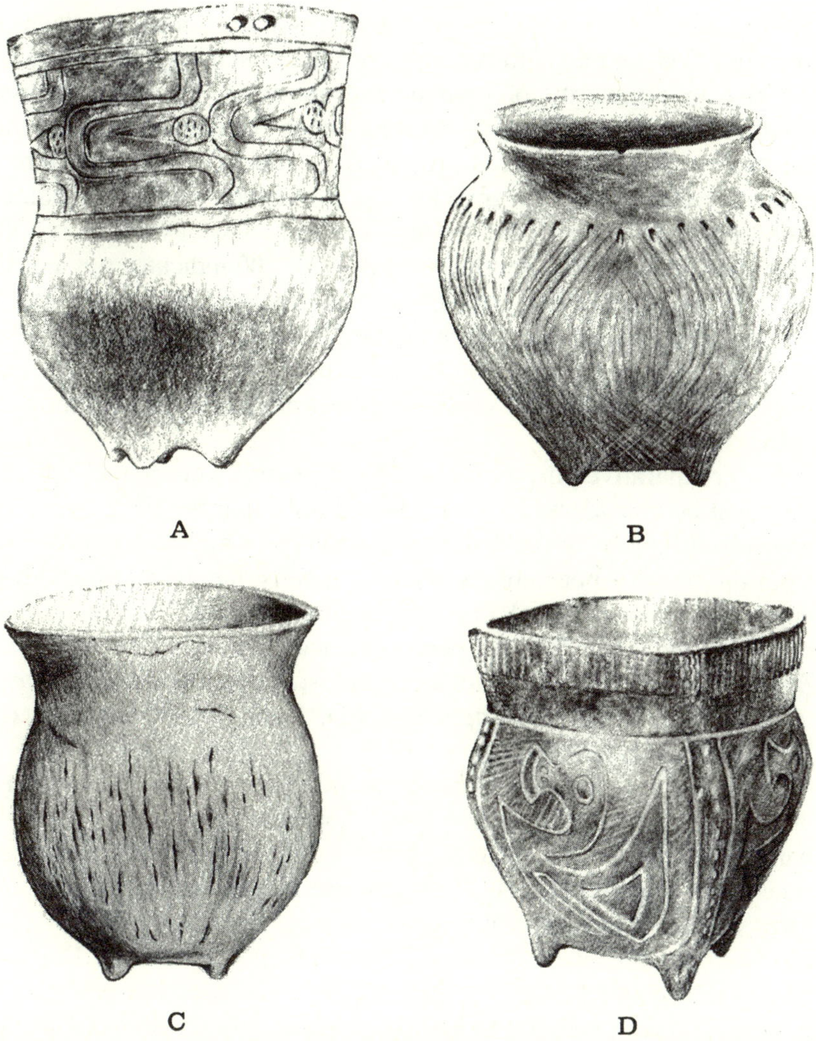

Figure 13-2. Tetrapodal Vessels Found in Middle Woodland Ceremonial Contexts: (A) Incised vessel from the Watkins mound, Logan County, Kentucky; Ht. 22.8 cm., (B) Simple Stamped/Brushed vessel from Mound City, Ross County, Ohio; Ht. 11.8 cm., (C) Cord-Impressed jar from Yent Mound, Franklin County, Florida; Ht. 11.5 cm., and (D) Zone-Stamped jar from Mound City, Ross County, Ohio; Ht. 12 cm. Average capacity of these vessels is .5 liters (2 pints).

Southeastern series with ceramic sequences in the South Appalachians and Gulf Coastal Plain indicate that the Ohio assemblage dates prior to the rise in popularity of complicated stamping. Based upon these Southeastern data, it appears that the major collapse of the Hopewell Interaction Sphere occurred around A.D. 200. If a similar pattern of exchange continued after this time the proportion of the later complicated-stamped ware would be much higher. Also, evidence of Ohio Hopewell trade in the Southeast after A.D. 200 indicates a major decline in the level of intensity of such interaction. Major late Middle Woodland mortuary sites, such as the classic Copena mounds, which have been dated to A.D. 200 to 500, exhibit only a superficial resemblance—mainly restricted to a few copper artifact styles—to the Ohio sites.

For comparative purposes, the Ohio Hopewell ceremonial center at Seip will be considered. It was selected for a number of reasons. The mounds at Seip have yielded large quantities of raw materials derived from the South Appalachians (steatite, greenstone, mica, and perhaps copper and bear canines), and Seip is one of the few Ohio sites where extensive excavations have been conducted in circum-mound areas. Based upon a number of radiocarbon dates, the Seip earthworks appear to have been constructed between A.D. 1 and 400 (Prufer 1968:153; Baby and Langlois 1979; Greber 1979).

Baby and Langlois (1979) have recently reported the excavation of an area half-way between the central mound at Seip and the outer embankment. Eight rectangular structures of the single-post construction type were exposed. Those illustrated are nearly identical in size and form to the structures found by Butler at Yearwood (1977:9). Two radiocarbon dates were obtained from the Seip structures: A.D. 230 ± 80 (DAL 116) and A.D. 280 ± 55 (DIC 281). The later date was derived from Structure 4, which is thought to postdate at least three of the other structures. Baby and Langlois (1979:18), in describing the contents of these structures, note that:

> All contained large numbers of bladelets, mostly broken, and mostly utilized. All contained a random scattering of a few intact and some broken projectile points and bifacial tools. All contained scattered potsherds, primarily plain or cordmarked, with occasional incised, rocker-stamped or other decorative ware, including several rimsherds and tetrapods. All contained fragments of mica, and of burned and unburned animal bone.

The Hopewellian Vacant Ceremonial Center

Prufer (1964:71) has characterized the Ohio Hopewell settlement pattern as having a central, elaborate vacant ceremonial center surrounded by scattered hinterland villages. Obvious activities conducted at these ceremonial centers were the construction of mounds and earthworks and burial of the dead. It may be inferred that large numbers of people congregated at these centers periodically to participate in these activities. Less obvious activities are suggested in the data reported by Baby and Langlois (1979) from the circum-mound area at Seip. The structures found at Seip contain evidence of food preparation, production of items from exotic raw materials, and the manufacture and sharpening of lithic implements.

Four aspects of the Seip data are of particular import to this present discussion: location of the structures, structure form, the presence of quantities of animal bone, and artifactual content. The most obvious characteristic is their location within the earthworks in proximity to, yet spatially removed from, the large burial mound. This location suggests that these were specialized structures built and used as part of the ritual activities conducted at the ceremonial center. Their rectangular (or square) form also appears to be of importance. Brown (1979:212), based on research into structure form and function by Hunter-Anderson (1977), has pointed out that whereas a round floorplan structure is the strongest structure type, and requires less expenditure of energy to build, it is limited in the planned use of space. On the other hand, a rectangular structure affords a floorplan arrangement conducive to multipurpose, spatially extensive functions. In sum, the vertical walls of rectangular structures provide a maximum volume of usable roofed space. Such maximization of the area of roofed space suggests that a variety of activities may have been conducted in such structures, and as Brown (1979:212) has noted, perhaps ritual, social-political activities involving display.

The recovery of quantities of animal bone within these structures and their structure form and size suggest that some of the functions conducted within them are paralleled with types of activities conducted in charnel houses (Brown 1979). Seeman (1979b) has recently made a strong case that Hopewellian ritual included "feasting with the dead," that is, ritual feasts conducted in association with mortuary activities.

Based upon a high number of occurrences of food remains, especially animal bone, in Ohio Hopewell charnel house contexts, Seeman has argued that ceremonial feasting and concomitant redistribution were an integral part of Hopewell mortuary ritual. Ethnohistoric accounts of Natchez and Choctaw mortuary ritual are cited by Seeman in support of his argument. Based on these data he suggests that ". . . the charnel house provided the focal point for chiefly management of game resources. In a word, we are dealing with redistribution—the flow of things (especially meat) toward a center (the charnel house) and out again (to the feasting populace)" (1979b:46).

The interpretation implied by these Ohio Hopewell data is that at the vacant ceremonial centers structures, often rectangular in shape, were constructed for a variety of ritual functions. Certain structures served primarily as charnel houses where dead, accompanied by status-related artifacts, were processed and displayed. Other structures, such as those in the circum-mound area at Seip, may have functioned as short-term ritual-specified roofed enclosures where ceremonial food was prepared and exotic materials (such a mica) were shaped into objects which ultimately were buried with the dead.

The final point to be considered is the nature of the cultural materials found in these ceremonial structures. Two categories of artifacts—prismatic blades and specific types of pottery—are especially common within and around these structures. The prismatic blades are clearly not common Middle Woodland utilitarian tools. This observation is supported by their occurrence in quantity at ceremonial sites (they are virtually absent in other contexts in some regions) and in the fact that, although types of local lithic materials from which they could have been manufactured were available, these blades are largely made of exotic or source-specific materials such as obsidian or multihued Flint Ridge chalcedony. The production of prismatic blades provides a maximum of functional edge per volume of core. If it is assumed that outlying or distant populations traveled periodically to the ceremonial centers, the transportation of blades and/or the small cores used in their production would have been less costly in terms of energy expenditure and required packing space. A recent functional study of a sample of such blades from the Napoleon Hollow site in Illinois indicates that these implements were used for cutting and light scraping (Michael Wiant: Personal Communication 1980). In light of these proposed functions combined with their form and context, it may be postulated that blades were utilized in the dissection of cadavers and in cleaning remaining skeletal elements. Such blades may also have been used in the preparation and serving of venison and other foods used and consumed during the ritual feasts.

The ceramics found in the Seip structures, and at other Hopewellian ceremonial centers, are of two basic types. First, there are medium to large sized utilitarian vessels most frequently made in traditional forms and with local finish treatments. Second, a relatively high percentage of the pottery at these sites consists of small, highly decorative jars and bowls made at distant places or copied from such exotic wares. William Sears (1973) has made a strong case, based largely upon ceramic materials from the Southeast, that there was a distinction in form and decoration between the types of pottery made by particular peoples for utilitarian use and for ritual use. Sears documents numerous examples of this distinction between the kinds of pottery found in village middens and in burial mounds and other ritual contexts. Milanich and Fairbanks (1980) provide additional examples of this ceramic dualism in their summary of Florida prehistory (Cades Pond is one classic example, p. 97). In his section on Middle Woodland ceramics, Sears (1973:35) notes that "while the entire Hopewell ceremonial assemblage is distinct, specialized ceramics are a part . . . Rocker stamping, zoned texturing, resist decoration, and tetrapodal bases . . . are common in ceremonial context, rare in village middens. Foreign vessels . . . are relatively common too. Most of them are of Southeastern origin."

One of the intriguing aspects of Sears' study is that this ceramic dualism is clearly traceable through later prehistoric times into the Mississippian period (Sears 1973:37–38). Assuming that this practice continued into the historic period, significant insight into the function of sacred ceramics is provided by Swanton from an ethnohistoric account of Natchez food offerings made to the dead.

> I saw a number of little earthen pots, platters and cups, and little cane baskets, all well made. This is to serve up to the spirits of the deceased chiefs, and the temple keeper finds his profits in it [1911:158].
>
> They give the dishes to the guardian, who carries them to the side of the basket in which are the bones of the dead; this ceremony lasts only one moon. The dishes are afterward placed on the palisades which surround the

temple and are abandoned to the fallow deer [1911:269; quoted by Seeman 1979b:44].

Based upon Sears' study, and upon ethnographic analogy, it may be postulated that the Hopewell and Southeastern series ceramics found at the Ohio centers were composed of small ceremonial vessels that were used to contain votive offerings of food for the dead. The larger, more normal sized vessels found at these centers may have been used to prepare ritual food and to serve this meal to the living, whom we may assume had more immediate need for large quantities of food. One morphological characteristic shared by these sacred ceramics, other than their diminutive size, is that most of these vessels are free standing. Flat or slightly rounded bases and tetrapodal supports are particularly common on these vessel forms in contrast to the conoidal or fully rounded bases of utilitarian vessels. It appears that the sacred vessels were made so that they would stand on a flat surface, perhaps for display during the mortuary ritual. The large numbers of ceramic vessels used and broken at these ceremonial centers and the nature of the activities conducted during the rituals result in a high ratio of sherds to lithic artifacts at such sites.

In regard to the five South Appalachian sites discussed earlier, these comparative data suggest that they were functional equivalents of the much larger Ohio Hopewell vacant ceremonial centers. These ceremonial encampments, or microceremonial centers, contain evidence of virtually identical ritual activities as those conducted at the northern microceremonial centers.

These activities may be summarized as follows:

1. *Congregation of large, and at times ethnically diverse participant populations*. The quantities of exotic ceramics found at these early Middle Woodland sites suggest that nonlocal populations or population segments were involved, perhaps with the local group serving as hosts (Ford 1979:237–238). The vast differences in both spatial extent and temporal span of reuse between the Ohio and South Appalachian centers suggest wide variation in the numbers of participants, probably reflecting differences in both regional and population density and level of socioeconomic complexity. Seeman (1979b) and others have argued that the Ohio evidence indicates that some of these groups were organized into chiefdoms. Similar

data from South Appalachian sites suggest that these mountain territories were occupied by intensive hunting and plant-harvesting bands and perhaps a few acephalous tribes (Walthall 1980).

2. *Ritual feasts in which large quantities of meat were consumed.* Extant seasonal data indicate that these feasts were conducted during warm weather, for example, during early fall when sizable harvests of seed foods and deer were available.
3. *Preparation and processing of the dead for interment and construction of burial facilities and tumuli.* Skeletal material recovered at Hopewell sites indicates elaborate preinhumation processing of the corpses. Defleshing and dismemberment, often followed by cremation, was a common treatment. The variety of burial types present in Hopewell mounded cemeteries ranges from flexed and extended flesh burials, to bundle burials, to cremations. While the type of mortuary processing afforded an individual may have been based upon status differentiation, it also seems possible that a specific type of treatment may have been dictated by the temporal duration between death and the next ritual assembly. That is, individuals who died shortly after a mortuary ceremony would have had to have been stored until the next. These individuals may have been processed into bundle burials or cremated while individuals who died at some interval nearer to the next ceremonial gathering may have been interred in the flesh.
4. *Redistribution of food and raw materials and finished items.* Seeman (1979b) and other researchers (Ford 1979) have argued that Hopewell exchange involved not only exotic materials used in social and ritual contexts but also basic subsistence goods such as food. Ford (1979:238) has recently observed that:

> Exchange of exotic goods has long been a hallmark of Hopewell. But the exchange mechanisms and raison d'etre were probably multiple.
>
> At the local level, trade and exchange may have brought food from areas of plenty to areas of want, or, more likely, economic and social exchange brought *people* from villages of scarcity to villages with a surplus. Formal visitations were undoubtedly coordinated by village leaders, included ceremonial presentations, feasting, and the exchange of durable goods such as beads and scarce items for food, and they may have facilitated marriages between groups.
>
> Supralocal or regional gatherings may have been periodic events related to

what we see as mortuary activities or earthworks. Again, planning and preparation were required for multivillage gatherings at these places.

5. *Rituals that were scheduled.* The data recovered from the sites under consideration indicate that they functioned as periodic loci for ritual activities. The congregation of sizable, often culturally diverse, populations at these centers suggests that these gatherings were scheduled. Yengoyan (1972) has made a distinction between the two types of intergroup ritual: the "unscheduled," time-independent communal rituals of low-density hunters and gatherers, and the "scheduled," time-dependent or calendric rituals of higher-density populations. Flannery (1972:129), in a commentary on Yengoyan's paper, notes that "ritual interaction among scattered groups of Australian hunter-gatherers is *ad hoc*, occurring only 'under favorable environmental conditions which permit local groups to cluster for several days.' This interaction . . . cannot be sustained on a scheduled basis because of the unreliability of food and water; the ritual is triggered by unpredictable moments of abundance."

In contrast, among successful food producers and among high-density hunter-gatherers, where harvests occur at predictable times of the year, time-dependent rituals occur with marked temporal regularity. While the Middle Woodland cultures under consideration practiced horticulture, paleobotanical evidence indicates that hunting and gathering were of primary economic importance (Ford 1979). However, in the rich eastern deciduous forests wild resources (deer, fish, seeds, etc.) were seasonally available in quantity. It may be predicted that Hopewell ceremonial gatherings were scheduled to coincide with warm weather seasons of plenty. Early fall when nuts and deer are harvested, and late spring when fish, greens, and garden produce are available, appear to likely times for such feasting.

Conclusions

The primary goals of this paper have been to provide a model of the Hopewellian vacant ceremonial center and to record its presence in the southern highlands. It would appear from the data presented that Hopewellian interaction involved not only the exchange and redistribution of materials and goods, but also information flow concerning ideological and ritual patterns of behavior. The concept of a spatially segregated, limited-activity locality for ritual gatherings, what has been called a vacant ceremonial center in this presentation, was widely disseminated and incorporated into local cultural systems throughout the East.

Such ceremonial centers are characterized by evidence of repeated, brief occupations by congregations of ethnically diverse groups at times of ritual activities related to mortuary processing and communal feasting. The material culture found at these centers is typified by the remains of relatively large numbers of sacred pottery vessels possibly used to serve votive offerings of food to the dead. In the South Appalachians such Middle Woodland sacred vessels usually took the form of the small tetrapodal jar. This vessel shape, originally foreign to the region, was derived from earlier Coastal Plain Gulf Tradition ceramics (Walthall 1980).

The five South Appalachian sites discussed in this paper appear to represent the same settlement type, a ceremonial encampment, which has not previously been recognized in the region. These sites also can be conceived of as initial nodes of Hopewell contact with indigenous highland peoples. As Griffin (1967) has noted, the distribution of Hopewell trade items and the spatial relationship of certain raw material source areas to consumer territories suggest that a major vehicle for this interaction was the trading party. Such trading parties may have included individuals well versed in ritual practices.

A close similarity between the Ohio macroceremonial centers and the South Appalachian ceremonial encampments, in terms of site functions and material culture, has been demonstrated. These observations raise two intriguing possibilities. First, that these five sites were actually visited, and briefly occupied, by Ohio Hopewell trading parties during their quests for exotic raw materials and routes to the coastal provinces to the south. Second, that these visits may have been reciprocated by South Appalachian groups who made pilgrimages northward to participate in the ritual activities conducted at the massive Ohio ceremonial centers.

Acknowledgments

This chapter represents an expanded version of a paper presented by James A. Brown and the author at the 1982 Southeastern Archaeological Conference in Memphis. I would like to thank Dr. Brown for his comments on draft versions of this paper and for the hours he spent discussing this topic with me. I would also like to thank Kenneth Farnsworth, James B. Griffin, and Richard Jeffries for their helpful comments and criticisms.

Tim Kennedy of the Illinois Department of Transportation contributed the illustration of the tetrapodal vessels, and his colleague, William Belair, prepared the accompanying map. I would also like to thank Jack Schock for providing an illustration of the Watkins mound tetrapodal jar which served as the basis for the drawing of this vessel.

14 • STANLEY SOUTH AND MICHAEL O. HARTLEY

Deep Water and High Ground: Seventeenth-Century Settlement Patterns on the Carolina Coast

Introduction

The importance of topography as a criterion for interpreting the settlement patterns of prehistoric Southeastern Indians was demonstrated by Joffre Coe (1964) in his work at the Yadkin River Archaic sites, where he recognized that the archaeological record was dependent upon an appreciation of the relationship between the cultural needs of the people and the physiographic factors present. Coe found the hourglass narrowing at river gorges, the attraction of shallow water, and the funneling effect these had on human travel along river courses to be major variables in the location of occupation sites on the same ground over thousands of years. This observation of the relationship between physiographic features and human behavior allowed him to hypothesize a highly predictable means for locating stratified occupation sites. These variables were no less important in the settlement patterns of the first Europeans who set foot on the eastern shores of North America. Two such variables were deep water and high ground (South and Hartley 1980).

When the leaders of the Port Royal Expedition of 1670 chose to establish the first English colony in South Carolina on the Ashley River rather than at Port Royal, they selected the high ground of a peninsula that touched the deep-water channel of the access creek to the site (Cheves 1897; South 1971). The Spanish, in settling their fledgling capital city of Spanish Florida at Santa Elena in Port Royal Sound over one hundred years before, had chosen a very similar site, one where high ground met the deep-water channel of the access stream to the site (Hoffman 1978; South 1979). Both sites provided bow-on fire from the high ground against any enemy ships trying to reach the secure footing of the settlement. The deep-water channel was the intercontinental highway of the settlement period, and to place a settlement away from this highway to the rest of the world was unthinkable.

At Jamestown, Virginia, the first fort and settlement was placed on high ground adjacent to the deep-water channel of the river. Subsequent erosion seems to have removed much of the early settlement site. These three early settlements in the Southeast—Santa Elena, Jamestown, and Charles Towne—also were characterized by having low marshy ground between the high ground of the settlement and the mainland, which served as a protective barrier against possible Indian attack from that direction. Thus, the early settlements were protected by a fort, and, in the case of Santa Elena and Charles Towne, by a marsh and creek, which would force an enemy vessel into a bow-on position of vulnerability in approaching the fort and town. The location of these important sites in the early history of this nation, therefore, was no accident, but rather represented a well-thought-out strategy for defense, as well as providing an easy access to the shipping channels of the world.

Given the above considerations, it follows that those individuals most likely to acquire the sought-after deep water and high ground would be those of higher status and financial ability to develop such land and landing locations. In 1975, South suggested that this association of deep water, high ground, and status might well be a major consideration in the development of continental frontier settlement in the American Southeast (South 1977:189). Such settlement would likely center around a major entrepot (Lewis 1977:151–201), with individuals seeking the deep-water and high-ground sites as a cluster of plantations on rivers and streams convenient to the major settlement center. Charleston, South Carolina, which grew out of the original Charles Towne settlement of 1670, is an excellent example of such a situation.

The Thornton-Morden Map of 1695 and the Maurice Mathews Map of 1685

Two maps provide the documentary basis for this study. A map published in 1695 (Figure 14-1), dedicated to John Thornton and Robert Morden, is based on a map surveyed around 1685 by Maurice Mathews (Cumming 1962:162, 166). These documents locate over 250 plantations or settlers' sites within 15 years of the first landing at Charles

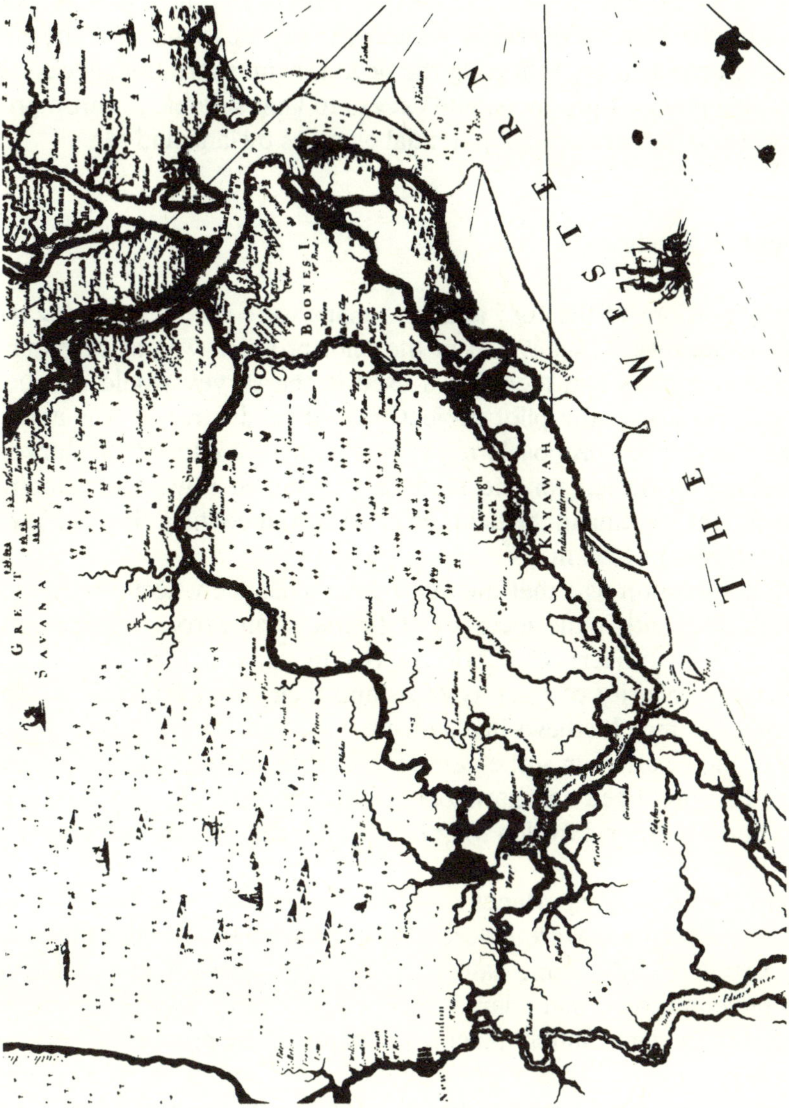

Figure 14-1. The Area of the 1695 Thornton-Morden Map of Interest in the Pilot Study (Caroliniana Library, University of South Carolina).

Towne in 1670, and thus are valuable records of colonial settlement patterns in the Charleston area (Cumming 1962:162, 166). These maps offer an opportunity to test the ideas of deep water, high ground, and status outlined above as critical variables in site location during the first years of colonization, reflecting the need for transportation, access to goods, shipping of products, and access to land suitable for crop production and defense against potential enemies by land and sea.

Research Design

Only portions of the 1685 and 1695 maps were used in outlining the project, because a major goal of the pilot program was to determine whether methods and techniques used in the survey would produce positive results. If the pilot project proved productive, it was anticipated that further proposals might be outlined to expand the survey. The research design for the study was oriented toward developing methods for locating in the field the seventeenth-century sites depicted on the 1685 and 1695 maps.

An assumption was that the maps gave reasonably accurate site locations. This faith in the accuracy of the maps came from a comparison of them with modern Geodetic Survey maps, which revealed a remarkable similarity of river systems and their tributary streams. Apparently, Maurice Mathews had done far more than simply draw a sketch map of the Charleston settlement area in 1685. Being a surveyor, Mathews had produced a remarkably accurate map of the area involved. Also, the Thornton-Morden Map had been highly refined before it was published.

One question of importance was whether the symbols shown beside names on the maps were indeed placed accurately enough to allow a pinpointing of sites. Some names had no house symbol shown, which may have indicated that a large tract of land was involved in that area for that individual. Simply placing the name of the property owner on the creek in some cases might well have been sufficient. In so doing, however, the pinpointing of sites of seventeenth-century occupations might be a chancy proposition, because such a site could have been located anywhere along the stream where the name was written on the map. In cases where a general site location was indicated by a name only, the position of the name was taken as a clue to the location of a "possible site" (Figure 14-2).

By using the sites with house symbols as a beginning, it was thought that the degree of accuracy of the symbols could be assessed, and from the location of such sites in relation to elevation, topography, marshland, high ground, deep-water channel, etc., a model would be in hand for use in locating the more generally indicated sites.

Testing the direct historical approach through the use of the 1685 and 1695 maps as research tools was a major goal of the project. Therefore, simply finding fragments of seventeenth-century pottery on a site located by means of the maps would be sufficient verification of the validity of the maps as a locational device for such sites. No statistical manipulation of the data was anticipated beyond simply determining the presence or absence of seventeenth-century materials. The extent to which seventeenth-century sites were found to be located on deep water and high ground in a patterned manner would be used to test the hypothesis regarding site location.

The correlation between social status and the pattern of sites discovered would depend on considerable research in archival records for clues to status levels of the individuals whose occupation sites were indicated on the maps, a project outside the scope of the present research design. However, some clues to status are available and will be referred to when applicable.

A primary goal of the project was to document information on the location of seventeenth-century sites. Some eighteenth- and nineteenth-century data are mentioned as they are deemed pertinent to the seventeenth century, but the goal is not the detailed recording of these sites of later occupation. Table 14-1 lists the relevant sites on the Stono River and North and South Edisto rivers.

Steps in the research procedure were as follows:

1. Background research on sites involved in the study area.
2. Drafting of maps of the research area using Geodetic Survey data and pinpointing potential site locations.
3. Field visits to search for surface indications of seventeenth-century occupation, study the lay of the land, draw sketch maps, make verbal observations, and talk to local informants and landowners.
4. Analysis of the data, artifacts, synthesis of results, and drafting of maps illustrating results.

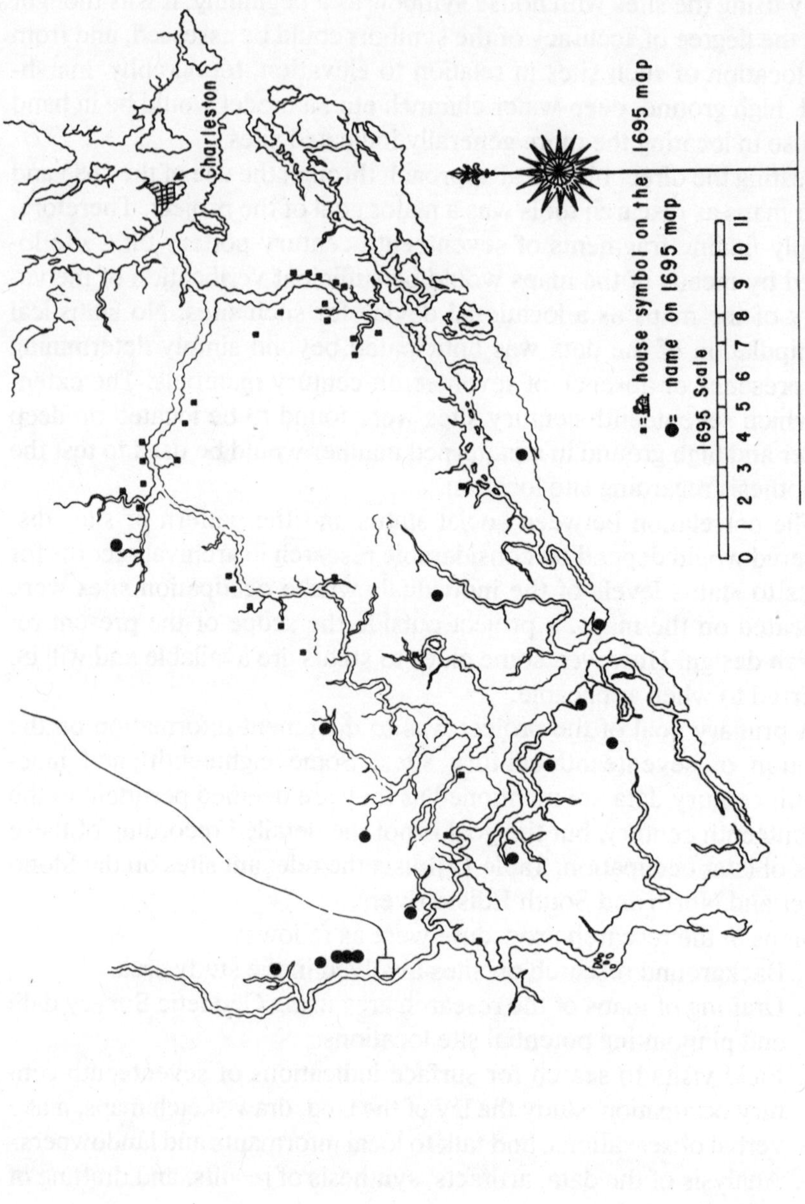

Figure 14-2. A Tracing from the 1695 Thornton-Morden Map Showing the Sites Indicated by a House Symbol and Those with a Name Only.

Table 14-1. A Listing of Some Sites from the 1695 Thornton-Morden Map between the Stono and Edisto Rivers.

Indian Sites

Indian settlements at the north entrance of Edisto River. Edestow settlements south of the north entrance of Edisto River. Indian Settlements on the west bank of Bohickock Creek.

Extinct Towns

New London

Sites on the North Bank of the South Edisto River

Sr. Peter Colleton Precinct Lotts	Mr. Green
Mr. Wilcocks London	Mr. Rose
Mr. Miller	Chebasah
Mr. Smith	

Sites on the South Bank of the South Edisto River

Russell
Mr. Crabb
Grimballs

Sites on the North Edisto River Drainage

Land^{r} Axtel	Warricks Island
Wappo	Land^{r} Morton
Governor Morton	Stone
Dr. Williams	

Site on Kayawagh Creek

Mr. Grice

Sites on the North Side of Stono River

Mr. Blakes	Mr. Morris	Mr. Goffe
Mr. Peters	Whitemarsh	Mr. Walkin
Cap. Bristows	Pell	Caffin
Mr. Farr	Hall	Mr. Beaman
Wilson	Ralph	Cap Clap
Joseph	George	

Sites on the South Side of Stono River

Mr. Seabrook	Conway	Ashley
Waight Land	Farr	Brackhurst
Cowens Land	Napper	Mr. Staniard
Jacob Waightlan	Mr. Petter	Dr. Woodward
Mr. Cowen	Mr. Davis	

5. Writing the conclusions, synthesis, and recommendations for further work based on results of the pilot study, as well as evaluation of the results of the methods used.

Methods

Site Data Recording

The major record of each site is the *verbal commentary* made at the time of the visit, in which the relationship of the actual site to the map location is discussed. The second basic type of data is the *artifact inventory* from the site, which is of primary value through the ceramic types present. Because no quantitative analysis was undertaken as a part of the research design, the presence of artifact classes or ceramic types was used instead. These data allow the fixing of general temporal information within relatively short intervals of time in some cases, a sensitivity deemed adequate for the present study where the major goal was the identification of seventeenth-century sites. The verbal commentary and listing of artifact classes and types for each site from which data were collected are published elsewhere (South and Hartley 1980).

When a specific site was being sought, the name of that site as indicated on the 1685 and 1695 maps is used as the site name. In fact, this name may be used for one or more sites found in the area indicated on the maps. If the site is limited to a specific point of high ground beside the deep-water channel of a creek, for instance, and seventeenth-century objects are found on the surface of a nearby road or field, then there is an excellent chance that the site found is that indicated on the maps.

In cases where a more general designation, consisting simply of a name written on the map in the area of a creek, several high points of ground may well touch the deep-water channel in that area; thus the pinpointing of the site is not so easy. In such cases, the sites are designated, for example, "Napper East," "Napper West," or simply "Napper," depending on the relationships involved. This allows several sites in the area shown on the 1685 and 1695 maps as "Napper" to be assigned site names.

This system has been very successfully applied at the site of Santa Elena on Parris Island, where various areas of the same large site have been designated through the use of a capital letter attached to the site number. Thus, sites 38BU162A, 38BU162B, and 38BU162C are all areas of the same 38BU162 site, where, for analytical purposes, areas of a site must be separated. The same system was used in this survey, with the verbal site *name* being designated as "Napper North," etc., and the site *number* being accompanied by a letter designation to separate it from other nearby sites that, although physically related to the Napper site, may well be different functional areas of a single working plantation. This system allows for a maximum of flexibility in the search for large occupational complexes, such as plantations, with their many structures and large areas of land.

In the case of the site indicated on the 1685 and 1695 maps as "Govern[r] Morton," no symbol for a structure was used, and thus a huge tract of land may well have been indicated. The authors realized that this did not allow them to pinpoint the site, as was possible in some instances where a specific symbol was used. The search for the Governor Morton site, therefore, resulted in some sites called "Governor Morton South" on the south side of Toogoodoo Creek (38CH483). Later, after talking with local informants who had used a land plat showing Governor Morton's land on the north side of Toogoodoo Creek, and who had found what appeared to be a seventeenth-century cellar hole, two sites on the north side of Toogoodoo Creek (both related to the Morton family) were designated "Governor Morton North" (38CH238). This was a case where local informants had more specific information than the surveyors were able to glean from the maps.

The approach was to photocopy specific areas of the USGS map whereon one or more of the seventeenth-century sites were thought to be, as suggested by the 1685 and 1695 maps. A circle was then drawn on each of these site maps to focus attention on the area where a search would be carried out. Once the site was found, a more detailed map was drawn. In some cases, a very strong indication of the location of the sites was deduced from the terrain, the 1685 and 1695 maps, and a close correlation with the USGS map (Figures 14-3 and 14-4).

In addition to the *verbal commentary* and *artifact inventory* records of each site, a *photograph* usually was taken of each site, and a *sketch map* was made to show specific on-site relationships to be used in re-

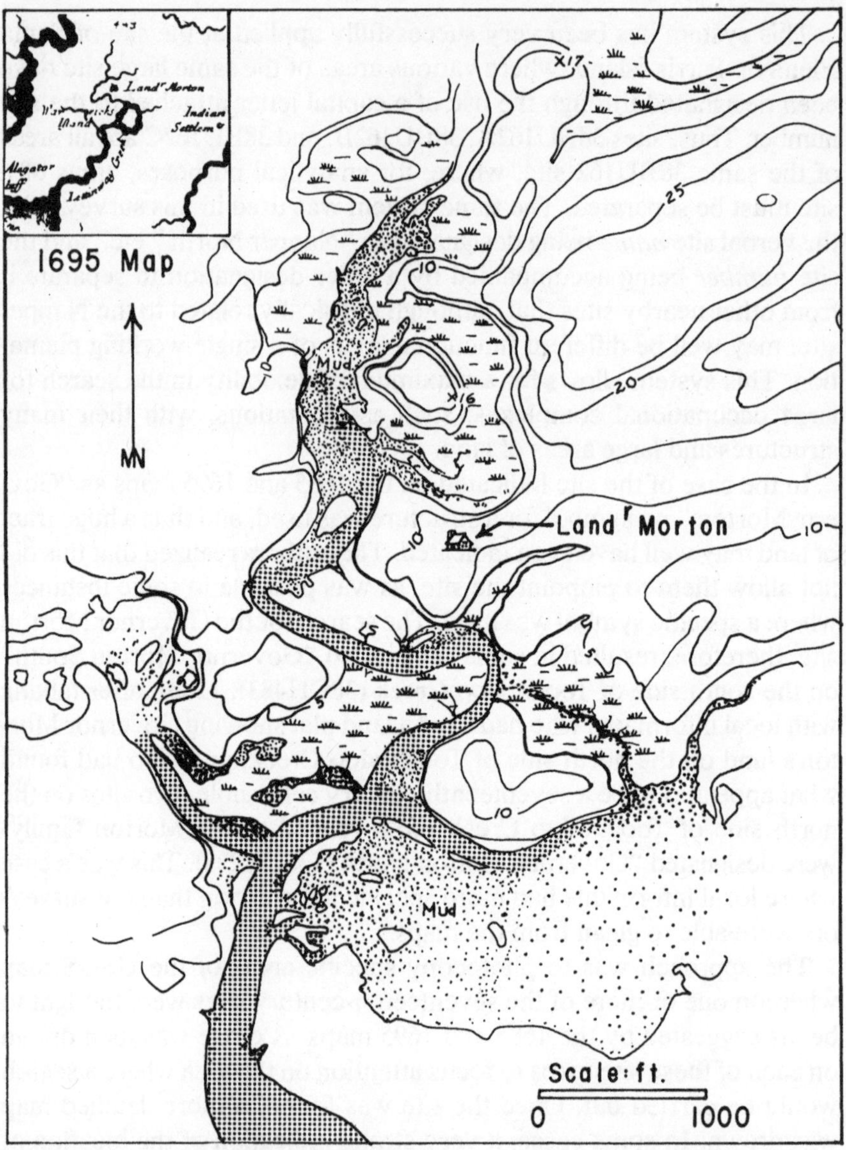

Figure 14-3. An Example of the Technique Used to Match the 1695 Map Showing a House Site, "Land^r Morton," and the USGS Map of the Same Area. (Note that although no artifcats were recovered due to local conditions the site location is known from the map correlation.)

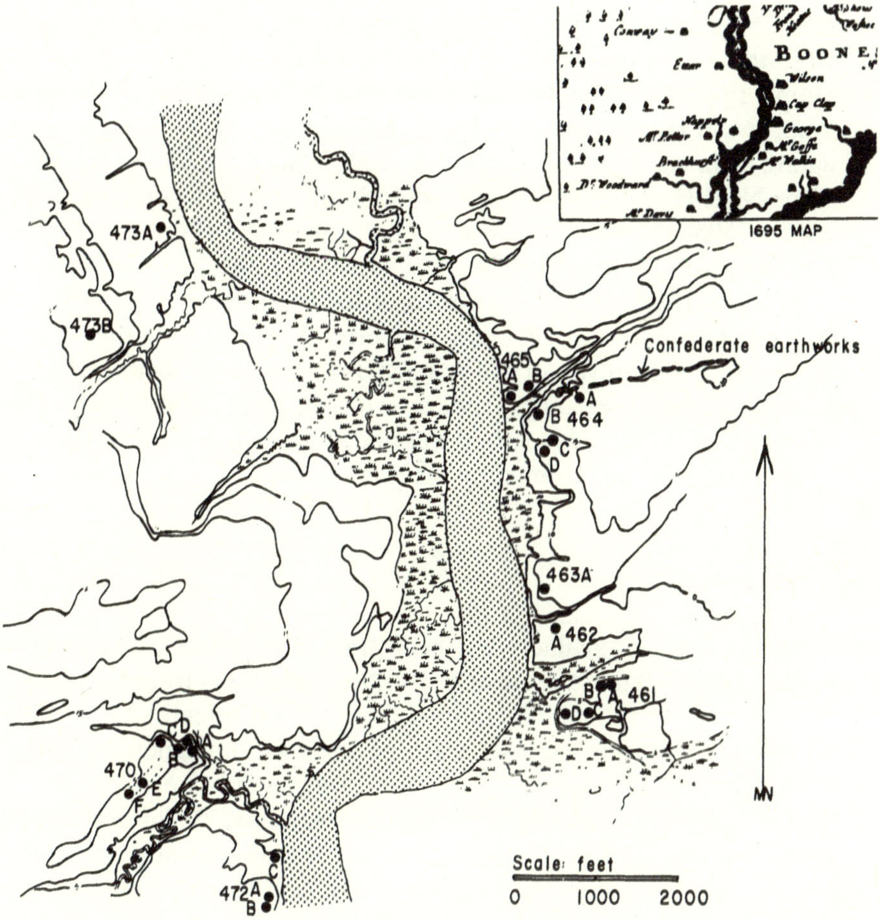

Figure 14-4. Sites on the Stono River at the Eastern Edge of the Pilot Study. (Note the correspondence with the 1605 map of the same area.)

locating the site. The photograph and sketch map form a third and fourth basic type of data collection carried out in the fieldwork phase of the study.

Artifact Data Recording

The primary data of interest in this project were those identifying the occupation of a site during the seventeenth century. The presence of ceramics of the seventeenth century was considered the best indicator of such occupation. Pottery types considered important in this regard were the Bellarmine-type stoneware jug, dating ca. 1620–1700 (Noël Hume 1970:55–57; South 1977:210); North Devon Gravel-Tempered Ware (Noël Hume 1970:104–105, 133; South 1977:211; Watkins 1960), dating from ca. 1650–1775; Combed Yellow Slipware, dating ca. 1670–1795 (Noël Hume 1970:107, 134–136; South 1977:211); and Delft, dating ca. 1600–1802. Delft, having such a wide range of use, is relatively nondiagnostic, given the small fragments usually found in surface surveys.

Artifacts from each site were recorded by type or class, with frequency of occurrence not being considered as a variable for the purpose of this study. The inventory of artifacts from each site, therefore, is not a fragment inventory but an indicator of what types and classes of artifacts are present. This method was adequate to determine the general temporal period represented by the artifacts.

Artifact Analysis

The analysis of artifacts has been limited to pottery, which is the major class of artifact represented in the collections from the survey. Nine pottery types manufacturered from the seventeenth through the nineteenth centuries were selected for analysis as diagnostic of occupation periods at the sites. The pottery types indicative of late seventeenth- and early eighteenth-century occupation are Bellarmine, North Devon Gravel-Tempered Ware, Combed Yellow Slipware, Delft, and Westerwald (South 1977:210–212). White Salt-glazed Stoneware reflects an occupation after ca. 1720, and its absence on a site, when no later types are present, suggests an occupation ending prior to its introduction in 1720. The same is true of Creamware, which dates after ca. 1762; its absence, and that of later types, suggests an occupation ending prior to that date. Ironstone-whiteware is a similar indicator of nineteenth-century occupation, with a beginning date around 1820 (South 1977:210–212).

The presence of a set of seventeenth-century pottery types suggests occupation in the seventeenth century. Sometimes, occupation continuing into the eighteenth century and into the nineteenth century would be indicated by presence of the diagnostic types of those periods. Other sites revealed that they were occupied at two different times, first in the seventeenth century and later in the nineteenth century. These placements were determined by the absence of mid-eighteenth-century pottery types, such as White Salt-glazed Stoneware (suggesting an occupation ending prior to 1720) and Creamware (suggesting an occupation ending prior to 1762). With the presence of such types, however, a continuous occupation was inferred.

The distribution of pottery types by sites is given in Table 14-2, where the types are arranged in chronological order from left to right. The diagonal line from the upper left to lower right reveals the temporal occupation of the sites as reflected by the presence and absence of pottery types of progressively later time periods of manufacture. If one used the presence of Bellarmine jug fragments as an indicator of seventeenth-century occupation, only eight sites would be used. If, however, one also included North Devon Gravel-Tempered Ware, nine more sites would be included in the seventeenth-century group. By including Combed Yellow Slipware, 11 more sites would be added. However, Combed Yellow Slipware occurs in association with pottery types of the late eighteenth century because of the long manufacture range of the type, and it cannot be used alone as an indicator of seventeenth-century occupation. The data in Table 14-2, therefore, suggest that the first 17 sites are those that can be said, on the basis of survey data, to have been occupied in the seventeenth century. Other sites were apparently occupied in the mid-eighteenth century, others in the late eighteenth and early-to-mid-nineteenth century, and still others into the twentieth century. These latter sites were located but have not been included in the analysis, since this most recent period is far less important to the goals of the project than the seventeenth- and eighteenth-century sites.

Using the mean of the median manufacture dates for the total number of pottery types present on each site, one can derive a "mean ceramic date" for each site. When two occupations are represented by the pottery types, as indicated by the absence of White Salt-glazed Stoneware or Creamware, it is then possible to determine a *terminus ad quem* for the occupation of the site as revealed by the types dating prior to that time. In such cases, a mean ceramic date for the second occupation of the site also can be derived. When continuous occupations are in-

Table 14-2. Presence of Some Pottery Types on the Survey Sites.

Site No. 38CH		BALLARMINE 1620–1700 (1660) = median mfg. date	N. DEVON GRAVEL T. WARE 1650–1775 (1713)	COMBED YELLOW SLIPWARE 1670–1795 (1733)	DELFT 1600–1802 (1650)	WESTERWALD 1700–1775 (1738)	WHITE SALT-GLAZED STONEWARE 1720–1805 (1763)	CREAMWARE 1762–1820 (1791)	PEARLWARE 1780–1890 (1805)	IRONSTONE–WHITEWARE 1820–1900 + (1860)	COLONO–WARE	CHINESE PORCELAIN
485C	"Joseph" C	X	X	X	X	X	X					X
461C	"Walkin" C	X	X	X	X	X	X	X	X	X	X	
463A	"George" A	X	X	X	X	X	X	X	X	X	X	X
467B	"Dr Woodward" B	X		X	X	X	X		X	X	X	
472B	"Mr Petter" B	X			X	X	X			X		
468A	"Dr Woodward" West A	X		X	X		X	X	X	X	X	X
470B	"Napper" B	X		X	X	X						
483B	"Gov Morton" South B	X						X	X	X		
238A	"Gov Morton" North A		X	X	X	X	X					X
466B	"Mr Davis" B		X	X	X	X		X		X		X
470F	"Napper" F		X	X	X	X	X	X	X	X	X	X
466A	"Mr Davis" A		X		X	X	X			X	X	
473A	"Mr Ettar" A		X	X			X			X	X	X
232A	"Russell" A		X	X		X	X	X	X			X
239A	"Mr Blake" A		X		X	X	X	X	X	X		X
489B	"Cap Bristows" B		X	X				X	X	X		

58	"New London"	x	x								
202C	"Grimballs" C		x	x		x					
470E	"Napper" E		x	x		x				x	x
464B	"Cap Clap" B		x	x			x	x		x	x
472C	"Mr Petter" C		x	x	x		x	x	x		x
465A	"Wilson" A		x	x	x		x	x	x		x
483A	"Gov Morton" South A		x			x	x	x	x		
461A	"Walkin" A		x					x	x	x	
202A	"Grimballs" A		x				x	x	x		x
202D	"Grimballs" D		x				x	x	x		x
238D	"Gov Morton" North B		x				x	x	x	x	
200	"Sir P. Colletons"		x								
462A	"Goffe" A			x			x	x	x		
461B	"Walkin" B			x			x	x			
488A	"Mr Farr" A			x			x	x			x
472A	"Mr Petter" A				x	x	x	x	x		
467A	"Dr Woodward" A				x		x	x	x	x	x
468A	"Dr Woodward" West B				x		x		x		x
469A	"Brackhurst" A				x		x	x	x		x
202F	"Grimballs" F				x		x		x		
487A	"Mr Grice" A						x	x	x	x	x
464D	"Cap Clap" D						x	x			
202B	"Grimballs" B						x		x		
485A	"Joseph" A						x		x		
201A	"Edisto Settlemt" A						x	x	x		
485B	"Joseph" B							x	x		
202E	"Grimballs" E								x		
470C	"Napper" C								x		
483C	"Gov Morton" South C								x		
473B	"Mr Ettar" B								x		

*part of Elaine Herold Collection, Charleston Museum.

volved, covering some two hundred years, a single mean ceramic date must be determined.

Using the method of deriving mean dates from the median manufacture date for each pottery type, one arrives at the dates seen in Table 14-3. The first twenty sites are likely seventeenth-century sites as revealed by the pottery types present, which expands the presence and absence list by three sites. Eighteenth- and nineteenth-century sites are also indicated by the use of mean ceramic dates.

If more extensive samples from the sites were available through test squares or excavation, it might well be found that some of the eighteenth-century sites would reveal seventeenth-century materials. However, the purpose of this pilot project was to determine if a surface survey approach alone would yield data reflecting seventeenth-century occupation, and 20 such sites were indeed located through such an approach.

In addition to these 20 sites, others were geographically located from the association of deep water with high ground, thus permitting sites to be pinpointed. In the absence of artifacts, however, such sites were not assigned numbers.

Deep Water and High Ground

One of the hypotheses to be tested by this pilot study was whether seventeenth-century settlement by Europeans was at sites located at the point where high ground met the deep-water channel of rivers and streams (South 1977:189). By high ground we mean those elevations above the five-foot contour, and by deep water we mean navigable streams having at least three feet of water at mean low water. Most of the sites located in the survey are within 100 feet of such deep water (Table 14-4). Some, however, such as those to the northwest of the site of New London, have a wide, very low ground area between the high ridge and the river, and it is thought that the occupants of these sites made use of the deep-water access available at New London, later known as Willtown (Smith 1909:20–32). The seventeenth-century site at Walkin C also may not have been on a deep-water channel; however, a canal leading to the site today may well have been a deep-water creek three hundred years ago, allowing this site also to fit the pervasive pattern of

Table 14-3. Mean Ceramic Dates for Pottery Types (Derived from Median Manufacture Dates) from the Survey Sites (South 1977:210–212).

Site No. 38CH		Mean Date for 17th c. Occupation	*Terminus Ad Quem*	Mean Date for Continuous Occupation & 18th c. sites	Mean Date for Second Occupation & 19th c. sites
485C	Joseph C	1709.5	(1762)		
461C	Walkin C			1745.9	
463A	George A			1745.9	
467B	Dr. Woodward B	1708.8	(1762)**		1832.5
472B	Mr. Petter B	1695.3	(1720) *		1860.0
468A	Dr. Woodward West A			1751.7	
470B	Napper B	1695.3	(1720)		
483B	Gov Morton South B	1660	—		1797.3
238A	Gov Morton North A	1719.4	(1762)**		
466B	Mr Davis B	1708.5	(1720) *		1825.5
470F	Napper F			1756.6	
466A	Mr Davis A	1716	(1762)**		1860.0
473A	Mr Ettar A	1736.3	(1762)**		1860.0
232A	Russell A			1757.2	
239A	Mr Blake A			1760.0	
489B	Cap Bristows B	1723.0	(1720) *		1818.7
58	New London	1723.0	—		
202C	Grimballs C	1715.3	(1762)**		
470E	Napper E	1715.3	(1762)**		
464B	Cap Clap B	1691.5	(1720) *		1798.0
472C	Mr Petter C			1762.8	
465A	Wilson A			1762.8	
483A	Gov Morton South A			1790.4	
461A	Walkin A			1799.3	
202A	Grimballs A			1797.3	
202D	Grimballs D			1797.3	
238B	Gov Morton North B			1797.3	
200	Sir P. Colletons	1733.0	(one sherd)		
462A	Goffe A			1801.5***	
461B	Walkin B			1782.0***	
488A	Mr Farr A			1782.0***	
472A	Mr. Petter A			1791.4	
467A	Dr. Woodward A			1798.5	
468B	Dr. Woodward West B			1796.3	
469A	Brackhurst A			1798.5	
202F	Grimballs F			1796.3	
487A	Mr Grice A				1818.7
464D	Cap Clap D			1798.0	
202B	Grimballs B				1825.5
485A	Joseph A				1825.5
201A	Edisto Settlm' A				1818.7
485B	Joseph B				1832.5
202E	Grimballs E				1860.0
470C	Napper C				1860.0
483C	Gov Morton South C				1860.0
473B	Mr Ettar B				1860.0

*determined by absence of white salt-glazed stoneware
**determined by absence of creamware
***1750 Delft date used

Table 14-4. Sites in Relation to Elevation, Deep Water Access, and Distance to the Landing.

Site No. 38CH	Site Name	Elevation				Deep Water Access		Distance to Landing				
		5′	10′	15′	20′	Yes	No	100′ or less	100-500′	500-1000′	1000-1500′	1500-2000′
485C	Joseph C	x				x		x				
461C	Walkin C	x				x?			x			
463A	George A		x			x			x			
467B	Dr Woodward B		x			x				x		
472B	Mr Petter B		x			x		x				
468A	Dr Woodward A	x				x					x	
470B	Napper B			x		x			x			
483B	Gov Morton South B		x			x		x				
238A	Gov Morton North A			x		x		x				
466B	Mr Davis B		x			x		x				
470F	Napper F			x		x			x			
466A	Mr Davis A		x			x		x				
473A	Mr Ettar A			x		x						x
232A	Russell A	x				x		x				
239A	Mr Blakes A		x			x?		x				
489B	Cap Bristows B		x			x			x			
58	New London				x	x		x				
202C	Grimballs C	x				x		x				
470E	Napper E			x		x				x		

464B	Cap Clap B		x		x	x				
472C	Mr Petter C	x			x	x				
465A	Wilson A		x		x	x				
483A	Gov Morton South A		x		x	x				
461A	Walkin A	x			x?		x			
202A	Grimballs A	x			x	x				
202D	Grimballs D		x		x				x	
238B	Gov Morton North B			x	x			x		
200	Sir P. Colletons	x			x	x				
462A	Goffe A	x			x		x			
461B	Walkin B	x			x?		x			
488A	Mr Farr A		x		x					
472A	Mr Petter		x		x	x				
467A	Dr Woodward A		x		x			x		
468B	Dr Woodward West B	x			x			x		
469A	Brackhurst A	x			x		x			
202F	Grimballs F	x			x	x				
487A	Mr Grice A		x		x					x
464D	Cap Clap D		x		x		x			
202B	Grimballs B	x			x	x				
485B	Joseph B		x		x			x		
202E	Grimballs E		x		x					x
470C	Napper C		x		x			x		
483C	Gov Morton South C		x		x	x				
473B	Mr Ettar B		x		x		x			

deep-water access to occupation sites located on high ground. No seventeenth-century sites were found on low ground, i.e., below the five-foot contour, and most were between the five- and ten-foot elevations (Table 14-4).

The access to deep water and the use of water as the major route of communication with neighbors resulted in residences and plantations being grouped in clusters forming interacting communities, with kinship ties, a feature still seen in the area. The 1685 and 1695 maps reveal several of these clusters of dwellings on both sides of a river (Figure 14-1). Today, we find that the river is a barrier to communication from one side to the other, but since river traffic was *the* major means of communication in the seventeenth century, the river became a connective link for people living on both sides. Therefore, clusters of settlements grew up with the river between as a major connecting link. These clusters or communities made use of the sought-after high ground for plantations with access to the transportation, communication, and shipping lanes afforded by the deep-water channels of streams and rivers.

Analytical Summary

The seventeenth-century site survey project, using the 1685 and 1695 maps as a locational guide, was successful in locating 20 sites with seventeenth-century artifacts. Fifteen of these sites are among the 50 shown on the 1695 map, thus 30 percent of the sites listed on the Thornton-Morden Map revealed seventeenth-century artifacts. The additional five sites are cases where more than one seventeenth-century site was found on a plantation. The location of the 50 sites is shown on the original Thornton–Morden Map (Figure 14-1). The locations of those on which seventeenth-century data were recovered are shown in Figure 14-5.

Notes on Status and Function

It is interesting to note that, after three hundred years, many of the sites in the survey area are still serving as domestic dwelling places surrounded by grassy lawns, a function they served originally. Also, the use of the high ground adjacent to the residences for agricultural purposes by the seventeenth-century settlers is replicated today by huge

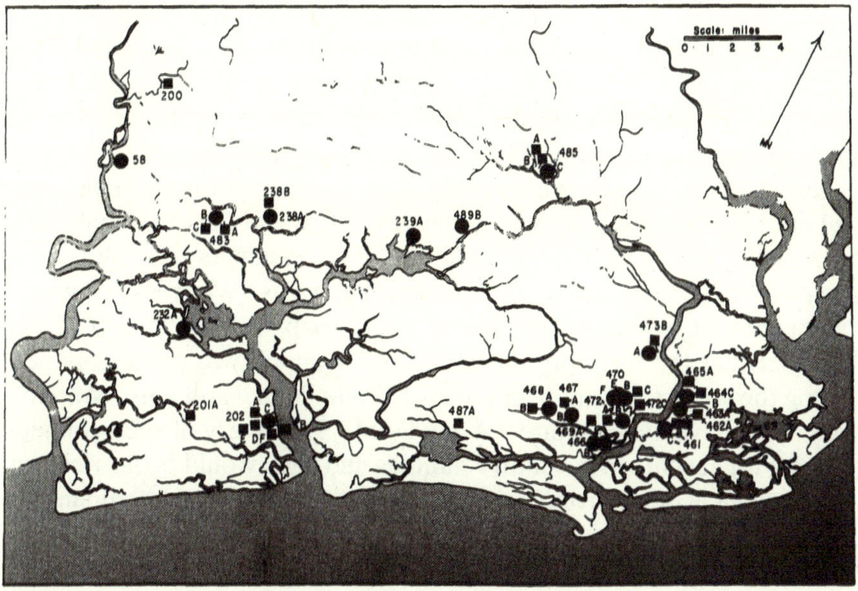

Figure 14-5. The Pilot Study Area Showing the Location of Seventeenth-Century Sites (round dots) and Eighteenth- and Nineteenth-Century Sites (square dots) determined by the Presence of Artifacts.

fields of corn, tomatoes, cucumbers, etc., operated on a scale characteristic of modern agri-business corporations.

The seventeenth-century sites shown on the 1695 map include those of such people as "Dr. Woodward," "Gov. Morton," "Cap Clap," "Landgrave Morton," "Landgrave Axtel," and "Sir Peter Colleton," obviously individuals of upper social status. Detailed research on the other names, no doubt, would reveal others in the upper social level of the period. It is interesting to note that at the present time the properties at the landing sites are still in the hands of affluent individuals. Large tracts of farmland are operated as agri-businesses through the use of migrant labor, large machines, etc. A major difference is that transportation of the produce to the market is by trucks on highways rather than by boat on the waterways once so important in relation to such high, level ground.

We have found that family ties are strongly woven among the low-country plantations where the sites for which we have searched are located. Some of these ties extend into the past for three hundred years, as we found with Governor Morton and Dr. Woodward, whose descendants still live in the area. A study designed to elicit such information might well establish the fact that many of the seventeenth-century families have descendants still working the same land.

Some place names have survived, such as "Russel Creek" in the area where "Russell" was shown on the 1695 map, and the "Grimball" site is still known by that name today by local residents. An interesting possible survival is seen in what today is known as "White Point," which is located where the seventeenth-century map showed "Wappo." We suspect that the local pronunciation of "Wappo" was misunderstood along the way as a pronunciation for "White Point," and thus "Wappo" may well have evolved into "White Point." Discovery of such connections with seventeenth-century families and sites would be far richer if a sociological or anthropological study were designed to accompany an archaeological survey such as we have conducted.

The survival of place names and family names from the seventeenth century reflects the continuity of land use that characterizes the area. The fringes of the area are being encroached upon by industrialization as the Charleston area becomes more densely populated. The core of the area, however, remains an agricultural system with deep roots in the past system. The variables of land use, upper-status control of land, close family ties, and close community ties within river and creek systems are important factors insuring that power remains within the same hands. Close family and community relationships are status-enforcing mechanisms that serve to keep the land, and thus the economic base, within the control of the power center (South 1977:41).

A variable of recent interest in status studies of seventeenth- and eighteenth-century sites is Colonoware, thought to be made by black slaves (Ferguson 1978:68). Twelve sites located in this study contained sherds of this ware (Table 14-2). An artifact that might reflect an upper-class status is Chinese export porcelain (Stone 1970:73). Twenty sites in the survey area contained Chinese export porcelain (Table 14-2). It is interesting to note that these sites are evenly divided between the seventeenth and eighteenth centuries, reflecting an interest in porcelain throughout this time period by those who could afford it. When quantitative studies are made on sites located in this survey, these wares will be a major attribute for examining function and status questions.

Project Assessment

This pilot study was directed at assessing seventeenth-century archaeological resources in the Stono/Edisto river area, as revealed on the 1685 Maurice Mathews Map and the 1695 Thornton-Morden Map. Thirty percent of the sites were found to contain seventeenth-century material, primarily in the form of pottery sherds. A strong settlement pattern based on the nexus of deep water and high ground was demonstrated. These sites are thought to be primarily those of high status individuals, it being highly unlikely that the mapmaker, Maurice Mathews, would have bothered to record the site locations of slaves, indentured servants, fishermen, poor whites, widows, hunters, trappers, or prostitutes, even if he knew the locations of their dwellings.

As the project developed, it became apparent that further survey of areas shown on the 1685 and 1695 maps, beyond that covered in the present study, would need to be built upon a much broader base than was used for this study. A settlement pattern study must be approached from the widest possible perspective to elicit the most information. Before this study began, we suggested that these seventeenth-century sites were being destroyed by industrialization and population increases. However, what we have found is that the geographic area remains remarkably untouched by modern intrusions, though inroads are now beginning in the fringe areas of the study area south of Charleston.

Other findings of this study take on a different perspective than would be the case if site destruction were the pattern rather than the exception. We have found a fascinating cultural subsystem in operation in this geographic area, having roots deeply buried in the seventeenth century. Continuity of land use, continuity of family ties, continuity of focus on wealth, continuity of land ownership, and continuity of economic resources being exploited by high-status individuals provide an opportunity to study this cultural system not only from an archaeological perspective, but from a social and cultural one as well. Of particular use to such a study are the valuable informants located during the survey.

Given these insights into the area, we recommend that future research projects be multidisciplinary in nature, focusing on the specific sites as seen on the 1685 and 1695 maps, with the goals of studying not only the continuation of occupation found on many of these sites through time, but the interlocking fabric of family and community relationships characterizing the area. Such a project would require the expertise of a cultural anthropologist, a historical geographer, an archaeologist, and a historian.

This project has demonstrated that there is indeed a very real predictive relationship between the topographic features of an occupation site and the needs of the individuals occupying those sites. The data happen to be from the historic period, relating to the settlement pattern of the first Englishmen of South Carolina. Such studies, regardless of their time period, demonstrate the value of archaeological methods in the study of culture process.

Epilogue • JAMES B. GRIFFIN

Joffre Lanning Coe: The Quiet Giant of Southeastern Archaeology

In the history of American archaeology, seldom has the development of knowledge about the prehistory of one of the states been so intimately connected with an individual as is that of North Carolina and Joffre Lanning Coe. North Carolina archaeological studies can indeed be divided into two major periods, B.C. and A.C.—Before Coe and After Coe. This is not to say that archaeological work had not been done in the state before his involvement, but that his part in its growth is associated with a significant shift toward a professional approach to archaeological problem solving. Nor was he alone in his youth in having a desire to see acceptable work done in the state, for his career was aided by a number of other North Carolinians.

Joffre was born in Greensboro, North Carolina, on July 5, 1916. Joffre's legal birthday is July 6, 1916; however, he was actually born shortly after midnight on July 5, 1916. His mother's birthday was July 4, and so he asserted himself from the very beginning by being sure he had his own birthday. The physician in attendance was Joffre's Uncle Sam, and Uncle Sam got mixed up on the date. Joffre's mother when she later found out the error replied: "Well, I guess I know. I was there." She well remembered hoping he would arrive before midnight on her birthday. His father was a building contractor whose business fluctuated with the ebb and flow of demand. There were winter trips to Florida and temporary residence in the Orlando-Titusville areas, and as a consequence Joffre changed schools many times. His maternal grandfather was a Methodist minister circuit rider, and Joffre's mother was born in Robbinsville, North Carolina, in Cherokee country. The grandfather was an active outdoorsman with skills in hunting, fishing, and other such activities. He acquired baskets, spoons, and other examples of Indian handicraft, as he and the grandmother provided them with food. As a result of these experiences, he told his grandson many stories of his association with the Cherokee. This apparently led to an interest in reading books about Indians and collecting arrowheads, some of which he probably did on trips with his grandfather. One of these trips took them overnight from Greensboro to what was then called Frutchey Mound and later became known as Town Creek. During his participation in Boy Scout activities, arrowhead collecting was part of his program, and he soon began to realize that there should be more to it than simply possession.

In Florida, during his junior and senior years in high school, he became more and more interested in archaeology, and during the summer of 1932 was writing to Dr. Carl E. Guthe at Ann Arbor in his capacity as Chairman of the National Research Council Committee on State Archaeological Surveys. Joffre was interested in learning about projectile point classification, surveying, recording methods, and excavating. Guthe sent him a copy of the "Guide Leaflet for Amateur Archaeologists," prepared by F. C. Cole, C. E. Guthe, A. V. Kidder, and N. Judd for the *Reprint and Circular Series, National Research Council*, No. 93, and issued in Washington in 1930. He was also referred to W. K. Moorehead's *The Stone Age in North America*. In one of his letters Guthe wrote: "It is a pleasure to learn that one as young as you is taking a serious interest in the study of materials left by the American Indians." In other letters Guthe complimented Joffre on his observations regarding a shell mound near Lake Poinsett on the Upper St. Johns, and on a map he made of the Pine Island mound, and he referred him to a former pole vaulter at the University of California, Matthew W. Stirling. Stirling, then the chief of the Bureau of American Ethnology, had done work in Florida and upon hearing from Joffre sent him publications. There were also instructions from Guthe the following years on how to dig a sand mound, catalog and care for specimens, information on where excavations were being conducted, additional publications, references to other reports, and advice on the courses Joffre should take in order to qualify him to enroll at the University of Michigan. In the late winter or early spring Joffre visited the excavations of Stirling at or near Canaveral Island in Florida and met two of Matt's young colleagues, George Woodbury and Erik Reed.

Coe had graduated from Orlando High School in the spring of 1933 but was unable to continue his schooling in 1933–1934 because of the Depression. In the fall of 1934, he enrolled at Brevard College, as the family by the spring of 1934 had returned to Greensboro. This brought him back to his association with Guy Johnson of the University of North Carolina. Johnson, who helped organize the Archaeological Society of North Carolina in 1933, had corresponded with Joffre before the society was formed, and Joffre became a charter member at the age of sixteen. Howard Odum, a nationally prominent sociologist at Chapel Hill, was interested in incorporating anthropological studies into the Department of Sociology. Bronislaw Malinowski, a charismatic social anthropologist, visited Chapel Hill on his way back from the Trobriand Islands in 1925, and a later lecture by W. K. Moorehead also stimulated Johnson's interest in this relatively little-known academic field. Clark Wissler helped in organizing a course that Johnson gave in 1930 in anthropology, which used Wissler's *Social Anthropology* as a text.

Joffre's interest in North Carolina prehistory was supported by such members of the University faculty as Wallace Caldwell in Ancient History, J. P. Harlan in Classical Studies, and James Bullitt in the Medical School. Letters were sent to 20 or 30 people with a known interest in North Caroina Indian history, such as Douglas L. Rights, a Moravian minister, and Burnham Colburn, a wealthy collector of prehistoric artifacts in Asheville. There was a meeting in Chapel Hill of some 10 to 12 individuals to discuss the formation of a society. One of the results was that Guy Johnson was named secretary, and he proceeded to draw up the preliminary by-laws. Upon hearing about this informal meeting, Coe went to Chapel Hill to see Johnson, and so began their long-time association.

The first annual meeting of the Archaeological Society of North Carolina was held at Colburn's home in Biltmore Forest near Asheville on October 7, 1933. Invited speakers were John R. Swanton on Indians of the Southeast, and Neil M. Judd on the problems of establishing a state society, the importance of an archaeological survey of the state, and the danger of allowing the commercial value of artifacts to be emphasized in the United States. Joffre gave a paper at the next meeting of the Society, which was held in Raleigh on April 28, 1934. In the *Bulletin of the Archaeological Society of North Carolina*, Vol. 1, No. 2, September 1934, the editor said: "The author of this paper is a young man from Greensboro who was shown a deep interest in the Society and has devoted most of his spare time to reading, thinking, and exploring during the past year. He is Chairman of the Committee on Survey and will have something to say about the survey work at the Charlotte meeting." Joffre's paper was entitled "Planning an Archaeological Survey in North Carolina." At the Charlotte meeting, on October 6, 1934, the title of Coe's paper was "Next Steps in our Archaeological Survey." (It is of some interest to note that the annual dues of the Society were $1.50, a single bedroom at the Hotel Charlotte $2.50 and up, and a double occupancy room was $4.50 and up.)

As a freshman at Brevard College, Joffre was instrumental in establishing the short-lived *Bulletin*, the initial number of which appeared in May 1935. The president of the Brevard College Society, Professor Carl H. Trowbridge, said in his foreword: "Fortunately, in its student secretary, Mr. Joffre L. Coe, the society has a very unusual asset. Mr. Coe's personal acquaintance with many prominent American archaeologists, his contagious enthusiastic interest in the prehistoric period of America, and his valuable experience in this and other states have solved many difficulties and made fascinating every step of the program." Listed in the six specially prepared talks was "The Place of Archaeology in History" by Guthe, who was enticed by Joffre to travel to Brevard to present it, stimulate the young society, and encourage their survey of Transylvania County. Coe received other statements for the *Bulletin* from F. C. Cole, N. C. Nelson, F. H. H. Roberts, Jr., and J. R. Swanton.

At Guthe's suggestion, Joffre applied to Cole and to Ralph Linton for summer excavating experience with either the University of Chicago or the University of Wisconsin. He had had extensive survey experience in Montgomery County and was preparing to study the site of Keyauwee in Randolph County, but was also aware of the need for more formal field experience. Although he was accepted by both Cole and Linton, the program in Wisconsin did not materialize, so in the summer of 1935 he appeared at the "Black Hole" of Kincaid, where the work that summer was under the direction of Thorne Deuel. The University of Chicago field training program had had a little over 10 years of development, and had benefited from the hundreds of students who had participated over the years. It was certainly the best-known summer archaeological program in the country. Joffre's participation was at a level usually assigned to new arrivals and undergraduates, and he was probably the youngest of the crew. At Kincaid, he learned about the excavation strategy for the mounds and limited areas of the village, read the report on the 1934 excavations by John C. "Pinky" Harrington, who had been the active field director the year before, and studied the available collections. During his stay he also became aware of a certain rigidity of techniques that pervaded the organizational structure for some years. The methods, many of which were used primarily because they had been used before, sometimes were a hindrance to the uncovering and preserving of features and materials in order to study and interpret relationships within and between cultural remains (Maxwell 1977:ix–x).

In mid-September of 1935, Joffre wrote to Guthe to tell him that he had returned from southern Illinois and had enrolled at the University of North Carolina in Chapel Hill. Guthe replied: "It is good to know that you did have an opportunity to work in the field with the University of Chicago group. I am sure that you must have found the work interesting, because Dr. Deuel has written me in some detail of the conditions under which the party lived and the interesting remains which were found. Sometime, if you feel it, I should like to have your reactions to your summer experience." I have no record that Joffre ever felt like it. Guthe continued to provide publications such as the printed survey form of the Wisconsin Archaeological Survey introduced to the Midwest in 1928, and my mimeographed comparative analysis of Fort Ancient sites prepared for the American Anthropological Association meeting in Pittsburgh in December 1935. My paper was the forerunner of the major Fort Ancient study, which was completed in 1939 but not published until 1943. Let it be recorded that Joffre found at least part of my trait list categories "ambiguous."

Joffre's transfer to the Chapel Hill campus was aided by Guy Johnson and other faculty members. The Johnsons had acquired a home with space that Coe occupied in return for babysitting and miscellaneous household chores—good training for later years of servitude. He remained with the Johnsons for a number of years, and in 1938 when they built a new home outside the city limits, Joffre was left during the summer to complete the installation of a septic tank and disposal/field. In this endeavor, as in the field and laboratory, his association with his contractor father had given him valuable experience. The disposal system worked perfectly for years until the area was taken into the city.

At Chapel Hill, Coe had a base of operation and faculty support adequate to begin a North Carolina archaeological program. It is uncertain whether he regarded his academic courses as a help or a hindrance in this endeavor. Certainly there was difficulty with some of the required courses and foreign languages. Nevertheless, he held a University Scholarship in 1936–1937 and a Service Scholarship in 1937–1939. In the spring of 1936, with funds provided primarily by Burnham Colburn, excavations were begun by Joffre and his associates at the Keyauwee village site in Randolph County. Archaeological society members served as free labor, the State Museum furnished some field equipment (with Joffre building whatever else was needed), and the University came through with laboratory space and a vehicle. This fieldwork cost a total of $143.50.

A preliminary report on the Keyauwee project was published in Vol. IV, No. 1 of the *Bulletin* of the Society. Two large areas were opened so that the relationships of features could be observed. Soil from pits was carefully screened, and three of the burials were encased in plaster of paris so that they could be carefully excavated in the laboratory. It should be emphasized that from the beginning, the field and laboratory program was "problem oriented." The initial Keyauwee work was undertaken to test the hypothesis that the occupation there was that of a Siouan village visited by John Lawson in 1700. This was an example of the direct historical approach followed by quite a few archaeologists in the late nineteenth and early twentieth centuries. The Keyauwee work initiated an attempt to ascertain and correlate the several complexes of the Carolina Piedmont Siouan tribes.

The summer of 1936 found Coe participating in a Midwest excavation. This was a field program jointly sponsored by the Milwaukee Public Museum, under the direction the direction of Will C. McKern, and the University of Wisconsin Department of Sociology and Anthropology, at several mounds along the Clam River in Burnett County, Wisconsin. This must have been in many ways a more pleasant summer than the preceding one at Kincaid. Along with Joffre in the Clam River field crew were John Adair, William R. Bascom, Leland Cooper, Harry

Figure E-1. Field Crew at the Rice Lake Site, Barron County, Wisconsin, Summer of 1936. Left to right: G. Lidberg, Joffre Coe, John Adair, William McKern (director), George Quimby, Albert Spaulding, and L. Cooper.

Geiger, Thomas James, George Lidberg, George I. Quimby, Albert C. Spaulding, David B. Stout, and George Topping (Figure E-1). Seven of these men were later to have distinguished careers in American anthropology. The crew was quite varied in its academic training and personalities. Coe particularly enjoyed the discussions and camaraderie of the group, led in the evenings by McKern.

While the excavations and associated archaeological activities were rigorous, there were frequent explanations of the reasons for the techniques, and reasonable flexibility when unforeseen conditions called for modification of established procedures. During the excavation of the Spencer Lake mound, a horse skull was found and described as being clearly an inclusive feature. This has been McKern's published opinion since 1936 and has been upheld in more recent years by Coe, Quimby, and Spaulding. The radiocarbon age and the recovered artifacts, however, strongly suggest that the mound was constructed in stages from the sixth to the tenth centuries after Christ (Crane and Griffin 1968:72–

73). The perplexing story is presented in the "Book Review" section, and statements by Robert Ritzenthaler and McKern, in Volume 45:2 of the *Wisconsin Archaeologist*.

This summer training completed Joffre's initial association with the three major archaeological leaders of the period in the Midwest—Guthe, Cole, and McKern. It was a period of major interest in the McKern classification and formal presentation of the reasons behind an archaeologist's recognition of cultural relationships. Following the field program, Joffre made his way to Ann Arbor and appeared unannounced at the door of our first residence on the outskirts of town. This was, I believe, the first time we had met. Joffre stayed with us for a few days, during which he made his initial firsthand acquaintance with the Museum of Anthropology facilities and its small staff. My wife was later to remark that he was the quietest guest we had ever had. Joffre expressed an interest in attending the University of Michigan, as he had stated in his correspondence earlier with Guthe.

During Joffre's short stay in Michigan, he visited the excavations of the Riviere au Vase multicomponent Late Woodland site in Macomb County, under the direction of Emerson F. Greenman. The field notes for Burial 38 include an interesting paragraph:

> Beneath and an inch to the N of the middle portion of the shaft of this femur was found a section involving the elbow of gritty material somewhat resembling a historic white clay pipe. There is a guilloche pattern and also a chevron design on it. This was first found and jarred loose by Jimmy Guthe. There is a possibility that it was planted by Coe of North Carolina who was visiting the dig. Ted (Guthe) saw him with a bowl of a pipe which he said he made himself and which he was going to plant on Holmes (Ellis), who was brushing off this burial.

The first letter I wrote to Joffre of which I have a copy, was on October 5, 1936, and I enclosed a statement of the pottery traits of A. R. Kelly's material from Macon, Georgia. I told of seeing McKern a week before I wrote and that he was very complimentary of Joffre's ability as a field archaeologist. In the reply of October 15, 1936, Joffre thanked me for the list and also for sending a copy of W. B. Hinsdale's publication on "Perforated Indian Crania in Michigan." He inquired about the measurements of our collection cabinets, drawers, and the manufacture of them. At that time, he was also working on a classification of about 4,500 projectile points that had been acquired from five sites, along with percentages and graphs to demonstrate any correlations that might appear.

My reply on October 23 alerted Joffre to the possibility of receiving financial support for fieldwork if he could certify that he had reasonable evidence that one or more sites had been occupied by Siouan tribes. There was a longstanding opinion that Siouan tribes had occupied the Ohio Valley, and it was believed that the identification of material culture from known Siouan sites in North Carolina would provide documentation that would aid in identifying the Ohio Valley sites. In his reply, Joffre mentioned a Saponi Town on the Yadkin, Lower Saratown on the Dan, Keyauwee, and the Leak site. This information was turned over to Eli Lilly and Glenn Black. Glenn visited Coe in 1937 to get firsthand information on the project, and as a result felt confident enough to also encourage Lilly to provide for further research funds. Joffre sent the Keyauwee pottery collection to Ann Arbor for study and a report. Most of the work on it was done by Spaulding and Stout, who were studying for M.A. degrees and working part-time in the Museum. The analysis of almost 2,300 sherds was done by surface finish and by field location (whether undisturbed or in the plowzone). Sherd counts and percentages were provided according to surface finish and location of the different types in the site.

In Vol. IV, No. 1 of the *Bulletin of the Archaeological Society of North Carolina*, there was an eight-page statement on the 1936 excavations with three plates of the site survey, a plan of the excavated area, and cross-sections. There were sections on excavation techniques, descriptions of features and materials, and cautious support of the identification of the site as the Keyauwee Siouan village. A major activity in 1937 was work at the Frutchey Mound (later to become known as Town Creek) in Montgomery County, North Carolina. This project, begun under the Works Progress Administration, was sponsored by the University of North Carolina and by the State Museum. Coe was assistant director, a title which probably meant that he did all of the work in the field and was responsible for the collections and a report. In 1938, the work was continued as a National Youth Administration operation. There was also survey work in the Roanoke River as a part of the Siouan problem research.

In the late winter-early spring, I had alerted Joffre to the projected plans for a meeting in Ann Arbor to inaugurate a format for the description and identification of pottery types, and a similar notice was also sent to a majority of those actively engaged in federally sponsored fieldwork. I mentioned some of those who were planning to attend and with whom Joffre might be able to get a ride, both to Milwaukee for the Central Section of the American Anthropological Association and the Society for American Archaeology meeting. On May 1, 1938, Coe wrote that he expected to make the trip to Milwaukee with Arthur Kelly and Gordon Willey. He also said that on the advice of Gordon, who was kept informed by James A. Ford from Ann Arbor, he had named three pottery types Clarksville Cord Impressed, Clarksville Wicker-fabric Impressed, and Caraway Net-fabric Impressed. Following the Milwaukee meeting, a number of archaeologists drove to Ann Arbor. Coe did attend with Kelly and later produced a description of Dan River types with Ernest Lewis, which was published in *Prehistoric Pottery of the Eastern United States* (Griffin 1952b).

By the fall of 1938, Joffre had met and/or corresponded with a high proportion of the active archaeologists and anthropologists interested in the Southeast and Mississippi Valley, contacts that were to be of continuing value to him over the years. A casual meeting that fall, however, was to have a more lasting impact than all those he had earlier or later. One afternoon when Coe returned to Guy Johnson's home after having been in the field all day, he was introduced to a young woman, who with her sister and friend were there, by a previous arrangement, for the purpose of picking up a sociology graduate student. The women had decided to pay a Sunday afternoon call on Dr. and Mrs. Johnson. After being introduced to Sally Denton, Joffre sat down in a small rocking chair listening to the conversation with arms folded and forefinger wagging, hardly participating and not displaying much visible reaction to Johnson's guests. This behavior puzzled Miss Denton, who normally witnessed a more overt impact on young males by her presence. She had recently arrived in Chapel Hill from Marks, Mississippi, to join her older sister, Alice, who was assistant director of Child Welfare Services in Raleigh. Sally had had two years of college with an interest in dramatic art, first at Alabama College in Montevallo and then at Millsaps in Mississippi. By 1937–1938, she was enrolled at Miss Hardbarger's Business School in Chapel Hill and had obtained work at the University's Institute for Research in Social Science, which was connected with Joffre's archaeology program. It was not until February 1939, however, that Joffre asked Sally to go on a double date to a movie in Durham. After that there was trial by survey collecting and other such tests or suitability studies by both parties. The relationship was found to be mutually satisfactory and was approved by State and Church in Chapel Hill on June 29, 1940. Of this union were born two sons, Joffre Lanning Coe II and Damon Denton Coe. At the present writing Joffre and Sally have two grandsons and one granddaughter, of whom they are very proud.

The work at Town Creek continued in 1939 and, indeed, until World War II put a stop to this and many other archaeological excavations. Also in 1939, the Research Laboratories of Anthropology was established. It has continued to this day as a focal point for the pursuit of North Carolina archaeology. This research center would not have been accepted if senior faculty members had not supported its program and had not been impressed with Joffre's accomplishments and promise. As was written in the Greensboro *Daily News* on Octoer 22, 1939, under the heading "Indian Lore is Unusual Hobby of Joffre Coe, U. N. C. Senior":

> One would not get the impression that Coe is a person of the distinction he has won. Tall and slender with brown, curly hair, his manner is quiet and modest, his facial expression is one of thoughtfulness. He would never boast, but he must be proud of his achievements—and he has a right to be.

In 1939, a statewide archaeological Works Progress Administration program was approved with the University of North Carolina as the primary sponsor, and the State Museum, the Division of State Parks, and the North Carolina Historical Commission as co-sponsors. Mr. Harry Davis, director of the State Museum, pushed this program through the maze of state and federal offices and served as the sponsor's representative until the fall of 1940. At that time, Robert Wauchope came to Chapel Hill to teach anthropology and was appointed sponsor's representative of this program in archaeology, with Joffre continuing to serve as statewide supervisor. Wauchope's stay was only two years, for in 1942 he was appointed director of the Middle American Research Institute at Tulane University.

Also in the fall of 1940, the Indiana Historical Society, sponsors of the Siouan research program, asked me to visit Chapel Hill for a preview of the results that had been obtained. As a result of this trip, I learned a bit about the Siouan occupations and submitted a report to the Indiana group, a copy of which went to Joffre, who replied that "it seems to cover the ground pretty well." He later made a more adequate statement to Lilly in return for his support.

The first report on Town Creek appeared in 1940 as *Occasional Contributions from the Laboratory of Anthropology and Archaeology*, No. 1. This statement reveals the high level of excavation skills that had been developed, and the care and patience with which the investigations were conducted, on this project. As with many other relief labor operations, records were kept of the total man-hours worked, total cubic feet of earth moved, total cubic feet of earth moved per man-hour in primary excavation, total burials located, cleaned, and removed, total features located, cleaned, and removed, total photographs taken, and total specimens cataloged. There was a "Daily Progress Record" form, "Burial Data" form, and "Photographic Data" form.

Shortly before Coe went into the army on June 11, 1942, at Fort Bragg, he packed and stored the artifacts and records that had been gathered at the University of North Carolina. Although they had been moved a number of times, these materials were to be in pretty good shape when he returned. Joffre was selected to become an aviation cadet at Lowrey Field in what was then the Army Air Force. This operation was later transferred to Yale University where he was graduated in February 1943, as a second lieutenant. He was assigned to the Columbia Air Base as an assistant photographic officer to a base squadron and was promoted to first lieutenant in June 1944. His development of photographic techniques in bombing and gunnery training at several air bases led to an appointment to a crash course in photographic interpretation and intelligence at the Orlando Air Base and an eventual assignment to Manila, where he participated in the interpretation of the damage from the Hiroshima bombing. From Manila, he was sent to Tokyo where he remained until November 1945. In Tokyo, he was a captain in the Intelligence Division of the Far Eastern Air Force. Later, he was promoted to the rank of major in the Air Force Reserve before he chose to go on inactive reserve status. He was discharged from active duty in March 1946.

With the help of the G. I. Bill and Sally, Joffre entered the graduate school of the University of Michigan in September 1946. During the 1947–1948 school year, he held the Aboriginal North American Research Fellowship supported by Eli Lilly. He received his M.A. in Anthropology in June 1948 and was elected to Phi Kappa Phi Honor Society in the spring of 1948. He was regarded as being on leave from the University of North Carolina during his service in the war and while he was in graduate school. In the fall of 1948, he entered the teaching program at Chapel Hill and thus had academic professional status. As such, he was included in the dinner for new faculty. As a part of this ceremony, the new people were introduced to President Frank Graham. Graham, who had been one of Joffre's supprters for some years, embraced the young man and said "Welcome home, son."

With the expansion of staff following the war years and changes in administration, there was a continuing problem of preserving the Laboratory's independence and preventing its incorporation into first, the Department of Sociology and Anthropology and then, the Department of Anthroplogy. Such actions are almost inevitable in the minds of tidy administrators who object to seeing small units of a university dangling unattached on an organizational chart. Or occasionally it results from a chairman of a department who feels that he has been retained to control all activities of units that are allowed to use an academic term indicating relationship to his unit. These attitudes seem to be endemic in large bureaucratic organizations and can be expected to reappear every few years with personnel changes. Another handicap probably faced Joffre as the result of his long association with the University, where he was cast in the role of a bright and promising young man, but where his growing stature and reputation were not adequately understood and respected by his superiors.

In 1949, the first number of *Southern Indian Studies*, which has had valuable papers by a large number of authors, was issued. Although Coe founded this series and has been its editor from the beginning, papers by him appear only in the first number. In the first number was a brief notice of the Morrow Mountain site and the Doerschuk site near Badin, excavated in 1948, in which Coe identified sequential occupational levels separated by flood deposits to a depth of fifteen feet. A notice also appeared of a small grant from the Carnegie Research Fund to continue work on the Morrow Mountain site in 1949, and of a much larger appropriation from the Division of State Parks for a two-year continuation of the research and restoration at Town Creek.

There was also a list of anthropological courses that could be studied for an undergraduate major, the M.A. in Anthropology, and a minor in Anthropology for the Ph.D. degree. Coe was listed as one of the instructors in General Anthropology, for the Archaeology of North America, Research Methods in Archaeology, and with Guy Johnson for Indians of North America. In 1948, he was named executive secretary of the Archaeological Society of North Carolina, and began a six-year term as director of research for the Eastern States Archaeological Federation.

Between 1949 and 1952, field work was concentrated along the Yadkin River from Badin Lake to below Morrow Mountain, where the experience of 1948 had provided Coe with the knowledge that, at certain types of favorable locations in Piedmont floodplains, remains of occupations thousands of years old could be found. These excavations, and their data on relatively short-lived settlements with a limited range of artifact forms, provided a lesson that archaeologists in the East have been slow to learn. It was possible to identify artifact styles in use during short time periods and their major functions and associations. The overall significance of this work for the study of Eastern United States prehistory was as "revolutionary" as the identification of extensive Archaic occupations along the Tennessee River had been in the mid-1930s. The major publication on this work did not appear until 1964. At the Seventh Southeastern Archaeological Conference in mid-October 1950, Joffre presented his data from the excavations along the Yadkin. Over the succeeding years, his results were discussed informally at many meetings and should have become well known.

Joffre's chapter, "The Cultural Sequence of the Carolina Piedmont," was the last of the contributions received (March 1950) for *Archeology of Eastern United States*, finally published in 1952. Robert Wauchope's (1953:139) review in *American Antiquity* said:

> Coe's chapter on the Carolina Piedmont is well organized, extremely well written, stresses the cultural significance of his materials, and reflects many fresh viewpoints. I know of no clearer or more readable exposition of an archaeological sequence, or one that gives, without straying too far from the facts and artifacts, a more vivid feeling that you are reading of real people who practiced real cultures. . . . In my opinion, Coe's paper ranks with the best archaeological writing yet published. It should be read by all anthropologists, both for instruction and for the sheer pleasure of reading.

A General Education Board Fellowship enabled Coe to return to the

University of Michigan for his third year of graduate work and paid enough tuition so that he could receive his Ph.D. on completion of his thesis. The department at Ann Arbor was growing, and, in 1952, David Aberle, William Schorger, and Emilio Willems were added to those instructors of Coe's earlier years. Among the graduate students with whom he interacted were William Sears, Hale Smith, Charles Fairbanks, Gary Vescelius, and Wesley Hurt.

By the early 1950s, Joffre had a number of students at the University of North Carolina who participated with him in outstanding excavations, surveys, and analyses of an increasing body of data. His Ph.D. dissertation, accepted in 1959, was regarded as outstanding. As a result of support from A. V. Kidder and a peer review by James A. Ford, it was accepted by the American Philosophical Society for its *Transactions* series, which finally appeared in 1964. This volume has been reprinted three times (1971, 1975, and 1979). Few other theses have had such success. As I remember it, I found the temporal and typological equivalence of the Hardaway points with Mississippi Valley Dalton forms difficult to swallow. The Hardaway forms, which were made of rhyolite, andesite, and argillite, did not have the appearance of the Daltons, which were made from fine-grained cherts. As usual, however, it turned out that Joffre was right. In the acknowledgments of the thesis, reference was made to the valuable help for three years of Stanley South, in the work in the Roanoke Rapids Basin, and to Lewis Binford, for his enthusiasm and assistance as well as the map preparation for the Roanoke work. Probably his most important expression of gratitude, however, was to Sally Denton Coe whose participation in cooperative efforts toward his degree did not end until final typing in the Museum of Anthropology in the spring of 1959. One of the practical results of his completion of the Ph.D. was a promotion to associate professor in 1960 and to professor in 1965.

The thesis was the result of a program designed to investigate and define complexes of the Archaic with more precision that could be done by surface survey, shallow midden excavations, or excavations done in arbitrary cuts to make the photographs appear clear-cut and soundly scientific. Coe recognized that the hydrologic factors responsible for finely stratified floodplain deposits in the Piedmont produced occupation zones available to Archaic peoples for short periods of time, and consequently that had a narrow range of temporally specific tool forms.

The success of such investigations in rich floodplain deposits has since been duplicated in the lower Kanawha Valley in West Virginia by Broyles (1971) and in eastern Tennessee by Chapman (this volume). One result was the recognition that the earliest levels of the large shell middens in northern Alabama began to be built during the Morrow Mountain period (about 4000 B.C.), and was the *coup de grace* to the idea that there had been a pre-lithic "bone complex" in northern Alabama. The ceramic sequence was clearly built on changes in vessel form, surface treatment, and decoration accompanied by other changes in material culture that led up to the historic period.

In the 1950s and 1960s a struggle continued for the preservation of the integrity of the Research Laboratories of Anthropology. When the Society for American Archaeology held its twenty-ninth Annual Meeting in Chapel Hill in early May 1964, the Laboratories was located in Person Hall. Here there were exhibits, research collections, and remarkably ordered records of North Carolina's prehistory. In terms of "hard money" appointments, however, it was still essentially a one-man show. At present, the staff of the Laboratories and the scope of its anthropological research has been expanded and perhaps solidified and entrenched in the University structure. A major research effort of the late 1960s and 1970s involved the identification and delineation of the growth of the prehistoric cultures that developed into the historic Cherokee and Siouan tribes. This work resulted in several important monographs and papers, some of which have been published, and it provided a training program for a large number of graduate students who have become professional archaeologists (Figure E-2). Initially, as we have seen, the Michigan-North Carolina archaeological interaction was one of nurturing activity provided from Michigan, as graduate students came to Ann Arbor from Chapel Hill. However, a shift gradually took place when an increasing number of students in archaeology went from Ann Arbor to get their doctoral training under Coe.

On November 20, 1980, Joffre was, so to speak, "canonized" at the Annual Meeting of the Historic Preservation Society of North Carolina. He received the Ruth Coltrane Cannon Award for his long excellence in historic preservation, restoration, and research in the state of North Carolina. As a token of this honor he received an engraved silver cup. The citation which accompanied the award read as follows:

Figure E-2. Joffre Coe with University of North Carolina Students at the Cold Morning Site, New Hanover County, North Carolina, Fall of 1979.

Dr. Joffre Lanning Coe's name is synonymous with the archaeology of the state and of the Eastern United States. Archaeological research has been carried out in North Carolina for nearly fifty years. These decades of research have resulted in a solid chronological framework for some ten thousand years of prehistory. The wide and frequent citation of his work "The Formative Cultures of the Carolina Piedmont" attests to the strength and accuracy of Dr. Coe's research.

Dr. Coe's role as a leader is not limited to the academic world. He was a founder of the Archaeological Society of North Carolina, an organization which has provided contact between lay interests and professional archaeologists since 1933.

Dr. Coe was integrally involved in the development of Town Creek Indian Mound as a State Historic Site. Town Creek, North Carolina's only prehistoric National Historical Landmark, is today reconstructed as it existed some 500 years ago, thanks to Dr. Coe's superb excavations, research, and analysis. He has also contributed significantly to the state's historic preservation program. He has served as the prehistoric archaeologist on the State Professional Review Committee since it was created in 1971. While on the committee he nominated some of the state's most significant archaeological sites to the National Register of Historic Places. Through his cooperation and assistance, the Historic Preservation program's Archaeology Branch has added thousands of sites to the Division's inventory to aid in review and compliances under the requirements of the National Historic Preservation Act.

The purpose of this essay has been to give some indication of the long, slow, and difficult path that Joffre has followed to reach one of his major aims, which was to place the record of North Carolina's prehistory in a leading position in the Southeast. No longer can it be said that nothing much is known about North Carolina archaeology. Much of the advancement and diffusion of knowledge on that subject can be traced one way or another to Joffre Coe. It is a remarkable achievement of steadfastness of purpose and refusal to be discouraged by temporary setbacks or diversions. Even the United States military forces were used as a means of improving his skills in photography and mapping for his archaeological work. Perhaps one of the facets of his early involvement in archaeology most difficult for some contemporary archaeologists to comprehend is the evidence presented here that Joffre was a prolific correspondent. This volume of papers by students and colleagues is a warm tribute to the affection they have for him and for his role of leadership in archaeological research.

Bibliography

Ames, Kenneth

1981 The Evolution of Social Ranking on the Northwest Coast of North America. *American Antiquity* 46:723–742.

Ayers, Harvard Glen

1972 *The Archaeology of the Susquehanna Tradition in the Potomac Valley.* Ph.D. dissertation, Catholic University. University Microfilms, Ann Arbor.

Baby, Raymond S. and Suzanne M. Langlois

1979 Seip Mound State Memorial: Nonmortuary Aspects of Hopewell. In *Hopewell Archaeology: The Chillicothe Conference*, edited by David S. Brose and N'omi Greber, pp. 16–18. Kent State University Press, Kent, Ohio.

Barka, Norman F.

1979 Archaeology of Flowerdew Hundred: Stone House Foundation Site. Ms. on file, Southside Historic Sites, Inc., Williamsburg.

Barka, Norman F. and Ben C. McCary

1976 Early Shell Tempered Pottery in the James River Valley, Virginia. *Eastern States Archaeological Federation, Bulletin* 36.

Bartlett, M. S.

1950 Tests of Significance in Factor Analysis. *British Journal of Psychology, Statistical Section* 3:77–85.

Bartram, William

1940 *Travels of William Bartram,* edited by Mark Van Doren. Dover Publications, New York.

Bass, Quentin R.

1977 *Prehistoric Settlement and Subsistence Patterns in the Great Smoky Mountains.* Unpublished Master's thesis, Department of Anthropology, University of Tennessee, Knoxville.

1979 An Analysis of the Lithic Artifacts from the Calloway Island Site. In *Archaeological Investigations at the Howard (40MR66) and Calloway Island (40MR41) Sites,* by Jefferson Chapman, pp. 186–255. Report of Investigations No. 27, Department of Anthropology, University of Tennessee, Knoxville.

Bennett, John W.

1943 Recent Developments in the Functional Interpretation of Archaeological Data. *American Antiquity* 9:208–219.

1946 Empiricist and Experimental Trends in Eastern Archaeology. *American Antiquity* 11:198–200.

Benthall, Joseph L.

1978 Archaeological Investigation at Daugherty's Cave, Russell County,

Virginia. Ms. on file, Research Laboratories of Anthropology, University of North Carolina at Chapel Hill, Chapel Hill.

Binford, Lewis R.

1963 A Proposed Attribute List for the Description and Classification of Projectile Points. In *Miscellaneous Studies in Typology and Classification*, edited by Anta M. White, Lewis R. Binford, and Mark L. Papworth. Anthropological Papers, No. 19, Museum of Anthropology, University of Michigan, Ann Arbor.

1964 *Archaeological and Ethnohistorical Investigation of Cultural Diversity and Progressive Development among Aboriginal Cultures of Coastal Virginia and North Carolina*. Unpublished Ph.D. dissertation, Department of Anthropology, University of Michigan, Ann Arbor.

1968 Archaeological Perspectives. In *New Perspectives in Archaeology*, edited by Sally R. Binford and Lewis R. Binford, pp. 5–32. Aldine, Chicago.

1977 *For Theory Building in Archaeology*. Academic Press, New York.

1978a Dimensional Analysis of Behavior and Site Structure: Learning from an Eskimo Hunting Stand. *American Antiquity* 43:330–361.

1978b *Nunamiut Ethnoarchaeology*. Academic Press, New York.

1979 Organization and Formation Processes, Looking at Curated Technologies. *Journal of Anthropological Research* 35:255–273.

1980 Willow Smoke and Dogs' Tails: Hunter–Gatherer Settlement Systems and Archaeological Site Formation. *American Antiquity* 45:4–20.

1981 *Bones, Ancient Men and Modern Myths*. Academic Press, New York.

1982 The Archaeology of Place. *Journal of Anthropological Archaeology* 1:5–31.

Binford, Lewis R. and Sally R. Binford

1966 A Preliminary Analysis of Functional Variability in the Mousterian of Levallois Facies. *American Anthropologist* 68:238–295.

Binford, Lewis R., Sally R. Binford, Robert Whallon, and Margaret Ann Hardin

1970 *Archaeology at Hatchery West, Carlyle, Illinois*. Memoirs of the Society for American Archaeology, No. 24.

Blaker, Margaret C.

1950 Pottery Types from the Townsend Site, Lewes, Delaware. *Eastern States Archaeological Federation, Bulletin* 9.

1952 Further Comments on Simple-Stamped Shell-Tempered Pottery. *American Antiquity* 17:257–258.

Boyce, Douglas W.

1978 Iroquoian Tribes of the Virginia–North Carolina Coastal Plain. In *Northeast*, edited by Bruce G. Trigger, pp. 282–289. Handbook of North American Indians, vol. 15, William G. Sturtevant, general editor. Smithsonian Institution, Washington, D.C.

Braun, Lucy E.

1950 *Deciduous Forests of Eastern North America*. Hafner Publishing Company, New York.

Brewer, Andrea J.

1973 Analysis of Floral Remains from the Higgs Site (40L045). In *Excavation of the Higgs and Doughty Sites, I–75 Salvage Archaeology*, by Major C. R. McCollough and Charles H. Faulkner. Tennessee Archaeological Society, Miscellaneous Paper 12:141–144.

Brose, David S.

1978 Comments. *Current Anthropology* 19:729–731.

1979 A Speculative Model of the Role of Exchange in the Prehistory of the Eastern Woodlands. In *Hopewell Archaeology: The Chillicothe Conference*, edited by David S. Brose and N'omi Greber, pp. 3–8. Kent State University Press, Kent, Ohio.

Brown, James A.

1979 Charnel Houses and Mortuary Crypts: Disposal of the Dead in the Middle Woodland Period. In *Hopewell Archaeology: The Chillicothe Conference*, edited by David S. Brose and N'omi Greber, pp. 211–219. Kent State University Press, Kent, Ohio.

Broyles, Bettye J.

1966 Preliminary Report: the St. Albans Site (46KA27), Kanawha County, West Virginia. *The West Virginia Archaeologist* 19:1–43.

1971 *Second Preliminary Report: the St. Albans Site, Kanawha County, West Virginia, 1964–1968*. Report of Archaeological Investigations 3. West Virginia Geological and Economic Survey, Morgantown.

Buchannan, William T., Jr., and Edward F. Heite

1971 The Hallowes Site: a Seventeenth Century Yeoman's Cottage in Virginia. *Historical Archaeology* 5:38–48.

Bullen, Ripley P., and H. Bruce Greene

1970 Stratigraphic Tests at Stallings Island, Georgia. *Florida Anthropologist* 23:8–28. Gainesville.

Bushnell, David I.

1922 *Villages of the Algonquian, Siouan, and Caddoan Tribes West of the Mississippi*. Smithsonian Institution Bureau of American Ethnology Bulletin 77. Washington, D.C.

Butler, Brian M.

1977 The Yearwood Site: a Specialized Middle Woodland Occupation on the Elk River. *Tennessee Anthropologist* II(1):1–15.

1979 Hopewellian Contacts in Southern Middle Tennessee. In *Hopewell Archaeology: The Chillicothe Conference*, edited by David S. Brose and N'omi Greber, pp. 150–156. Kent State University Press, Kent, Ohio.

Byers, Douglas S.

1959 The Eastern Archaic: Some Problems and Hypotheses. *American Antiquity* 24:233–256.

Cable, John S., Charles E. Cantley, and Jim S. Sexton

1978 *A Study of Prehistoric Utilization of the Inter-Riverine Piedmont: the U.S. 176 By-pass Survey from Union to Pacolet, South Carolina*. Institute of

Archeology and Anthropology, University of South Carolina, Research Manuscript Series 131. Columbia.

Caldwell, Joseph R.

1952 The Archeology of Eastern Georgia and South Carolina. In *Archeology of Eastern United States*, edited by James B. Griffin, pp. 312–321. The University of Chicago Press, Chicago.

1954 The Old Quartz Industry of Piedmont Georgia and South Carolina. *Southern Indian Studies* VI:37–39. Chapel Hill, N.C.

1958 Trend and Tradition in the Prehistory of the Eastern United States. *American Anthropological Association, Memoir* 88. Springfield, Illinois.

1964 Interaction Spheres in Prehistory. In *Hopewellian Studies*, edited by Joseph R. Caldwell and Robert L. Hall. Illinois State Museum Papers 12:135–143.

Callen, E. O.

1963 Coprolites. In *Science in Archaeology*, edited by Donald Brothwell and E. Higgs, pp. 186–194. Thames and Hudson, London.

Calmes, Alan R.

1967 Test Excavations at Two Late Archaic Sites on Hilton Head Island, Beaufort County, S.C. Ms. on file, Institute of Archeology and Anthropology, University of South Carolina, Columbia.

Canouts, Veletta

1971 *Towards a Reconstruction of Creek and Pre-Creek Cultural Ecology*. Unpublished Master's thesis, Department of Anthropology, University of North Carolina, Chapel Hill.

1976 Excavation Strategies and Results at a Shallow Lithic Site on a Piedmont Ridgetop. Paper presented at the 33rd Annual Southeastern Archaeological Conference, Tuscaloosa.

1977a Management Strategies for Effective Research. In *Conservation Archaeology: a Guide for Cultural Resource Management Studies*, edited by M. B. Schiffer and G. J. Gumerman, pp. 121–127. Academic Press, New York.

1977b Problem Domains in the Santa Rosa Wash Project, Arizona. In *Conservation Archaeology: a Guide for Cultural Resource Management Studies*, edited by M. B. Schiffer and G. J. Gumerman, pp. 135–143. Academic Press, New York.

Canouts, Veletta, Ernest E. May, Neal H. Lopinot, and Jon D. Muller

1977 An Archaeological Assessment of the Upper Cache Watershed Project. Ms. on file, Department of Anthropology, Southern Illinois University, Carbondale.

Carbone, Victor A.

1976 *Environment and Prehistory in the Shenandoah Valley*. Ph.D. dissertation, Catholic University. University Microfilms, Ann Arbor.

Carson, Cary, Norman Barka, William Kelso, Garry Stone, and Dell Upton

1981 Impermanent Architecture in the Southern American Colonies. *Winterthur Portfolio* 16:135–196. The University of Chicago Press, Chicago.

Casteel, R. W.

1977 Characterization of Faunal Assemblages and the Minimum Number of Individuals Determined from Paired Elements: Continuing Problems in Archaeology. *Journal of Archaeological Science*, 4:125–134.

Cattell, Raymond F.

1965 Factor Analysis: an Introduction to Essentials: I. The Purpose and Underlying Models. *Biometrics* 21:190–215.

Cavallo, John A.

1979 A Compendium of New Jersey Paleo-Indian Settlement Pattern: Data, Directions, and Dialogue. Paper presented at the Middle Atlantic Archaeological Conference. Rehoboth Beach, Delaware.

Chapman, Jefferson

1973 *The Icehouse Bottom Site, 40MR23*. University of Tennessee, Department of Anthropology, Report of Investigations 13. Knoxville.

1975a *The Rose Island Site and the Cultural and Ecological Position of the Bifurcate Point Tradition in Eastern North America*. Ph.D. dissertation, Department of Anthropology, University of North Carolina, Chapel Hill.

1975b *The Rose Island Site and the Bifurcate Point Tradition*. University of Tennessee, Department of Anthropology, Report of Investigations 14. Knoxville.

1976a Early Archaic Site Location and Excavation in the Little Tennessee River Valley: Backhoes and Trowels. *Southeastern Archaeological Conference, Bulletin* 19:31–36. Knoxville.

1976b The Archaic Period in the Lower Little Tennessee River Valley: the Radiocarbon Dates. *Tennessee Anthropologist* I(1):1–12.

1977 *Archaic Period Research in the Lower Little Tennessee River Valley-1975: Icehouse Bottom, Harrison Branch, Thirty Acre Island, Calloway Island.* University of Tennessee, Department of Anthropology, Report of Investigations 18. Knoxville.

1978 *The Bacon Farm Site and a Buried Site Reconnaissance*. University of Tennessee, Department of Anthropology, Report of Investigations 23. Knoxville.

1979 *Archaeological Investigations at the Howard [(40MR66)] and Calloway Island [(40MR41)] Sites*. University of Tennessee, Department of Anthropology, Report of Investigations 27. Knoxville.

1981 *The Bacon Bend and Iddins Sites: the Late Archaic Period in the Lower Little Tennessee River Valley*. University of Tennessee, Department of Anthropology, Report of Investigations 31. Knoxville.

Chapman, Jefferson and Bennie C. Keel

1979 Candy Creek–Connestee Components in Eastern Tennessee and Western North Carolina and their Relationship with Adena–Hopewell. In *Hopewell Archaeology: The Chillicothe Conference*, edited by David S. Brose and N'omi Greber, pp. 157–161. Kent State University Press, Kent, Ohio.

Chapman, Jefferson and Robert Newman

1979 Archaeological Investigations at the Citico Site. In The 1978 Archaeological Investigations at the Citico Site (40MR7), edited by Jefferson Chapman, pp. 1–41. Ms. on file, Frank H. McClung Museum, University of Tennessee, Knoxville.

Chapman, Jefferson and Andrew Brewer Shea

1977 Paleoecological and Cultural Interpretations of Plant Remains Recovered from Archaic Period Sites in the Lower Little Tennessee River Valley. Paper presented at the 34th Annual Southeastern Archaeological Conference, Lafayette.

1981 The Archaeobotanical Record: Early Archaic Period to Contact in the Lower Little Tennessee River Valley. *Tennessee Anthropologist* VI(1):61–84.

Charles, Tommy C.

1981 *Dwindling Resources: an Overture of the Future of South Carolina's Archaeological Resources*. Institute of Archeology and Anthropology, University of South Carolina, The Notebook 13. Columbia.

Cheves, Landgon (editor)

1897 The Shaftesbury Papers and Other Records Relating to Carolina and the First Settlement on Ashley River prior to the Year 1676. *Collections of the South Carolina Historical Society* V. Richmond, Virginia.

Chomko, Stephen and Gary Crawford

1978 Plant Husbandry in Prehistoric Eastern North America: New Evidence for its Development. *American Antiquity* 43:405–408.

Ciolek-Torrello, Richard S.

1978 *A Statistical Analysis of Activity Organization: Grasshopper Pueblo, Arizona*. Unpublished Ph.D. dissertation, University of Arizona. University Microfilms, Ann Arbor.

Claflin, William H., Jr.

1931 The Stalling's Island Mound, Columbia County, Georgia. *Papers of the Peabody Museum of American Archaeology and Ethnology, Harvard University* XIV(1). Cambridge.

Clark, Wayne E.

1980 The Origins of the Piscataway and Related Indian Cultures. *Maryland Historical Magazine* 75(1).

Clarke, David

1973 Archaeology: the Loss of Innocence. *Antiquity*, 47:6–18.

Cliff, Norman and Charles D. Hamburger

1967 The Study of Sampling Errors in Factor Analysis by Means of Artificial Experiments. *Psychological Bulletin* 68:430–445.

Cobb, James E.

A Preliminary Report on 40KN49: an Early Archaic Site in Knox County, Tennessee. Ms. on file, Department of Anthropology, University of Tennessee, Knoxville.

Cobb, James E. and Charles H. Faulkner

1978 *The Owl Hollow Project: Middle Woodland Settlement and Subsistence Patterns in the Eastern Highland Rim of Tennessee*. Final Technical Report

Submitted to the National Science Foundation in Accordance with the Requirements of Grant BNS76-11266. University of Tennessee, Knoxville.

Cochran, William G.

1977 *Sampling Techniques*. John Wiley and Sons, New York.

Coe, Joffre L.

1937 Keyauwee—a Preliminary Statement. *Bulletin of the Archaeological Society of North Carolina*, Chapel Hill 3(1).

1940 Quarterly Report of the WPA-UNC Archaeological Project. *Occasional Contributions from the Laboratory of Anthropology and Archaeology* 1. Chapel Hill.

1951 Minutes of the Seventh Southeastern Archaeological Conference. *Newsletter of the Southeastern Archaeological Conference* 3(1):4.

1952 The Cultural Sequence of the Carolina Piedmont. In *Archeology of Eastern United States*, edited by James B. Griffin, pp. 301–311. University of Chicago Press, Chicago.

1964 The Formative Cultures of the Carolina Piedmont. *Transactions of the American Philosophical Society* 54(5). Philadelphia.

1975 Discussion of Papers. In *Lithic Technology, Making and Using Stone Tools*, edited by Earl B. Swanson. Mouton Press, Chicago.

1983 Through a Glass Darkly: an Archaeological View of North Carolina's More Distant Past. In *The Prehistory of North Carolina: an Archaeological Symposium*, edited by Mark A. Mathis and Jeffrey J. Crow, North Carolina Division of Archives and History, Department of Cultural Resources, Raleigh.

Coe, Joffre L. and Ernest Lewis

1952 Dan River Series Statement. *Prehistoric Pottery of the Eastern United States*, Museum of Anthropology, University of Michigan, Ann Arbor.

Colquhoun, Donald J., Mark J. Brooks, William H. Abbott, Frank W. Stapor, Walter S. Newman and Richard R. Pardi.

1981 Location of Archeological Sites with Respect to Sea Level in the Southeastern United States. In *Florilegium Florinis Dedicatum*, edited by L. K. Königsson and K. Paabo, pp. 144–150. Striae 14. Uppsala.

Cowgill, George L.

1970 Some Sampling and Reliability Problems in Archaeology. In *Archéologie at calculateurs: problèmes sémiologiques et mathématiques*, edited by Jean-Claude Gerdin and Mario Borillio, pp. 161–172. Colloques Internationaux de Centre National de la Recherche Scientifique, Paris.

Crane, H. Richard and James B. Griffin

1968 University of Michigan Radiocarbon Dates XII. *Radiocarbon* 10:61–114.

Cumming, William P.

1962 *The Southeast in Early Maps with an Annotated Check List of Printed and Manuscript Regional and Local Maps of Southeastern North America during the Colonial Period.* University of North Carolina Press, Chapel Hill, N.C.

Custer, Jay F.

1978 Broadspears and Netsinkers: Late Archaic Adaptation Indicated by Depositional Sequences from Four Middle Atlantic Archaeological Sites of the Ridge and Valley Province. Paper presented at the Middle Atlantic Archaeology Conference, Rehoboth Beach, Delaware.

Cuthbert, Mabel J.

1948 *How to Know the Fall Flowers*. William C. Brown Co., Dubuque, Iowa.

Davis, R. P. Stephen, Jr.

1980a A Summary Report of Probabilistic "Non-Site" Sampling in Tellico Reservoir, 1979. In *The 1979 Archaeological and Geological Investigations in the Tellico Reservoir*, edited by Jefferson Chapman, pp. 59–90, Report of Investigations No. 29, Department of Anthropology, University of Tennessee, Knoxville.

1980b *A Preliminary Report of Probabilistic and Nonprobabilistic Archaeological Sampling in Industrial Area II, Tellico Reservoir, Tennessee*. Tellico Archaeological Survey Report No. 2, Department of Anthropology, University of Tennessee, Knoxville.

1981 Archaeological Survey in the Lower Little Tennessee River Valley: a Comparison of Probabilistic and Nonprobabilistic Sampling Strategies. Paper presented at Upland Archaeology in the East: a Symposium, James Madison University, Harrisonburg, VA, February 28, 1981.

Davis, R. P. Stephen, Jr., Larry R. Kimball, William Baden and Jefferson Chapman

1980 *A Research Design and Proposed Budget for Archaeological Survey and Resource Assessment within Tellico Reservoir, Tennessee*. Submitted to the Division of Land and Forest Resources, Tennessee Valley Authority, Norris, Tennessee.

Deetz, James

1967 *Invitation to Archaeology*. The Natural History Press, Garden City.

Delcourt, Hazel

1979 Late Quaternary Vegetation History of the Eastern Highland Rim and Adjacent Cumberland Plateau of Tennessee. *Ecological Monographs* 49(3):255–280.

Delcourt, Paul A.

1980a Quaternary Alluvial Terraces of the Little Tennessee River, East Tennessee. In *The 1979 Archaeological and Geological Investigations in the Tellico Reservoir*, edited by Jefferson Chapman, pp. 110–121, Report of Investigations No. 29, Department of Anthropology, University of Tennessee, Knoxville.

1980b Quaternary Terraces along the Little Tennessee River, Southeastern Tennessee. Paper presented at the 37th Annual Southeastern Archaeological Conference, New Orleans.

Delcourt, Paul A. and Hazel R. Delcourt

1979 Late Pleistocene and Holocene Distributional History of the Deciduous

Forest in the Southeastern United States. *Veroff. Geobot. Inst. ETH, Stuftung Rubel, Zurich* 68:79–107.

1980 Pollen Preservation and Quaternary Environmental History in the Southeastern United States. *Palynology* 4:215–231.

Dennell, R. W.

1976 The Economic Importance of Plant Resources Represented on Archaeological Sites. *Journal of Archaeological Science* 3:229–247.

1979 Prehistoric Diet and Nutrition: Some Food for Thought. *World Archaeology* 10:121–135.

Dickens, Roy S., Jr.

1964 The Stone Mountain Salvage Project, Dekalb and Gwinnett Counties, Georgia, Part I. *Journal of Alabama Archaeology* X(2):43–49. University, Alabama.

1971 Archaeology in the Jones Bluff Reservoir of Central Alabama. *Journal of Alabama Archaeology* XVII(1):1–107. University, Alabama.

1975 A Processual Approach to Mississippian Origins on the Georgia Piedmont. *Southeastern Archaeological Conference, Bulletin* 18, pp. 31–42.

1976 *Cherokee Prehistory: the Pisgah Phase in the Appalachian Summit Region*. The University of Tennessee Press, Knoxville.

1978 Mississippian Settlement Patterns in the Appalachian Summit Area: the Pisgah and Qualla Phases. In *Mississippian Settlement Patterns*, edited by Bruce Smith, pp. 115–139. Academic Press, New York.

1979a *Archaeological Investigations at Horseshoe Bend National Military Park, Alabama*. Special Publications of the Alabama Archaeological Society 3. University, Alabama.

1979b The Origins and Development of Cherokee Culture. In *The Cherokee Indian Nation: a Troubled History*, edited by Duane King, pp. 3–32. The University of Tennessee Press, Knoxville.

1980 Ceramic Diversity as an Indicator of Cultural Dynamics in the Woodland Period. *Tennessee Anthropologist* V(1):35.

Dreimanis, A.

1968 Extinction of Mastodons in Eastern North America: Testing a New Climatic-Environmental Hypothesis. *Ohio Journal of Science* 68:257–272.

Dunnell, Robert C., Lee H. Hanson, Jr., and Donald L. Hardesty

1971 The Woodside Component of the Slone Site, Pike County, Kentucky. *Southeastern Archaeological Conference*, Bulletin 14.

Earle, Carville V.

1979 Environment, Disease, and Mortality in Early Virginia. In *The Chesapeake in the Seventeenth Century*, edited by Thad W. Tate and David L. Ammerman. W. W. Norton and Company, New York.

Edwards, Robert L., and Arthur S. Merrill

1977 A Reconstruction of the Continental Shelf Areas of Eastern North America for the Times 9500 B.P. and 12,500 B.P. *Archaeology of Eastern North America* 5:1–43.

Edwards, William E.

1965 Preliminary Report on Excavations at Sewee Indian Mound. Ms. on file, Institute of Archeology and Anthropology, University of South Carolina. Columbia.

Egloff, Keith T.

1971 *Methods and Problems of Mound Excavation in the Southern Appalachian Area*. Unpublished Master's thesis, Department of Anthropology, University of North Carolina, Chapel Hill.

1979 Croaker Landing Site. Ms. in preparation. Virginia Research Center for Archaeology, Yorktown.

1980 White Bank Park Site (44CF67) in a Fall Zone Study Area. Ms. on file, Virginia Research Center for Archaeology, Yorktown.

Egloff, Keith T., and Celia Reed

1980 Crab Orchard Site: a Late Woodland Palisaded Village. *Quarterly Bulletin of the Archeological Society of Virginia* 34:130–148.

Evans, Clifford

1955 A Ceramic Study of Virginia Archaeology. Smithsonian Institution *Bureau of American Ethnology Bulletin* 160. Washington, D.C.

Fairbanks, Charles H.

1942 The Taxonomic Position of Stalling's Island, Georgia. *American Antiquity* 7:223–231.

Faulkner, Charles H., and J. B. Graham

1965 *Excavations in the Nickajack Reservoir, Season I*. Tennessee Archaeological Society, Miscellaneous Paper 7. Knoxville.

1966a *Westmoreland–Barber Site (40MI11), Nickajack Reservoir, Season II*. Department of Anthropology, University of Tennessee, Knoxville.

1966b *Highway Salvage in the Nickajack Reservoir*. Department of Anthropology, University of Tennessee, Knoxville.

Feest, Christian F.

1978 Virginia Algonquians. In *Northeast*, edited by Bruce G. Trigger, pp. 253–270. Handbook of North American Indians, vol. 15, William G. Sturtevant, general editor. Smithsonian Institution, Washington, D.C.

Fenneman, Nevin M.

1938 *Physiography of Eastern United States*. McGraw-Hill Book Company, New York.

Ferguson, Leland G.

1971 *South Appalachian Mississippian*. Ph.D. dissertation, Department of Anthropology, University of North Carolina at Chapel Hill. University Microfilms, Ann Arbor.

1978 Looking for the "Afro-" in Colono-Indian Pottery. *The Conference on Historic Site Archeology Papers* 12:68–86. Institute of Archeology and Anthropology, University of South Carolina. Columbia.

1980 Looking for the "Afro-" in Colono-Indian Pottery. In *Archaeological*

Perspectives on Ethnicity in America, edited by Robert L. Schuyler. Baywood Publishing Company, New York.

Fernald, Merritt L.

1950 *Gray's Manual of Botany*. American Book Company, New York.

Flannery, Kent V.

1972 Summary Comments: Evolutionary Trends in Social Exchange and Interaction. In *Social Exchange and Interaction*, edited by E. N. Wilmsen. Anthropological Papers No. 46, Museum of Anthropology, University of Michigan, Ann Arbor.

Flannery, Regina

1943 Some Notes on a Few Sites in Beaufort County, S.C. Smithsonian Institution *Bureau of American Ethnology Bulletin* 133:147–153. Washington, D.C.

Florer, Linda E.

1972 Palynology of a Post-glacial Bog in the New Jersey Pine Barrens. *Bulletin, Torrey Botanical Club* 99(3):135–138.

Ford, James A.

1954 On the Concept of Types. *American Anthropologist* 56:42–53.

Ford, Richard I.

1979 Gathering and Gardening: Trends and Consequences of Hopewell Subsistence Strategies. In *Hopewell Archaeology: The Chillicothe Conference*, edited by David S. Brose and N'omi Greber, pp. 234–238. Kent State University Press, Kent, Ohio.

Forde, C. Daryll

1934 *Habitat, Economy, and Society*. Methuen and Company, London.

Gardner, Paul S.

1981 Analysis of Carbonized Plant Remains from 38An8, Anderson County. In *Archaeological Data Recovery in the Richard B. Russell Multiple Resource Area: The Anderson County Group (Interim Report)*, edited by W. Dean Wood. Southeastern Wildlife Services, Inc., Athens, Georgia.

Gardner, William M.

1974 The Flint Run Complex: Pattern and Process during the Paleo-Indian to Early Archaic. In *The Flint Run Paleo-Indian Complex: a Preliminary Report 1971–73 Seasons*, edited by William M. Gardner. Archeology Laboratory, Department of Anthropology, The Catholic University of America, Occasional Publication 1:5–47.

1976 Archaeological Excavations at 18Pr141, 18Pr142, and 18Pr143 near Piscataway, Maryland. Ms. on file, Maryland Historical Trust, Annapolis.

1978 Comparison of Ridge and Valley, Blue Ridge, Piedmont, and Coastal Plain Archaic Period Site Distribution: an Idealized Transect. Ms. on file, Maryland Historical Trust, Annapolis.

1980a The Archaic. Paper distributed at the Middle Atlantic Archaeology Conference, Dover.

1980b Settlement-Subsistence Strategies in the Middle and South Atlantic Portions of the Eastern United States during the Late Pleistocene and Early

Holocene. Paper presented at the Annual Meeting of the American Anthropological Association, Washington.

Garner, H. F.

1974 *The Origin of Landscapes*. Oxford University Press, New York.

Goad, Sharon I.

1980 Patterns of Late Archaic Exchange. *Tennessee Anthropologist* V(1): 1–16.

Goodyear, Albert C.

1974 *The Brand Site: a Technofunctional Study of a Dalton Site in Northeast Arkansas*. Arkansas Archeological Survey, Research Series 7. Fayetteville.

1975a General Research Design for Highway Archeology in South Carolina. *Institute of Archeology and Anthropology, University of South Carolina, The Notebook* 7(1):3–38. Columbia.

1975b Research Design for the Study of Dalton Settlement-Subsistence Activities in the Cache River Basin. In *The Cache River Archeological Project: an Experiment in Contract Archeology*, assembled by M. B. Schiffer and J. H. House, pp. 205–216. Arkansas Archeological Survey, Research Series 8. Fayetteville.

1977 Regional Model Building in the Contract Framework: the Hecla Projects of Southern Arizona. In *Conservation Archaeology: a Guide for Cultural Resource Management Studies*, edited by M. B. Schiffer and G. J. Gumerman, pp. 413–426. Academic Press, New York.

Goodyear, Albert C., John H. House, and Neal W. Ackerly

1979 *Laurens–Anderson: an Archeological Study of the Inter-Riverine Piedmont*. Institute of Archeology and Anthropology, University of South Carolina, Anthropological Studies 4. Columbia.

Goodyear, Albert C., L. Mark Raab, and Timothy C. Klinger

1978 The Status of Archaeological Research Design in Cultural Resource Management. *American Antiquity* 43:159–173.

Gould, Richard A.

1977 Ethno-archaeology; or, Where do Models Come from? In *Stone Tools as Cultural Markers, Change, Evolution and Complexity*, edited by R. V. S. Wright, pp. 162–168. Australian Institute of Aboriginal Studies, Prehistory and Material Culture Series 12. Canberra.

Greber, N'omi

1979 A Comparative Study of Site Morphology and Burial Patterns at Edwin Harness Mound and Seip Mounds 1 and 2. In *Hopewell Archaeology: The Chillicothe Conference*, edited by David S. Brose and N'omi Greber, pp. 27–38. Kent State University Press, Kent, Ohio.

Griffin, James B.

1952a *Archeology of Eastern United States*. The University of Chicago Press, Chicago.

1952b *Prehistoric Pottery of the Eastern United States*. Museum of Anthropology, University of Michigan, Ann Arbor.

1966 The Arctic Denbigh Complex. In *New Roads to Yesterday: Essays in Archaeology*, edited by J. R. Caldwell. Basic Books, New York.

1967 Eastern North American Archaeology: A Summary. *Science* 156:175–191.

1979 An Overview of the Chillicothe Hopewell Conference. In *Hopewell Archaeology: The Chillicothe Conference*, edited by David S. Brose and N'omi Greber, pp. 266–280. Kent State University Press, Kent, Ohio.

Griffin, James B., Richard E. Flanders, and Paul F. Titterington

1970 *The Burial Complexes of the Knight and Norton Mounds in Illinois and Michigan*. Museum of Anthropology, University of Michigan, *Memoir* 2. Ann Arbor.

Griffith, Daniel, and Richard Artusy, Jr.

1977 Middle Woodland Ceramics from Wolf Neck, Sussex County, Delaware. Sussex Society of Archeology and History, *The Archeolog* 28(1):1–28.

Guilday, John E., and David S. Berman

1969 Mastodon and Paleo-Indian in West Virginia. *West Virginia Archaeologist* 22:1–3.

Gumerman, George J., and David A. Phillips, Jr.

1978 Archaeology beyond Anthropology. *American Antiquity* 43:184–191.

Hack, John T.

1957 Submerged River System of Chesapeake Bay. *Bulletin, Geological Society of America* 68:817–830.

Hall, Alan

1976 *The Wild Food Trailguide*. Holt, Rinehart, and Winston, New York.

Hally, David J.

1975 Complicated Stamped Pottery and Platform Mounds: the Origin of South Appalachian Mississippian. Discussion. *Southeastern Archaeological Conference, Bulletin* 18, pp. 43–47.

1981 Plant Preservation and the Content of Paleobotanical Samples: a Case Study. *American Antiquity* 46:723–742.

Hally, David J., Patrick H. Garrow, and Wyman Trotti

1975 Preliminary Analysis of the King Site Settlement Plan. *Southeastern Archaeological Conference, Bulletin* 18:59–62.

Harrington, J. C.

1948 Plain Stamped, Shell Tempered Pottery from North Carolina. *American Antiquity* 13:251–252.

1952 Historic Site Archeology in the United States. In *Archeology of Eastern United States*, edited by James B. Griffin, pp. 335–344. The University of Chicago Press, Chicago.

Harrington, Mark R.

1922 *Cherokee and Earlier Remains on Upper Tennessee River*. Museum of the American Indian–Heye Foundation, New York, Indian Notes and Monographs 24.

Harrison, W., R. J. Malloy, Gene A. Rusnak, and J. Terasmae
1965 Possible Late Pleistocene Uplift, Chesapeake Bay Entrance. *Journal of Geology* 73(2):201–229.

Hemmings, E. Thomas
1970a *Emergence of Formative Life on the Atlantic Coast of the Southeast.* Institute of Archeology and Anthropology Research Manuscript Series 7. Columbia.
1970b Preliminary Report of Excavations at Fig Island, S. C. *Institute of Archeology and Anthropology Notebook* 2(2–3):9–15. Columbia.

Hodges, Charles
1979 Flowerdew Ceramics. Ms. in preparation, Flowerdew Hundred Foundation, Hopewell, Virginia.

Hodges, Mary Ellen Norrisey
1980 Excavation of a Nineteenth Century Trash Pit on the Pamunkey Indian Reservation, King William County, Va. Ms. in preparation, Virginia Research Center for Archaeology, Yorktown.

Hoffman, Michael A., and Robert W. Foss
1980 Blue Ridge Prehistory: a General Perspective. *Archeological Society of Virginia Quarterly Bulletin* 34:185–210.

Hoffman, Paul
1978 Sixteenth Century Fortifications on Parris Island, South Carolina. Ms. on file, National Geographic Magazine. Washington.

Holland, C. G.
1966 Archeology and Ethnohistory: an Illustration. Archeological Society of Virginia. *Quarterly Bulletin* 12:2–8.

Holmes, William H.
1884 Illustrated Catalogue of a Portion of the Collections Made by the Bureau of American Ethnology during the Field Season of 1881. 3rd Annual Report of the *Bureau of Ethnology*, pp. 427–510. Smithsonian Institution, Washington, D. C.

House, John H. and David L. Ballenger
1976 *An Archeological Survey of the Interstate 77 Route in the South Carolina Piedmont.* Institute of Archeology and Anthropology, University of South Carolina, Research Manuscript Series 104. Columbia.

House, John H. and Ronald W. Wogaman
1978 *Windy Ridge, a Prehistoric Site in the Inter-Riverine Piedmont in South Carolina.* Institute of Archeology and Anthropology, University of South Carolina, Anthropological Studies 3. Columbia.

Hunter–Anderson, Rosalind L.
1977 A Theoretical Approach to the Study of House Form. In *For Theory Building in Archaeology*, edited by L. R. Binford, pp. 287–315. Academic Press, New York.

Jeffries, Richard W.

1976 *The Tunacunnhee Site: Evidence of Hopewell Interaction in Northwest Georgia.* Anthropological Papers of the University of Georgia 1. Athens.

1979 The Tunacunnhee Site: Hopewell in Northwestern Georgia. In *Hopewell Archaeology: The Chillicothe Conference*, edited by David S. Brose and N'omi Greber, pp. 162–170. Kent State University Press, Kent, Ohio.

Jenkins, Ned. J.

1979 Miller Hopewell of the Tombigbee Drainage. In *Hopewell Archaeology: The Chillicothe Conference*, edited by David S. Brose and N'omi Greber, pp. 171–180. Kent State University Press, Kent, Ohio.

Johnson, Stephen C.

1967 Hierarchical Clustering Schemes. *Psychometrika* 32:241–254.

Jones, Charles C., Jr.

1873 *Antiquities of the Southern Indians, Particularly of the Georgia Tribes.* D. Appleton and Company, New York.

Kauffman, Barbara, and Joseph Dent

1978 Preliminary Flora and Fauna Analysis at the Shawnee Minisink Site (36MR43). Paper presented at the Middle Atlantic Archaeology Conference, Rehoboth Beach, Delaware.

Kavanagh, Maureen

1980 Archaeological Resources Assessment of the Monocacy River Region, Frederick and Carroll Counties, Maryland, Phase III (draft). Ms. on file, Maryland Historical Trust, Annapolis.

Kay, Marvin, Frances B. King, and Christine K. Robinson

1980 Cucurbits from Phillips Spring: New Evidence and Interpretations. *American Antiquity* 45:806–822.

Keel, Bennie C.

1976 *Cherokee Archaeology: a Study of the Appalachian Summit.* The University of Tennessee Press, Knoxville.

Keeler, Robert W.

1978 *The Homelot on the Seventeenth-Century Chesapeake Tidewater Frontier.* Ph.D. dissertation, University of Oregon. University Microfilms, Ann Arbor.

Keeley, Lawrence H.

1980 *Experimental Determination of Stone Tool Uses: A Microwear Analysis.* University of Chicago Press, Chicago.

Kelly, John E.

1972 *An Archaeological Survey of the Piedmont Region in North Central South Carolina.* Unpublished Master's thesis, Department of Anthropology, University of Wisconsin, Madison.

Kelso, William M.

1975 Historical Archaeology at Kingsmill: the 1973 Season. Ms. on file, Virginia Research Center for Archaeology, Yorktown.

1976 Historical Archaeology at Kingsmill: the 1974 Season. Ms. on file, Virginia Research Center for Archaeology, Yorktown.

Kimball, Larry R.

1976 Early and Middle Archaic Lithic Assemblages of the Lower Little Tennessee River Valley. Paper presented at the 33rd Annual Southeastern Archaeological Conference, Tuscaloosa.

1978 An Analysis of Early Archaic Lithic Technology from Three Stratified Sites in the Lower Little Tennessee River. Paper presented at the 35th Annual Southeastern Archaeological Conference, Knoxville.

1980a *The 1977 Archaeological Reconnaissance and an Overall Assessment of the Archaeological Resources of Tellico Reservoir*. Tellico Archaeological Survey Report No. 1, Department of Anthropology, University of Tennessee, Knoxville, in press.

1980b A Quantitative Pattern Recognition Model of Temporal Variability in Debitage for Early Archaic through Historic Cherokee Lithic Assemblages in the Lower Little Tennessee River Valley. Paper presented at the 37th Annual Southeastern Archaeological Conference, New Orleans.

Kimball, Larry R. and William W. Baden

1980a Quantitative Model of Woodland and Mississippian Ceramic Assemblages for the Identification of Surface Collections. In *The 1977 Archaeological Reconnaissance and an Overall Assessment of the Archaeological Resources of Tellico Reservoir*, by Larry R. Kimball, Tellico Archaeological Survey Report No. 1, Department of Anthropology, University of Tennessee, Knoxville, in press.

1980b Statistical Analysis of Select Tellico Assemblages by Activity Groups. In *A Preliminary Report of Probabilistic and Nonprobabilistic Archaeological Sampling in Industrial Area II, Tellico Reservoir, Tennessee*, by R. P. Stephen Davis, Jr., pp. 88–95. Tellico Archaeological Survey Report No. 2, Department of Anthropology, University of Tennessee, Knoxville.

Kinsey, W. Fred, III

1972 *Archaeology in the Upper Delaware Valley*. Pennsylvania Historical and Museum Commission, Anthropological Series 2. Harrisburg.

1975 Faucett and Byram Sites: Chronology and Settlement in the Delaware Valley. *Pennsylvania Archaeologist* 45(1-2):1–103.

Kneberg, Madeline

1952 The Tennessee Area. In *Archeology of Eastern United States*, edited by James B. Griffin, pp. 190–206. University of Chicago Press, Chicago.

Kraft, John C.

1976 Geological Reconstructions of Ancient Coastal Environments in the Vicinity of the Island Field Site, Kent County, Delaware. *Transactions, Delaware Academy of Science* 5–6:83–117. Newark, Delaware.

Kraft, John C., and Chacko J. John

1978 Paleogeographic Analysis of Coastal Archaeological Settings in Delaware. *Archaeology of Eastern North America* 6:41–60.

Krieger, Alex D.

1944 The Typological Concept. *American Antiquity* 9:271–288.

Kroeber, Alfred L.
1939 *Cultural and Natural Areas of Native North America*. University of California Publications in Anthropology. University of California Press, Berkeley.
Küchler, A. W.
1964 *Potential Natural Vegetation of the Coterminous United States*. American Geographical Society, Special Publication 36. New York.
Lafferty, Robert H. III
1978 The Early Woodland Chronological and Cultural Affinities at Phipps Bend on the Holston River, Northeast Tennessee. *Journal of Alabama Archaeology* XXIV(2):132–150. University, Alabama.
Larson, Lewis H., Jr.
1972 Functional Considerations of Warfare in the Southeast during the Mississippian Period. *American Antiquity* 37:383–392.
Lawson, John
1967 *A New Voyage to Carolina*, edited by Hugh T. Lefler. The University of North Carolina Press, Chapel Hill.
Lewis, Kenneth
1977 Sampling the Archeological Frontier: Regional Models and Component Analysis. In *Research Strategies in Historical Archeology*, edited by Stanley South, Academic Press, pp. 151–201. New York.
Lewis, Thomas M. N.
1956 The Middle Period Cultures in Eastern Tennessee. *Newsletter of the Southeastern Archaeological Conference* 5:34–37.
Lewis, Thomas M. N. and Madeline Kneberg
1941 *The Prehistory of the Chickamauga Basin in Tennessee: A Preview*. Tennessee Anthropology Papers 1. Knoxville.
1946 *Hiwassee Island: an Archaeological Account of Four Tennessee Indian Peoples*. University of Tennessee Press, Knoxville.
1947 *The Archaic Horizon in Western Tennessee*. University of Tennessee Record, Extension Series 23(4), Tennessee Anthropology Papers 2. Knoxville.
1955 The A. L. LeCroy Collection. *Tennessee Archaeologist* XI(2):75–82.
1956 The Paleo-Indian Complex on the LeCroy Site. *Tennessee Archaeologist* XII(1):5–11.
1957 The Camp Creek Site. *Tennessee Archaeologist* XIII(1):1–48.
1959 The Archaic Culture of the Middle South. *American Antiquity* 25:161–183.
Lewis, Thomas M. N. and Madeline Kneberg Lewis
1961 *Eva: an Archaic Site*. University of Tennessee Press, Knoxville.
Lipe, William D.
1974 A Conservation Model for American Archaeology. *The Kiva* 39:213–245.
Logan, John H.
1859 *A History of the Upper Country of South Carolina from the Earliest Periods to the Close of the War of Independence*. Vol. 1. S. G. Courtenay and Company, Charleston.

Lowie, Robert H.

1954 *Indians of the Plains*. McGraw-Hill Book Company, New York.

MacCord, Howard

1965 The DeShazo Site, King George County, Virginia. *Archeological Society of Virginia, Quarterly Bulletin* 19:98–104.

1969 Camden: A Postcontact Indian Site in Carolina County. *Archeological Society of Virginia, Quarterly Bulletin* 24:1–56.

McCary, Ben

1976 A Surface Collection of Indian Artifacts from the Richmond Site, Moysonec. *Archeological Society of Virginia, Quarterly Bulletin* 31:1–30.

McCollough, Major C. R.

1973 Supplemental Chronology for the Higgs Site (40L045), with an assessment of Terminal Archaic Living and Structure Floors. *Tennessee Archaeologist* XXIX(2):63–68.

McCollough, Major C. R. and Charles H. Faulkner

1973 *Excavation of the Higgs and Doughty Sites, I–75 Salvage Archaeology*. Tennessee Archaeological Society, Miscellaneous Paper 12. Knoxville.

McKinley, William

1873 Mounds in Georgia. *Smithsonian Institution Annual Report*, 1872, pp. 422–424. Washington, D.C.

McKusick, Marshall

1973 *The Grant Oneota Village*. Office of the State Archaeologist of Iowa Report 4. Iowa City.

McNett, Charles W.

1975 Excavation at the Spring Branch Site. *Archeological Society of Virginia, Quarterly Bulletin* 29:97–123.

Malinowski, Bronislaw

1961 *Argonauts of the Western Pacific*. E. P. Dutton, New York.

Manson, Carl

1948 Marcey Creek Site: An Early Manifestation in the Potomac Valley. *American Antiquity* 13:223–226.

Marrinan, Rochelle

1975 *Ceramics, Molluscs, and Sedentism: the Late Archaic Period on the Georgia Coast*. Unpublished Ph.D. dissertation, Department of Anthropology, University of Florida.

Martin, Paul S.

1958 Taiga-Tundra and the Full-Glacial Period in Chester County, Pennsylvania. *American Journal of Science* 256:470–502.

Mathews, Maurice

ca. 1685 A Plat of the Province of Carolina in North America (the south part actually surveyed by Mr. Maurice Mathews), Joel Gascoyne. Copy on file, Institute of Archeology and Anthropology, University of South Carolina, Columbia.

Maxwell, Moreau
1977 Foreword. In *For the Director, Research Essays in Honor of James B. Griffin*, edited by Charles E. Cleland. Anthropological Papers, Museum of Anthropology, University of Michigan 61. Ann Arbor.

Milanich, Jerald T. and Charles H. Fairbanks
1980 *Florida Archaeology*. Academic Press. New York.

Miller, James F.
1973 *Weed Identification*. University of Georgia Cooperative Extension Service Bulletin 632. University of Georgia, Athens.

Mooney, James
1894 *The Siouan Tribes of the East*. Smithsonian Institution Bureau of American Ethnology Bulletin 22. Washington, D.C.

Moore, Clarence B.
1915 Aboriginal Sites on the Tennessee River. *Journal of the Academy of Natural Sciences of Philadelphia* (2nd series) 16:171–422.

Morrison, Alexander H. II
1979 An Improved Method for Excavating Post-in-the-ground Structures. Paper presented at the 1979 meeting of the Society for Historical Archaeology, Nashville.
1980 Excavation at the Van Sweringen Site: Problems and Plans. Paper presented at the 1980 meeting of the Middle Atlantic Archaeological Conference, Dover.

Mouer, Daniel L.
1981 Powhatan and Monaceen Regional Settlement Hierarchies: A Model of Relationship between Social and Environmental Structure. *Archeological Society of Virginia, Quarterly Bulletin* 36:1–21.

Munson, Patrick J., Paul W. Parmalee, and Richard A. Yarnell
1971 Subsistence Ecology of Scovill, a Terminal Middle Woodland Village. *American Antiquity* 36:410–431.

Myer, William E.
1928 Indian Trails of the Southeast. *42nd Annual Report of the Bureau of American Ethnology*, 1924–1925, pp. 727–857. Smithsonian Institution, Washington, D.C.

Neiman, Fraser D.
1980 Field Archaeology of the Clifts Plantation Site, Westmoreland County, Virginia. Ms. on file, Robert E. Lee Memorial Foundation, Stratford.

Nelson, Thomas C.
1957 The Original Forests of the Georgia Piedmont. *Ecology* 38:390–397.

Newman, Walter S., and Gene A. Rusnak
1965 Holocene Submergence of the Eastern Shore of Virginia. *Science* 148:1464–1466.

Nöel Hume, Ivor
1962 An Indian Ware of the Colonial Period. *Archeological Society of Virginia, Quarterly Bulletin* 17:1–16.

1969 *Historical Archaeology*. Alfred A. Knopf, New York.
1970 *A Guide to Artifacts of Colonial America*. Knopf, New York.
1979 First Look at a Lost Virginia Settlement. *National Geographic* 155:737–767.

Oliver, Billy L.
1981 *The Piedmont Tradition: Refinement of the Savannah River Stemmed Point Type*. Unpublished Master's thesis, the Department of Anthropology, University of North Carolina, Chapel Hill.

Oosting, Henry J.
1942 An Ecological Analysis of Plant Communities of Piedmont North Carolina. *The American Midlands Naturalist* 28:1–126.

Opperman, Antony F.
1980 *A Study of the Prehistoric Ceramics from Maycock Point, Prince George County, Virginia*. Unpublished Senior thesis, Department of Anthropology, College of William and Mary.

Outlaw, Alain
1978 Governor's Land Archaeological District Excavations: the 1976 Season. Ms. on file, Virginia Research Center for Archaeology, Yorktown.

Overstreet, William C. and Henry Bell III
1965 *The Crystalline Rocks of South Carolina*. Geological Survey Bulletin 1183.

Owens, James P., Karl Stefansson, and Leslie A. Sirkin
1974 Chemical, Mineralogic, and Palynologic Character of the Upper Wisconsin-Lower Holocene Fill in Paris of Hudson, Delaware, and Chesapeake Estuaries. *Journal of Sedimentary Petrology* 44(2):390–408.

Painter, Floyd
1970 Cypress Swamp Knobbed: A Unique Early Ceramic Ware. *The Chesopiean* 8:101–104.
1977 The Beaker Makers of Currituck Sound. *Archaeology of Eastern North America* 5:43–61.

Parmalee, Paul W.
1962 Faunal Remains from the Stanfield-Worley Bluff Shelter, Colbert County, Alabama. *Journal of Alabama Archaeology* VIII(1-2):112–114. University, Alabama.

Peterson, Lee
1977 *A Field Guide to Edible Wild Plants of Eastern and Central North America*. Houghton Mifflin, Boston.

Phelps, David S.
1980 *Archaeological Salvage of the Thorpe Site and Other Investigations along the U.S. 64 Bypass, Rocky Mount, North Carolina*. Department of Sociology and Anthropology, East Carolina University, Archaeological Research Report 1. Greenville.
1981 *The Archaeology of Colington Island*. Department of Sociology and Anthropology, East Carolina University Archaeological Research Report 3. Greenville.

Potter, Stephen R.

1982 *An Analysis of Chicacoan Settlement Patterns*. Unpublished Ph.D. dissertation, Department of Anthropology, University of North Carolina.

Prufer, Olaf H.

1964 The Hopewell Complex of Ohio. In *Hopewellian Studies*, edited by J. R. Caldwell and Robert L. Hall, pp. 35–84. Illinois State Museum, Scientific Papers No. 12. Springfield.

1968 *Ohio Hopewell Ceramics: an Analysis of the Extant Collections*. Anthropological Papers No. 33, Museum of Anthropology, University of Michigan, Ann Arbor.

Radford, Albert E., Harry E. Ahles, and C. Ritchie Bell

1964 *Guide to the Vascular Flora of the Carolinas*. The Book Exchange, The University of North Carolina, Chapel Hill.

Rathje, William L. and Michael B. Schiffer

1982 *Archaeology*. Harcourt Brace Jovanovich, New York.

Ray, Clayton E., Byron N. Cooper, William S. Benninghoff

1967 Fossil Mammals and Pollen in a Late Pleistocene Deposit at Saltville, Virginia. *Journal of Paleontology* 41:608–622.

Reeves, Brian

1973 The Concept of an Altithermal Cultural Hiatus in Northern Plains Prehistory. *American Anthropologist* 75:1221–1253.

Reid, J. Jefferson

1967 *Pee Dee Pottery from the Mound at Town Creek*. Unpublished Master's thesis, Department of Anthropology, University of North Carolina at Chapel Hill.

1973 *Growth and Response to Stress at Grasshopper Pueblo, Arizona*. Ph.D. dissertation, University of Arizona. University Microfilms, Ann Arbor.

1975 Comments on Environment and Behavior at Antelope House. *The Kiva* 41:127–132.

Reid, J. Jefferson, editor

1982 *Cholla Project Archaeology: Introduction and Special Studies*. Arizona State Museum Archaeological Series 16(1). Arizona State Museum, University of Arizona, Tucson.

Reid, J. Jefferson, Michael B. Schiffer, and Jeffrey M. Neff

1975 Archaeological Considerations of Intrasite Sampling. In *Sampling in Archaeology*, edited by James W. Mueller, pp. 209–224. University of Arizona Press, Tucson.

Reid, J. Jefferson, Michael B. Schiffer, and William L. Rathje

1975 Behavioral Archaeology: Four Strategies. *American Anthropologist* 77:864–869.

Ritchie, William A.

1961 *A Typology and Nomenclature for New York Projectile Points*. New York State Museum and Science Service Bulletin 384. Albany.

1969 *The Archaeology of New York State*. Natural History Press, Garden City, N.J.

Roberts, Wayne D.

1977 *An Analysis of East Tennessee Dalton Projectile Points*. Unpublished Master's thesis, Department of Anthropology, University of Tennessee, Knoxville.

Rostlund, Erhard

1952 *Freshwater Fish and Fishing in Native North America*. University of California Publications in Geography 9. Berkeley.

Rouse, Irving J.

1972 *Introduction to Prehistory: a Systematic Approach*. McGraw-Hill Publishing Company, New York.

Rummel, R. J.

1967 Understanding Factor Analysis. *Conflict Resolution* 11:444–480.

Runquist, Jeannette

1979 *Analysis of the Flora and Faunal Remains from Protohistoric North Carolina Cherokee Indian Sites*. Unpublished Ph.D. dissertation, Department of Zoology, North Carolina State University, Raleigh.

Salo, Lawr V. (editor)

1969 *Archaeological Investigations in the Tellico Reservoir, Tennessee, 1967-1968: an Interim Report*. Report of Investigations No. 7, Department of Anthropology, University of Tennessee, Knoxville.

Schiffer, Michael B.

1972 Archaeological Context and Systemic Context. *American Antiquity*, 37:156–165.

1976 *Behavioral Archaeology*. Academic Press, New York.

1977 Toward a Unified Science of the Cultural Past. In *Research Strategies in Historical Archaeology*, edited by Stanley South, pp. 13–40. Academic Press, New York.

Schmitt, Karl

1952 Archaeological Chronology of the Middle Atlantic States. In *Archeology of Eastern United States*, edited by James B. Griffin, pp. 59–70. University of Chicago Press, Chicago.

Schroedl, Gerald F.

1975 *Archaeological Investigations at the Harrison Branch and Bat Creek Sites*. University of Tennessee, Department of Anthropology, Report of Investigations 10. Knoxville.

1978 *Patrick Site (40MR40), Tellico Reservoir, Tennessee*. University of Tennessee, Department of Anthropology, Report of Investigations 25 and Tennessee Valley Authority Publications in Anthropology 22. Knoxville.

Schubel, J. R., and C. F. Zabawa

1972 *A Pleistocene Susquehanna River Channel Connects the Lower Reaches of the Chester, Miles, and Choptank Estuaries*. Johns Hopkins University, Chesapeake Bay Institute, Special Report 24. Baltimore.

Sears, William H.

1962 The Hopewellian Affiliation of Certain Sites on the Gulf Coast of Florida. *American Antiquity* 28:5–18.

1973 The Sacred and the Secular in Prehistoric Ceramics. In *Variations in Anthropology: Essays in Honor of John C. McGregor*, edited by D. Lathrup and J. Douglas. Illinois Archaeological Survey Publications, Urbana.

Seeman, Mark F.

1979a The Hopewell Interaction Sphere: the Evidence for Interregional Trade and Structural Complexity. Indiana Historical Society, *Prehistoric Research Series* 5(2):237–438. Indianapolis.

1979b Feasting with the Dead: Ohio Hopewell Charnel House Ritual as a Context for Redistribution. In *Hopewell Archaeology: The Chillicothe Conference*, edited by David S. Brose and N'omi Greber, pp. 39–46. Kent State University Press, Kent, Ohio.

Shelford, Victor E.

1963 *The Ecology of North America*. University of Illinois Press, Urbana.

Slattery, Richard G.

1946 A Prehistoric Indian Site on Seldon Island, Montgomery County, Maryland. *Journal of the Washington Academy of Sciences* 36(8):262–266.

Smith, Arlo I.

1979 *A Guide to Wildflowers of the Mid-South*. Memphis State University Press, Memphis, Tennessee.

Smith, Bruce D.

1975 *Middle Mississippian Exploitation of Animal Populations*. Museum of Anthropology, University of Michigan, Anthropological Papers 57. Ann Arbor.

Smith, Gerald P.

1971 *Protohistoric Sociopolitical Organization of the Nottoway in Chesapeake Bay–Carolina Sound Region*. Unpublished Ph.D. dissertation, Department of Anthropology, University of Missouri.

Smith, Henry A. M.

1909 Willtown or New London. *South Carolina Historical and Genealogical Magazine* 10:20–32.

Smith, Jason W.

1976 *Foundations of Archaeology*. Glencoe Press, Beverly Hills.

South, Stanley

1959 *A Study of the Prehistory of the Roanoke Rapids Basin*. Unpublished Master's thesis, the Department of Anthropology, University of North Carolina, Chapel Hill.

1971 *Archeology at the Charles Town Site on Albemarle Point in South Carolina*. University of South Carolina, Institute of Archeology and Anthropology, Research Manuscript Series 10. Columbia.

1975 Preliminary Plan for a Research Proposal for Submission as a Grant Request. Ms. on file, Institute of Archeology and Anthropology, University of South Carolina, Columbia.

1977 *Method and Theory in Historical Archeology*. Academic Press, New York.

1978 A Pilot Study for the Location of Certain Seventeenth Century Sites in Charleston and Berkeley Counties, South Carolina. Ms. on file, Institute of Archeology and Anthropology, University of South Carolina, Columbia.

1979 *The Search for Santa Elena on Parris Island, South Carolina*. Institute of Archeology and Anthropology, University of South Carolina, Research Manuscript Series 150. Columbia.

South, Stanley and Michael O. Hartley

1980 *Deep Water and High Ground: Seventeenth Century Low Country Settlement*. University of South Carolina, Institute of Archeology and Anthropology, Research Manuscript Series 166. Columbia.

Spaulding, Albert C.

1960 The Dimensions of Archaeology. In *Essays in the Science of Culture in Honor of Leslie A. White*, edited by Gertrude E. Dole and Robert L. Carneiro. Crowell Publishing Company, New York.

Spencer, Edgar W.

1965 *Geology: a Survey of Earth Science*. Thomas Y. Crowell, New York.

Stephenson, Robert L.

1963 *The Accokeek Creek Site: A Middle Atlantic Seaboard Culture Sequence*. Museum of Anthropology, University of Michigan, Anthropological Papers 20. Ann Arbor.

Stern, Theodore

1951 *Pamunkey Pottery Making*. Southern Indian Studies Vol. III:1–78. Chapel Hill, N.C.

Steward, Julian and F. Seltzer

1938 Function and Configuration in Archaeology. *American Antiquity* 4:4–11.

Stewart, R. Michael

1980 *Prehistoric Settlement and Subsistence Patterns and the Testing of Predictive Location Models in the Great Valley of Maryland*. Unpublished Ph.D. dissertation, Department of Anthropology, Catholic University of America, Washington, D.C.

Stoltman, James B.

1972 The Late Archaic in the Savannah River Region. In *Fiber Tempered Pottery in the Southeastern United States and Northern Columbia*, edited by R. P. Bullen and J. B. Stoltman, pp. 37–62. Florida Anthropological Society Publications, No. 6.

1974 *Groton Plantation: an Archaeological Study of a South Carolina Locality*. Monographs of the Peabody Museum 1. Cambridge.

Stone, Garry W.

1970 Ceramics in Suffolk County, Massachusetts Inventories 1680–1775—a Preliminary Study with Divers' Comments Thereon, and Sundry Suggestions. *The Conference on Historic Site Archeology Papers* 3:73–90. Institute of Archeology and Anthropology, University of South Carolina. Columbia.

1978 The Carpentry Evidence of Timber Molds and Holes. Ms. on file, St. Mary's City Commission, Maryland.

1982 *Society, Housing, and Architecture in Early Maryland: John Lewgar's St. John's.* Unpublished Ph.D. dissertation, Department of Anthropology, University of Pennsylvania, Philadelphia.

Strong, Duncan

1936 Anthropological Theory and Archaeological Fact. In *Essays in Anthropology in Honor of A. L. Kroeber*, edited by Robert Lowie. University of California Press. Berkley.

Swanton, John R.

1911 *Indian Tribes of the Lower Mississippi Valley and Adjacent Coast of the Gulf of Mexico.* Smithsonian Institution Bureau of American Ethnology Bulletin 43. Washington, D.C.

1922 *Early History of the Creek Indians and their Neighbors.* Smithsonian Institution Bureau of American Ethnology Bulletin 72. Washington, D.C.

1928 Social Organization and Social Usages of the Indians of the Creek Confederacy. *42nd Annual Report of the Bureau of American Ethnology* 1924–1925, pp. 23-472. Smithsonian Institution, Washington, D.C.

1946 *The Indians of the Southeastern United States.* Smithsonian Institution Bureau of American Ethnology, Bulletin 137. Washington, D.C.

Talmage, Valerie, Olga Chesler, and Staff of Interagency Archeological Services

1977 *The Importance of Small, Surface and Disturbed Sites as Sources of Significant Archeological Data.* National Park Service, United States Department of the Interior, Washington, D.C.

Tatsuoka, Maurice M.

1971 *Multivariate Analysis: Techniques for Educational and Psychological Research.* John Wiley and Sons, New York.

Taylor, Richard L.

1979 *A Synthesis of Archeological Resources of the South Carolina Piedmont.* Institute of Archeology and Anthropology, University of South Carolina, Research Manuscript Series 155. Columbia.

Taylor, Richard L. and Marion F. Smith

1978 *The Report of the Intensive Survey of the Richard B. Russell Dam and Lake, Savannah River, Georgia and South Carolina.* Institute of Archeology and Anthropology, University of South Carolina, Research Manuscript Series 142. Columbia.

Taylor, Walter W.

1948 *A Study of Archaeology.* American Anthropological Association Memoir 69. Menasha.

Thomas, Cyrus

1894 Report on the Mound Explorations of the Bureau of Ethnology. *12th Annual Report of the Bureau of American Ethnology*, 1890-1891, pp. 3–730. Smithsonian Institution, Washington, D.C.

Thomas, David H.

1975 Non-Site Sampling in Archaeology: up the Creek without a Site? In *Sampling in Archaeology*, edited by James W. Mueller, pp. 61–81. University of Arizona Press, Tucson.

Thomas, Ronald A.

1974 An Archaeological Inventory of Delaware Prehistory. *Delaware Historic Plan* 2:328–360.

1976 A Brief Survey of Prehistoric Man on the Delmarva Peninsula. *Transactions, Delaware Academy of Science* 5–6:119–140. Newark, Delaware.

Thornton, John and Robert Morden

ca. 1695 This New Map of the Chief Rivers, Bays, Creeks, Harbors, and Settlements, in South Carolina Actually Surveyed and Humbly Dedicated by John Thornton and Robert Morden. Ms. on file, Institute of Archeology and Anthropology, University of South Carolina, Columbia.

Tippitt, V. Ann and William H. Marquardt

1982 Interassemblage Variation in a Stratified Site: a Piedmont Example. *South Carolina Antiquities* 14:1–23.

Trimble, Stanley W.

1974 *Man-Induced Soil Erosion on the Southern Piedmont 1700–1970*. Soil Conservation Society of America, Ankeny, Iowa.

Trinkley, Michael

1976 *A Typology of Thom's Creek Pottery for the South Carolina Coast*. Unpublished Master's thesis, Department of Anthropology, University of North Carolina at Chapel Hill.

1980 *Investigation of the Woodland Period along the South Carolina Coast*. Unpublished Ph.D. dissertation, Department of Anthropology, University of North Carolina at Chapel Hill.

Trinkley, Michael and H. Trawick Ward

1978 The Use of Soil Science at a South Carolina Thom's Creek Culture Shell Ring. *Florida Anthropologist* 31(2):64–73.

Tuck, James A.

1978 Regional Cultural Development, 3000 to 300 B.C. In *Northeast*, edited by Bruce G. Trigger, pp. 28–43. Handbook of North American Indians, vol. 15, William G. Sturtevant, general editor. Smithsonian Institution, Washington, D.C.

Turnbaugh, William A.

1975 Toward an Explanation of the Broadpoint Dispersal in Eastern North American Prehistory. *Journal of Anthropological Research* 31:51–68.

Turner, E. Randolph

1976 *An Archaeological and Ethnohistorical Study on the Evolution of Rank Societies in the Virginia Coastal Plain*. Unpublished Ph.D. dissertation, Department of Anthropology, Pennsylvania State University, University Park.

Ubelaker, Douglas H.

1976 Prehistoric New World Population Size: Historical Review and Current

Appraisal of North American Estimates. *American Journal of Physical Anthropology* 45:661–665.

Van Buren, G. E.

1974 *Arrowheads and Projectile Points*. Arrowhead Publishing Company, Garden Grove, California.

Vaught, Claire C. B.

1979 Archaeobotanical Remains. In *Archaeological Investigations at Horseshoe Bend National Military Park, Alabama*, by Roy S. Dickens, Jr., pp. 171–187. Special Publications of the Alabama Archaeological Society 3. University, Alabama.

Walthall, John A.

1973 *Copena: a Tennessee Valley Middle Woodland Culture*. Unpublished Ph.D. dissertation. Department of Anthropology, University of North Carolina, Chapel Hill.

1980 *Prehistoric Indians of the Southeast, Archaeology of Alabama and the Middle South*. University of Alabama Press, University, Alabama.

Ward, H. Trawick

1980 *The Spatial Analysis of the Plow Zone Artifact Distributions from Two Village Sites in North Carolina*. Unpublished Ph.D. dissertation, Department of Anthropology, University of North Carolina, Chapel Hill.

Waring, Antonio J., Jr., and Lewis H. Larson, Jr.

1968 The Shell Ring on Sapelo Island. In *The Waring Papers: the Collected Works of Antonio J. Waring, Jr.*, edited by Stephen Williams, pp. 263–280. Papers of the Peabody Museum of American Archaeology and Ethnology, Harvard University 58. Cambridge.

Waselkov, Gregory A.

1982 *Shellfish Gathering and Shell Midden Archaeology*. Unpublished Ph.D. dissertation, Department of Anthropology. University of North Carolina.

Watkins, C. Malcolm

1960 North Devon Pottery and Its Export to America in the Seventeenth Century. *Contributions from the Museum of History and Technology. United States Museum Bulletin* 225(13). Washington, D.C. pp. 17–59.

Watts, W. A.

1970 The Full-Glacial Vegetation of Northeastern Georgia. *Ecology* 51:17–33.

1971 Postglacial and Interglacial Vegetation History in Southern Georgia and Central Florida. *Ecology* 52:666–690.

1975 Vegetation Record for the Last 20,000 Years from a Small Marsh on Lookout Mountain, Northeastern Georgia. *Geological Society of America Bulletin* 86:287–291.

1979 Late Quaternary Vegetation of Central Appalachia and the New Jersey Coastal Plain. *Ecological Monographs* 49:427–469.

1980 Late-Quaternary Vegetation History at White Pond on the Inner Coastal Plain of South Carolina. *Quaternary Research* 13:187–199.

Wauchope, Robert

1953 A review of "The Cultural Sequence of the Carolina Piedmont." (One of a collection of chapter reviews of *Archeology of Eastern United States*, edited by James B. Griffin), *American Antiquity* 19:187–188.

1966 Archaeological Survey of Northern Georgia. *Memoirs of the Society of American Archaeology* 21. Salt Lake City.

Webb, William S.

1938 *An Archaeological Survey of the Norris Basin in Eastern Tennessee*. Smithsonian Institution Bureau of American Ethnology Bulletin 118. Washington, D.C.

1939 *An Archaeological Survey of Wheeler Basin on the Tennessee River in Northern Alabama*. Smithsonian Institution Bureau of American Ethnology Bulletin 122. Washington, D.C.

1946 *Indian Knoll, Site Oh2, Ohio County, Kentucky*. University of Kentucky, Reports of Anthropology and Archaeology IV (3, Part 1). Lexington.

Webb, William S., and David L. DeJarnette

1942 *An Archeological Survey of Pickwick Basin in the Adjacent Portions of the States of Alabama, Mississippi, and Tennessee*. Smithsonian Institution Bureau of American Ethnology Bulletin 129. Washington, D.C.

Webb, William S., and C. G. Wilder

1951 *An Archaeological Survey of the Guntersville Basin on the Tennessee River in Northern Alabama*. University of Kentucky Press. Lexington.

Wendland, W. M., and R. A. Bryson

1974 Dating Climatic Episodes of the Holocene. *Quaternary Research* 4:9–27.

Wesler, Kit W.

Typology and Sequence in the Maryland Archaic. *Southeastern Archaeology* 2(1), in press.

White, John W., and Albert C. Goodyear, III

1981 A Preliminary Report: an Examination of the Inter-Riverine Late Archaic of the South Carolina Piedmont. Paper presented at the 38th Annual Southeastern Archaeological Conference, Asheville.

Whitehead, Donald R.

1965 Palynology and Pleistocene Phytogeography of Unglaciated Eastern North America. In *Quaternary of the United States*, edited by H. Wrights, Jr. and D. Frey, pp. 417–432. Princeton University Press, Princeton.

1972 Developmental and Environmental History of the Dismal Swamp. *Ecological Monographs* 42:301–315.

Whitehead, Donald R. and Elso S. Barghoorn

1962 Pollen Analytical Investigations of Pleistocene Deposits from Western North Carolina and South Carolina. *Ecological Monographs* 32:347–369.

Whitmore, Frank C., K. O. Emery, H. B. S. Cooke, and Donald J. P. Swift

1967 Elephant Teeth from the Atlantic Continental Shelf. *Science* 156:1477–1481.

Whittlesey, Stephanie M.

1978 *Status and Death at Grasshopper Pueblo: Experiments Toward an Archaeological Theory of Correlates.* Ph.D. dissertation, University of Arizona. University Microfilms, Ann Arbor.

Wiessner, Polly

1982 Beyond Willow Smoke and Dogs' Tails: a Comment on Binford's Analysis of Hunter-Gatherer Settlement Systems. *American Antiquity*, 47:171–178.

Wilke, Steve, and Gail Thompson

1974 Interim Report on the Kent County Archaeological Research Project. Ms. on file, Maryland Historical Trust, Annapolis.

Willey, Gordon R., and Philip Phillips

1958 *Method and Theory in American Archaeology.* The University of Chicago Press, Chicago.

Willey, Gordon R., and Jeremy A. Sabloff

1980 *A History of American Archaeology.* Thames and Hudson, London.

Williams, C. B., and D. H. Hill

1920 *Corn Book for Young Folks.* Ginn and Company, Boston.

Wilson, Jack H., Jr.

1977 *Feature Fill, Plant Utilization, and Disposal among the Historic Sara Indians.* Unpublished Master's thesis, Department of Anthropology, University of North Carolina, Chapel Hill.

1980 Charred Plant Remains from the Plum Grove Site, Tennessee. Ms. on file, Laboratory of Archaeology, Georgia State University, Atlanta.

Winters, Howard D.

1968 Value Systems and Trade Cycles of the Late Archaic in the Midwest. In *New Perspectives in Archaeology*, edited by Sally R. Binford and Lewis R. Binford, pp. 175–221. Aldine, Chicago.

Witthoft, John

1953 Broad Spearpoints and the Transitional Period Cultures. *Pennsylvania Archaeologist* 23(1):4–31.

1959 Notes on the Archaic of the Appalachian Region. *American Antiquity* 25:78–85.

Wobst, H. Martin

1978 The Archaeo-Ethnology of Hunter-Gatherers or the Tyranny of the Ethnographic Record. *American Antiquity* 43:303–309.

Wood, W. Dean

1981 Archeological Data Recovery in the Richard B. Russell Multiple Resource Area: the Anderson County Group (Interim Report to Interagency Archeological Services–Atlanta), edited by W. Dean Wood. Southeastern Wildlife Services, Inc., Athens, Georgia.

Wood, W. Dean and Thomas H. Gresham

1980 *Archeological Test Excavations at 38LU107.* Draft report submitted to the United States Department of the Interior, Heritage Conservation and Recreation Services, Interagency Archeological Services–Atlanta, Purchase Order No. A-54130(80). Southeastern Wildlife Services, Inc., Athens, Georgia.

Wright, Henry T.

1959 A Preliminary Sequence for the Upper Potomac Valley. *West Virginia Archaeologist* 11:9–21.

1973 *An Archeological Sequence in the Middle Chesapeake Region, Maryland*. Maryland Geological Survey, Archeological Studies 1. Baltimore.

Yarnell, Richard A.

1971 A Study of Archaeological Plant Remains from Two Sites (Au7 and Lo32) in the Jones Bluff Reservoir, Alabama. In *Archaeology in the Jones Bluff Reservoir of Central Alabama*, by Roy S. Dickens, Jr., pp. 108–111. Journal of Alabama Archaeology XVII(1), University, Alabama.

1976 Plant Remains from the Warren Wilson Site. In *Cherokee Prehistory: the Pisgah Phase in the Appalachian Summit Region*, by Roy S. Dickens, Jr., pp. 217–224. University of Tennessee Press, Knoxville.

Yengoyan, Aram A.

1972 Ritual and Exchange in Aboriginal Australia: an Adaptive Interpretation of Male Initiation Rites. In *Social Exchange and Interaction*, edited by E. N. Wilmsen. Anthropological Papers 46, Museum of Anthropology, University of Michigan, Ann Arbor.

Contributors

Veletta Canouts, Institute of Archeology and Anthropology, University of South Carolina, Columbia, SC 29208

Jefferson Chapman, Department of Anthropology, University of Tennessee, Knoxville, TN 37996-0720

R. P. Stephen Davis, Jr., Research Laboratories of Anthropology, University of North Carolina, Chapel Hill, NC 27514

Roy S. Dickens, Jr., Research Laboratories of Anthropology and Department of Anthropology, University of North Carolina, Chapel Hill, NC 27514

Keith T. Egloff, Virginia Research Center for Archaeology, Yorktown, VA 23186

Albert C. Goodyear III, Institute of Archeology and Anthropology, University of South Carolina, Columbia, SC 29208

James B. Griffin, Museum of Anthropology, University of Michigan, Ann Arbor, MI 48109

Michael O. Hartley, Institute of Archeology and Anthropology, University of South Carolina, Columbia, SC 29208

Alexander H. Morrison II (deceased), St. Mary's City Commission, St. Mary's City, MD 20686

Billy L. Oliver, Archaeology Branch, North Carolina Division of Archives and History, Raleigh, NC 27611

J. Jefferson Reid, Department of Anthropology, University of Arizona, Tucson, AZ 85721

Stanley South, Institute of Archeology and Anthropology, University of South Carolina, Columbia, SC 29208

Michael B. Trinkley, Environmental Section, South Carolina Department of Highways, Columbia, SC 29202

John A. Walthall, Illinois Department of Transportation, Springfield, IL 62764

H. Trawick Ward, Research Laboratories of Anthropology, University of North Carolina, Chapel Hill, NC 27514

Kit W. Wesler, Department of Sociology and Anthropology, Murray State University, Murray, KY 42071

Jack H. Wilson, Jr., Historic Sites Section, North Carolina Department of Cultural Resources, Raleigh, NC 27611

Index